PENGUIN BOOKS

# UNLEASHING THE VAJRA

Sujeev Shakya is a thought leader who traverses many worlds. He earned the title of Nepal's CEO, 'chief eternal optimist', for the optimism he projected in his book *Unleashing Nepal* (2009). He writes and speaks extensively on business, development, economy and leadership. In 2008, after spending two decades in one of Nepal's leading business groups, he founded Beed Management, an international management consulting and advisory firm based in Kathmandu, Nepal. He is also the founder and chair of the Nepal Economic Forum.

A chartered accountant, he has a diploma in international marketing from Boston University and a certification in coaching from Columbia University. He was awarded the Hubert H. Humphrey Fellowship by the US State Department in 2002. He writes a regular column for the *Kathmandu Post* and his world can be viewed through www.sujeevshakya.com.

T0158275

# UNLEASHING THE VAJRA

## NEPAL'S JOURNEY BETWEEN INDIA AND CHINA

## SUJEEV SHAKYA

PENGUIN BOOKS

An imprint of Penguin Random House

PENGUIN BOOKS

USA | Canada | UK | Ireland | Australia
New Zealand | India | South Africa | China

Penguin Books is part of the Penguin Random House group of companies
whose addresses can be found at global.penguinrandomhouse.com

Published by Penguin Random House India Pvt. Ltd
4th Floor, Capital Tower 1, MG Road,
Gurugram 122 002, Haryana, India

Penguin
Random House
India

First published in Viking by Penguin Random House India 2019
Published in paperback in Penguin Books in 2021

ISBN 9780143456209

Typeset in Adobe Garamond Pro by Manipal Technologies Limited, Manipal
Printed at Replika Press Pvt. Ltd, India

www.penguin.co.in

MIX
Paper from
responsible sources
FSC® C016779

*To everyone who believes in the*
*potential of Nepal*

# Contents

*Introduction*                                                            ix

## I: THE PAST

1. Nepal Chronicles Its Existence: Nepal Era, 879 CE                      3
2. Shah Rule: From Regional Hub to Isolation, 1776–1846                  18
3. Shah Puppets: Rana Autocracy, 1846–1950                               31
4. Shahs' Rise and the Fall of the Partyless Panchayat: 1950–90          45
5. Fall of Shahs: Restoration of Multiparty Democracy,
   Conflict and End of Shah Dynasty, 1990–2008                           71
6. Years of Transition: 2006–18                                         110
7. The Leap: The 'Unleashing Nepal' Journey, 2006–18                    134

## II: THE CONTEXT

8. Cartelpreneurs: The World of the Nepali Private Sector               159
9. Donorpreneurs and the Business of Development                        195
10. Global Nepalis: Migration, Diaspora and Remittance                  220
11. Nepal's Future in between China and India                           243
12. Capitalist Welfare State: In between Capitalism
    and Socialism                                                       270

# III: ACTION TIME

13. Vision 2030 and Beyond 295
14. Making 'HATS and I' Happen 323
15. Unleashing Transformation 350


*Acknowledgements* 377
*Notes* 379
*Index* 393

# Introduction

By 2040, it is projected that China will be the largest economy in the world, followed by India. The two put together will have nearly a third of the world's population and GDP. This is similar to the glories of Asia in the sixteenth and seventeenth centuries, when India and China accounted for nearly 70 per cent of the global GDP. Nepal, till the seventeenth century, was known for being a trade link between China and India. The wealth accumulated by the Malla rulers of that time helped to create great architectural marvels with superb handcrafting skills, as well as trade with both nations. Now, there exists an opportunity for Nepal to unleash its potential and return to the time when it had the advantage of being in between two prospering neighbours. This book tries to understand the past in order to learn how to get the future right—Nepal now has just two decades to relive its glorious past.

Writings on Nepal began with the British arriving in the subcontinent, and these were supplemented with accounts in the English language written by explorers. Together, this literature provides the background to Nepal's history. Little is known about Nepal in the period before the Shah dynasty was established in 1776. The Newa language was then the lingua franca, and much of the history was transmitted orally. Archiving systems were poor and interest in history was limited. With the ban on the Newa language, the Shahs, and later the Ranas, decided what the narrative should be, and how it would be taught in schools. However, with the advent of multiparty democracy in 1990, the history recounted by the Shah kings began to be questioned and new narratives emerged.

After the fall of the Shah dynasty in 2008, with the extensive penetration of the Internet and the emergence of social media platforms, many new narratives came to the fore. Historians like 100-year-old Satya Mohan Joshi, who has seen major events in Nepal occur in his lifetime, started to openly talk about the past. His descriptions[1] of the Newa craftsman Arniko who went to China and built temples and cities in Lhasa and Beijing spread far and wide and were not censored. The growing numbers of young and educated Nepalis were curious, and more stories started to emerge in Nepali magazines, books and online portals. In this book, I attempt to look at Nepali history from the year the Nepal era, popularly called the Nepal Sambat, began, in 879 CE. I try to piece together information from different sources, including the stories that we inherited from our ancestors.

Knowledge of the state of Nepal's economy and society is understood from reports written by various development partners, including multilateral and bilateral agencies. These served a specific purpose and had a limited scope; very few explored history, culture and societal contexts. With the late development of the private sector and the concept of corporations, there was limited investment in research by business concerns as the core occupation remained trading, which was basically taking an arbitrage position on either taxes or the open border with India. The presence of only a few professional companies with foreign investment and the fact that Nepal was not a sought after investment destination were further hindrances in conducting studies on the impact of history, culture and consumer behaviour on business. This is in contrast to other countries, where it has become a major staple for consulting companies to produce reports.

The use of the English language was limited; moreover, with the improvement of technology, the use of Nepali in typing and translation applications became more widespread, which restricted content availability in English. Many parts of this book have benefited from my effort of writing columns in Nepali; I had previously been inspired to write a book in Nepali titled *Arthat Arthatantra* (It's the Economy) in 2018.[2] The interactions after the publication of this book provided multiple lenses for me to look at issues. I present them here.

Nepal has been widely perceived to be linked to India in many ways. It shares an open border and a fixed currency with India as well as a special treaty for transit and trade. Nepal's rulers historically had links with India: the Lichhavis, Mallas, Shahs and Ranas. Even post-1990, most people at the helm of affairs in Nepal had educational, marital or other relationships with India. Tibet was Nepal's other immediate neighbour, and it was only after 1960 that Nepal had to deal with China. The 1962 war between China and India led Nepal to consider a policy of allowing China and India to compete to provide aid to Nepal, but this was short-lived as both countries were fighting their own internal economic battles of population explosion and poverty. China continued to maintain that Nepal needed to deal with India for its internal security and trade issues. At that time, China just wanted to ensure that Nepal accepted the One China policy, and never allowed its soil to be used for uprisings or anything that posed a security challenge. It was only after the earthquake of April 2015 that mainland China started to take an interest in Nepal, and with the Indian blockade in September 2015, China got interested in Nepal—it has not looked back since. After a very successful visit by Indian Prime Minister Narendra Modi in August 2013, followed by commitments at the SAARC summit in November 2014, and the assistance for relief and rebuilding after the earthquake, it was felt that there has been a recalibration in the Nepal–India relationship. This joy was short-lived and the relations that nosedived after the blockade are yet to return to normal. Even in PM Modi's second term, there is hardly any indication of change. An Eminent Persons Group of six people, three each from India and Nepal, was formed to review the 1950 treaty, and their tenure expired in July 2019 without the report being accepted and implemented.

In the meantime, with the global churn of events in Europe, the US and the UK, China started to emerge as the new custodian of globalization, and the implementation of the One Belt One Road idea into a powerful programme under the acronym BRI (Belt and Road Initiative) accelerated. India did not join the BRI, but for Nepal this became a good opportunity to get out of being 'India-locked'. New treaties were signed, and when Chinese President Xi Jinping visited Nepal in October 2019, he provided a new impetus to Nepalis by announcing that Nepal was now a strategic partner for China. A Nepal–China Trans-Himalayan Multi-Dimensional Connectivity Network has been formed that will expedite land links with China, with the potential of railway links when the rail link to the southern parts of the Tibet Autonomous Region is built. A new chapter thus begins, and new opportunities open up for Nepal to define its relations with China. This book looks at some historical perspectives, and at cultural and practical on-the-ground issues to understand what Nepal's journey has been, and what the future of Nepal's journey in between China and India will be.

*Unleashing Nepal* was one of the first books that was published in the post-Shah period and had the liberty to question the conduct of the Shah kings, which till 2008 was not possible. When I reflect now, it is very interesting to understand how the obvious was not stated, and despite Nepal being under multiparty rule, there was little evaluation of the conduct of the Shah kings. There was only political sloganeering, but no questions on how they messed up the education system; how they propagated crony capitalism; how they were isolationists and did nothing to promote investment but rather were happy to get the begging bowl out. In 2008, Nepal's journey as a Federal Democratic Republic began; there were changes, but some were for the worse. Some leaders of the country travelled with more fanfare than the erstwhile kings, the culture of VIP treatment proliferated with feudal practices being encouraged rather than eradicated. Entitlement became the norm as political leaders travelled on taxpayer money for expensive medical treatments. Religious functions substituted kings and royalty with newly crowned rulers, and *chakari* or the culture of sycophancy bloated as more people had to be pleased than at the time of the royals. In the decade after the publication of *Unleashing Nepal,* I thought about the need for understanding culture and society more deeply through observing basic behaviour and little things rather than big ones. This made me believe that economic transformation required not just financial and management skills, but also societal transformation, moving towards an equitable society with sound civic behaviour, empathy and integrity. Therefore, from *Unleashing Nepal,* where I used the lenses of a corporate executive who spent twenty years looking at businesses, in this book I use the lens of an observer questioning the basics.

After the publication of *Unleashing Nepal,* I got the opportunity to interact with many people during book discussions, events and other platforms that gave me more perspectives. I travelled extensively and discussed Nepal within Nepal and with the diaspora that has grown phenomenally. Using the book as the foundation, I designed a course on business environment for the MBA programme at Kathmandu University School of Management, Nepal's premier business school. Interactions with students who took this course helped me ask questions from different perspectives. Nepali society has moved dramatically in the past ten years. The end of the conflict meant that people could move freely within Nepal and that led to a boom in domestic tourism that surpassed revenues from international tourists.[3] With extortion becoming passé, people were willing to show off their wealth, buying houses, apartments, cars and jewellery. Educational institutions mushroomed throughout the country and large domestic investments started being made in private hospitals. With very little regulatory oversight on both, it encouraged many people to pool in money to start schools and hospitals. With more women joining the workforce and the shift to nuclear families, there was more proliferation of new eateries. Internet penetration, reduction in smartphone prices and better electricity connectivity along with reliability changed the way people consumed content, disrupting the entertainment and media industry. Nepalis started to travel outside the country for work, education and pleasure like never before, creating pressure at Nepal's only airport in Kathmandu and forcing new international airports to open in Bhairahawa and Pokhara. The book looks at the journey of the decade closely in terms of what changed dramatically for the better and what for the worse.

*

The book has been divided into three parts. The first part deals with the past and narrates the turn of events, breaking it into seven distinct parts. The first chapter deals with the 900 years prior to Shah rule. The subsequent ones examine the Shahs over four distinct divisions— the first till the Ranas took over; the second about them as puppet kings; the third their resurgence; and, finally, their end. The period between 2008 and 2018 has been viewed from the perspective of the challenges as well as transformations in two different chapters. This part provides the necessary background to understand the current state of Nepal in terms of the challenges of economic growth, the inward-looking isolationist mindset, the never-ending migration and the sense of apathy.

The second part sets the context to understand the key issues that drive Nepal's economy. The section deliberately leaves out omissions on the part of the government because much has already been written and said about the challenges of bureaucracy and the failure of politicians to deliver. Criticizing politicians has been the best excuse of non-performance, therefore I did not dedicate a separate chapter to this; instead, I try to examine the other key sectors—the private sector and the development sector—closely to understand the different distortions that exist in the society, from cartel behaviour to rent-seeking. This section also deals with the emergence of the global Nepali, and the dichotomy as Nepal itself continues to be inward-looking. With more than a sixth of its population outside the country, different kinds of Nepalis have emerged around the world. Remittances sent by Nepalis around the world to Nepal have swelled and equal nearly a quarter of the country's GDP. This in turn has impacted prices of land, consumption patterns and societal behaviour. In the chapter on Nepal's location between India and China, I try to look at its relationship with the two countries from different dimensions, setting the stage for the direction in which Nepal could head in the days to come. In the final chapter of this section, the discussions centre around the choice Nepal has between capitalism and socialism. I continue to discuss the capitalist welfare state, a concept that I have been propagating for nearly two decades since the publication of the chapter in the book *State of Nepal* edited by Shastri Ramachandaran and Kanak Mani Dixit in 2001. I continue to argue that free enterprise regulated as per global standards will generate enough revenues for the government to solve the problem of poverty. We have to find ways to deal with both extreme poverty as well as extreme wealth.

In the third part, we discuss what can be done. It is important to articulate a vision, but an execution plan is also necessary. The prescriptions are laid out, and perhaps timelines can be inserted and executed. The second chapter in this section looks at the sectors that Nepal needs to focus on and provides fresh perspectives to known topics. In addition to hydropower, agriculture and tourism; the services sector and infrastructure is examined. The final chapter is perhaps the core of the book, and reflects upon the need for societal transformation. I sincerely believe that after interacting with change agents, many of the issues raised will be internalized at individual levels, and perhaps help to build a better society. If one can focus on one's own cleanliness and the cleanliness of one's house and surroundings, the collective behaviour will lead to a cleaner neighbourhood, city and country.

*

Readers of *Unleashing Nepal* questioned me about how I could be so positive about Nepal. I always maintain that I can only speak for myself, and I have no complaints about the opportunities Nepal has provided me. After returning from my studies in India, I started my career at the Soaltee Hotel as a trainee and in just over a decade and a half became the group president of one of the largest business groups in Nepal. Thereafter, in 2008, I went on to start Beed Management, a management consulting firm. In over a decade of operations, we have completed assignments in six countries. It is possible to run a global business based out of Nepal. I founded a think tank called the Nepal Economic Forum, and within a decade—with the help of some great members of the advisory board and the dedication of volunteerism from the Beed team—we have been able to make it to GoTo Think Tank lists, producing a review publication every quarter, conducting events regularly and ensuring social media buzz with blog posts on different issues relating to the economy. I served as the secretary general of Himalayan Consensus for five years and hosted four world-class global events in Kathmandu in the form of the Himalayan Consensus Summit. I have incubated and delivered more programmes than I can count. This is a land of opportunity.

I continue to believe in Nepal's potential. Nepal is landlinked to the two fastest-growing economies in the world. It has access to markets in the most populous parts of India; and with Bangladesh, the numbers add up to more than half a billion. Nepal has the opportunity to reap demographic dividends with half of its population under the age of twenty-five, and 70 per cent of people under the age of thirty-five. Women, who form half the population, have not integrated into the economy fully, but there has been rapid progress in this regard, and that will create great changes. Finally, I believe that with federalism and 753 local bodies, political leaders will emerge from different parts of Nepal who will one day take on the leadership role of not only transforming their sphere of influence in their village, town, city or province, but in Nepal as a whole.

*

The phrase 'unleashing the vajra', I believe, will be used as a metaphor in the future where it will denote the unleashing of Nepal's potential between its two neighbours by hitching its wagon to their fast-moving engines. The vajra can have different meanings for people of different faiths and beliefs, but for me it is a symbol that denotes potential. It is also an assurance of a dream that cannot be put down due to the indestructible powers represented by the diamond, the dream of millions of Nepalis across the world. Finally, it is the irresistible force of the thunderbolt that will bring about positive transformation.

# I

# The Past

The first seven chapters attempt to bring to the fore critical events in the history of Nepal that have had an impact on its society as well as the economy. From 879 CE when the Nepal Era (Nepal Sambat) helped provide a reference to Nepal's history up till 2019, 1140 years of the country's journey is discussed. Many important events are examined to understand how they shaped the Nepali way of life, society and the economy. The historical linkages with India and China are examined in the context of events taking place elsewhere in the world.

It is important to understand Nepal's past in order to understand its present and shape its future.

# The Past

# Nepal Chronicles Its Existence: Nepal Era, 879 CE

## Journey till 1776: Licchavis and Mallas; India and China

At a time when the Buddhist dynastic rulers of the Pala dynasty were ruling north-eastern India, the Tang dynasty was nearing its end in China, and the Tibetan empire was declining, history was being written in the Kathmandu valley—a new calendar was announced to honour a benevolent merchant called Sankhadhar Sakhwa. On 20 October 879 CE, the Nepal Sambat (Nepal Era) began—the date chronicled by history in different tablets, temples and scriptures.

Sakhwa was a merchant in what is now Bhaktapur. Legend has it that as per an astrologer's prediction, the sand present in the confluence of two rivers would turn into gold overnight. One day, the king of Bhaktapur ordered the sand to be collected. When the merchant saw this being done, he decided to buy the collected sand. Next day, when it changed to gold, he decided to use that to pay off the debts of farmers rather than keep it for himself. This benevolence was honoured with the creation of a calendar beginning from that time, which would serve as the official calendar of Nepal till the Rana rulers replaced it with the Bikram Era[1] calendar in the 1850s.

The chronicling of Nepal's history has been made easier with the Nepal Sambat calendar, but many of the events before this era do not have definitive dates. The major reference point is the life of the Buddha, who was born in modern-day Kapilvastu in Nepal in 623 BCE. So the major references after this period have an association with the Buddha or Buddhism.

The modern-day history of Nepal has been written under the 250-year aegis of the Shah kings and Rana rulers glorifying their rule and achievements. The fact that people could not write or speak against the rulers led to them being the sole recorders of history.

## Buddhism, the Connector

The history of Nepal is laden with stories of wealth, business and trade from the time of the Buddha, with references to rich traders in the sutras who were benevolent *upasakas* or followers. Thereafter, there are stories of King Ashok coming to the Kathmandu valley, building a pillar in Lumbini and four stupas in the prosperous kingdom of Patan in the Kathmandu valley. He left his daughter Charumati behind, and she constructed another stupa that is currently known as Chabahil. The valley's inhabitants were rich enough to not only feed themselves, but also take care of visitors, embrace art and culture as well as build some historical structures, some of which are still well preserved today.

The other story well-documented in Tibetan writings is about Princess Bhrikuti, who was married to the Tibetan king Songtsen Gampo and has been credited with spreading Tibetan Buddhism in Tibet. Princess Bhrikuti was the daughter of Anshuvarman of the Licchavi dynasty. She brought with her Newa[2] craftsmen and crafts made by them that were housed in the Jokhang temple in Lhasa. Princess Bhrikuti is referred to as Bhelsa Tritsun or 'Royal Lady' in the Tibetan language, and also as 'Green Tara' in iconography, treated as a reincarnation of Goddess Tara.[3]

The other important figure in Tibetan Buddhism is Padmasambhava or Guru Rinpoche, who traversed through the Himalayan kingdom in the eighth century. A Buddhist master born in today's Pakistan, much of the history of that time and era can be accessed in writings about him. Guru Rinpoche meditated in the Asura cave, which is in the town of Pharping in the southern part of the modern-day Kathmandu valley, making the valley his transit point during journeys between India and Tibet.

It is important to look at Nepal through the lens of Buddhism as it was the link between China and India, the two big countries bordering Nepal. Buddhist missionaries from India to China travelling through Nepal till the eleventh century were the connectors of those times and they cemented the trade route, which also has been referred to as the Spice Silk Road. There are no records available after that period as the fall of Buddhism began in India, with Brahminism taking over and the start of large states being fragmented into smaller kingdoms.

There are many legends of debates and fights between Adi Shankaracharya, who was brought in by the Malla kings, and the Newa Vajracharya priests who presided over the Vajrayana Buddhist faith.

The marital relationship between the Licchavi kings of Nepal and the Tibetan empire led to major trade and economic ties between the two kingdoms. These continued with other rulers of the Tibetan kingdom and the Malla kings till the Shah kings decided to wage wars with Tibet. Major trade operations existed for agricultural produce being exchanged for silver and salt from Tibet.

A mid-1600s treaty between Kathmandu and Tibet established the route through the Kathmandu valley as the only trade link to be used by Tibet for trade with India. Nepal was also to mint silver coins for Tibet for which the latter provided silver or paid in gold. As the sole entrepôt for Tibet, the Kathmandu valley flourished not only as a trade hub but also as a value-adding manufacturer, most prominently through its artisans and craftsmen. They could rent-seek on the trade route by simply trading and not producing much. Produce from the highly fertile Indo-Gangetic plains flowed into the Tibetan kingdom where the rulers, who also served as religious figures, had gold and silver to mine and spend to buy everything, from essentials to items of luxury. The monopoly of Nepal's geographical position ended only a century ago in 1905 when an expedition of the British officer Francis Younghusband camped in Kalimpong in India and mainstreamed the route through the

Chumbi valley passes of Jelap La and Nathu La in Sikkim—which was an independent kingdom then and is now part of India.

## Shakyas: From Kapilvastu to the Kathmandu valley

The history of Nepal has always been linked with Gautama Buddha, born as Prince Siddhartha in the Shakya clan in Kapilvastu. A Kshatriya king, he went on to renounce his kingdom and attain enlightenment and bring about stiff competition to the strong Hindu culture, beliefs and traditions he was born to. His manner of conversing in the local Pali language rather than Brahminical Sanskrit attracted common people. Farmers, merchants and traders—the middle class which was the bulk of the population at that time—could identify with him and not the Hindu religion that was associated with richness, power and opulence in day-to-day practice. By the time he passed away, most of his people in the kingdom had either turned to monkhood or were serving monks as upasakas. When Kapilvastu was attacked, they moved towards the Kathmandu valley and settled in by continuing the Buddhist traditions.

This changed their economic fortunes forever. Even though they were Kshatriya, they went on to become either priests in temples along with the Vajracharya priests or traders and craftsmen who then got various titles based on their occupation. Later, due to haphazard segregation by caste, they got further divided into different sections and orders. In the Kathmandu valley, they began the tradition of monastic living around *bahas* or monasteries and smaller *bahis* or offshoots of the bahas. The Shakyas did not have to be celibate but could practise as priests. These practices are reflected today. For instance, at the Golden Temple (Hiranyavarna Mahavihara) in Nepal, the tradition of taking turns to become its caretaker for one month once in a lifetime continues in the families there.

## Arniko Builds Beijing

When Emperor Kublai Khan established the Yuan dynasty and moved his capital to Beijing in the thirteenth century, he was responsible for building the city of Beijing. Arniko, a Nepali engineer, was summoned to his court to help. A plaque at the white pagoda at Miaoying temple acknowledges it was 'built under the supervision of Nepali architect Arniko in 1271'. The temple has a dominating Buddhist stupa that is 50.9 metres tall, with a diameter of 30 metres, in the Newa architecture of the Kathmandu valley. Perhaps Arniko is the most prominent Nepali in history whose biography is among the very few foreigners mentioned in Chinese history books. He was given the title of the duke of Liang, and a memorial stela marks the spot where he was cremated in Hsiang Sheng near Beijing.

The writings on Arniko emerged after historian and cultural commentator Satya Mohan Joshi visited China and discovered him in greater detail after years of research. The Shah and Rana rulers were never keen to showcase a Newa, considered their enemies. Arniko was born in current-day Patan in 1244. He went on to have many children from his ten wives in places that included Mongolia and China. When Sakya Lama Drogon Chogyal Phagpa requested King Jayabhimdev Malla to send one hundred artists to build monasteries in Tibet, eighty were selected. At the age of seventeen, Arniko was one among the eighty artisans.[4]

Kublai Khan declared Tibetan Buddhism the state religion and appointed the Sakya Lama as the Imperial Preceptor. Henceforth, all the successors of Kublai Khan appointed Sakya Lama Drogon Chogyal Phagpa to take care of religious affairs with the title of Dishi, 'Teacher of the Emperor'. It was this Sakya Lama who introduced Arniko to Kublai Khan. The adoption of Buddhism also created a market for Newa craftsmen and traders, making this perhaps the second wave of migration from the Kathmandu valley after the one begun by Princess Bhrikuti.

## Bahas of Beijing

Bahas or courtyards have been a prominent hallmark of the inner cities that comprise the Kathmandu valley. They house the places of worship dedicated to Gautama Buddha and follow the Vajrayana tradition of worship. The word 'baha' is used in the Newa language to explain the conglomeration of monasteries or viharas. The bahas[5] have essentially become a way of living by historically fostering the continued congregation of people from various walks of life.

When Arniko, at the behest of Emperor Kublai Khan, travelled to China to design the Buddhist monasteries and the city of Beijing, he might have taken the contemporary living systems of the place he came from as an inspiration. In this context, walking through the *siheyuans* of Beijing felt a lot like navigating Kathmandu's bahas. Siheyuan, which literally translates to 'four sides of a courtyard with the garden in the centre', were ubiquitous in some parts of Beijing. The hutongs or narrow lanes connect the various courtyards with a striking resemblance to Patan's bahas. The chatter among residents, the sense of knowing each other and the lingering warmth of the historical places feel similar to Kathmandu's streets.

The more one explores the inside courtyards of Beijing, the more similarities one can find with the courtyards of the Kathmandu valley, with the structures of lions and tortoises along with other animals that line entrances, the frescos on the walls and the beautifully detailed wooden gate structures, doors and windows.

It's interesting to note that many of these old courtyards have also aged in similar ways. While some have given way to multistorey large structures, it's clear that both countries recognize the historical and social value of these architectural designs and are actively working to preserve them in innovative ways. The usage of exposed bricks in courtyard areas illuminates a sense of 'historical modernity'—which has grown increasingly popular as a tourism strategy. In both countries, some traditional courtyards have been converted into boutique hotels.

## Marco Polo and Arniko

When we look at dates of their travels, Marco Polo and Arniko were perhaps in Beijing at the same time, interacting with Emperor Kublai Khan. Polo, a merchant, explorer and writer, recorded his travels in the book *Livre des Merveilles du Monde* (Book of the World's Marvels), published around the year 1300. In English, this book is also known as *The Travels of Marco Polo*[6] and it describes—among other things—

Polo's travels along the Silk Road and in various Asian regions and cities, including China.[7] This book defines China as we know it now and has been a point of reference when it comes to discussing the Belt and Road Initiative (BRI), a policy adopted by China in 2013. However, it is very strange that Arniko is not mentioned in the extensive narratives of Marco Polo nor is Marco Polo mentioned in Chinese imperial history books, like Arniko is amongst the many foreigners mentioned in them. The fact that the Great Wall of China is not mentioned in the writings of Marco Polo has been raised by many to doubt his observations.

## Newa Script and Language

With the recent popularity of Tibetan Buddhism and the mushrooming of Tibetan Buddhist monasteries worldwide, prayer wheels have become one of the most popular sights, with 'Om Mane Padme Hum' inscribed on them. These words are written in the Ranjana script that derives its origin from the Brahmi script. Formulated in that was the script in which the Newa language was written in the Nepa Mandala and elsewhere. In the volumes of Tibetan Buddhist scriptures that were translated from Sanskrit into the Tibetan language, the headlines and covers were written in the Ranjana script. It is believed that when the Mughal invasion and destruction began, many Sanskrit texts were taken to Tibet through Nepal where they got translated and written in the Tibetan language in a script that was derived from the Ranjana script.

The valley residents spoke the Newa language which is the Sino-Tibetan language and written in multiple scripts, including Ranjana. This language remained the official language of the country till the Shah kings replaced it with the Khas (*khen bhaye* in Newa) language, which started being referred to as the Nepali language only in the early part of the twentieth century.

## Imperial History of Nepal

When it comes to the history of Nepal before the Shah dynasty, it is generally seen through the lenses of European travellers, especially as writings in Chinese and Tibetan were not accessible due to translation issues. Therefore, much of the history we get to read is only from the seventeenth century. Newa culture, which primarily defined and contributed to the history of the Kathmandu valley, is largely based on the oral tradition, and consequently, it is difficult to retrieve clear descriptions from it. Further, the ban imposed on the Newa language and Buddhism in the 104 years of the Rana regime ensured that whatever little would have remained in the mid-1850s in terms of oral tradition vanished.

Now, Nepali scholars studying in China are discovering a wide range of literature in various Chinese languages that fill some of these historical gaps. With archival processes in China improving and old texts and documents being made more accessible, researchers with the required linguistic skills will undoubtedly uncover more of these historical and cultural threads of similarities.

## The India Connection

From historical times, Nepal forms a part of the Indian subcontinent in terms of politics and culture and is distinct from the Chinese civilization. Sita, wife of Lord Ram in the Ramayana, hails from modern-day Janakpur, and in the Mahabharata, the Kirata kingdom is mentioned along with King Yalambar who is killed by Lord Krishna.

The kingdom of Kapilvastu that belonged to Prince Siddhartha, who became Gautama Buddha, was annexed by the kingdom of Kosala (modern-day Uttar Pradesh in India). The Licchavi rulers who belonged to Vaisali (current-day Bihar) ruled Nepal approximately from 450 to 700 CE. The Malla kings who ruled Nepal from 1200 CE took the title 'Malla' from the word for 'wrestler' in Sanskrit. They are credited with promoting the culture and language of the Mithila people from Bihar. Many of the historical writings suggest strong marital connections as well as relations of trade, education and culture between the different kingdoms of modern-day India and Nepal.

The invasion of India by Mohamad of Ghazni in 1000 CE marked the beginning of the rule of Muslim kings in India, which lasted till the Battle of Plassey in 1757, after which the East India Company, a business incorporated in Britain in 1600 CE, took over. During these 750-plus years of wars, feudal fights and religious squabbles, the Kathmandu valley recorded only one invasion by an external army. In 1345, Sultan Shams ud-din Ilyas of Bengal attacked the valley and destroyed many monasteries and stupas. During this period when the Malla kings ruled the valley, it was known for its wealth and prosperity. Buddhists from Bengal and other parts of India came to visit Swayambhu, and Hindus came to visit Pashupatinath. They took back stories of golden taps, stupas and temples that prompted the Bengal ruler to launch an attack to plunder these riches. Unlike in Kashmir, where they attacked and stayed back to rule, they did not do so in Nepal and retreated, carrying back wealth and riches.[8]

Many writings from India exist that link the rulers of the Nepa Mandala[9] to Karnataka in south India. It is believed that these people from what is now the south Indian state of Karnataka were Marathi- or Kannada-speaking barons or military chiefs from the Deccan who followed the victorious armies of Vikramaditya between 1040 and 1069 AD.[10] This is also explained by many through the linkages in food items with Karnataka, be it wo (bara), chatamari (uttapam) or yomari (modak). The usage of conch shells and coconuts in rituals in a place that has none indicates the influence of external forces.

Nepal during the reign of the Malla kings was well linked for trade and business with India and China. The merchants of the valley and other parts of Nepal did not only do business with India, Tibet and China but also travelled to other parts of Asia. Apart from the Newa community, the Manange from Manang district in the Himalayan part of Nepal were the other transnational traders that traded across modern-day Myanmar, Thailand, Malaysia and Singapore. They brought back wealth to build monasteries and made enough surplus to support one-fifth of the male population that lived in these Buddhist monasteries.[11]

## Guru Nanak in Nepal

The valley was also known for visits of religious saints from India. One of the most notable ones was Guru Nanak, founder of the Sikh sect.

It is believed that he travelled to Nepal in the sixteenth century during the reign of King Jay Jagat Malla. The myth is that when Guru Nanak cured a Malla royal family member with an unsound mind, the Malla kings invited him to visit Nepal. Oral recorded history says that he came to Nepal in his third Udasi and spent a few months in Kathmandu. He meditated in six places and a shrine was built at each site in commemoration. The king apparently gave around 200 acres of land to build a gurudwara. The Pashupatinath temple complex still houses copies of the Guru Granth Sahib, the holy scripture of the Sikhs.[12]

## Kashmiri Muslims in Nepal

The first set of Muslim traders that came to Nepal were Kashmiri; they were followed by Iraqi, Persian and Afghan traders. The Raqi Bajar in Indrachowk is said to have been named for the traders from Iraq. The Kashmiri Muslims were interlocutors for the Malla kings with the Delhi Sultanate. The Malla kings wanted to benefit from trade with Kashmiri Muslims to Tibet and invited them to use Nepal as transit point. They were even allowed to set up a mosque called the Kashmiri Takiyah. While many of them spoke Urdu, they went on to learn the Newa language. Descendants of these Muslim families are organized under the Newa Muslim Samaj in pockets of Kathmandu and Patan.

## Religious Tourism and Pilgrimages

The concept of religious pilgrimages is many millennia old, with the belief that a visit to religious shrines and places of pilgrimage would cleanse people of their sins or get them a better place in heaven or the afterlife. This ensured that there was a lot of movement of people that resulted in the economics of transportation, be it carriages and human carriers or rest houses and stores selling everything from essential wear to religious artefacts. Nepa Mandala remained an important place of pilgrimage for both Buddhists and Hindus, thereby attracting people from the region. This perhaps provided the foundation of religious tourism that still forms the bulk of tourist arrivals in Nepal and will continue as both the Indian and Chinese outbound population has grown in recent years.

Nepalis also travelled to religious places in India. The pilgrimage to four abodes (*char dham*) was essential to many Nepali Hindus—Badrinath in Uttarakhand, Dwarka in Gujarat, Puri in Odisha and Rameswaram in Tamil Nadu are the four must-visit places to ensure that one's soul achieves salvation. Similarly, Nepali Hindus, after a death in the family, went for rituals to Haridwar, Gaya, Kashi (Varanasi) and Prayag (Allahabad). The cultural and religious ties between India and Nepal are so entangled and strong that they have not been impacted by the political challenges faced by both countries for the past two centuries, since the signing of the Treaty of Sugauli in 1812.

Many of the Nepa Mandala rituals had an Indian influence. For instance, the Rato Machendranath (Red Machendranath) god is taken around in a chariot each year in Patan before the rains, as per the lunar calendar. This idol has been brought from Kamakhya (Kamrupa) in modern-day Assam. While the Hindus worship him as an incarnation of Shiva, the Buddhists worship him as the god of compassion, a manifestation of Avalokitesvara. The origins of Charya singing and dance can be traced back over one thousand years, originating in East Bengal (currently Bangladesh), but the way it is presented reflects the milieu of cultures. While the singing is in Sanskrit, the moves resemble the temple dances of south India, while the headgear and attire have a strong Tibetan and Chinese influence.

## Malla Caste System

In the fourteenth century, when King Jayasthiti Malla decided to organize the people into four varnas[13] and sixty-four castes with the help of five Brahmins from the Indian plains, no one imagined that it could have an impact for centuries to come. From entrepreneurs to people in agricultural, trade and religious practices, the valley Newas were suddenly put into pigeonholes of professions they should rent-seek on. The most productive folks in the farms, the Jyapus, were relegated to the lower caste. Within the Shakyas, if someone was in the profession of tailoring, his name would be changed to a tailor in the Néwa language and then he would be relegated further to a lower untouchable caste (Damai). So if a trader used a scale (*tula*) to sell his wares, he got branded as Tuladhar (the holder of scales), and if one was a painter, then one became Chitrakar and was banished to the lower caste. The various castes had to follow specific rules pertaining to occupation, residence, dress, housing and a number of social and ritual matters.[14] These got even more complicated during the Shah rule which shall be discussed in the next chapter. The caste system rewarded people who did less work and ordered others around while the real workers got relegated to lower castes. This has resulted in rent-seeking in one's own higher caste and looking down on people who do actual work, a practice that has become one of the biggest impediments to fostering entrepreneurship in Nepal.

## What Was Happening Elsewhere

Nepali history has always been written and read in isolation. But it is important to understand what was going on in the world when the Malla kings ruled the Nepa Mandala. At that time, in many areas of Asia, major building projects which included that of palaces and temple complexes were being undertaken. In China, Kublai Khan was building the Forbidden City, in Tibet, major monasteries like the Jokhang temple were being built. The Chola dynasty of India had spread to the Far East. Major structures like Angkor Wat were being built in Cambodia, and the stories of the Borobudur temple in Java, Indonesia, had spread. In Europe, the Italian Renaissance had begun. The exploration of other worlds had begun, and people like Christopher Columbus and Vasco da Gama were discovering new lands and etching out new routes.

 Much of the history we read of Nepal and South Asia looks at events only through political lenses. However, most of the conquests, wars and exploration were for economic motives—to meet consumption from imports, create demand for new items of luxury, and to explore new economic vistas. The introduction of tea in Europe laid the foundations of a new economy that led to plantations and jobs. Similarly, the demand for high-end silk or porcelain in Europe created trading economies in China. The transport of beer over long distances required innovation, therefore Indian Pale Ale (IPA) was born.

Similarly, tea could earlier only be transported in liquid form to Britain as loose tea leaves were not allowed to be imported, and this created the requirement of brewing tea in ships in the high seas. This led to a lot of marks being left on porcelain cups. The accidental discovery of brewing milk with tea solved this problem.

## Himalayan Kingdoms

During the time of the Malla kings, a lot was happening elsewhere in the Himalayas. In Ladakh, the Buddhist kings were trying to save themselves from successive invasions by Muslim invaders. As Ladakh was being managed by Tibet, the palaces there were also built with Newa craftspeople. The Stok Palace was constructed in the fourteenth century, and Ladakhi legend has it that the Dalai Lama was so jealous that he ordered a bigger palace of the same design to be constructed in Lhasa. This resulted in the building of the Potala Palace in the mid-1600s.[15] This rivalry between rulers in constructing palaces and monasteries ensured that the Newa craftsmen from Nepal continued to get work and so they travelled to these places. In 1620, Shabdrung Ngawang Namgyal of Bhutan commissioned a few Newa craftsmen from the Kathmandu valley in Nepal to make a silver stupa to contain the ashes of his father, Tempa Nima.[16]

In the east, the contours of modern-day Sikkim were created by a monk, Phuntsog Namgyal, in 1604, along with the Namgyal dynasty whose kings had the title Chogyal or 'Dharma king'. Namgyal, meaning 'the victorious one', was also a dynasty in Ladakh that started in 1460 CE. Bhutan in its current form was founded in the seventh century, and its first ruler, Shabdrung Ngawang Namgyal, died in 1651. His death was kept a secret for decades.[17] The Himalayan kingdoms kept fighting with each other but also had intermarriages among them and commonality in religious beliefs, practices and cultures.

Vocation, profession, nature of tribes and opportunities were very important in how ethnic groups got associated with prosperity or poverty. For instance, the stories of the Sherpas are interesting. Sher (East) and Pa (People), literally, people from the East, migrated from the Tibetan Kham province—now the border of the Sichuan province—in the fifteenth century, and settled in the Khumbu valley, to the east of Kathmandu. With strong vocational and entrepreneurial pursuits, their economic fate took a turn for the better. After the opening of the mountains for climbing, they are now associated with climbing around the world.

## Tibet and Newas

Nepal, especially Kathmandu, had a roti–beti (literally, 'bread–daughter'; figuratively, 'intimate') relationship with Tibet, very much like the Madhesis' relationship with the neighbouring Indian states of Bihar and Uttar Pradesh, or the relationships that the Ranas and Shahs shared with Rajasthan and other princely states of India. While growing up, we were told that Shigatse, the second largest city in Tibet, was christened by Newa traders. At one point in time, this village had around ten houses, and therefore, in the Newa language it was called 'Zhikha', meaning ten, and 'chhen', meaning house. As the Mallas of the Kathmandu valley minted coins for Tibet, Newa traders returned with Tibetan wives. In the *bhoey* (feasts) of Nagbaha, the baha[18] with the largest number of Tibetan business folks in Patan, known as 'Lhasa Newas', phing and tofu found their ways into different Nepali dishes. Long before the habit of drinking Darjeeling or Assam tea with milk and sugar after the British colonized India, tea was drunk like in Lhasa, using chiyari or bhakchu with salt and butter. Mah-jong, a Chinese board game, was more popular than cards. Centuries of doing business with Tibet had also established the Newa merchant community as the primary link between Indian traders to the south, and the Tibetan traders to the north. The control of the Newa community over this trade route is demonstrated by reports that place the Newa as the single largest group of foreigners in Lhasa.[19]

## Gorkhas and Newas

To the west of the Nepa Mandala was the Gorkha kingdom, a confederation of twenty-four kingdoms popularly known as Chaubisi Rajya. Their boundary with the Malla kingdom was the Trishuli River. The kingdom was founded by Prince Dravya Shah in 1559. His father and ancestors belonged to the group of Rajputs who settled and founded Udaipur in current-day Rajasthan. It is said that when the Rajputs refused to get their daughter married to Emperor Akbar, he went on a rampage, and the survivors were forced to flee. The Gorkha kingdom kept waging wars with Malla kings at different times for nearly two hundred years before finally conquering the Nepa Mandala. The Mandala had split into three separate kingdoms and there could not have been a better time for invasion as the internal squabbles were endless.

The Gorkhas and the Newa people were like chalk and cheese. The Gorkhas were Hindu devotees and a martial race that was battle-hardened, having to keep control of twenty-four kingdoms. The Newas were their complete opposite—people who were tolerant and peaceful. The other big difference was that the Newa people used alcohol and meat in their offerings to Hindu gods, and therefore the Gorkhas clubbed them with the alcohol-offering and drinking group commonly known as the Matwalis. So an entire tribe of Newas became a caste in the eyes of the Gorkhas. This understanding continues till date. The Gorkhas regarded the Newas as meek people who were very scared, thereby dubbing them akin to cowards. For the Newas, the Gorkhas represented the *kheys* or the dumb people who spoke the *khey bhaye* (Khas language). This difference in perception ensured that Gorkha king, Prithvi Narayan Shah took over the Nepa Mandala on the day of the festivities of Indrajatra, putting an end to six centuries of Malla rule and beginning the new dynasty of the Shah kings.

## 2

# Shah Rule: From Regional Hub to Isolation, 1776–1846

When Prithvi Narayan Shah was crowned the king of Gorkha in 1743, he had already set his sights on the Kathmandu valley. His interest in the valley was not surprising, given its affluence and power. The valley was home to one of the wealthiest kingdoms in the entire Mahabharata range. Situated on the primary trade route between South Asia and the northern kingdoms of Tibet and China, the three kingdoms of Bhaktapur, Lalitpur and Kathmandu benefited from an extensive trade network and a prosperous agricultural economy. In taking over the Kathmandu valley, Prithvi Narayan Shah gained the advantage of a monopoly over the trade between India and Tibet. The economic sway of these three kingdoms over the entire hill region is attested to by the fact that its entire monetary requirement was met through coinage minted in these kingdoms. When he attacked the Kathmandu valley, he was well aware of the impending squabbles between the Malla kings and the Tibetan ruler. The infighting between the Malla kings had cost them dear and they started mixing copper in silver coins. This led to protracted altercations which resulted in a war.

Prithvi Narayan Shah understood that Gorkha was not a wealthy nation. Had he heard of Adam Smith's definition of wealth as the annual produce of the land and the labour of a society, he would have agreed. Born in the same year, both Shah and Smith shared an interest in the wealth of nations. However, if Adam Smith's motivations are widely believed (rightly or wrongly) to have been philosophical and intellectual, Prithvi Narayan Shah's are generally seen as real and practical—he strove for personal and national enrichment. He had a modest upbringing for a prince—eating sugar cane for a treat and keeping pigeons as a hobby. An annual clothing budget of six and a half rupees and pocket money counted in quarters—all in the coinage of the valley kingdoms—were his other, equally unimpressive royal privileges. This austere upbringing, coupled with a long-standing family desire to capture the wealth of Kathmandu, undoubtedly inspired him to lead Gorkha on a warpath towards Kathmandu.

Prithvi Narayan Shah ruled over a predominantly Newa population and was fortunate that this community came to accept Gorkhali rule without putting up too much of a fight, though they initially had reasons to do so. The prolonged war and blockade instituted by the Gorkhali army had created a shortage of food supplies in the valley and had seriously disrupted trade, the Newa mainstay. With the Gorkhali conquest of Kathmandu, however, Newa traders suddenly found themselves in the capital city of an expanding empire and at the central trade hub for the entire hill region of Nepal. A Newa farmer who traditionally produced and traded mustard oil with Tibet suddenly found previously restricted markets in the western regions of Nepal opening up for trade.

## New Caste System

Prithvi Narayan Shah reworked the caste system of Nepal created by the Malla kings to ensure that he could use religion and caste as a weapon to cement his authority. The Newas, who had their own caste system, were now clubbed together under the Matwali group—which meant people who offered alcohol to the gods. The Newa priests were replaced by priests from India. Christian missionaries and Kashmiri merchants were expelled in the quest of making Nepal a true Hindu nation. The Newa rulers and custodians of their religion suddenly found themselves dominated by the new Gorkha rulers. This pushed them to either migrate or simply focus on the business profession they had adopted.

The initial resentment at being conquered quickly vanished as the Newas started capitalizing on these undeniable business advantages. This resurgence of trade within and beyond the borders of the empire led to an economic boom.

Having secured a firm financial base for his empire, Prithvi Narayan Shah quickly moved south and conquered the three Terai kingdoms of Makwanpur, Vijaypur and Chaudandi by 1774. It is without a doubt that the prosperity of these regions made them prime targets. They were not only the primary gateway for trade into India, but were also rich in resources. The vast forests that dominated the southern expanses of Nepal provided a lucrative base for the trade of resources like wax, honey, musk, herbs and timber. In addition to this, major commodities like paddy, oilseeds, cotton, jute, tobacco and sugar cane were produced in the region in sufficient quantities to export to cities as far off as Patna and present-day Kolkata.

Although a sense of nationalism and the cause of defending the Hindu nation from occupation and subjugation by the British and the Muslims are commonly cited as political and personal motives behind Prithvi Narayan Shah's conquest, the economic rationale cannot be underestimated. Indeed, an economic analysis of his expansion indicates that his continued success in both conquest and rule hinged on the acquisition of a strong financial base. Shah was a visionary and an astute tactician; it is not without reason that he has been glorified as a nationalist hero and the unifier of the nation in every Nepali textbook. However, given his personality traits of having vision and a strategic acumen, it is hard—and perhaps even dishonest—not to add the incentives of wealth, power and glory to his drive. Without the income secured from his initial conquests, it is unlikely that the Gorkhali empire would have been able to sustain its expansion until well after his death in 1775.

## The Tumultuous Years

During the years after the death of Prithvi Narayan Shah in 1775 and the Treaty of Sugauli in 1816, there were many tussles between his successors. The rise of the prime ministers and the deadly feud between the families began as well. The Thapa and Pandey families engaged in bitter feuds, marking the culture of having puppet kings and giving rise to the era of powerful prime ministers. Also, during these years, two expensive wars were fought. In 1789, the Nepali army repelled the invasion from the Tibet side and signed the Treaty of Kerung. As per the treaty, Nepal was to give back the territories it captured and in return receive a tribute of Nepali Rupees (NPR) 50,001 each year. However, the Tibetan rulers asked for help from the Qing rulers in Beijing and they invaded Nepal. After protracted battles, Nepal agreed to sign the Friendship Treaty of Betravati on 2 October 1792. After this, Tibet was no longer required to pay the tribute; instead, the Nepal government was mandated to pay tributes to the Qing ruler in Beijing every five years.[1] The Newa traders in Lhasa and other parts of Tibet who were harassed and whose belongings were taken away got a respite. However, this ended the Shah rulers' dream of expanding their kingdom beyond the Himalayas in the north.

## The Invisible Hand versus the Visible Fist

A year after Prithvi Narayan Shah's death, Adam Smith would publish his magnum opus, *The Wealth of Nations*.[2] In his book, Smith presents the notion of the invisible hand as a natural force which guides free-market capitalism through the competition for scarce resources, regulating it in the absence of state control. Smith believed that the greatest benefit to a society is brought about by individuals acting freely and in self-interest in a competitive market—leading to specialization and diversification in the economy. However, even if Smith himself were the personal adviser to the kings of Nepal on all economic matters, he would have found it an extremely arduous and painstaking job, if not an impossible one, to convert the late-eighteenth-century feudal rule of Nepal into a free-market economy. The difficulty of such a task lay in the stark contrast between the conditions in Europe and in Nepal. Although Europe was also largely dominated by some form of feudalism during the eighteenth century, it had established a number of semi-autonomous institutions of scientific research and education. Financial and monetary systems had already been institutionalized in order to manage the extensive trade networks while the lack of a caste system allowed for mobility of labour between occupations. The mobility and flexibility in Europe's labour market is perhaps best illustrated by the rise of Napoleon from a common solider to emperor of the French republic. Such a feat would have been unheard of and socially unacceptable in Nepal. Most importantly, the involvement of the individual in the economy and the general perception of the economy in Europe were fundamentally different from Nepal's situation. The rise of trade and capitalism had allowed Europe to perceive the economy as a distinct entity in its own right, an entity in which the state itself was a player. However, in Nepal, the economy was perceived as belonging to the state. This perception was further supported by the Nepali government's landownership system (which will be described later), limitations on private enterprise, and restrictions on the workforce. The Nepali economy was clearly ruled by the iron-fisted and very visible hand of the state.

The lack of favourable social and institutional conditions in Nepal was not the sole reason for its failure to enter a capitalist economy—the nature of the leadership was also to blame. When *The Wealth of Nations* was published, it practically founded the science of economics, at a time when the words 'economics' and 'capitalism' were not even in common use. The American nation had just come into being in 1776, while Germany was about a century away from establishing itself as a nation. Nepal, however, lacked leaders like Thomas Jefferson and Benjamin Franklin, who were raised during the Age of Enlightenment and taught in the progressive scientific tradition that was establishing itself in the West. Thus, it is not surprising that ideas of free-market capitalism and universal suffrage were even further off. The maximization of efficiency and productivity, the hallmarks of any capitalist society, were not central to the Nepali economy. Instead, the focus seemed to be on maximizing revenues and state control while maintaining the status quo, rather than creating the conditions necessary for economic growth and expansion.

The caste system is a classic example of this erroneous focus. Taken as an economic system for the division of labour, the caste system shows an understanding of the importance of labour specialization. However, as a state-instituted regime, it became a hierarchical social order that restricted labour migration and led to a stifled economy.

Before his death, Prithvi Narayan Shah was able to present a vision for the nation popularly known as *Divya Upadesh*.[3] The dictated vision of Nepal's conquering king contains the seeds of a Nepali national identity, a strong affinity for the traditional Hindu caste system, and a tacit acknowledgement of the diversity present in Nepal. His realization of the need for a strong administration and judiciary are apparent in his emphasis on a system that is fair and just. He not only outlined a code of conduct for his citizens, but also demanded austerity and conservatism from his own descendants and the nobility. Unfortunately, he was unable to institutionalize this code of conduct. Additionally, he made strong statements that advocated a protectionist monetary economy based on nationalistic principles. This economic protectionism and his strong warnings against the British played a significant role in Nepal's hostile stance towards the British and its adoption of isolationist policies. These protectionist policies continued till 250 years later, even after the demise of the Shah dynasty he had founded.

The state of Nepal was structured by a feudal system that centralized the ownership of land with the state, which was synonymous with the king. The nobility and feudal lords of Nepal, unlike the feudal lords of England and Germany, thus could not assert any independent authority based on the ownership of land. All feudal lords in Nepal enjoyed their rights to hold land only at the discretion of the king. This traditional system of administration, called the *pajani* system, was carried forward by Prithvi Narayan Shah because he believed it would allow the king to be the defender of justice. Under the system, each feudal lord's performance with his land grant, vis-à-vis revenue collection, would be reviewed, leading to either renewal or termination dependent upon performance levels. This system of administration held true for everyone working for the government, from the nobility to soldiers.

In simple terms, the pajani system was meant to ensure that the right man was matched with the right job, thus ensuring the productivity of land as an asset, and that all the nobility remained loyal to the crown. Its weakness was its overdependence on a single individual, the king, as the guarantor of justice, a responsibility which he did not always conduct according to the stated rules. This resulted in a tenuous system of land administration where, lacking any guarantee of continued rights to the land, nobles preferred to wage war or attend at court to impress the king, rather than develop a viable political relationship with the populations in their territories.

## Sowing the Nepali Rent-Seeking Mentality

There is a rich tradition in Nepal which encourages the aristocracy and rich landowners to do nothing but tend to the renting out of their land. Upper-caste males of the Brahmin, Chhetri and some Newa castes frowned upon the idea of working. The belief was that work was meant for the lower castes, and the only dignified service for upper-caste persons was religious activity (for Brahmins) or military service (for Chhetris). The pattern of elite members of society showing an aversion to work, remaining content with doing nothing other than collecting rent and being socially praised for such inactivity, is what I call here the rent-seeking mentality. It has its roots in Nepal's early history and is a disposition to economic activity that resurfaces in various forms to this day. We are yet to become a society that believes in the dignity of labour, and finds doing a task as respectable as ordering a task to be done.

With an agrarian economy lacking private enterprise and facing mounting administrative and military expenses, the Nepali state could only respond to a shortfall in funds by exploiting its primary asset: land. Prithvi Narayan Shah was quick to realize that the lack of a strong cash economy and his inheritance of a weak government revenue and expenditure system ensured that land remained his primary asset. He had to maximize the productivity of the land he owned as it was the only means of increasing state revenue. He therefore made land central to the feudal and economic structure of Nepal and controlled access to it through the pajani system in which there was no guarantee of continued rights to the land. Now I will describe the various land tenure systems and ownership modalities that were already in operation in Nepal, and explain how, combined with pajani, they eventually weakened the empire.

*Birta*s were land grants given out by the state to individuals,[4] with the individual retaining all rights to the produce of the land, along with the rights to earn an income from litigations, administrative fees and taxes on the surrounding area. This system placed the *birtawals*[5] as the effective rulers over the tracts of land which they were renting from the state in return for supplying troops, weapons and ammunition to the expanding empire. If birta land grants were an effective way to rent out state-owned land to ensure productivity, the *jagir* system was an ingenious way to continue the expansion of the empire while running the government at a deficit. Adapted from a system that was introduced by the Muslim rulers in India during the thirteenth century, jagirs were short-term land grants which were mostly given for military services in lieu of cash salaries. This greatly reduced the cash burden on a state that lacked a strong cash economy, ensured productivity in newly acquired lands, and was a successful means of payment, as a large number of land-hungry hill men thought the promise of fertile land in the Terai was worth more than the risk of death in military service.

Besides the birta and jagir systems of land grants, *guthi* land grants were given to temples and monasteries for the benefit of the local community. *Rakam* land grants were given to craftsmen and skilled workers as payment for their labour. Birta and jagir started to replace other forms of landownership under Prithvi Narayan Shah's rule. For instance, *kipat* land was part of a more traditional form of communal landownership practised in the eastern regions of Nepal by Rai and Limbu ethnic groups. Large tracts of kipat land were converted into birta and jagir lands to fund the expansion of the Nepali state. Although the land system adopted by the new state of Nepal facilitated its expansionary steps, in the long run it was to prove a disastrous and costly system for the state. Under this system, the direct relationship between the state and the peasantry was replaced and superseded by the birta or jagir tenant. Thus, the administration of justice and the protection of the peasantry, which, according to Prithvi Narayan's *Divya Upadesh*, were the direct responsibility of the king and state, were never experienced in that way by the peasants. For the peasantry, the state was effectively replaced by the birtawal or *jagirdar*. The word jagirdar is still popularly used to refer to someone who has a plum 'rent-seeking' job that includes working as a driver in a non-governmental organization (NGO).

To make matters worse, the one relationship the peasantry had left with the state was of exploitation through taxes. The state did not tax birta and jagir grant-holders as the grants were given with a tax exemption, and so the burden of paying taxes to the state fell on the underprivileged class of peasants who owned small tracts of land compared to the vast tracts owned by the birtawals and jagirdars.

This required peasants to work on birta and jagir land, paying a rental fee for the rights to cultivate that land. These rents were often preposterously high as both the birtawals and jagirdars tried to maximize their income during their limited tenure on the land. The pajani system ensured that there was no guarantee of continued rights to it. Since the bulk of birta and jagir owners were members of the nobility, they rarely presided over the lands they were granted. Being in Kathmandu made it easier to secure the blessing of the king and earn larger land grants. This meant that they had to contract out the actual administration of the land, further removing the peasantry from any direct contact with the state. This contractual hiring of administrators, called the *ijara* system,[6] was also deployed by the state to collect taxes from the peasantry. Till date, the system is perpetuated by political parties which use different village representatives to collect money and propagate the party ideology; this method stems from the same mindset that was operating at that time.

After Prithvi Narayan Shah's death in 1775, the expansion of the state continued but successive rulers were unable to institutionalize either a strong governance system or a progressive economic policy. The empire thus made little progress—the traditional feudal economic system that was prevalent in Gorkha and the surrounding regions continued. The financial pressures on the Nepali state were tremendous; in 1772, three years before Prithvi Narayan Shah's death, the annual cost of maintaining an army of around 9000-strong persons was about NPR 4,50,000, while its revenues amounted to at most NPR 3,00,000 for the same year.[7]

The nobility's dependence on birta grants and jagir assignments for their own individual affluence created a lot of competition between them. These systems were also in stark contrast to the political and administrative system of the British East India Company, which followed a more modern system of landownership, taxation and governance. The two systems came into conflict in the Terai, where local landholders would get rights to land from the British as well as from Kathmandu and declare themselves and their land as belonging to either party, depending on what was convenient at any given time. The British were used to having clearly demarcated boundaries and found it difficult to adapt to the more ambiguous Nepali land system. Land rights under the Nepali system also included rights to adjudicate in, administer and tax these lands, further confusing the British East India Company's administration. These land disputes eventually led to the 1814–15 Anglo-Nepal war.

## The End of Empire

Given Nepal's weak financial situation due to its extensive expansion efforts, it is surprising that the country entered into a war against the British East India Company. A heavy loss to the Chinese in the 1792 Sino-Nepal war had already considerably weakened the Gorkhali army and empire. Additionally, the Nepali army had been weakened by a prolonged but unsuccessful siege at Kangra which had ended in a clash with the Sikh ruler Ranjit Singh in 1809. In contrast, by 1813, the Company had expanded its control over most of India, aside from the kingdoms of Punjab and Nepal. The Company's military and financial superiority to the newly formed Gorkhali empire was evident in its accomplishments. The empire's continued expansionary efforts despite these known facts and its eventual war with the British point to the weak governance and lack of foresight of its ruling aristocracy.

Unlike the agrarian Nepali state, the British East India Company's military power was the result of a commercial enterprise that grew out of a monetary economy. The East India Company had been established through a royal charter as a joint stock company in the year 1600. It functioned as a commercial organization with state-granted monopolies over the trade of certain goods or forms of labour. It began trading in India in 1608, and by 1813 had commercial and political control over most of the Indian subcontinent, aside from Punjab and Nepal. However, much like Nepal, the Company was on the brink of bankruptcy, with its wars of expansion in India having drained its coffers. In an attempt to stave off bankruptcy, the Company petitioned Parliament, leading to the British Crown asserting its sovereignty over its Indian territories but extending the administrative rule of the Company within those territories in 1813.

In effect, the Anglo-Nepal war was fought between the state of Nepal and a Company which had been hired to manage the administration of British territories in India. On the eve of the war, Nepal's annual state revenue was no more than approximately NPR 8,00,000. During the same time period, the annual revenue of the British government totalled 16 million pounds. Thus, the much-acclaimed historical David-and-Goliath battle between the two nations was more a case of Nepali recklessness than courage, and more arrogance than foresight. By the end of the war in 1816, Nepal had lost considerable tracts of agriculturally productive lands in the Terai, Sikkim and a significant portion of territory west of the Mahakali River. For a kingdom that was so heavily dependent on land, the loss of over 64,000 square km of territory was a significant blow to the national ego. Nonetheless, the fact that the Gorkhali empire eventually retained an area of over 1,36,000 square km, having started with a kingdom of less than 250 square km, is a good measure of its success.[8] Even so, given the economic value of the one-third of lands lost to the British, Nepal was crippled by this territorial and economic defeat. The defeat to the British, which was preceded by defeats at the hands of the Chinese and the Sikhs, effectively ended Nepal's expansionary attempts and its attempts to establish itself as a regional power. Forced to acknowledge its disadvantage in both military size and economic power in comparison with the two major powers in the region, from 1816 onwards Nepal followed an increasingly isolationist policy. The way the war ended did sow a big problem between the inhabitants of the lowland region of Nepal called the Terai and the folks from the mid-hills of Nepal. This kept haunting the government in Kathmandu for the next 200 years, eventually leading to the Indian blockade at the border in September 2015 that changed the future of the region's geopolitics.

## The Uncertainty and the Fall of the Shahs: 1816–46

After losing a major proportion of territory and lots of money in the war with the British, the Shahs started becoming more inward-looking, with major skirmishes taking place within the key minister families of the Thapas and Pandeys. Bhimsen Thapa became a *mukhtiyar* or prime minister after a massacre that killed ninety-three people, and ruled for a full decade. After his death, the Pandey family took over as the ministers, ending a long period of Thapa rule. The internal squabbles never ceased. In four decades, another massacre took place on 14 September 1846, when Jung Bahadur Kunwar and his brothers went on a rampage, ending eighty years of Shah supremacy and leading to a different way of governing Nepal.

3

# Shah Puppets: Rana Autocracy, 1846–1950

The fallout from the end of empire was that the nobility and feudal lords of Nepal all returned to Kathmandu from different parts of Nepal. No longer able to win honours and land grants through their military prowess, the feudal pajani system made it necessary for the nobles to cosy up to the royal family in order to secure their land rights and increase their wealth. The result was a chaotic power struggle between the various families of the nobility—most notably the Thapa, Pandey and Basnet families. Court intrigue, political manoeuvring and assassinations became a regular occurrence in these turbulent times. This culminated in the 1846 Kot massacre, orchestrated by Jung Bahadur Kunwar and his brothers, resulting in the death of over fifty high-ranking and prominent members of the nobility and military. In one bloody night, within the precincts of the royal court, Jung Bahadur successfully eliminated all his enemies and propelled himself into the position of prime minister of Nepal. Jung Bahadur is, in many ways, Nepal's Napoleon. Coming from a minor aristocratic family, the Kunwars, Jung Bahadur made a name for himself through his sheer recklessness and daring character. He was a man who would do anything for the right price. By 1846, having moved up the aristocratic ladder, he had successfully annihilated most of the aristocracy, reduced the king and queen to mere puppets and assumed absolute power over Nepal. To commemorate his accomplishment, he took on the title of Rana, marking the beginning of the Rana regime. The name 'Rana' was adopted by all his kinsmen.

By eliminating the most prominent members of all the other aristocratic families and banishing their remaining family members to British India, Jung Bahadur was able to assert absolute control over the Nepali court. He also utilized the pajani system to ensure that all offices of responsibility and all land rights were offered to his own family and supporters. Jung Bahadur did not appoint himself as king, choosing instead to retain the monarchy as a symbolic institution and severely curtailing the movements and activities of the king and queen.

From the end of the Anglo-Nepal war in 1816 till the time of Jung Bahadur's ascendancy, little changed in the way Nepal was governed. However, unlike his predecessors, whose relations with Britain were cold, Jung Bahadur realized the futility of trying to stand against them. With the British annexation of the Sikh empire in 1849, early on in Jung Bahadur's career, he understood the ability of the British empire to humble the expansive kingdoms of the south. Although cautious, Jung Bahadur sought to befriend the British, a strategy which was to work in his favour. Unwilling to allow British and Indian traders into Nepal, he nonetheless saw the benefits of trading with them. He was keen on restoring the monopoly Nepal had once possessed on the trade between India and Tibet. Using the mistreatment of Nepali traders in Tibet as an excuse, Jung Bahadur launched an offensive against Tibet in 1855. His intelligence on the Chinese was undoubtedly facilitated by the British, who were gearing up for the second Opium War of 1856. Thus, the inability of the Chinese to assist Tibet, which had, in the past, thwarted Nepali expansion, was effectively insured. This eventually led to Nepal's 1856 treaty with Tibet which granted Nepal similar privileges in Tibet as it had enjoyed during the Malla reign in the sixteenth and seventeenth centuries and subsequently lost during the late eighteenth century, but it still remained a tributary state to China. Importantly, this reinstated Nepal's trade relations with Tibet which had taken a serious hit since the 1792 Sino-Nepal war.

## Traversing the Black Waters

In pursuit of friendlier relations with Britain, Jung Bahadur became the first prince from the subcontinent to travel across what were then known as the 'black waters' to England. His voyage across the black waters, forbidden by the Hindu religion, required him to return, for purposes of purification, via Rameswaram in southern India. Many people thereafter referred to Jung Bahadur as impure, since he had crossed oceans and started behaving like a westerner.

Jung Bahadur's voyage to Europe allowed him to see Britain at the height of its industrial revolution, possessing the most powerful navy in the world and in command of an empire that had expanded throughout the world. The technological and military supremacy of Britain reaffirmed Jung Bahadur's belief that the British could not be beaten through military means. Upon returning, some of the things he saw appear to have rubbed off on him—he went on to institute a number of reforms in an attempt to modernize the nation, such as keeping accounts for revenues collected by the state. Figures from this period show Nepal having revenues of slightly above NPR 1.4 million in 1851, which went up to NPR 9.6 million by the last year of Jung Bahadur's rule in 1877. Subsequent Rana rulers chose not to keep an account of revenues, although at the end of Rana rule in 1951, the state revenue was recorded at NPR 29 million. Although Jung Bahadur saw the value of good account-keeping and tried to institute it, he saw no reason to change the tradition of claiming all state revenues as his own personal income. Thus, the view of land as the property of the state and all income generated from the land as the income of the king remained.

In 1857, the sepoy rebellion in India allowed Jung Bahadur to cement his alliance with the British. He rode into India as the head of an army that assisted the British in suppressing the rebellion. This firmly established Nepal as an ally to the British empire and led to its eventual acknowledgement of Nepal as an independent and sovereign nation state. Jung Bahadur also promulgated and supported the active recruitment of Gorkhas[1] into the British army. This was a tradition that had started as early as 1815 with the formation of King George I's Own Gorkha Rifles by General David Ochterlony—who commanded the East Indian Army that was sent against Nepal. This concession on the recruitment of Gorkhas into the British army from Nepal, granted to the British as part of the peace treaty, led a Nepali general, Balbhadra Kunwar, to leave the country in disgust and go fight for the Sikh king Ranjit Singh in Lahore, which is the origin of the popular local Nepali title for mercenaries who join foreign armies—*lahure*. It also established a long-standing trend of Nepali workers leaving Nepal in search of a better future.

## Lucknow Loot

The quelling of the sepoy rebellion in India also provided unprecedented wealth to Jung Bahadur and his family members who were involved in the plundering of cities after the war. The term 'Lucknow Loot' is used to describe the riches that were brought back to Kathmandu after plundering palaces and homes after the cities fell to the Gorkhas in Company uniforms. There are many stories about the amount of loot that was brought back. There are accounts that describe people spotting 400 bullock carts laden with riches crossing the Indian border to Nepal.[2] The riches from this loot ensured that the Rana family could indulge in opulence, build palaces and compete with each other in terms of embracing luxury. Raj Krishna Shrestha describes in his book, *The Lucky Man*, the major sale of these items when the Rana regime started to wane due to internal squabbles, excessive indulgence in women and alcohol and the lack of purpose to their lives.

The role of the Ranas during the sepoy rebellion and later the faithful support of the British during World Wars I and II made them very unpopular with the people fighting for the independence of India from the British. This cost them dearly as the Rana regime ended in 1950, soon after India gained independence from the British.

## Procreation and Categorization

The family of Jung Bahadur between 1846 and 1950 multiplied in an unprecedented manner with polygamy and marriage with women of other castes and communities. Unlike the Newa families where marrying outside the community and caste was frowned upon, therefore limiting population growth, the Ranas went in for procreation with gusto. The growth created complications in succession and this gave rise to categorization. A-class denoted those born of high-caste wives and who were eligible for the roll of succession. B-class denoted children born of secondary high-caste wives and from alliances with princesses from the royal household. C were children from others.[3] In the absence of education and the desire to get exposed to what was happening around the world, the attention of the Rana men gravitated towards eating, drinking, gambling and women. The stories of men from three generations of the same Rana family running after a young Tamang girl became the reflection of those times.[4] While the A-class Ranas continued to protect their status, the B and C categories continued to fight for their rights. Further, children from the different wives of the A-class Ranas were jealous and mindful of the others. This created continuous infighting which led to the downfall of the Ranas. While the economic numbers are not available, it is interesting to ponder upon how a regime that owned all the land, had money to build opulent palaces and which amassed wealth from Lucknow Loot could last for just a hundred years. Perhaps this was a result of the structural problems they created while governing themselves.

This pattern can be seen later with the Shah kings and even the different democratic political forces in the country.

## To Greener Pastures

The practice of working in and migrating to India features prominently in Nepali history and is closely related to the stagnation of the national economy. Nepali interests were hampered and economic revenues affected when in 1904, the British opened a new route into Tibet that passed from Siliguri through Sikkim all the way up to Lhasa. This effectively made the trade route through Kathmandu redundant due to the closer proximity of the new route to present-day Kolkata and the shorter travel time required to reach Lhasa. As a result, a considerable number of Newa families involved in the trade business with Tibet shifted to Kalimpong. This Newa migration came at the tail end of a much more voluminous Nepali migration into the neighbouring regions of Darjeeling and Assam to work in the newly established tea estates and agricultural land from the 1850s onwards. The migration of Nepalis went beyond India to present-day Myanmar, Thailand and Malaysia.

The migration of a large number of Nepali people from the eastern hills and plains of Nepal into British-controlled areas of Darjeeling and Assam evinces the opportunities they saw across the border. Simultaneously, it highlights the limited opportunities and lack of hope that people felt in Nepal. The oppressive social hierarchy of the caste system and the totalitarian rule of upper-caste Hindus made it impossible for the lower castes to branch out into fields of work other than what their caste designation allowed them. Within such a confining social structure, these lower castes could not even escape via entrepreneurial spirit as they were forbidden from partaking in a business or occupation beyond their caste. The discouragement of business through state intervention, the lack of capital access and limited mobility due to a lack of investment in transportation infrastructure made Nepal a nation cut off from the progress and social transformation evident elsewhere. In such a dire situation, the people's desire to migrate in the hopes of a better future is understandable.

## Migration to Protect Identity and Cultural Stifling

The migration was also a result of the 'one language, one religion' policy of the Rana rulers. The Newa language and Nepal Sambat were banished and the Khas language, which went on to become the Nepali language only in 1920, was the official language. Speaking and teaching in other languages were banned. Buddhism and Buddhist practices were banned. Buddhist monks were banished from Nepal and they had to find solace in parts of India to continue their dhamma practice. Many laypersons[5] followed these monks to help them navigate their lives in a new country amidst a new culture, language and environment. Much of the valley's living traditions and culture vanished during this time as they were based on oral traditions and not written ones. This was applicable to other communities also. People from the Terai were not allowed to come to Kathmandu without a permit and hill communities that did not practise Hinduism or speak Nepali found living in one's own country suffocating.

The Ranas, like many other rulers in British India, were conservative Hindus who believed in the caste system and patriarchy. The role of women was restricted to household chores and child-bearing. To make matters worse, Jung Bahadur established the Muluki Ain in1854 —a civil code based on caste and class—and effectively reinstituted the caste system in Nepal, eliminating any chance of creating something like the Protestant revolution that was one of the cornerstones of the rise of capitalism and of the industrial revolution in Europe. The fact that the Muluki Ain went for a makeover in 2018 after 174 years demonstrates the challenges of bringing Nepal to a contemporary frame of mind. The code ensured that non-Hindus were placed below Hindus. Therefore, Newa priests were below the ranks of the Hindu priests and they were replaced. The Hindu priests from the Bahun community of the hills and India started to gain more prominence and legitimacy. The migration of the Bahuns into the Kathmandu valley during the Rana period changed the population mix of the valley, relegating the natives, the Newas, to the status of a minority within a century.

The non-Hindu women of the Newa and other hill communities lived a more liberal life compared to Shah and Rana women. For instance, Newa women who lost their husbands were never ostracized as they were by tradition married to the sun, so they could never become widows. They also took part in agriculture, crafts-making and trade. However, the Ranas detested this liberal status of women. My grandmother used to tell us stories about how the Rana men used to come on horseback looking for Newa girls, and therefore they were sent to places like Kalimpong in India as a safe haven and also for their education. The Rana rulers had the image of tyrants and therefore, when the time came to revolt against this regime, there was a lot of tacit support.

## Own Land versus the Lord's Land

One of the primary lures of migrating to Darjeeling and Assam was the availability of land. Coming from a country in which the state hoarded all land and allowed only limited landownership among its people, the story of land being given out by the government to farmers in India must undoubtedly have been an astounding and magical tale of hope for Nepali farmers. For farmers who had never owned the land they tilled, this was an opportunity beyond their wildest dreams. As previously mentioned, in Nepal, the burden of taxes on land was borne by the peasants, who were often forced to farm land belonging to big landowners in order to survive. Nepal's unwillingness to modernize, its insistence on maintaining a bigger than necessary army, its exclusionary landownership system and its inability to establish a sound economic and monetary policy were just some of the causes that led to the stagnation of the Nepali economy, forcing its people to go abroad for better opportunities.

## The Decline and Fall of the Ranas

For all of Jung Bahadur's audacity and daring, including his trip to England, he remained a child of tradition and was unable to push Nepal along a path of modernity. A classic example of how tradition held back reform and technology was when Jung Bahadur brought back a water pump to irrigate the fields of Kaski. A white man was needed to operate the pump, but since this would religiously and culturally 'pollute' the water, the pump became useless for all practical purposes.[6]

The Ranas' close relationship with the British in India was crucial to their control over Nepal. It legitimized and facilitated their rule by muffling any dissent against their regime in the south. The Ranas' power also depended on their military might, and so they maintained a strong standing army that was of considerable expense to the state. Although the army was to become a source of considerable revenue for the Ranas during the two World Wars, they believed that they could maintain a stronger grip over Nepal and rule for much longer if they kept it isolated from the world and did not expose the people of Nepal to the changes that were going on in the broader world. This strategy was to prove effective for the Ranas, but it was not to last. The industrialization of India and the eventual fall of the British Raj meant that the tide of change that had swept through India would inevitably reach the Nepali kingdom as well.

The Rana regime was also illustrative of a lack of ambition. In the early 1900s, Nepal already had hydroelectricity and a ropeway, but the use of both remained limited to building palaces. The opportunity technology afforded for economic growth and an increase in state and concurrently personal income went unheeded by the Rana regime. The Ranas focused on amassing personal wealth and assets in the Kathmandu valley, thereby alienating themselves from the rest of

Nepal, as Nepal and Kathmandu became synonymous. The people outside the Kathmandu valley referred to Kathmandu as Nepal, and this perception of a Kathmandu-centric Nepal would not change for decades to come.

The modernization projects they carried out were aimed primarily at impressing the British with their capacity to be western and modern. Although Prime Minister Juddha Shumsher (1932–45) did make a few progressive moves, such as printing currency notes, constructing factories and instituting a pension system to quell the growing resentment against the Rana regime, the power of the conservative elite comprising other members of the Rana regime did not allow him or his successors, Padma Shumsher and Mohan Shumsher, to go the full distance. Thus, modernization can safely be said to have entered Nepal early, but softly. Neither the rulers nor the people seemed to have much interest in it. They seem to have seen no great accomplishment worth deriving from it. The conservatism of the government and an overly strong emphasis on security seem to have been the primary culprits in the aforementioned lack of ambition.

## Isolation Continues

The Rana regime in Nepal coincided with one of the most important phases in world history. Political changes took place as colonization began and ended. The major colonizers, the British and the French, decided to end human slavery, as did the United States. Human movement got redefined, with automobiles ferrying goods and people at unprecedented speeds. Aviation went commercial in a big way, changing the way wars were fought and enabling humans to reach destinations in time frames that were unimaginable. Currency notes and banking penetrated commerce as it started to replace barter and other systems. Global standards were being fixed in terms of measures of length or weight. The number of explorers and travel writers increased. Along with the reduction in the cost of printing and distribution, print media became accessible and affordable.

Electricity changed the way people lived. Radio and television had entered households in many parts of the world. Education, knowledge and information was being dispersed in far-flung lands. Affordable multi-language dictionaries made translations easier. This was the time when the world made great strides. However, Nepal's engagement only took place during that time with the darker side of world affairs: the wars.

## Economics of Mercenaries in Foreign Uniform

After the Nepali association with the British in the suppression of the Indian sepoy rebellion of 1857, Jung Bahadur realized the economics of sending Nepali youth to fight other people's wars. The people who went to war were never from the ruling class or the dominant Bahun and Chhetris, but were Rais, Magars, Gurungs and Limbus. By World War I, Jung Bahadur's nephew Chandra Shumsher was already receiving an annual payment of a million rupees from the British. Therefore, during World War I, 2,00,000 soldiers were sent to join the fighting British Indian army, dispatched to Europe, where the war was being fought. When the population of Nepal was around 5 million, the number of people who went to fight was nearly one-fifth of able-bodied males in Nepal. With no education or exposure, they went to fight for money—for them the war was about being able to come back with salaries and pensions. They knew the perils of war. For every ten young men from the hills that went to fight, one did not come back and one was injured or incapacitated for life.

Similarly, during World War II, 2,50,000 Nepalis served in the British Indian army and there were 32,000 casualties. Compared to World War I, which was a European war far away from Nepal, World War II was closer to home and fought in the jungles of Burma and Malaysia. With limited economic opportunities in the oppressive Rana regime, selling their lives for other uniforms was the best way to fend for oneself and one's family. Further, the social and cultural norms in the hills of Nepal became associated with sending one's children to fight other people's wars. The tradition of sending one son from the family to join the army began very much like the tradition of sending the eldest son to a monastery to become a monk amongst the Buddhist hill communities. The entire social narrative of the hills changed forever. A hundred years later the same people are sending at least one of their sons to work in Qatar or Malaysia.

## The Institution of Chakari

Dr Ram Sharan Mahat, in his book *In Defense of Democracy*,[7] summarizes what he calls the Rana Shogunate, 'The Rana political system was undisguised military despotism with absolute total control over all aspects of public life.'[8] The Ranas institutionalized the *chakari* system to control political dissent. The system required the concerned nobles to formally and publicly attend the Rana courts for specified hours each day in order for them to remain in close proximity to the Ranas. This effectively controlled the movement and activities of potential troublemakers and conspirators. Furthermore, the practice of night-time curfews rendered night visits and activities impossible. The chakari system continues in Nepal and is a feature of political life till date. It makes proximity to people in power and hobnobbing with them more important than the performance of administrative duties.

The Ranas tried for long to restrict education among the Nepali people. They saw in more widespread education the seeds of their own downfall. Although they did establish a limited number of schools in Nepal, these were primarily meant to prevent Nepali youths from going to study in India. They were also tools for state propaganda and an attempt to ensure the loyalty of the educated class. This attempt had limited success, as education in India was considered of much higher quality. As long as the British remained in India, the Rana regime remained strong in Nepal, but with a growing class of Nepali citizens studying and growing up in India due to educational restrictions in Nepal, a new class of Nepali citizens was forming. They were mostly upper-class and upper-caste landowning Hindus and the children of those who had loyally served in the Rana bureaucracy. It was this class of citizens that both assisted the Indian National Congress in its fight for independence and eventually fought against the Rana regime in the 1940s. Anti-Rana sentiments were sometimes fostered within the Rana family itself, most particularly among lower-ranking Ranas who were not benefiting from the rule they were publicly associated with.

Although anti-Rana movements started in Nepal as early as the 1920s, the most comprehensive attempt to challenge the regime came from the Nepali Congress, constituted by the exiled children of Rana bureaucrats, India-educated and heavily influenced by Jawaharlal Nehru and Mahatma Gandhi. The Nepali Congress grew out of one of the earliest anti-Rana movements which was led by the Praja Parisad, a political party. A few members of the Praja Parisad were executed by the Rana rulers on charges of treason. The anger of the Nepali public about the executions only strengthened the opposition against the Rana regime. Surviving members of the Praja Parisad escaped to India and went on to establish the Nepali Congress in India, with the goal of establishing democracy in Nepal. Although initially propounding a non-violent movement following the way of Gandhi, the Nepali Congress was to take up an armed struggle against the Rana regime from 1947 onwards. In this, they were supported by King Tribhuvan, who had been crowned as the tenth Shah king of Nepal in 1911 at the age of five and been actively involved in the Praja Parisad. He was strongly opposed to the regime of the Rana prime ministers and wished to restore the Shah dynasty to its previous glory.

In April 1950, the Nepali National Congress led by B.P. Koirala, and the Rana dissidents, led by Suvarna Shumsher and Mahavir Shumsher, joined forces. This gave King Tribhuvan the impetus he needed to use pro-democratic forces to push his anti-Rana crusade, the eventual aim of which was to legitimize his own powers. This quest was further facilitated by an independent India which by policy supported the pro-democratic forces in Nepal. By 1951, as a result of these developments, the regime of the Rana prime ministers had fallen in Nepal, while Tibet had been annexed by the Chinese. King Tribhuvan had declared that a democratic government leading to a Constituent Assembly was to be established in Nepal. Under India's tutelage, an interim constitution was drawn up and plans for a Constituent Assembly leading to the establishment of a formal constitution were drafted. These years formed the first few years of Nepal's entrance upon the world stage and its first attempts at modernization towards an industrial society.

# Shahs' Rise and the Fall of the Partyless Panchayat: 1950–90

When King Tribhuvan drove from the Indian embassy (where he had taken refuge to save himself from the Ranas) to take the flight to Delhi on 11 November 1950, the end of the Rana regime was only a matter of time. After protracted negotiations with and help from the Indian government, he returned victorious to restore the glory of the Shah kings. On 18 February 1951 (Falgun 7, 2007 Bikram Sambat) a historical proclamation was made, and a new Constitution was promised. An opening was created for the first time in the twentieth century for Nepal to push for progress and better lives for its people.

What followed immediately after the fall of the Rana regime in 1950 was a foretaste of Nepal's continually stymied attempts to modernize, industrialize and democratize in the coming half century. Between 1951 and 1959, Nepal went through a series of short-lived governments based on an interim constitution entitled the Interim Government of Nepal Act, 1951. This Act was to be in effect until a Constituent Assembly was elected. Although this Act ended the Rana regime, it also made way for the authoritarian rule of King Tribhuvan by granting the king supreme executive, legislative and judicial powers. Further, the marital relations between the Shahs and Ranas continued. For instance, the position of chief of army remained with the Shumsher Jung Bahadur (SJB) Rana family till Gaurav SJB Rana retired in 2015, with a few in the position not belonging to the clan.[1]

The interim Constitution was a drastic change, at least in wording, from anything the Government of Nepal had ever attempted or stated in a document. For instance, for the first time in Nepali history, it categorically stated that the objective of the government was to promote the welfare of the people of Nepal by securing social, economic and political justice. While this was a heartening development in terms of political ideals, economically, Nepal remained isolated from contemporary developments. At a time when the post-War and post-colonial economies in the then developing regions of South and South East Asia started to enter larger transnational networks of trade and commerce, Nepal still had trade relations with only China and India. It also had few industries, with practically an entire population working on the farms and no monetary policy of its own, which meant that the fate of prices and the demand and supply of commodities was completely linked to India. Only 2 per cent of Nepal's entire adult population was literate, less than 1 per cent was engaged in modern industrial occupations, and 85 per cent of all employment and income was based on traditional agricultural practices. There were less than 5000 children in school, 200 doctors, 376 km of metalled roads and a currency that did not have any global value. The newly established government of 1951 faced daunting challenges such as these as it attempted to usher into Nepal the same economic and social changes that were taking place in the rest of South and South East Asia.[2]

## The Currency Curry

The first few governments in the early 1950s quickly realized that because the Indian rupee dominated trade and commerce, Nepal had no control over its own monetary policy, and consequently no control over its foreign currency holdings. The Indian rupee was by far the most prevalent medium of exchange throughout the country. The Nepali rupee remained in use only in Kathmandu and the surrounding hill areas, while the other parts of Nepal, especially the western and far western regions, continued to use the Indian rupee. All of Nepal's foreign exchange earnings went to the Central Bank of India, which in return provided all the foreign currency needs of the country. The existence of a dual currency system in the nation significantly restricted capital accumulation as people did not know which currency to save and which to spend. Government spending during these early years was curtailed as the transactions done in Indian rupees never formed part of the revenue streams for the government.

Responding to the needs of governance and development, the government instituted the Nepal Rastra Bank as the central bank of the nation under the Nepal Rastra Bank Act, 1955. As the central bank of the nation, it was charged with the responsibility of supervising all commercial banks and guiding the monetary policy of the nation. It also set out to regulate the issuance of paper money, mobilize capital, and develop the banking system in the country. Through the efforts of the central bank, a concerted effort was made to circulate the Nepali currency throughout the country as the primary medium of exchange. The Nepali rupee also entered the international currency market through a fixed exchange rate between Nepali and Indian currency in April 1960. Prior to this, the Nepali and Indian currencies were traded at market value with the value of 100 Indian rupees fluctuating between 71 and 177 Nepali rupees between 1932 and 1955.

The argument given by the Rastra Bank for the fixed exchange rate was that it helped lower the fluctuation in the price level of Indian products. This was stated as important because the majority of items imported into Nepal and used by the poor came from India. This argument, that a fixed exchange rate controls inflation, is standard for any fixed exchange rate system. However, the fixed exchange rate, which still persists in Nepal, also prevents the central bank from having any control over the nation's monetary policy, even though a strong monetary policy remains the primary means to ensure macroeconomic stability. Every time the Indian rupee appreciates or depreciates, Nepal has to adjust its currency to it. The fixed exchange rate policy of the Rastra Bank also makes it necessary for it to differentiate the Indian currency—as a freely convertible currency—from other currencies which are non-convertible within Nepal. The non-convertibility of other currencies allows the Rastra Bank to maintain a reserve of foreign currencies. Since 1960, the exchange rate has only been adjusted seven times. The last adjustment in February 1993 set the rate to NPR 1.6 to one Indian rupee, and it has remained that until now, in 2019. It is shocking that an exchange rate set over twenty-six years ago, before the civil war, before the remittance economy, and before the Indian economic boom still remains unchanged. If anything, it is a testament to the Nepali aversion to change that has been endemic since the 1810s.

## Varanasi Connection

The construction of Nepal post the 1950s has perhaps been heavily influenced by Varanasi. The houses of the people in Biratnagar who went to Varanasi to study emulate the ones in the latter city, lock, stock and barrel. The heady mix of religion and politics perhaps finds its foundation in Varanasi, as the control of religious trusts involving temples and the control of political parties can be discussed in the same breath. Therefore, the process of pushing Hinduism and conservative values in the name of religion and culture can be seen even now in Nepal. The caste system did not go away, and neither did the status of women change. Even the Nepali Congress developed a lexicon influenced by the ancient city, where every senior leader is addressed as 'Babu'.

Perhaps Nepali cities also resemble Varanasi in terms of the filth and dirt of the city, with citizens always screaming themselves hoarse demanding their rights but being unwilling to begin a discourse on responsibility. The anti-English tirade, which includes the creation of Sanskritized versions of words and meanings, having licence plates in Devanagari,[3] and considering English an enemy rather than a tool for facilitation, has kept both Varanasi and Nepal far away from globalization. A visit these days to the Pashupatinath temple area in Kathmandu makes one come across alleys that resemble Varanasi. Political power mixes with religion here in a reciprocal relationship—proximity to politics makes it easier to access temples while religious leaders seek to work with the politically powerful to enhance their own influence. Rather than reforming rituals and rites associated with birth or death, a heady mix of consumerism, social pressure and religious fear continue to distinguish Nepal from the rest of the global values embracing South and South East Asia.

## Foreign Aid Begins

The 1950s was also the time the first trickle of foreign aid started to flow into the country. A first aid grant of $2000 was provided by the United States to a tottering Rana regime that fell within a month of receiving it. The source of the money, the Marshall Plan,[4] to fight the rise of communism, was an indication of the direction and intention with which foreign aid was to flood the nation in successive decades. Nepal's two neighbours, despite themselves being aid recipients and decades away from experiencing the prosperity of the 1990s, also got into the aid act, starting with India in 1952 and China in 1956. Both countries showed a keen interest in assisting in infrastructure development projects which remained beyond the financing capabilities of the Nepali government. Indeed, till the mid-1960s, Nepal was entirely dependent on foreign aid to carry out all its development projects.

It is slightly ironic that a country which had remained isolated and detached from the world for over a century should, upon re-entering the world stage, immediately lapse into a state of acute dependency. However, such was the case with Nepal, and this dependency only grew with time. The average aid-to-GDP ratio of a mere 2 per cent in the 1960s grew to around 10 per cent by the 1990s. The government's revenues were perennially lower than its expenditure, thereby requiring it to borrow from aid agencies and obtain grants to meet the gap.

Being seen as a country chronically dependent on foreign aid has had serious economic implications for Nepal. Foreign aid has played a considerable role in shaping many of the sociocultural changes that Nepal has witnessed since the 1950s. It has played a part in introducing Nepal to the world, in influencing its international relations and in shaping the fate of democracy and governance. The tremendous impact of foreign aid on every aspect of its society, politics and economy will be discussed in detail in Chapter 8, but we can state here that it is far from certain that all the billions of dollars of aid money in cash, and cash equivalents like equipment, technology and training have had the desired results of peace, prosperity and development in Nepal.

## Flirting with Democracy

Nepal's entry on to the world stage during King Tribhuvan's rule in the 1950s was marked with considerable hope and aspiration for the future of the nation. However, King Tribhuvan, often referred to as the 'father of democracy' in Nepal, was a bit of an opportunist whose constant interference in the democratic process often impeded that process. For instance, in 1951, King Tribhuvan favoured as the first prime minister Matrika Prasad Koirala, who was supposedly backed by the Indian government, over his younger brother, B.P. Koirala, who was leading the Nepali Congress party at that time. The first cabinet under M.P. Koirala was created in a very inclusive way by today's definition, with five ministers coming from five different communities, namely M.P. Koirala, Narada Muni Thulung, Tripurawar Singh, Suryanath Das Yadav and Mahavir Shumsher Rana. Thereafter, in the last sixty years in Nepal, the government has only paid lip service to this policy of inclusion.

King Tribhuvan thereby privileged Indian patronage over popular democratic norms. After the fall of the government led by M.P. Koirala (due to internal squabbles in the Congress), King Tribhuvan played a role in splitting the Congress, following which M.P. Koirala headed a new breakaway party—the Nepal Praja Parisad. King Tribhuvan then reappointed M.P. Koirala to the post of prime minister in 1954, despite the obvious lack of support from the main Congress party.

King Tribhuvan's short post-Rana stint is also marked by the successful rise of the royal family back into its position of power, filling in the power vacuum left by the Rana prime ministers. The royals showed an increasing willingness to assert their executive power and reinstate their control over the army. In short, the power vacuum created during the period of the interim Constitution allowed for the Shah royal family to reconsolidate its power base. King Tribhuvan died in 1955 without having held the Constituent Assembly he had promised the Nepali people. His son, Mahendra, at age thirty-five, ascended the throne that very year and proved to be a man of vision as well as of action.

In 1959, under the leadership of King Mahendra, Nepal's first election was held, paving the way for a Nepali Congress victory, with the party taking seventy-four of the 109 seats. This set the stage for B.P. Koirala to be the first popularly elected leader of the Nepali people. Kamal Mani Dixit, an intellectual and writer, recalls that during the 1950s, after seven years of confusion, the Nepali people were fed up with the government's inaction and lack of resilience. But with the elections, he says that there was a renewed air of hope and excitement— his own aspiration at the time was '*Sachi nai aba desh banla jasto thiyo*' (It looked like the country would actually prosper now).

It is worth mentioning the framework of the interim Constitution within which the Koirala government had to work. The Constitution decreed two legislative houses, an Upper House and a Lower House. The 109-seat Lower House was elected by universal suffrage, and the thirty-six-seat Upper House was composed of eighteen members hand-picked by the king and eighteen elected from the Lower House. The leader of the majority in the Lower House was elected prime minister but was second in line to the king who could act and dismiss the prime minister without consulting the Lower House. Additionally, the king had complete control over the army and foreign affairs and could invoke emergency powers suspending all or part of the Constitution. Thus, the Constitution was, in effect, only as democratic as its king. Given such a political backdrop, the achievements of the Koirala government were reasonable. It was able to abolish the birta land system that granted state land to select individuals for purposes of administration, thus releasing more land for the ownership of common Nepalis. It revised the lopsided trade arrangements that favoured India unduly and signed a new Trade and Transit Treaty with India in 1960. Nepal would successfully get United Nations membership despite strong tactical opposition from India by demonstrating its identity using the Ranjana script and Newa language, which was distinct from the Nepali language written in the Devanagari script—a Brahmi script in which Sanskrit was also written.

During the Koirala government, and even before it, since the early 1950s, the difficulty of carrying out major development work without skilled human resources, capital and a proper long-term plan of action had become apparent. For this reason, five-year plans were instituted in order to facilitate development, with a major focus on transportation and communication. The lack of roads in its formidable terrain may have assisted the Rana regime's isolationist policy, but proved to be a serious challenge to the progressive Koirala government's attempts to ensure economic growth. The legacy of years of isolation, an administrative structure that had changed little since medieval times, and the shortage of people with the capability and capacity to manage development projects proved even bigger hurdles. As a result, the First Five-Year Plan's budget remained severely underutilized and none of the targets were met. For instance, out of 1450 km of roads planned during the First Five-Year Plan, only 565 km were built, and of a development budget of NPR 576 million, the government was able to utilize only NPR 383 million.[5] Sadly, this underutilization of budgets and the inability to fulfil development plans is a trend that continues to this day. A review in 2019 of the actual spending against the budgets of the Ministry of Finance reveal that since 1950, in no year was the government able to spend the total amount budgeted.

The 1950s were also marked by strong tensions between India and Nepal, with India trying to assert its dominance over all things Nepali. The primary objective of the Indian government was to keep Nepal completely under its own economic umbrella and integrate it completely into the Indian economy. For instance, Nehru himself in 1952 opposed the opening of the American embassy in Kathmandu on the simple grounds that 'it is rather naive to think this can come without any conditions or strings being attached to it'.[6] Facing an expansionist China to its north, which had only recently annexed Tibet and was embroiled in territorial disputes with India, India was not willing to allow Chinese influence to cross the Himalayan range into its backyard. Thus, it adopted a position as the dominant local power in the Himalayan kingdoms of Nepal, Bhutan and Sikkim. This was to eventually lead to the annexation of Sikkim and the imposition of Indian foreign and defence policies within Bhutan. This Indian position was to be a constant bone of contention for Nepal and assisted in the fostering of strong anti-India sentiments in Nepal. For instance, during the coronation of King Birendra, India was annoyed with the invitation to the chogyal (ruler) of Sikkim, and therefore it decided to send its vice president instead of the president to the ceremony, whereas India had sent its president to the Bhutanese king's coronation just a year before.

The increasingly liberal bent of the Koirala government—typified in the Second Five-Year Plan—was giving jitters to the army, former aristocrats and landowners (all three of which were mostly the same class and caste of people). When B.P. Koirala returned from India, he wore clothes like Jawaharlal Nehru and mimicked his style. Later, he quickly switched to dressing like Mahendra. The fact that he started wearing identical sunglasses did not go down well with Mahendra. Given his self-professed lack of belief in democracy and his tendency to transform his beliefs into action, it was hardly a surprise that on 15 December 1960, the king, with the support of the army, exercised his executive powers to dismiss the government and assume full power. Thus ended Nepal's first flirtation with democracy, following which the country became entrenched in three decades of what is popularly known as Panchayat rule, instituted by King Mahendra. The Panchayat system was a partyless, centralized democratic system controlled by palace officials, with sovereign powers vested in the king. The three-tier Panchayat system was comprised of village and town panchayats ruled by a local autocracy, district panchayats, ruled by the king's appointees, and the national panchayat, an appointed Parliament.

However, looking back, B.P. Koirala, while being charismatic, also believed in an economic system that would not have worked towards the inclusive development that he dreamt of. His excessive belief in socialism led him to build an economy based on a system that failed miserably given the fact that by 1978, China was forced to open up its economy and the Soviet Union disintegrated in 1988. The Nepali Congress that believed in pursuing his vision was converted into a party of multiple internal squabbles and dynastic rule, like the Indian National Congress. Therefore, now one can see that the general discontent of the people meant that they did not mind the royal takeover in 1960 as Nepal experienced a similar situation thirty-two years later with King Gyanendra's reign from 2001–08. The biggest challenge of those times was that the rulers, be it Mahendra or B.P. Koirala or others, were Kathmandu-centric in their thinking and did not consider what was happening elsewhere in the country.

## The Panchayat System: Back to Autocracy

The Panchayat system successfully tamed its opposition when the king ordered the arrest of the deposed prime minister, B.P. Koirala, in 1960 and held him in prison for eight years. By the time Koirala was released, the Nepali Congress party had splintered into three groups—leaving Koirala no option but to go to India to muster support against the autocratic rule of the king. However, India's defeat at the hands of the Chinese in 1962 went in the king's favour, with the Indian government unwilling to alienate Nepal for fear of pushing it into the Chinese sphere of influence. It also confirmed King Mahendra's belief that getting too close to any one nation could seriously threaten the sovereignty of Nepal. Thus, unlike his father, who was a staunch supporter of India, King Mahendra chose to maintain an equidistant relationship with India and China. His cool stance towards India also served him well in terms of popular sentiment, by allowing him to act as a saviour of Nepali sovereignty from Indian hegemony. This was later emulated by K.P. Oli after the blockade of 2015.

Mahendra was astute and could develop a good personal relationship with leaders. He managed to develop a personal rapport with Nehru; therefore, he did have some good Indian thought leaders in his team. Similarly, he charmed Chou En Lai, the powerful Chinese leader. He also managed to invite Queen Elizabeth on a royal hunt and aspired for the leadership of the Non-aligned Movement (NAM), an alliance of countries that did not want to ally themselves to any bloc.

Nepal's quest for membership to the United Nations during the rule of Prime Minister Mohan Shumsher Rana in the 1950s had been unsuccessful due to the Cold War competition between the Soviet Union and the United States. Prabhakar Rana, who briefly worked at Nepal's foreign ministry at that time, recalls that in 1956, Nepal seized the opportunity to oppose both the Suez Crisis and the invasion of Hungary so that it could be seen as a neutral country. This stance of neutrality facilitated its entry into the United Nations. Nepal's neutral position also made Hrishikesh Shah, the first Nepali ambassador to the United Nations, quite popular in the international community. He stood a very good chance of becoming the UN secretary-general in a year when the seat was reserved for Asia, when even India would not have opposed his candidacy. That honour eventually went to U. Thant from Burma, because Hrishikesh Shah was called back to Nepal by King Mahendra, exactly when Nepal had the opportunity to be on the global centre stage. The days of autocracy were returning.

King Mahendra proclaimed that Panchayat rule was based on the spirit of democracy and Nepal's classical tradition of local governance. A loyal army, a business community protected by the protectionist policies of the state and feudal powers who opposed the land reforms of the Congress became the main proponents of Panchayat rule. They claimed that historically, each caste group in Nepal had its own panchayat (literally: a council of elders) which functioned as the local governance unit. The 1960s Panchayat system, in their justification, merely scaled this local-level unit up to the regional and national level, with the national-level Panchayat functioning as a council of ministers who advised the king. The king, in this system, remained the source of all power and authority.

## Caste to Class

Further, as a kind of modernization effort, King Mahendra sought to organize people into classes—peasants, labourers, students, women, former military personnel and college graduates—as a substitute to the traditional caste system. These classes were instituted as part of the political system as a replacement for trade and labour unions with ideological and political leanings. This division was continued post-1990 (when the Panchayat system ended) and the political parties continued to exploit the rent-seeking that was instilled within these classes. The price of politics relating to labour unions and the disruption by student unions that the Nepali economy has had to pay has been heavy.

The Panchayat Constitution not only emphasized the irrelevance of political parties within the Panchayat system, but also banned them outright as illegal. Although King Mahendra claimed that the Panchayat system was a political expression of Nepali cultural identity, its similarity to the Panchayat system in India suggests that its roots lay outside Nepal.

The royalist vision of the Panchayat system as an embodiment of Nepali identity and of the king as the divine representation of God on earth is a vision that assumes and accepts an inherently hierarchical and unequal society. While in comparison to the autocratic Rana regime, Panchayat rule was significantly more progressive and oriented towards development, it also retained some of the autocratic and ultimately detrimental features of the Rana regime, including direct access to the royal treasury for the king without any legitimate account-keeping. It did not provide a respite for non-Hindus and other marginalized groups as the Nepali language and Hinduism continued to be imposed, continuing the oppressive practices of earlier Shah and Rana rulers. It also allowed for the fickle creation of laws at the whim of the king and maintained the system of chakari which required, as a surveillance measure, that palace officials and other concerned nobles attend the court formally and publicly at specified times. Further, the mixed economy model that King Mahendra adopted only helped to prolong and accentuate Nepal's nepotistic chakari-based tradition, since the centralized power structure based in Kathmandu meant that the getting of jobs and the securing of contracts were all a matter of knowing the right people in the right places.

Dr Bhekh Bahadur Thapa, only the second Nepali citizen to earn a PhD in economics, was the secretary of planning in the 1960s. He says that given the limited opportunities in Nepal, there was no option for Nepali traders but to attempt to expand their reach to include the consumers of Uttar Pradesh, Bihar and Bengal in India. This prompted the Nepal government to charge a lower duty on imports than India did, thereby giving incentives to people to import consumable goods into Nepal and sell them in the aforementioned markets of India. In one example, the government encouraged industries that manufactured household steel utensils to set up operations in Nepal. They would import steel, paying lower duties for it than India would and thereby make finished products at a lower cost than factories in India. India had a major problem with this, as cheaper goods from Nepal were affecting its own domestic industry which imported raw materials while paying a very high duty, and it therefore had to price goods uncompetitively as compared to imports from Nepal. Dr Thapa recalls a conversation with Indian commerce secretary K.B. Lall, who accused Nepal of trying to subvert Indian economic structures. Dr Thapa challenged Lall, stating, 'I have a solution for you—if you fear Nepal's liberal policies, then why not make India more liberal?'

## Mixed Economy or Failed Concoction?

Although the Panchayat government sought to maintain its distance from India, it survived with the support of the Nehru government, which had been weakened by its defeat in the 1962 Sino-Indian war, and thus needed to cultivate Nepal's support before China did. Ironically, King Mahendra was considerably influenced by the then prime minister of India, Jawaharlal Nehru, and his support for Fabian socialism. Like Nehru, King Mahendra saw the public sector as the primary means of achieving long-lasting economic development. The loss of faith in capitalism caused by the Great

Depression in the United States and the seemingly potent powers of communism on the rise in the Union of Soviet Socialist Republics (USSR) had increased the appeal of the mixed economy model. However, with the benefit of hindsight, many believe that Fabian socialism and the mixed economy model adopted by Nehru for India and Mahendra for Nepal have failed. While Nehru's staunch belief in liberalism, tolerance and democracy set the foundations for a robust Indian democracy, advocates of minimal state control are of the view that his economic policies hampered growth by allowing excessive state interference in industry and thus impairing productivity, quality and profitability. Nepal, under King Mahendra's autocratic quasi-democracy, lost out on both fronts— neither was a robust democracy allowed to develop nor was a vibrant economy allowed to flourish.

Proponents of the mixed economy model claimed that utilizing the *best* of both capitalism and communism would allow the state to take the lead in industrializing the nation. In reality and practice, the mixed economy for both India and Nepal turned out to be anything but the perfect balance between capitalism and communism. The problem with the mixed economy system lay not in conceptualization but in implementation. One of the primary problems inherent in the system as observed in both India and Nepal was the high level of corruption it invited due to the heavy reliance on politicians and bureaucrats within the system. The individual politicians and bureaucrats quickly lost their ability to see the difference between serving their interests and those of the state, as they themselves were the state. This hegemony of the bureaucracy, due to its extensive and invasive rules and regulations, discouraged entrepreneurs from engaging with the state. The state was seen as an autocratic, nepotistic, unfriendly and a kind of extortive mafia where all employees worked not for the benefit of the nation but for their own individual benefit. Bribery and commissions grew to be an accepted part of this system and were necessary for carrying out tasks as mundane as paying electricity bills and getting a driving licence.

## Private Sector: Another Tool to Consolidate Power

The private sector in Nepal took its first steps in 1951 when a new Companies Act was implemented for private limited companies. Previously, the Nepal Companies Act of 1936 only provided for the incorporation of industrial enterprises on a joint stock principle with limited liabilities. The first such firm, Biratnagar Jute Mills, was established in 1936, in a collaborative venture between Indian and Nepali entrepreneurs. By the mid-1960s, over ninety private companies had been established but they remained ineffective in scaling up due to heavy reliance on the import of resources and too many restrictions on business. Following the Fabian economic model advocated by Nehru, King Mahendra's government gave little attention to facilitating the growth of these private companies and instead focused its efforts on the establishment and expansion of existing and new public companies.

A fundamental flaw in King Mahendra's regime was its perception of the role of government towards its people. The Panchayat government saw the nation through the traditional eyes of the Shah kings and saw the activities carried out by the government for its people as a gift from the monarch to his loyal subjects. Everything in the nation belonged to the crown and all acts of governance were acts of philanthropy carried out by the owner of those lands. The prevalence of this attitude is confirmed by an analysis of most big private-sector investments that occurred during the Panchayat era. All businesses ran on nepotism and required the special blessing of the royal family in order to effectively start up and function. This was typified in the use of language in particular. The king and royal family members were addressed in a grammatical form that could not be used for common citizens. It contained a lot of Urdu usage and an exclusive vocabulary to describe food, eating, sleeping and other daily activities. As knowledge of this language was a major advantage in gaining proximity to the power centres around the palace, it functioned as a means of excluding people who were unfamiliar with it. On top of it all, most major businesses started during this time were owned by members of the royal family. For instance, the hotels Soaltee and Annapurna were established in the early 1960s by the king's brothers as the premier hotels in the country. Both hotels benefited from a growing tourism sector, royal patronage and a government which saw its best interest in ensuring their success.

The case of the Salt Trading Corporation demonstrates how the royal family interfered in various ways with the operation of business enterprises. The company was established in 1963 without royal intervention, as a public–private venture between existing private salt traders who were licensed by the government to import salt, but the company was formed with the special approval of the government. Kamal Mani Dixit, one of the company's initial promoters, recalls how the price of salt used to fluctuate based on market demand for it, especially when people from the hills came to the market to buy salt. As salt is an essential commodity, the government decided to regulate the salt trade through the Salt Trading Corporation. However, when the Salt Trading Corporation wanted to get into manufacturing vanaspati ghee, it was not granted a licence. Instead, it had to buy a licence for manufacturing vanaspati ghee from Deepak Singh, King Mahendra's son-in-law, paying him in Salt Trading Corporation shares. This is one example of how difficult it was to do business without getting members of the royal family quite closely involved.

Another of the many controversial decisions taken by King Mahendra during his regime was to give people from Manang (popularly known as Mananges) preferential treatment—they were allowed to import goods into Nepal with a reduced duty. This was argued to be a continuation of the facility given to the Mananges by the former Rana rulers of Nepal. The Ranas, fearing an ethnic revolt from this strong ethnic group, had granted them permission to trade outside Nepal. This had allowed the Mananges to trade from Tibet with colonial India, Burma, Thailand and Laos. Dr Thapa explains that King Mahendra had decided to give the Mananges preferential treatment because of their entrepreneurial spirit and their traditional occupation as nomadic traders. The preferential policy allowed anyone from Manang to obtain a passport without hassle during a time when obtaining a passport was a difficult task. These benefits were misused by many non-Mananges, including Marwari and Newa business people, who used Mananges as carriers for their goods, which they could now pass through customs at a reduced duty fee. This facilitated the establishment of Nepal as a centre for smuggling goods into India. Smuggling became big business and continued even into the 1990s—for instance, more than 25 million umbrellas were imported annually into Nepal at a time when the entire population of the country was less than the number of umbrellas it was importing. Since every Nepali does not have an umbrella collection, it is obvious that these umbrellas were being smuggled across the border into India. The high import duties in India coupled with restrictions on foreign exchange made Kathmandu and the border towns of Dhulabari in the east of Nepal among the biggest shopping attractions for Indians. The carrying of goods across the border in collusion with customs and border authorities on both sides of the border is a highly lucrative business for many people till date.

With smuggling becoming the most profitable business in Nepal, actual production and manufacturing came to be of only peripheral importance, especially once the state started to monopolize industries. Stories of losses in efficiency and productivity due to a business atmosphere structured to favour a particular business group or industry are common knowledge in Nepal. One such example is of Hetauda Cotton Textile Mills, which was a state-owned enterprise set up with Chinese assistance. The mill functioned as the sole producer of cotton textiles in the central region of Nepal for decades without any competition due to the protectionist policies of the state. However, this lack of competition and the guarantee of survival meant that the company did not have to worry about efficiency or quality. It was quite simply the only large-scale producer of cotton textiles produced on the sole machine that could produce cloth of a certain length. This allowed it to dictate the terms on which it provided its products, regardless of considerations of quality or price. In a competitive market, the company would not have been able to survive without developing quality products and minimizing costs.

## The Education Mishap

A grave shortcoming of the entire Panchayat era was its educational policy. A New National Education Plan was launched in 1972 with the objective of focusing on job-oriented vocational education. However, the plan later on became a tool to produce people loyal to the Panchayat regime. Community-owned schools were nationalized and cosmetic changes were brought about by aping the US educational system—colleges were now called 'campuses', and there were 'internal assessments' of students, suggesting a mild degree of autonomy. Although the government was successful in establishing new schools and expanding their coverage throughout the nation, the quality of education remained poor. The increasing number of schools could not be followed up with an increase in the number of teachers, leading to an acute shortage of teachers, with most being barely qualified to teach. In the early 1980s, around 60 per cent of all primary school teachers and 35 per cent of all secondary school teachers were untrained.[7]

Further, the imposition of King Mahendra's 'one country, one language' policy throughout the nation, promoting the Nepali language above all others, had a significantly detrimental effect. Not only was it seen as a sign of state-sponsored caste-based repression, but it also deterred the development of an English curriculum. At the higher education level, Nepal's first university, Tribhuvan University, was established in 1959. However, given the lack of quality at the primary and secondary level, it is hardly a surprise that very few students made it past the School Leaving Certificate (SLC) exams which acted as an iron gate to higher education. Education remained the exclusive domain of the urban elite, with a further stratum being created through the distinction between the English boarding school and the Nepali government school. The mastery of English that was offered at the former type of institution, combined with a standard of education that the government schools were unable to match, encouraged anyone with the means to either send their children to one of the English boarding schools or abroad, to India. The lack of human resources was acutely felt by the government, which led to it sponsoring a large number of its finest and brightest minds to go and study abroad in the universities of Europe, America and India.

## Tourism of the 1950s: A Success Story

The only success story from the 1950s that endures is the growth of the tourism sector. When Sir Edmund Hillary and Tenzing Norgay Sherpa climbed Mount Everest in 1953, Nepal arrived on the global tourism map as a forbidden Shangri-La, mystical and adventurous. Prabhakar Rana, a member of the first Tourism Master Plan Committee and the first general manager of Soaltee Hotel, says that credit has to be given to Boris Lissanevitch, who started the Royal Hotel and brought in the first batch of tourists in 1955. Boris convinced King Mahendra of the potential of Nepali tourism at a time when the Nepali people wondered why tourists would come to an underdeveloped country like theirs. This resulted in King Mahendra's visit to Switzerland and the arrival in Nepal of people like Toni Hagen, who became the first foreigner to trek throughout Nepal and conduct an extensive geological survey. This also set the stage for allowing Nepali entrepreneurs to enter the tourism business. With tourists being brought over by international groups like American Express and spending considerable amounts of money, tourism quickly became a thriving business. Even Air India started to include Nepal in its brochures to attract tourists to India from the US and Europe. The Department of Tourism was established in 1957 and a Tourism Act enacted in 1964.

It is worth noting that two of Nepal's oldest and most prestigious hotels, Soaltee Hotel and Annapurna Hotel, were established in 1960 and 1965 respectively. Both hotels were established by the brothers of King Mahendra. Further, the expansion in the 1970s of the Royal Nepal Airlines Corporation locally and internationally attracted a considerable amount of tourists to a previously closed Shangri-La. Airplane and helicopter services to areas of Nepal previously completely untouched by modernity further lured tourists in droves. The establishment of Casino Nepal in 1968, the promotion of Nepal's role in the Hindu world and the attraction of shopping the world's delights in Bishal Bazaar that began in the mid-1970s, when Indians faced many foreign exchange restrictions at home, also contributed to a dramatic increase in the number of Indian tourists.

In 1972, a vision document called the Tourism Master Plan was prepared, which emphasized investments in tourism by both the public and private sectors, with a view to creating more jobs and more revenue for the government. Though a good plan, it was never updated. During Dr Harka Gurung's tenure in 1977–78 as tourism minister, the big debate over the quality versus the quantity of tourists began, and perhaps a lot of potential focus on quality was thereby lost. With the arrival of the hippies in the 1970s, Nepal started receiving a lot of backpacker tourists who came in search of instant nirvana in a country where marijuana and other drugs were not yet illegal. They outnumbered the high-end tourists who were brought in by leading international tour operations. Prabhakar Rana says that though many objected to the poor quality of budget tourists in Nepal, the hippies were without a doubt the primary marketing tool for Nepal, providing the best publicity for the destination at a time when the government could not afford advertisements.

The opening up of the hotel sector for foreign investment and management allowed the Oberoi and Sheraton groups to enter Nepal, thereby providing wonderful training opportunities; this made hospitality services one of the key job opportunities for

Nepali people in Nepal and abroad. The government started Royal Nepal Airlines in 1966 and by 1990 had a fleet of four jets, eleven Twin Otters, two Pilatus Porters and three Avros flying 6,00,000 passengers a year. Tourism grew in the 1980s at an annual rate of 10 per cent, and by the 1990s Nepal received close to 3,00,000 tourists, the tourism industry had a share of 4 per cent of the GDP, while foreign exchange earnings from the sector were close to $50 million.

## Transportation: Roads to Prosperity

The Panchayat government was also successful in developing the infrastructure of the country, which did facilitate the growth of business even into the 1990s. Before the Panchayat government fell, it had successfully developed its road network from a mere 276 km in the early 1950s to 7330 km by 1990. Although significant tracts of the country still remained inaccessible by motorized transport, the achievements, given Nepal's terrain, are remarkable. Without a doubt the development of these roads contributed significantly to the growth of the private sector. The roads that were built during that era were logically defective, since both roads out of Kathmandu linked the eastern parts of the country by going through the western cities of Hetauda or Narayangarh.

## King Birendra: Failed Attempts at Change

King Birendra was crowned the king of Nepal in 1972 after the death of his father, King Mahendra. He followed the non-aligned policy of his father and went a step further in declaring Nepal a zone of peace. This was partly to protect Nepal from a situation like that of the kingdom of Sikkim which in 1974 was annexed into an Indian Union that feared a Chinese invasion in the politically unstable region. It was also an attempt to counter the anti-royal fervour that was gripping India and the Indian government after the abolition of the Privy Purse[8] in 1971. A decade later, in the

1980s, the sending of Indian peacekeepers into Sri Lanka and the imperialistic model of a Big Brother that India was adopting in the region caused increasing concern in Nepal. Simultaneously, the rise of the Gorkhaland movement in 1986 and the growing clamour for a separate state in the Darjeeling region was increasingly worrisome to India. The Indian government did not want to deal with a separatist insurgency in its backyard when it was trying to establish itself as a regional power. The attempts of King Birendra's regime from 1972 to 1990 were not so much a product of anti-Indian sentiment as of a growing concern in Nepal about its own sovereignty in the face of a liberalizing and expanding Indian influence in the region, especially when Rajiv Gandhi was the prime minister from 1984 to 1989. The dominance of India in Nepal was constantly felt. When Dr Thapa, then ambassador to the United States, discussed the possibility of American investments in Nepal during King Birendra's visit to the United States in 1984, American companies were reluctant to invest as they saw Nepal as a small economy positioned to work with India better than the US. They advised the Nepali government to focus on India, indicating that making a deal in water resources with India would be the best scenario.

Although he inherited an autocratic regime from his father, King Birendra was of a considerably more liberal bent than his father. He instituted a number of economic reforms, including the Industrial Enterprise Act of 1974, which shifted the government's emphasis from the public to the private sector as the primary medium for economic growth. Birendra was influenced by the Americans. Recalls Prabhakar Rana, chairman emeritus, Soaltee Hotel Limited, and a relative of the royal family: 'He tried to decentralize the nation and, in those days when communication and travel was difficult, he decided to take the power away from Kathmandu for two months each year by operating out of one of the development regions. This was quite unlike his father who used to only tour around and never stick around.' While this was a great idea, it started becoming an expensive hobby when ministers and government officials had to shuttle between Kathmandu and those cities, along with the flowering of the business of chakari built around such visits. More people wanted to be seen at the palaces or king's retreat as part of the chakari mode of royal surveillance.

King Birendra's regime also instituted the Social Services National Coordination Council (SSNCC) in 1975, which attempted to bring the growing number of NGOs and INGOs under a single umbrella. Headed by Queen Aishwarya, the council had six committees, generally headed by individuals close to the royal family. Membership to the council was a privilege granted to the elite, and all NGOs were required to be registered with the council so that the state could monitor the people who formed NGOs, their objectives and their activities. By 1990, there were 219 NGOs registered with the SSNCC. The council was converted to a foreign aid coordination body after the 1990 Constitution came into effect, wherein all NGOs that received foreign aid or grants had to be registered with the SSNCC.

Despite its liberal bent, King Birendra's regime also carried forward many traditional forms of royal patronage and business. A striking example of this was the establishment of the King Mahendra Trust for Nature Conservation in 1982, the Lumbini Development Trust in 1985 and the Pashupati Development Trust in 1987. All these trusts, established under specific Acts, were set up with the stated objective of protecting, preserving and conserving their specified areas of interest. The establishment of these organizations and their laudable objectives speak well of King Birendra's regime. However, the lack of regulation, transparency or accountability in these organizations, especially during the royal regimes, significantly undercut their benefits. Not only were funds not flowing to the organizations' desired objectives, but quite often the organization was being used to channel money for activities that were in no way related to and sometimes even contrary to its stated objectives.

# 1979 Referendum: Panchayat Survives

With a growing population that found itself unemployed and unable to find employment, King Birendra's regime came under increasing pressure to liberalize. By 1979, in response to widespread student protests, he held a referendum in which the Panchayat system won by a narrow margin against the multiparty system, allegedly by rigging. After the referendum, the royal establishment shifted its focus to power retention. An all-powerful Panchayat Policy, Enquiry and Investment Committee formed in 1980 reported directly to the king. This committee could take action against anyone they perceived as acting against the 'interest of the nation' and the action of the committee could not be questioned in any court of law. Dr Ram Sharan Mahat says, 'The Panchayat Policy's rationale rested on three founding ideals, viz. nationalism, economic development and indigenous character based on tradition and religion. The concept of nationalism was based on the shallow concept of one language, one crown and one country.' The creation of this all-powerful body fuelled a growing sense of dissent against the regime.

## Zone of Peace: Failed Attempt

In 1972, when King Birendra ascended the throne of Nepal, he made a call to the international community asking for the recognition of Nepal as a Zone of Peace. This proposal was a political manoeuvre in keeping with the non-aligned philosophy Nepal had adopted to manage its neighbours India and China. Birendra may or may not have seen the dark irony of calling Nepal a Zone of Peace, given the nation's violent history. Nepal was forged through conquest and held together by sheer brute force. Little to nothing of Nepal's early history suggests that the Nepali nation and identity predated the late 1700s Shah conquest or that the conquerors, the Hindu Chhetris of Gorkha, and the conquered people of various ethnicities, indigenous cultures and religions, had a common identity. The Nepali unification under Prithvi Narayan Shah was not a Gandhian non-violent nationalist movement but a product of a monarch's vision, ambition and leadership.

Panchayat rule began and ended with politics in the forefront while the economic agenda remained second. Prabhakar Rana says, 'The sad part of the Panchayat period was that it did not utilize and develop its own resources like hydropower but went with a begging bowl to other countries. It was a tremendous loss of face for Nepal and Nepalis.' Between 1960 and 1990, Nepal's GDP grew at an average of merely 1.5 per cent per annum from $0.6 billion to $3.6 billion. During the same period Singapore's GDP grew from $0.6 billion to $36 billion and Thailand's from $2.76 billion to $85 billion. Malaysia's GDP grew from $2.5 billion in 1963 to $44 billion in 1990.[9] The growing population in Nepal was faced with limited employment opportunities and was already clamouring for change. The people wanted to capture the promise of a growing economy and follow the dream of becoming another Switzerland. These many dissatisfactions were to reach their culmination in a widespread popular agitation called the Jana Andolan in 1990, following which King Birendra agreed to step down and allow for the establishment of a constitutional monarchy and multiparty democratic system, paving the way for Nepal's second stint with democracy.

5

# Fall of Shahs: Restoration of Multiparty Democracy, Conflict and End of Shah Dynasty, 1990–2008

When King Birendra gave in to popular protest in April 1990 and agreed to become a constitutional monarch, he must never have fathomed that the Shah dynasty would end within eighteen years. That period was no different than the early 1950s when King Tribhuvan had vowed to establish a democratic Nepal. In the eighteen years, practically all forms of governments were witnessed, from the elected single-party rule of the Nepali Congress to the various permutations and combinations that included democratic forces who fought for the restoration of democracy and those who suppressed it. Nepal saw prime ministers change fourteen times, with someone like Girija Prasad Koirala coming to power four times. The period also saw a ten-year conflict (1996–2006) end, with the Communist Party of Nepal (Maoist) fighting the state and ruling parts of Nepal. The royal massacre of 2001 killed King Birendra and his entire family, while his brother, King Gyanendra—who became the king afterwards—took on a role that he had never expected to. He got ambitious, and within a year of being crowned, usurped power

71

and decided to rule directly. The underground Maoist and other democratic forces joined hands to fight for the end of monarchy.

  This chapter will discuss one of the most eventful eighteen years that saw the biggest changes in Nepal's economic history.

## Nepal Decides to Globalize

If the 1990 Jana Andolan, a people's movement for democracy, represented the spirit of the times, the first budget speech of 1991 by the finance minister represented the monetized expression of that spirit. The changes demanded in the Jana Andolan were to be brought about through the budgetary allocation of resources by the first elected government in over three decades. This belief in the political power of the budget was in itself a statement about the changing times. The Nepali public no longer trusted individuals to deliver their country from poverty, but instead placed their trust in the institution of democracy. The public presentation of the budget displayed the nation-building project transparently while reflecting the aspirations of the Nepali people who had voted in the new government. The fall of the Berlin Wall and the collapse of the USSR reinforced this belief in the triumph of democracy and liberal market capitalism over socialist or authoritarian institutions. Riding the airwaves via their newly acquired television sets, Nepali people witnessed scenes of change at home and abroad.

## Indian Embargo, Nepali Democracy

The fall of the Panchayat government in 1990 provided considerable insight into the geopolitical location and role of the Nepali state. In March 1989, before the Jana Andolan, a trade embargo had been placed on Nepal by the Indian prime minister, Rajiv Gandhi. The reason given by an increasingly irate Indian government, however, was the Nepali government's unwillingness to sign a single treaty covering trade and transit agreements between India and Nepal.

The rumour mills in Kathmandu ran stories as to how this was the result of a non-Hindu Sonia Gandhi not being allowed to enter Pashupatinath Temple.[1] In truth, New Delhi was infuriated with its smaller neighbour's agreement for the purchase of arms from the Chinese government, which directly violated a secret treaty of 1965 between India and Nepal. The 1965 treaty required that Nepal purchase its arms from India whenever possible, and when it was not, to inform India of the purchase of arms from other countries as well as transport of such arms through India. King Birendra's government had pushed the equidistance card too far and New Delhi made it all too apparent how dependent the Nepali economy was upon India. If this political scenario provided the foundation for the 1990 Jana Andolan, a youthful proletariat opposed to the traditional feudal structures of Nepal was the immediate catalyst of the popular movement.

The Indian embargo provided the ideal opportunity for Nepal's democratic forces to unite and accuse the Panchayat government of ineptitude and inability to rule. This, together with the government's rampant corruption, restriction of freedoms and most importantly, its inability to meet the basic needs of the neediest, made the democratic movement unstoppable. During the height of the embargo, India closed down thirteen of its fifteen transit points into Nepal and severely limited the flow of goods from India to Nepal. Critically, it cut off the supply of petroleum to Nepal, which led to petroleum prices soaring from NPR 8 a litre to NPR 80 a litre in the grey market, causing an acute energy shortage. This had a direct impact on industries as well as on the average citizen through limitations on the transfer and transportation of goods and raw materials. However, the embargo did bring about two realizations—the importance of being energy independent and the need to tap into the extensive hydropower resources present within the country. The direct effect of the trade embargo was the opening up of space for the political parties to manoeuvre and initiate an anti-government and pro-democratic movement, which the Indian government tacitly supported.

The first Jana Andolan brought about the fall of the Panchayat government and the establishment of an interim government under the leadership of the Nepali Congress leader Krishna Prasad Bhattarai. Following this, on 1 July 1990, New Delhi lifted the year-long trade embargo in recognition of a democratic Nepal. With the establishment of a democratic government formed of political leaders who had been nurtured in India, Nepal's flirtation with China also ended. Nepal was effectively entrenched within the Indian sphere of influence, and India in turn became more willing to cooperate with a neighbour that acknowledged it as the Big Brother in the region.

## Economic Liberalization Follows Democracy

For the first time in 1990, the Nepali people felt like they were part of a global family clamouring for change. Colour televisions started receiving satellite images, hoardings of international products and services dotted the streets, restaurant chains started opening up for business, department stores mushroomed, shopfronts started getting an international look, old buildings gave way to new structures and the latest models of cars started plying the streets. Expectations were high, and the politicians, during the first election post-1990, promised even more—they promised to turn Nepal into the Switzerland of Asia. An economic boom like that seen in the countries known as the Asian Tigers, namely South Korea, Singapore, Taiwan and Hong Kong, was anticipated—it was expected that a sea of opportunities would flood the nation. Liberalization of markets, unrestricted expansion of trade networks, and industrialization were all expected to follow from an unshackled and reinvigorated private sector. The dividends from economic growth would facilitate the development and modernization of rural Nepal. The Nepali Congress, the leader of the democratic movement, had also shifted gears, abandoning the Fabian socialist model[2] advocated under B.P. Koirala in favour of a more progressive liberal market economy during the election of 1991.

Sure enough, in keeping with the spirit of the times, the Nepali Congress won a majority of 110 seats in the 205-seat Parliament.

Following a comprehensive victory in the 1991 elections, the Nepali Congress government formed under Girija Prasad Koirala forged closer links with India and looked towards liberalizing the economy to encourage private-sector–led economic growth. With this objective in mind, the government instituted some sweeping reforms. It set forth the Industrial Policy 1992 as a programme statement, and passed the Foreign Investment and One-Window Enterprise Act, 1992; the Industrial Enterprise Act, 1992; and the Foreign Investment and Technology Transfer Act, 1992. These Acts were initiated with the objective of making it easier to do business in Nepal by removing hurdles to start businesses and encouraging investment by both foreign and local investors. The government wanted to change its role from being a 'process stopper' to a 'process facilitator', where they would treat businesses like businesses treat customers.

The government also loosened its stranglehold over foreign currency exchange by incorporating free convertibility into the current account. This allowed individuals the freedom of converting and holding foreign currencies in special accounts without requiring explicit permission from the government. Import-licensing requirements were also abolished, except for a few commodities, reducing the hassle of obtaining permits for securing foreign currency and importing foreign goods. Further, with the reduction in the restrictions placed upon foreign banks, commercial banks were encouraged to open, operate and expand. The subsequent boom in the banking sector allowed for a considerable increase in savings while simultaneously increasing access to capital. Taxation laws were reformed, import tariffs reduced drastically, income tax rates cut significantly and tax sops for investments announced.

A private sector can only develop to meet the needs of the market if it is allowed to enter any market where it sees a gap and an opportunity to create profit. If the private sector is to be an engine for growth, it must be allowed to ply its wares anywhere and test the waters of all available markets. Towards this end, the government instituted the Privatization Policy, 1991, which was followed by the formation of a separate privatization cell in the Ministry of Finance. This eventually led to the endorsement by Parliament of the Privatization Act, 1994, that June. The preamble of the Act read, 'To mitigate the financial administrative burden to the Government, and to usher in all round economic development of the country by broadening the participation of the private sector in the operation of such enterprises, it is expedient in the national interest to privatize such enterprises and to make arrangements thereof.'

The government believed that given the opportunity, the private sector could enter any sector and turn it into a profitable, national revenue-generating and economically self-sustaining industrial behemoth. The government opened up sectors that had for decades remained the exclusive domain of the state. Most significantly, it opened up the skies for private airlines to enter the domestic market; it opened up the financial sector for the rapid growth of banks, finance and insurance companies; and it opened up the energy sector, allowing for private-sector involvement in the generation of hydroelectricity and other forms of energy.

Following the Keynesian economic model advocated by the World Bank and International Monetary Fund (IMF), the next logical step for the government was to reform the capital market with the establishment of the Securities Board and the Nepal Stock Exchange, which opened for trading in January 1994. The establishment of the stock exchange was expected to create opportunities for the common Nepali to invest in companies and be able to enjoy a share of the profits. The stock market was seen as a primary resource in ensuring the prosperity of not just a select few industrialists but the growing middle class as well. With NPR 70 million worth of shares being transacted during just the first six months of the year, public offerings of stocks became a viable way for companies to raise capital to finance their expansion activities. It wasn't just the private sector that was upbeat; the donor community in Nepal was also eager to see Nepal as an ideal example of the success of the democratic liberal market economy, and thus lined up to get a cut of the action. From infrastructure to education, from health to hydropower, it was willing to inject the necessary capital into Nepal to create a major economic boom.

## 1993–94: Dream Run for the Nepal Economy

Sure enough, the economy seemed to surge forward to match the policy leap towards a liberal market economy. The fiscal year of 1993–94 turned out to be a dream year, with a 7.9 per cent increase in GDP. The agricultural sector alone recorded an unprecedented 7.6 per cent growth rate, and tourism had forged ahead to contribute 4 per cent of the GDP. In manufacturing, the carpet industry had established itself as a major foreign exchange earner, accounting for half of all of Nepal's exports. This fuelled a near tripling of the value of exports in 1994 to NPR 19.3 billion, compared to the total of NPR 7.3 billion in 1991. The garment industry followed in the footsteps of the carpet industry, and carpets and garments combined accounted for 80 per cent of Nepal's total exports.[3]

For that one year, Nepal was a model child for development economists and their development theories at the big financial institutions. Confirming predictions made using the Lewis Model,[4] the booming carpet and garment industry in the urban sector resulted in a relocation of labour from the rural agricultural sector to the modern industrial sector. Simultaneously, the increase in development expenditure by the government and a real estate boom in cities created, in turn, a boom in the construction industry, which absorbed even more unskilled workers into its industrial machine. There were also concerted government efforts to reach rural populations, and this resulted in the spread of modern agricultural practices, new equipment and materials. An agricultural boom occurred in rural Nepal through a combination of supportive government policies as well as an increase in entrepreneurial activities that saw in the boom a good future for business. The development of road networks and trade routes further assisted in bringing excess production from rural to urban areas. Without a doubt, the Nepali economy was expanding—transactions were increasing and goods and services were in higher demand.

In addition to the urbanization and modernization process, a sociocultural upheaval was in the making in urban Nepal. Traditional norms and values were increasingly challenged and often found wanting. A new culture of consumerism, desire and pleasure developed among the general population after the pessimistic and fatalistic years of the autocratic Rana and Shah regimes. New urban lifestyles included eating out, partying and keeping up with global trends. Catering to these new desires, an industry of restaurants, bars, clubs and trendy stores sprang up. Concurrently, the alcohol and cigarette industries in Nepal experienced a major boom, with the establishment of Surya Tobacco as the premier Nepali cigarette brand and a host of internationally acclaimed beers and spirits introducing their brand into the Nepali market. The budding advertising industry, as the primary promoter of this new lifestyle, successfully utilized the commercialized airwaves of radio and television channels to disseminate the new religion of consumerism.

The children of the 1990s heralded a new age of youth in Nepal. They formed the first generation of children who were driven by the consumer culture that had finally made its way to Nepal. These children grew up not knowing a world without televisions or cellphones, not being able to imagine a world unhooked to the Web and with no remembered experience of the bureaucratic lethargy of the government-owned Nepal Bank. These youths formed the biggest consumer group to ever inhabit this country. Growing up under the spell of Bollywood and Hollywood while being nurtured by a traditional Nepal, they functioned as negotiators between the values of old and new. With the spread of the Internet and exposure to the world through education and travel, multiple cultures mingled with Nepali culture. The popularity of Korean television soaps, food, music and fashion was one of the big changes in society. On the side of tradition stood the values of family, moderation, conservatism and community, while on the newer side of things stood consumerism, individuality and progress.

## Bankers Have a Field Day

The reform of the financial sector through the liberalization of the banking system during the early 1990s has been a success story that endures to this day in Nepal. Prior to liberalization, the only banks in service were owned, managed and operated by the Government of Nepal. This banking monopoly had a detrimental impact on the quality of service, efficiency and competency of banks and their staff. There are horror stories of people who had to queue up for hours and then offer bribes ranging from tea money to full meals to tellers in order to withdraw their own money. This, unsurprisingly, had a detrimental effect on the economy by discouraging people from investing in banks or even opening a bank account. The opening up of the banking sector shifted the focus to providing premium customer service, with the growing number of banks increasingly having to compete with each other to secure the services of a limited client base.

Increasing competition also led to the introduction of more services like credit and debit cards along with a variety of loan and financing options, which dramatically increased access to capital for both businesses and individuals. Further, a growing emphasis on credit ratings and payback viability rather than patronage and connections in the process of giving loans ensured that capital was made available for the most promising projects. The development of professionalism and workforce capabilities through banks has been an important driving force in the expansion of the private sector, and has resulted in an increasing trend towards workplace professionalism and service delivery. The real estate boom that Nepal experienced during the first decade of the twenty-first century was largely financed by a dramatic increase in savings and a capital market which was easier to negotiate.

## Politics Trumps Economics: The Bubble Bursts

The bubble of reform that was seen as the advent of democracy and liberalization burst all too soon, and the economic boom that it had inspired lost steam all too quickly. The beginning of the downfall was signalled by the volatility of Nepali politics, with the toppling of Girija Prasad Koirala's majority government in 1994 due to infighting within the Nepali Congress party. Rampant corruption, bad governance and the ensuing political instability were to be the defining characteristics of Nepal's multiparty democracy and they quickly neutralized the economic spurt and spirit of the early 1990s. The very foundations upon which the economic growth of the early 1990s occurred proved to be enfeebled and weak. Even though the private sector was ready to take the helm in order to ensure economic growth, the politicians were not ready to take on the responsibilities of democracy. A weak and disoriented government quickly invited back the spirit of profiteering, racketeering and patronizing that had plagued the private sector during the Panchayat era.

The lack of staying power of successive governments and the swiftness with which they lost their political convictions prevented any political party from summoning up the will or the time to push any reform process to fruition. The moment a party was able to capture power, it immediately became embroiled in a fight to maintain that power. Conversely, the moment a party lost power, it engaged in knee-jerk dissent against those in power, with the hope that it might gain power in the near future. In such a cannibalistic environment, there was no time to think about the greater good of Nepal—ethical thinking broke down and the desire for power overcame better instincts. A complete sense of political hedonism ruled; the idea was to get in power, and grab what you could as quickly as you could before you got kicked out and someone else got the opportunity to pillage the country.

The myopia of government and the protectionist approach of business and trade unions were to have a tremendously negative impact on the national economy. This situation of policy without conviction was exemplified during the nine-month rule of the Communist Party of Nepal (UML [Unified Marxist–Leninist]) in 1994—with the leaders remaining wedded to the old socialist rhetoric even as they promised to liberalize the economy during meetings with donors or when seeking funds from the business community. On top of all this, the push for liberalization that the multilateral and bilateral agencies demanded from the government, heedless of local context, did not help.

The fall of the communist government in 1995 and the series of coalition governments that were formed from then onwards made a mockery of the political system. The political parties showed a lack of strong ideological conviction or the motivation to really move beyond electoral preparation, and feeble attempts at power retention. If anyone on the street during the mid- and late 1990s was questioned on the role of the political parties, his or her response would have been 'to keep their seats' (stay in power). Sadly for the nation and its people, the political parties proved incapable of getting their act together and maintaining a government structure for longer than two years. The astounding statistic of eleven prime ministers in the ten years between 1990 and 2000 speaks volumes about the political instability that characterized the Nepal government.

This political myopia had a major impact on Nepal's external image. From a country of hope that could pursue an economic agenda using diplomatic channels to woo investors, it was relegated to a state where countries were willing to give aid but not trade with it.

Overall, the squandering of the unique opportunities provided by the 1990s was a direct result of the government's lack of commitment to any specific reform policy. This left the nation in the doldrums, going neither here nor there, and ultimately led to stagnation. Each successive government lacked the courage to either wholly embrace a capitalist welfare state, or to follow the discredited Nehruvian model. This confused approach was evident in both the promulgation of pro-labour laws and the manner in which state enterprises were privatized. For instance, a Company Act came into force which accepted the concept of public joint stock companies but required the wide dispersal of shareholding. The Act required large and unwieldy quorums for shareholders' meetings, not to mention the obligation to take on public shareholders. The state refused to accept the basic tenet that businesses are a capitalist phenomenon into which it is hard to inject a socialist ideological element. While laws relating to the registration of foreign investments and other domestic investments were reformed in 1992, the laws that could help a business close down came only in 2006 when the Bankruptcy Act was enacted. However, the provisions of the Bankruptcy Act required that a commercial bench of the judiciary be created to deal with such cases of bankruptcy. The business owners would have no legal options if the business failed and were thus less likely to take on the risk of starting a business at all.

## Bureaucracy: Feudalism under a Veneer

A major hurdle to efficient governance was the entrenched and dysfunctional bureaucracy, which continued as it was from the Panchayat system through the 1990 Jana Andolan and beyond. No major overhaul of the bureaucracy has ever been contemplated or attempted in Nepal, leaving it with the same antiquated system of governance that characterized the Panchayat years. Bureaucracy still has a working culture moulded out of the system of nepotism and chakari, which causes seekers of power and favour to spend most of their time displaying themselves regularly before authority to demonstrate their loyalty.

Additionally, the decrease in the quality of education during the Panchayat era led to a direct loss in the quality of service being provided by the bureaucracy. Simultaneously, the preferential propagation of the Nepali language inevitably led to the dominance of the hill culture of the Bahun and Chhetri ethnic groups within the bureaucracy. From 69 per cent of Bahun/Chhetri representatives in 1983–85, this was up to 81 per cent in 1992–93, a number which peaked at 98 per cent in 2000. The proportion of Newas who made it into the civil services during the same period was down from 19 per cent to 11 per cent over the same period, coming to rest at 1 per cent in 2000. The figure for the *janajati* category dipped from 3 per cent to 2.5 per cent to nil.[5] Finally, the bureaucracy became a playground for a party-affiliated reward system, a transposition of the traditional jagir system of the Shah kings via the political parties, where grants of land were replaced with posts in the bureaucracy.

The government also failed to decentralize and delegate responsibility properly to the local and regional levels. This created an evident disparity between Kathmandu and other regions of Nepal. This Kathmandu-centric governance model impacted business as well, with most businesses also remaining Kathmandu-centric. As an example of the dominance of Kathmandu over the entire Nepali economic landscape, it is worth noting that even in early 2008, although the valley had just 7 per cent of Nepal's population, 40–60 per cent of the sales of the majority of consumer goods took place there. The region by 2008 consumed around 45 per cent of the country's total electricity generation, used 75 per cent of all fixed telephone lines and 90 per cent of all mobile phone connections, and was home to 90 per cent of all cars and 80 per cent of all motorcycles.[6] This Kathmandu-centric approach has had a negative impact on the prospects of developing other urban areas and has detrimentally affected the environment and quality of life in the Kathmandu valley as well.

## Multiparty Democracy, Graft for All

Even after the Jana Andolan, the democratic movement of 1990, the Panchayat administrative system was not changed, other than being rechristened and put under the directives of the Ministry of Local Development. Thus the gau, nagar and zilla panchayats became *gau bikas samitis*,[7*] *nagar palika*s[†] and zilla bikas samitis[‡]. The bureaucracy by this time had expanded to over 1,00,000 civil servants and required considerable restructuring and streamlining. With this objective in mind, the democratic government took a number of initiatives, including the passing of a new Civil Service Act in 1993 which sought to strengthen the bureaucracy, increase accountability and decrease the ability of ministries to tamper with the bureaucracy. Unfortunately, these well-meaning attempts ran up against entrenched obstacles to efficiency, as will be outlined below.

With multiparty democracy, the art of graft that had formerly been limited to people in close circuits of power was also democratized. Corruption became rampant and started becoming accepted as a way of life. This can also be attributed to the sociocultural phenomenon where one does not ever hesitate to offer sweets, money or promises to gods. Dubbed the 'two-laddoo' syndrome, it encompasses the tendency to corrupt even the gods people worship, with offerings of sweets in return for favours. Such a mentality could only have led to the formation of a society where corruption was not taken as a social evil and people flaunted the wealth they acquired by graft or even talked about it openly. Phrases like '*kar ma basyo bhane ghar banincha, bhansar ma basyo bhane sansar banincha*', meaning, 'if you work at the tax department you can build a house and if you work at customs you will make your world', became common proverbial phrases of wisdom. The need for political parties to fund their elections and take care of their cadres and all their aspirations for better lifestyles also fuelled this culture of graft. Government positions started getting auctioned to the highest bidders behind closed doors, and the business–bureaucracy–politician nexus manufactured plenty of fodder for the vernacular tabloids.

The inability of the government to ensure accountability and transparency is attributable to a judiciary that remained weak and has never been independent. Although the stated aim of all political forces since the fall of the Rana regime has been to promote an independent judiciary, constant intervention by political figures and government officials has meant that practice is different from intention.

In the 1950s, major improvements in establishing a coherent set of laws and developing substantive procedural mechanisms had been made, in comparison to the arbitrary and punitive laws of the Ranas. However, the lack of a clear demarcation in the Panchayat system thereafter, of the limits of the judiciary versus the executive and the legislature, weakened the authority and independence of the judiciary. The heavy involvement of the government in the judiciary even during multiparty democracy and republicanism posed significant challenges to the integrity of the judicial system.

## Labour Woes

If the government followed a capitalistic bent in encouraging enterprise, capital formation and investment, its lack of will to go fully with the liberal capitalistic model was exemplified by its inability and unwillingness to address labour law issues. Of primary concern was the government's unwillingness to release the domain of labour–enterprise relations from its control and allow labour and enterprise to negotiate disagreements independently, without involving the government. Its weakness in addressing labour issues is perhaps best highlighted by the jagir system that is prevalent in the bureaucracy and state-owned enterprises, where jobs take the place of the old system of land grants as payments for favours. The jagir mentality also spills over into the private enterprises where workers consider their jobs to be for life, regardless of performance and efficiency. This assurance of the job or jagir makes it unnecessary to put one's full effort into the job, adding yet another layer of inefficiency to an already deeply ineffective system. The provisions of the labour laws make it impossible for workers in both private and public sectors to be fired on grounds of inefficiency and non-productivity. The workers, in order to shield themselves from being fired or taken to task, even now choose the route of unionization. Trade unions affiliated to political parties have members in huge numbers, increasing the total amount coming in as membership fees, and in return, the large union cadres turn up for a show of strength whenever the party requires it.

The labour laws and policies that were put into place since the 1990s have been unsuccessful in either creating a secure business environment or in securing the rights of workers, given that the unions were politically affiliated and followed party dictates. From the point of view of enterprise, the preamble of the Labour Act of 1992 only provides for the protection of the interests of the labour community and not those of the enterprise itself. Successive legislative interventions like the Labour Laws, 1993; Trade Union Act, 1992; and Labour Court Laws, 1995, were no better—each of them made labour and its unions more powerful while compromising the rights of the enterprise. With the strong advocacy of a few bilateral agencies and the support of a pro-socialist media owned by private businesses and empowered by their political clout, labour groups successfully took advantage of their necessity to enterprise and essentially held it to ransom. Labour unions and their leaders also started making investments in casinos and other ventures such as real estate. Therefore, they emerged not only as a formidable source of cadres but also as a source of money for political parties.

## Real Labour Loses, Politicians Gain

Although Nepal's legal framework provided for the protection of labour, over and above the fundamental rights of workers guaranteed by the International Labour Organization (ILO) conventions, the workers still suffered. They still did not have access to the rights that the government had secured for them. A large part of the problem was that all labour unions in Nepal were politically affiliated and labour rights were often just a pretext for achieving a strong vote bank amongst the labouring class. The rights of the workers were never the fundamental impetus behind labour movements and strikes in Nepal. The misuse of labour unions as a means to gaining political clout and voicing disagreements continues to inflict a tremendous cost on the Nepali economy. The labour union leaders go around in swanky expensive sport utility vehicles (SUVs) funded by bilateral agencies and become more important than the enterprise. The funding agencies have never realized that there will be no work for labour if the enterprises don't exist. The militancy of labour that such a culture has fostered has been a severe deterrent to both foreign and domestic investment, with labour issues remaining a primary source of concern for those wanting to do business in Nepal.

The reason why labour issues were not reformed is apparent. The politicians and political parties simply had too much to lose by challenging the labour unions they themselves had helped create and strengthen. The unions formed the core of their political voter base and simultaneously provided the strongest muscle power in their political arsenal.

However, in the bargain, labour lost the most, as the people who really wanted to work for a living chose to leave Nepal, owing to their uncertainty about Nepal's economic future and their inability to handle situations where they were called in to protest rather than work. Many factories shut down, with owners being forced to sell their properties. Businesses closing down meant not only the loss of overtime pay opportunities, of employee housing and profit-linked bonuses, but also the relocation of families in search of work to different parts of the country and abroad, to India.

## Bandhs Galore: The Business of Closure

The successful use of *chakka* jams and Nepal bandhs[8] during the Jana Andolan had highlighted the importance and strength of street-level agitation to the politicians. The strategy of closing down the nation or obstructing traffic to make a political statement is perhaps a remnant of the power of the Indian embargo in Nepal. Whatever the cause, the chakka jam and Nepal bandh soon became an integral part of Nepali society. Political parties, labourers, businesses, social workers and even grief-stricken family members took to the streets in some form of chakka jam or Nepal bandh the moment their rights were threatened or demands unmet. Websites like www.nepalbandh.com started providing advance information on such events, helping people to plan their days of travel and decide whether to keep offices open or shut. The popular currency of such digital representations of the bandh cycle in a nation that was not overwhelmingly tech-savvy is an indication of how deep a hold the bandh phenomenon had on the Nepali psyche.

Agitating cable operators cutting off transmission of their channels, taxis expressing grievances by parking along the Ring Road to obstruct traffic in and out of the airport, garbage piling up on the street when someone in the garbage chain is unhappy—these are all routine occurrences. Ironically, when upset, businesses and hotels which lamented the impact of bandhs on business and tourism resorted to calling for bandhs themselves. It was as if Nepal and bandhs were a match made in heaven—once in the country, everyone seemed to welcome bandhs and revel in them. For the by-now fatalist and escapist Nepali populace, the bandh was just another holiday. It was an excuse to drink excessively the night before and play cards all day long, so most Nepalis relished the many surprise vacations that the nation's political turmoil threw at them. Simultaneously, for the business-minded, it presented the ideal opportunity for racketeering and profiteering by providing more arbitrage opportunities to make that extra rupee. The vegetable vendors in Kalimati, Kathmandu, as well as the adulterated fuel gas stations prayed for that landslide in Krishnabhir or a strike by any organization—as long as life came to a standstill. Businesses that thrive by capitalizing on such windows of opportunity have served to further the culture of bandhs. The business atmosphere in Kathmandu runs on the same wavelength as Kolkata, which even after all its moves towards liberalization has yet to get rid of the image it impressed upon the world during the 1970s—as a city with more non-working days than working days. In the tourist or economic map of the world, Nepal, with its addiction to bandhs and chakka jams, has firmly established itself as Kolkata's younger sibling. Each day of the strike meant a loss of NPR 1.8 billion to the economy and its impact reduced the gross annual input by 1.38 per cent.[9]

## A Waste of Youth

At the heart of the bandh and chakka jam cycle are event coordinators such as student and trade unions. In yet another perversion of economic potential, the politicization of university campuses and trade unions created the need for a large number of young cadres to take to the streets to enforce bandhs and chakka jams as a real representation of political power. The use of youth as a means of political leveraging is, in effect, the squandering of the promise held by it. Unlike the youth in China, Thailand and Vietnam, who are driving the economic growth of their countries, young people in Kathmandu are either busy touting party propaganda or spending their nights partying. The youth who were not party material (in either sense of the word 'party') sought out opportunities to leave the country and work abroad. Unfortunately, having been raised in an educational system which lacked the standards that would allow its products to compete in the international market, most of these youth found their skills severely lacking and their degrees ephemeral comforts in a world that was more concerned about quality and brand than heart and intention. For parents, it became more important to provide $100 for a pair of Doc Martens shoes than buy books for just a tenth of the amount, since Nepali society generally seems to judge external looks only. For every ten beauty pageants there was one quiz contest held and while ever more places were available to go drink and smoke, there was no place to go and listen to a good lecture. While clubs and dance bars mushroomed, no museums or art centres got built. A business atmosphere that deterred investment for fear of militant labour, energy shortages and constant security concerns all stifled the growth of employment opportunities in the private sector. The rise in unemployment, dissatisfaction and militancy in such a scenario is thus, hardly surprising.

## The Tourism Jinx

Nepal's fate as a tourist destination was also afflicted during these years due to various local and international events. By 1996, the gold rush in the tourism industry had created a situation of oversupply of hotel rooms, while the poor infrastructure (aside from the boom in hotel rooms) could not cater to the rising number of tourists. There was no innovation in the tourism products that were being sold, and the novelty of the golden triangle of Pokhara, Chitwan and Kathmandu became stale. The Visit Nepal Year campaign of 1998 that was supposed to provide the impetus for a tourist influx paradoxically coincided with the decline of tourist arrivals in Nepal. The hijacking of an Indian Airlines plane on the Christmas Eve of 1999 dealt the first big blow, with flights from India to Nepal suspended for six months. Thereafter, a riot broke out in February 2001, sparked by rumours that an Indian film star had made derogatory remarks about Nepal. Then there was the closure of hotels over a service charge row between hotel owners and hotel workers. The already ailing industry was dealt another blow with the Royal Massacre in June 2001. Thereafter, the 9/11 attack on the World Trade Center in New York and the subsequent impact on global tourism made the slump continue till 2002. The escalation of the Maoist conflict in 2002 prompted negative travel advisories and tourist arrivals fell that year to as low as 1990 levels.

## Power Snaps

In retrospect, the twenty-odd years from 1990 to 2008 have been a rollercoaster ride for the Nepal economy. The restoration of democracy and the subsequent opening up of the economy sparked much hope, but the squandering of opportunity that began in 1994 was further aggravated by the ten-year conflict between the state and the Maoists. By the time the first prime minister of the Democratic People's Republic of Nepal took the oath of office in September 2008, the economy was worse off than in 1990.

The example of the energy crisis perhaps best explains this tremendous decline. The biggest impact of the Indian embargo of 1989 was on the supply of fuel from India, which abruptly stopped. At that time, major power cuts were anticipated and the government, in response, wanted to develop hydropower for energy security as well as rapid economic growth. A hydropower policy was instituted in 1992, which encouraged private investment in hydropower, including foreign direct investment. By 1997, Nepal had launched two of what were to be the only ten successful privately financed hydropower enterprises in that decade—Bhote Koshi and Khimti. Both had secured foreign investment.

Shortly thereafter, with the devaluation of the Nepali rupee and revenues pegged to the US dollar, these two projects drew a lot of flak and became everyone's favourite punching bags. In 1998, the then deputy prime minister and minister in charge of hydropower, Shailaja Acharya of the Nepali Congress, categorically stated to a business delegation that included this author that Nepal did not want the private sector, indigenous or otherwise, to develop power projects with a power generation capacity of more than 10 MW. With private investors out of the picture, foreign donors got into the action to fund the Kaligandaki and Middle Marsyangdi power projects, which were to be built and owned by the state-owned utility, the Nepal Electricity Authority (NEA). While the government waited for more donors to line up to build projects, all investors waited for the government to grant licences. A historic Power Trade Agreement signed between India and Nepal in 1996 to facilitate power trading between the two countries was approved by the Indian cabinet, but till date, successive Nepali governments have never managed to get the treaty approved at their end. Perhaps this was because of the speculation and hypothesis that Indian interest in commercial hydropower only began after the Bhote Koshi and Khimti projects were well under way in 1996.

Hydropower also generated big activists who stalled many projects. They opposed Arun III, a World Bank–initiated project, and a number of foreign investments in hydropower, especially Indian. The same people who opposed the Arun III project went on to lobby for a power project at Melamchi and worked as propagators for Chinese investment in West Seti. Keeping their offices running on expensive diesel generators, these lobby groups did not mind Nepal staying starved of electricity.

## Private Schools and Foreign Education

By the early 1990s, Nepal had made dramatic improvements to its educational system, with over 17,000 primary schools established by 1990 and an equal rise in the number of secondary- and tertiary-level institutes. However, the literacy rate had only increased to around 40 per cent by 1991 and the quality of this education was questionable. Most tertiary-level education occurred in the field of the arts, with very few opting to study technical subjects like engineering and medicine. This was largely due to weak primary education in English and the limited seats available for students to enter technical fields. The low quality of government education had fostered the growth of the private English boarding school industry from the 1980s onwards. After the liberalization of the 1990s, the private school industry experienced an economic boom. This had a very salutary effect on Nepal's educational sector and its economy overall. Charging higher fees, these schools could pay less to teachers than government schools did, but were able to teach English to their students from the primary school level on. Although many schools acted only as money-making ventures, it is without a doubt that private schools in general immediately set a new benchmark for education in Nepal and challenged the hegemony of a government school education among the Nepali middle class.

Suddenly in the early 1990s, three things shook up the educational sector: passport access was decentralized, an English-speaking generation was produced, and the educational consultancy industry was established. With limitations on both the capacity and quality of higher educational opportunities in Nepal, going abroad to study was an alluring prospect. The precedent had already been established by the older elite English boarding schools, and foreign degrees carried an undeniable prestige. Attached to the prospect of going abroad was the eventual opportunity to work and live on in the foreign country. It was an attractive prospect for many, to shed the Nepali image and acquire a lifestyle that fitted with their perception of the West.

Peer pressure forced rent-earning parents to sell their property or mortgage it in order to finance their children's overseas education. This was the only way for them to raise enough money to send their children abroad as they did not see a future for them in Nepal. It is not surprising that children, adopting their parents' world view, also saw a brighter future outside the country, one much better than anything imaginable in Nepal. The educational consultancy industry literally opened up a world of opportunity. An educational market that had thus far been cornered by students of the elite schools in Nepal was suddenly made accessible to the rising masses from newly established private English boarding schools. This is perhaps a story best told in terms of numbers—in 1994–95 only about 1000 Nepali students were present in the United States; by 2008 this number had risen to 8936 Nepali students per year, making it number 11 in terms of foreign students in the US.[10] The return rate among these students remains extremely low, with most choosing to stay on legally or illegally.

Given the establishment and rapid expansion of private English boarding schools throughout the nation and the subsequent rise of educational consultancies, it can be argued that education in Nepal has been an intrinsically market-driven phenomenon. With the limited scope and quality of government education in Nepal, there was an increasing demand for better educational standards and practices, especially with a growing number of educated middle-class parents who were increasingly aware of the opportunities a good education could provide their children. These children, educated in the private school system, were even more aware of the opportunities they could grasp and set their aspirations much higher than their parents did. Thus, the educational consultancy industry was born out of this demand for quicker and easier access to universities abroad. The 'secrets' of the application process, that only students at elite schools had been privy to in the past, were made available to all—for the right price.

## Private Institutions of Higher Learning

The impact of privatization was felt throughout the educational sector. Aside from the private school boom, perhaps the biggest revolution to shake the foundations of the Nepali educational system was the establishment of Kathmandu University. Established in 1991 through an Act (Kathmandu University Act, 1991), it is the first private institute of higher learning established in Nepal, posing the first direct challenge to the educational monopoly of Tribhuvan University. In 1992, Kathmandu University started its first class with intermediate-level courses only; since then the university has quickly expanded into undergraduate and postgraduate studies. It currently operates seven schools based on the disciplines of arts, education, engineering, law, management, medical science and science. More than 25,000 students have graduated in this period. Setting an educational benchmark that places it in a different league than the government-mismanaged Tribhuvan University, there is an increasing trend among private secondary and tertiary institutions to seek affiliation with Kathmandu University. Constant strikes, delays in examinations, delays in publishing results, and disillusionment with the entire quality of education on offer in Tribhuvan University means that any student with ambition shuns it.

Although privatization went a long way in improving the standard of education in Nepal, the lack of governmental regulation on private schools meant that a considerable amount of profiteering occurred. Although some private schools gave you all you paid for in terms of education, facilities and access, some, if not most of them, took the easier way out. By charging increasingly higher fees while doing nothing to improve the quality of education or the facilities of the school in return, it is safe to say that private schools often became a cash crop. By selling substandard uniforms through designated contractors, books through cartels of booksellers and book publishers associations, and charging parents for foundations, events, fairs or excursions, education became the best unregulated private sector. Its ability to deliver, albeit by charging such high fees, encouraged some Nepali students to study in Nepal.

The costs of all levels of private education remained relatively high, with the cheapest private schools in Nepal charging rates that were easily higher than those being charged in private schools of the same standard in neighbouring India. With school fees of up to NPR 1000 a month, private education was not a luxury that low-income people, with their low minimum pay, could afford to provide their children. These high fees have been a bone of contention between private schools and the government; add to it increasing pressure from the government to have control over such private schools, and soon private schools grouped together to form big cartels with strong negotiation powers. With 5 million children in school, this provided the largest base of customers that the service providers could profit from.

## The People's War: 1996–2006

Given the reasonably good success rate of armed insurgency in seizing political power in Nepal, the People's War started by the Communist

Party of Nepal (CPN-M)—also known as the Maoists—in February 1996 was a calculated and understandable strategy. The stated objectives of the People's War were to: 'remove the bureaucratic-capitalistic class and the state system, uproot semi-feudalism and drive out imperialism, in order to establish a New Democratic Republic with the view to establish a new socialist society'.[11] While the state system in this case was the monarchy, they attacked semi-feudalism as a system under the rule of kings and other feudal lords, which exploited people as a means to their own prosperity.

Dr Baburam Bhattarai, the senior Maoist leader who went on to become the prime minister, explained to this author that Nepal had been bestowed with many resources, but the feudal lords were parasitic, extractive and rent-seeking, and used these resources only for their own benefit. They were never interested in development but only in leisure and living luxuriously. The Maoist struggle was needed to ensure that this class could be removed, thereby allowing a model of people's participation in Nepal's future economic development.

Unlike past insurgencies, the Maoists were unique in that they wanted to capture and control land in Nepal, apart from challenging the state structure. This was a strategy that they took from Mao's books and it proved powerful enough to win the support of a vast number of Nepalis who had long suffered under the burden of poverty and oppression. Starting out in the districts of Rolpa, Rukum and Jajarkot in the mid-1990s, the Maoists started with the removal of select local 'tyrants' who formed the local elites and police force. They were very successful in these early phases, partly because of a government that did not care to act and partly because their strategy was immensely popular with the impoverished and exploited locals. This allowed them to set up their own local government structures in these regions, totally supplanting the government's administrative and judicial structures. After just three years of building, expanding, recruiting, extorting and raiding, the Maoists were able to formally announce the formation of the People's Army in February 1999. Although raids, sabotages, ambushes and kidnappings had formed the core areas of competency for the Maoist guerrillas, the establishment of the People's Army marked a new phase in the war. On 25 September 2000, the People's Army successfully launched their first full-scale assault on Dunai, the headquarters of Dolpa district in the western part of Nepal. The victory was a big boost to the Maoist war efforts and subsequently led to the escalation of the war.

The People's Liberation Army (PLA), during the course of the decade-long insurgency from 1996 to 2006, is estimated to have had anywhere from 4000 to 8000 core combatants with a support structure of 20,000 to 25,000 armed militia.[12] The Maoists had to have significant political and administrative capacities to operate such an army, as well as run a parallel government structure in roughly one-third of the entire nation. Part of the success of the Maoists has been their ability to not only manage and coordinate but also to ensure loyalty and respect for the command hierarchy within their organization. This partly stems from the fact that they were a militia, conducting extensive guerrilla training and compelling discipline. The Maoists were also successful in recruiting former British and Indian Gorkhas and ex-Nepal army personnel to lead their training exercises. This has allowed them to develop a level of professionalism and create a soldier's culture within the ranks of the PLA, which would not have been possible without specialist military trainers.

## Legacies of the Conflict

The conflict has relegated Nepal to a situation similar to West Bengal's in 1977 where after the Naxalite war, a Left Front government with coalition partners belonging to various left parties came together and won the elections. The only difference was that it was not the Naxalites that led the government in Bengal in 1977. After coming to power in Bengal, the Left Front worked on various ways to consolidate and stay in power, and they have done that brilliantly, with more than three decades of continuous rule. They came to power promising vigorous agrarian and political reforms, just as the Maoists in Nepal did.

They called for a 'reversal of the trend toward industrial stagnation by constraining monopoly capital, encouraging small-scale industry, promoting worker self-management and an expansion of the state sector. Corporate industrialization was to be minimized in favour of industrial cooperatives and the public sector.'[13] This is similar to the Maoist policy pronouncements in Nepal. What the Left Front in Bengal did was to woo the landless through distribution of land, get youth votes through various voluntary employment programmes and free largesse in the form of loans that did not need to be repaid, get the workers into the fold through strong unionization and patronize some business groups to enable control over business.

## War Economics: 'Business Opportunities'

The Maoists' major revenue was obtained through extortion and the levying of donations and taxes on the general populace. The donations and taxes in particular were most severe in Maoist-controlled areas where they targeted teachers, government officials and farmers in addition to local businessmen. The payment of a tax to the Maoists ensured protection from Maoist violence, but did nothing to protect the payer from the security forces or from opportunistic hoodlums. It is estimated that by the year 2000, the Maoists' extortion and tax racket had allowed them to accumulate over NPR 5 billion.[14] By 2001, the Second National Conference of the Maoists in February 2001 declared Pushpa Kamal Dahal or Prachanda the party chairman, and the party officially touted a doctrine that was popularly called 'Prachandapath'. The doctrine is an extension of the ideological line expounded by the Communist Party of Peru and is an attempt to localize the doctrines of Marxism, Leninism and Maoism in the Nepali context. It was also around this time that the People's Army was renamed the People's Liberation Army and placed under the direct command of Prachanda. It now boasted three divisions, nine brigades and twenty-nine battalions, and was far better equipped than before, thanks to the automatic weapons and explosives looted from police posts and army barracks. There are also unofficial rumours that suggest that the Maoists were successful in procuring AK-47 assault rifles from black markets in the Indian states of Bihar and Uttar Pradesh.

Cost estimates of financing the PLA vary from source to source, from around NPR 250–800 million.[15] What we do know is that the Maoists spent frugally on the payment and equipping of their forces; however, they did spend extensively on training them and preparing them for battle. At the individual level, it is estimated that each soldier received NPR 150 as monthly allowance, was given a non-vegetarian meal every week, and no more than NPR 17,000 in total a year was spent on each combatant.[16] Aside from extortion, looting and kidnapping, the Maoists were successful in raising funds from the trading and taxing of Yarchagumba plants. They were also able to tap poaching and the illegal trade in forest wood, for which they followed a similar informal taxation model to that of Yarchagumba, requiring direct payments to the Maoists based on the value or volume of goods. They also made levies in areas of their control where natural resources were exploited. Further, the Maoists were successful in establishing Nepali Maoist trade unions in countries where Nepalis worked, including in the Middle East and East Asia. These sympathizers were then able to channel considerable funds to support the Maoist movement.

The insurgency came with its own unique set of advantages. For one inclined to do business for the sake of profit without the restraints of ethics, these proved particularly bountiful times. Corruption allowed a great deal of trade in Nepal under the cover of the insurgency. From the smuggling of goods to poaching, and from printing counterfeit notes to the creation of artificial shortages, Nepal's swindlers and double-dealers had a field day. A weak state structure invites all these irregularities and promotes the proliferation of racketeering. The hugely popular use of blockades, chakka jams and strikes was particularly effective in creating artificial shortages that allowed businessmen in Kathmandu to make a few extra bucks on commodities ranging from kerosene to tomatoes. With no consumer protection laws and few alternatives, the people had to pay up.

These chakka jams, blockades, raids and lootings also meant that newsworthy events were now happening all over the country, and suddenly, Nepal was Kathmandu no longer. Nepal grew vast, and began to represent many places previously unheard of and unknown to the urban mind. Here was a crash course on Nepali geography that most people would have done better without.

## Prohibitive Cost of War

The ten years of conflict have done immeasurable damage to Nepal's economy, society and culture. A significant amount of infrastructural damage was caused by the Maoists in their quest to remove old feudal structures. For instance, they targeted many government installations as a way of attacking, destroying and superseding representatives of the state to demonstrate the state's weakness. Primary Maoist targets were the offices of village development committees (VDCs), school buildings, municipality offices, district development offices and other government offices. They also targeted communication installations, power relay stations and bridges as a way of gutting state infrastructure and creating a parallel administration and also because these targets were identified as components of the feudal state. In total, over a ten-year destructive spree, the Maoists were successful in vandalizing and destroying infrastructure worth NPR 30.55 billion in 1841 rural VDCs.[17] Some of these structures, which had been built over the course of forty years of development, are yet to be rebuilt.

The nation also had to bear the cost of a dramatic rise in spending on security forces and other necessities for the state's war against the Maoists. The security force used to be a 50,000-strong personnel army and a 50,000-strong police force, but it soon incorporated an entirely new branch—the paramilitary outfit of the Armed Police Force. By 2005, the combined security forces had expanded to over 1,00,000 strong. This was accompanied by a rise in budgetary spending on security from NPR 5.38 billion in 1996 to NPR 18.33 billion in 2005.[18] During this time, the government security forces and the army in particular were responsible for purchasing weapons, including 5000 M16 rifles and 5500 M246 Minimi rifles. The total budgetary spending on security forces during the ten years of insurgency totalled a whopping NPR 107.8 billion.[19] If this money had been used to build power plants, then Nepal would have had a 625 MW power plant!

It is estimated that the conflict cost the nation around 2.5 per cent of GDP growth per annum since the escalation of the violence due to the insurgency, starting from the year 2000.[20] The impact on GDP is the result of a combination of factors including the decline in tourists, losses in business, drying up of foreign direct investment, and loss in human capital. The conflict has impacted the ability of the government to provide basic needs to the people in the form of drinking water, education and health services and has affected the capacity and extent to which development work on such things as roads and communication has been carried out in rural Nepal. The most significant costs that the nation and the people have had to bear is the invaluable cost of the lives of over 15,000 Nepali citizens. This has had an impact on their families, relatives, friends and local communities. The war led to a mass migration of young men and boys fleeing out of fear of both sides. From 1,00,000 to 2,00,000[21] people have been displaced from their homes and been forced to shift to the urban centres, primarily Kathmandu, in search of safety, security and work.

## Psychological Impact of War

Given the substantial number of people the insurgency has directly and indirectly impacted, a strong undercurrent of resentment can be felt in Nepali society. Feelings of anger, hatred and revenge have established themselves in the minds and hearts of many Nepalis and pose an invisible danger to the social fabric. There is no way of predicting or being prepared for the possibly violent reactions of people who have themselves witnessed and suffered from violence. This invisible danger will be an investment risk for doing business in Nepal for the next two generations. The insurgency has also caused immeasurable damage to the intricate networks of trust and friendliness, for which Nepali society was once known throughout the world. Nepali people no longer walk the streets and implicitly trust those they cross paths with; there is an air of mistrust and suspicion. It is no longer considered safe to talk to people at random or be involved in discussions about politics and society out in the open. There is a fostering of the perception that there are eyes all around and one wrong move in front of the wrong set of eyes could have drastic consequences. For instance, during the conflict, it became difficult for a lodge owner to decide whether to rent a room to a stranger as both the Maoists and the state were keeping an eye on people's movements. If the guest was a Maoist, then the security forces went after the lodge owner, and if the guest had any level of allegiance to the state, then the Maoists went after the lodge owner. Spontaneous chatting in tea shops in villages, carrying parcels for a relative or acquaintance, or just travelling in a local bus became more and more difficult for the common citizen.

## Insurgency: A Great Excuse

The insurgency also provided an ideal excuse to the private sector and the development sector for their inefficiencies and failures. The insurgency, in this sense, became the tastiest scapegoat to have ever lived beyond two Dasains.[22] For the donors, the insurgency was the reason for the failure of many of their development programmes, even though many of these programmes had been in business—unsuccessfully—for far longer than the insurgency itself. It also gave the donors the excuse to quietly close down programmes that were not working without acknowledging their failures. Some donors were romantic about the promise of socialism and bought into it like a dream once lost. They continued to operate their programmes in Maoist-held territories, willingly paying the 10–15 per cent tax they had to bear in order to operate within these regions, despite knowing full well that their money was being used to buy weapons and finance extortions. Even so, the donors and international community in Nepal did not want to see a Maoist victory. This would have been dangerous in not only encouraging other such revolutions but also in terms of the instability it would invite into the region.

India had declared the Maoists a terrorist outfit much earlier than Nepal itself had, and it was well known that most Nepali Maoist leaders and troops were based out of India. Historically, it should be noted that any insurgency in Nepal has not succeeded without some form of explicit or silent support from India. The Indian government's inability to tackle the Nepal insurgency is either a sign of limitations in its ability to control its northern frontier or an indication of a much deeper political manoeuvre.

## The Illusion for Many

The Maoists who had fought the People's War continued to race ahead in the struggle for power, like any other political party, by using nepotism and money. Leaders who had walked in the jungles and found four-wheel vehicles the epitome of imperialism suddenly started to own them; leaders who had gained public sympathy by banning alcohol could now not live without their favourite imported Scotch; leaders who had burnt down private schools were now educating their own children in elite private schools. Maoist leaders started working closely with businesses to further their personal fortunes and used the party as a veil to hide the benefits of capitalism that they had discovered. Suddenly, the people who had lost their youth, relations and livelihoods during the ten-year insurgency started to question the necessity of the revolution.

## State Apathy

The government during the late 1990s was involved in a number of inter-party and intra-party squabbles that allowed the Maoists to operate without much state resistance. The lack of popular support behind the Maoists, especially in Kathmandu during their earlier days, made them of only fringe interest to the government at the time. Indeed, if anything, the political parties were willing to use the Maoists as leverage to play their own power games. This was perhaps best exemplified by the political shuffle within the Congress party when Krishna Prasad Bhattarai's government was displaced by his own party colleague Girija Prasad Koirala in March 2000. The stated reason for this shuffle was that Prime Minister Bhattarai's government was unable to initiate dialogue or tackle the Maoist problem. At this point, the Maoist violence had escalated to a considerable degree and was increasingly impacting the national economy. The inability of the government to effectively deal with the insurgency and the weakness of its administrative and security structures was quickly revealed. The police force was poorly trained, poorly equipped and extremely corrupt. The police structure was centralized with all recruitment and placements occurring in the capital, thus dissociating the police from the local community, to whom it appeared as a foreigner representing state repression. In many sections of the police, the insurgency suddenly created business opportunities in directing the placement of police officers around the nation. A nice bottle of Black Label whisky to a senior officer could be the difference between going to the heart of the Maoist insurgency in Rolpa or to the tamer town of Dharan. The police also lacked discipline and were guilty of harassment and prone to lash out randomly when threatened. With such a culture of corruption and unruliness, it is not surprising that the police were disliked and despised by people as a reckless and irresponsible group of hoodlums. Thus, when the

Maoists first attacked the police, there was actually considerable public sympathy for their actions.

## Army Stays Out

The government also faced major problems in mobilizing the army. Although the army was, in theory, under the control of the government through the National Defence Council, it retained its allegiance to the king. The king using his army to kill fellow Nepalis always became a moral issue that he had to address publicly to retain legitimacy. Therefore, he refrained from using the army despite the level of escalation in violence. The army, in turn, chose to abide by its traditional allegiance to the king, instead of following the wishes of the democratic government. Although the army had a good public image in comparison to the police, corruption was endemic in that budgets and spending were neither accountable nor transparent. The army's unwillingness to join the conflict in situations where it could have assisted police forces and its lack of cooperation with the prime minister and Parliament caused considerable consternation to the government.

For instance, during the Maoist attack on Dunai in September 2000, local army barracks opted not to intervene in the fight and allowed the Maoists to take off with NPR 50 million from the local bank, which had received this surplus money that very day. The unwillingness of the king to get the army involved and the lack of the army's interest in entering into the conflict forced the government into the formation of the Armed Police Force in 2001. It was primarily established as a paramilitary force to maintain law and order, contain the insurgency and fight terrorism. The general feeling among the Nepali people was also against the use of security forces by the government. This was largely due to a fear that the use of the army would lead to an escalation of the crisis. The constant political turmoil and infighting between political leaders further reduced the faith of the Nepali people in the ability of the democratic government to successfully manage the army and handle the conflict.

## Royal Massacre Complicates Politics

If the escalating violence due to the insurgency was not enough reason for worry, the Nepali nation was shocked in June 2001 by the massacre of the entire royal family and the ascension of Gyanendra Shah to the throne as the king of Nepal. Shortly thereafter, within two months of the World Trade Center attacks in New York, the Maoists launched a full-scale attack on an army barrack in Dang in western Nepal, breaking a ceasefire and leading, finally, to the government mobilization and deployment of the Royal Nepal Army. The timing of the Maoist attack seemed to be in line with their shift in propaganda, attacking American imperialism rather than Indian hegemony. In an interview, Prachanda himself states, 'In the process of waging war we managed to snatch a few rifles from the armed police. It is these rifles that are now capturing automatic weapons from the royal army. Thus, weapons sent by George Bush to suppress Nepalese people will soon be reaching the hands of Nepalese people, and will be directed against imperialism.'[23]

Although there were several peace talks between 2002 and 2005 between the government and the Maoists, none of them was successful in resolving the crisis. The primary reason for their failure was the government's unwillingness to cede to the Maoists' demands for a Constituent Assembly for the drafting of a new Constitution. There are also claims that the Maoists were only using the peace talks as a means to consolidate and strengthen. The argument goes that the peace talks were used by the Maoists as a time to recuperate, gather supplies and plan for their next offensive. There is some justification for this argument as after the breakdown of each talk, the Maoists became stronger and launched more and more daring raids.

## Gyanendra: The Last Shah King

King Gyanendra was crowned king for the first time when he was four years old on 7 January 1950 by the then Rana prime minister to have a puppet king as King Tribhuvan had left the country. With India not accepting this baby king, Gyanendra had to give way to his grandfather, King Tribhuvan. While it is rumoured that astrologers had told him he would become king once again, he could never have imagined that he would have to take the burden of the crown at the most difficult times for his family. His elder brother, King Birendra, had been ruling for thirty years before his rule came to a horrifying end. Crown Prince Dipendra gunned down his father, mother, brother, sister and many more family members after inviting them for a meal at his palace. Gyanendra's wife, Queen Komal, sustained major injuries but his children were saved. Dipendra killed himself in the end, and as per archaic traditions, he was still declared the king before finally being declared dead and making Gyanendra the king.

The way this royal massacre was handled at the beginning of the twenty-first century with sombre music played on radio and television in the days of mobile phones and the Internet was unfortunate. It allowed rumours to rule the roost, and Gyanendra still remains a suspect in the eyes of the bulk of the Nepali public. When he was advised to use a world-class communications firm to explain the matter, he refused. Furthermore, the government investigations were conducted in a ridiculous manner. Nepalis who witnessed the aftermath on television will never forget House Speaker Taranath Ranabhat making a fool of himself and the situation.

Gyanendra was seen by many as an astute businessman, but only insiders knew his problems and how he was a loner who listened to everyone but went his own way. He inherited the Soaltee Hotel and Himalaya Tea Garden business in the 1960s when his uncle and aunt, Prince Himalaya Shah and his wife, Princep Shah, died without leaving an heir. He had Princep Shah's brother, Prabhakar Rana, as a partner in the business, but it was the latter who operated the Soaltee Hotel and the Tea Garden. He was also an investor in Surya Tobacco (now Surya Nepal) but had to sell the bulk of his shares to pay off some liabilities before he took the throne. Having a son that had garnered a reputation that no father would like and a daughter who was married to a person seen as an opportunist did not help improve his image or business. He was also the chair of the King Mahendra Trust for Nature Conservation (now the Nepal Trust for Nature Conservation), started by his brother Birendra for him. But the fact that the institution was continuously mired in controversies and management challenges did not speak well about his management or leadership skills.

Gyanendra lived surrounded by a few of his family members and advisers. He was eloquent and could impress anyone with his articulate analysis of issues and solutions. However, everyone questioned his ability to deliver and walk the talk. Perhaps his way of functioning made him make successive erroneous judgements in politics and business. He also could not gain the confidence of the extended family members who believed in the institution of monarchy and the Nepal Army of which he was the commander in chief. Perhaps, looking back, he had the best opportunity in the modern times of Nepal post-1950 to emerge as a leader who could transform Nepal in all ways, but his myopia cost him dearly. In December 2005, his business partner Prabhakar Rana and his son decided to part ways, and the new entity Tara Management Private Limited was born, separate from the Soaltee Group. Having served twenty years with the Soaltee Group, I also parted ways with the parent company to take on a position as the group president of Tara Management. In the days to come, I had to continuously explain how the former king had very few investments, and perhaps it was not the political forces and Nepali people, it was Gyanendra who was responsible for the end of the institution of monarchy and the 240-year-old Shah dynasty.

## The End of the Shahs

By the time of the royal coup in February 2005, when King Gyanendra sacked the prime minister and began direct rule, the conflict had become a stalemate, with the Maoists controlling considerable tracts of the countryside while the government controlled the urban centres. After the coup, there was a crackdown on civil liberties, which caused considerable opposition to the royal regime. The Maoists were increasingly aware of their inability to defeat the army in a protracted military struggle and saw a unique opportunity in tying up with dissenting political parties and taking part in a non-violent campaign against the monarchy. A twelve-point agreement was signed in New Delhi between the seven parties on 22 November 2005, pledging to start a popular movement to end the monarchy. This was a Nepal that was well connected by powerful private media, mobile phones, radio and the Internet. Gyanendra could not see what was coming. India tried its best to explain to him the writing on the wall, but he did not understand or care. His days and the days of the Shah dynasty were numbered and he was just a guest for a few days at the Narayanhiti Palace. After the elections to the first Constituent Assembly that brought the Maoists to power, they declared Nepal a Federal Democratic Republic. On 11 June 2008, seven years after he was crowned the king, he departed the Narayanhiti Palace after addressing a press conference and making a press release. People lined up in the streets to see the last king of the Shah dynasty leave his palace.

# 6

# Years of Transition: 2006–18

## Open Moment: 2006

The year 2006 was an open moment in the history of Nepal. The country had emerged from a decade-long conflict after democratic forces joined with the then underground Maoists to fight the 240-year-old Shah rule, paving the way for a Federal Democratic Republic. After a nineteen-day non-violent street-level protest popularly referred to as the Jana Andolan II, the king stepped down and reinstated Parliament. The country completely moved away from the dual power of palace and Parliament as monarchy was abolished on 28 May 2008. An interim government under the leadership of Prime Minister Girija Prasad Koirala then led the nation to its first Constituent Assembly election, which subsequently led to the establishment of a Maoist-majority government in September 2008. This government set about the task of writing a new Constitution by 2010 with a new round of elections planned for 2011. Yet, it was not until 2015 that the second Constituent Assembly finally promulgated the new Constitution. In October 2017, the two largest communist parties—CPN (UML) and CPN (Maoist Centre)—decided to contest the elections together. The first federal and provincial elections under the new Constitution were held in December 2017. The Nepal Communist Party controlled nearly two-thirds of Parliament and K.P. Oli took over as the prime minister on 15 February 2018, leaving behind over two decades of being in a political quagmire and marking the end of an almost twelve-year political transition and the supposed beginning of a new economic future for Nepal. In this chapter, we will discuss the challenging political uncertainty and in the next chapter the societal transformation.

## The Rule of Uncertainty and Proliferation of Expectation Fatigue

The post-conflict transition process was not easy for Nepal. While the People's Movement of 2006 led to a drastic change in the political arena, it also created high expectations amongst the people. The political forces, however, worked as a political syndicate which people started referring to as a 'party-full Panchayat' system, similar to the 'party-less Panchayat' unitary system that ruled Nepal from 1960 to 1990. There was no opposition as a different permutation and combination of political parties ruled, producing as many prime ministers in as many years, including Supreme Court Chief Justice Khil Raj Regmi being appointed to lead a technocrat government. Political uncertainty continued to remain the only constant in Nepal. The frequent changes in government reflected the nature of short-term power equations between the various political forces that provided them with control over financial and other resources to be used for their own benefit while adversely impacting development. The long-term needs of having clear-cut policies, legislation and institutional frameworks were shelved in favour of working through ordinances and myopic decisions that benefited the few who were close to the corridors of power.

This uncertainty impacted the infrastructure industry the most as infrastructure projects became the fundamentals to rent-seek on the short-term power equations. While everyone admitted that infrastructure development was instrumental to economic growth, it remained neglected. Capital expenditure could not be fully utilized by the government, and infrastructure projects became synonymous with shabby jobs to be redone each year that kept party workers and people close to the party happy. For instance, Nepal, with its world-class resources, know-how and technology supported by multilateral and bilateral countries, could not manage to build 300 metres of a road in three years in my neighbourhood—this was the story of almost every neighbourhood. This reflected the impact of leveraging uncertainty for personal benefits at the cost of the nation's economy.

## Maoists Come above Ground!

It became an acceptable fact in Nepali lives that any tendering for government or quasi-government organizations would be rigged in favour of the party's cadres, be it for collection of tourist tax in Patan or contracts to build or break anything. With more cash flowing into the war chest of this erstwhile extortionist party, it started working with willing business people in real estate, and rumours of the party investing in banks, media houses and hospitals slowly started to be assumed as facts. Business people who were about to default on bank loans were provided informal credit, which not only earned them and the party some interest but also stemmed the sliding of the real estate prices that they had heavily invested in. Cadres who used to travel via public transport were suddenly seen driving expensive SUVs and making rounds of the cocktail circuits. From being part of an underground revolution, they moved into the dizzy social life of the Kathmandu elite and were introduced to expensive whisky, wine and gourmet restaurants. The leaders started to juggle between Mao's *Red Book*[1] during the day and Red Label whisky at night. The ideology of communism that they had been indoctrinated with had taught them about equality, and so they started becoming equals of the upper class of Kathmandu. This led to bitter infighting that finally resulted in the party's split. The common terms being used were 'Cash Maoist' for the UCPN, and 'Dash Maoist', or those whose hopes have been dashed, for the splinter group, the CPN (Maoist), which did not get its share of booty.

## All Combinations Tried

Nepal, after rejecting the autocratic direct rule of the king and ending the 240-year-old monarchy, went on to experiment with unprecedented combinations. The objective was simple in 2006: conduct the elections to the Constituent Assembly, write a Constitution and then conduct the federal and local elections. The elected government would then rule as per the provisions of the new Constitution. But the tendency of Nepalis to complicate processes led to losses of billions of dollars with repeated elections.

In the beginning, the Constituent Assembly could not be held on the designated date of 7 June 2007. It was postponed to 22 November 2007 (the date was decided by astrologers and the date of 26 November 2007 was changed to 22 November when a more powerful Indian astrologer overruled it[2]) but it was held finally only on 10 April 2008.

The election results sprung a surprise, with the Maoists coming first and the Nepali Congress and CPN (UML) coming second and third respectively. In the absence of a majority, coalition politics became the rule of the game. With inter-party and intra-party squabbles, it took four months before Pushpa Kamal Dahal became the prime minister in August 2008. In July 2008, Parliament also voted to elect a president, and Dr Ram Baran Yadav became Nepal's first. Dahal did not last even a year as he got embroiled in the critical issue of appointing Kul Bahadur Khadka as the chief of army, breaking protocol and tradition. He resigned as he could not appoint someone close to him instead of the then incumbent, General Rookmangud Katawal. This led to two successive prime ministers from the CPN (UML)—Madhav Kumar Nepal (May 2009 to February 2011) and Jhala Nath Khanal (February 2011 to August

2011)—leading the coalition. The Maoists were so unhappy with the arrangement that they continued threatening to withdraw from the peace process. In May 2010, they engaged in the tactic of spreading fear, engulfing the Kathmandu valley with their cadres by declaring a strike and capturing power. The situation was tense, but by the end of the fourth day, the citizens of the valley retaliated, making Dahal a frustrated erstwhile icon of terror as he spoke to the people and the press at a hurried function held at a hotel in Kathmandu.

The focus shifted away from Constitution-writing to usurping power and ensuring one does not leave the position of power. Each change in government meant the bureaucracy was shuffled and a new set of people got favours and contracts. This created a tremendous amount of enmity between various factions within the parties and resulted in destructive rather than constructive politics. The Constituent Assembly that was supposed to deliver a Constitution in two years got its tenure extended four times. Maoist leader Baburam Bhattarai became the prime minister in August 2011, and he went on to announce the dissolution of the Constituent Assembly in May 2012. With the Supreme Court's verdict of no extension, the role of the judiciary also got embroiled in the complicated quagmire of legislature.

The elections to the second Constituent Assembly were to be held in November 2012, but again, there was the issue of who would form the caretaker government. Uncertainty ruled again. In the end the parties decided to appoint Khil Raj Regmi, the chief justice of the Supreme Court, to lead an election government of technocrats. He took over as the prime minister in March 2013 and thereafter led the country through its second Constituent Assembly elections. The technocrat government did not function differently from the elected governments. The former government secretaries who were nominated to the position of ministers were more than happy to behave like politically elected ones. They started wielding power in terms of meddling in bureaucracy and also in public, where they enjoyed being chief guests, receiving garlands and gifts, and giving patronage to business people—there could not be a better post-retirement perk.

The sceptics who churned out reports selling uncertainty had a field day in talking about why the Constituent Assembly elections would not happen and the Constitution would not be written. From a takeover by India to the installation of a baby king (King Gyanendra's grandson) to the Maoists going back to the jungle—everyone had a theory. This period also saw an amazing number of international parachute analysts who started to paint a dismal picture of Nepal. In the name of social inclusion, a lot of money was already being spent on programmes and projects. Not being able to distinguish between their personal opinions and the opinion of the organizations, these analysts got sucked into the political squabbles. Finally, the elections to the second Constituent Assembly were completed successfully on 19 November 2013, but the CPN (Maoist), which was the largest party at that time, got relegated to a distant third, with the Nepali Congress making a comeback and UML ending up in second position. The royalist Rastriya Prajatantra Party that believed in Nepal reverting to a Hindu kingdom surprisingly won twenty-four seats, which became important in the game of numbers. With the Nepali Congress as the largest party but without a majority, different coalitions were experimented with. Initially, Sushil Koirala became the prime minister with the help of the UML but remained in power only from February 2014 to September 2015, stepping down after promulgating the Constitution. Thereafter, K.P. Oli (UML) led a government for a short period of time between October 2015 and August 2016. Next, the Nepali Congress had a deal with the CPN (Maoist) and decided to support Pushpa Kamal Dahal. As per the deal, Sher Bahadur Deuba became the prime minister for the fourth time in his life in June 2017 and oversaw the federal, provincial and local elections. Most interestingly, many of the dominant figures in Nepal politics since 1990 did not belong to the big three parties—for instance, Kamal Thapa and Bijay Gacchedar went on to be ministers and deputy ministers multiple times.

## Elections 2017

The local elections were held in 2017 for the first time in over two decades, and along with the federal and provincial elections, the political transition came to an end as Nepali voters entered into the reality of a federal Nepal. Ironically, their hopes were answered by Prime Minister Sher Bahadur Deuba—the same politician who had dissolved local bodies in 2002 and throttled Nepal's decentralization journey when he previously served as prime minister.

In October 2017, the CPN (UML) and the CPN (Maoist Centre)—the two largest communist forces in the country—decided to form an alliance for the federal and provincial elections. This move came as a surprise to the Nepali Congress (the oldest political party in Nepal; also the largest party in the dissolved Parliament) as well as India, which continued to have tremendous strategic interest in Nepali politics. The alliance brought together two parties with strong grass-roots organizational structures and paved the way for their historic win: they secured 116 out of the 165 directly elected representative seats and 58 out of the 110 proportional representation seats. When the parties actually united in early 2018, they held 174 of the 275 parliamentary seats and 42 upper house seats. This means they had nearly a two-thirds majority in Parliament.

The Nepali Congress, which was the leader of the coalition government at the time of elections, was now in the Opposition with just 63 seats. Despite receiving the same number of votes as the CPN (UML), Nepali voters rejected the Nepali Congress leaders who were contesting the elections. This loss has been attributed to several problems. First, the negative image of Sher Bahadur Deuba as the party leader and prime-ministerial candidate eroded public trust. Second, the old guard which had been 'holding fort' for nearly thirty years was reluctant to give way to a new generation of party leaders who might be better received by voters. Third, the citizens were fed up with the infighting in the Nepali Congress. Fourth, the Nepali Congress was seen to be hostage to the Indian meddling in Nepali politics. Notably, the party's failure to oppose the 2015 Indian blockade was unforgivable to many Nepalis. The final nail in the coffin was the party's list of candidates, which included known criminals and business people with dubious credibility.

So what made the Left Alliance comprising the Maoists and UML preferable? First, they peddled nationalism—which in Nepal means being anti-India—and voters saw CPN (UML) leader and former prime minister K.P. Oli as someone who could stand up to India as a result of his actions during India's blockade. Second, the alliance made stability and development the key message. For example, the parties took credit for Nepal's miraculous transition from suffering daily eighteen-hour power cuts to no power cuts. Third, knowing that the Nepali Congress was at the weakest point in its history, the CPN (UML) went into the 2017 elections all guns blazing. It particularly targeted incumbent Prime Minister Sher Bahadur Deuba and convinced voters in many far-flung areas that the Nepali Congress was the key reason for Nepal's underdevelopment.

On 15 February 2018, K.P. Oli, as per a power-sharing agreement with Dahal, as the co-chairs of the Nepal Communist Party (NCP), became Nepal's twelfth prime minister in as many years since the end of the monarchy in 2006 and the thirty-eighth prime minister since 1950. It was his second stint at a time when the world was witnessing many individual leaders as the focal point of election victories. He joined the list of contemporary leaders known for their strong personalities, like Donald Trump in the United States, Narendra Modi in India, Xi Jinping in China, Vladimir Putin in Russia, Recep Tayyip Erdogan in Turkey and Viktor Orban in Hungary.

## No Opposition

In a democracy, the system of checks and balances is based on a strong opposition that checks the party in power. In Britain, where democracy began, they even have shadow ministers to track functions.

However, in Nepal, pursuing a political syndicate, the concept of opposition was done away with. Since the political parties knew they had to ally with another force, they decided to do away with being in opposition and instead created a cartel that would ensure a proper channelling of resources to their cadre and party. The business folks loved it as they could just deal with a cartel and never run out of favour with any of the parties.

The All Party Mechanism (APM) that was introduced in the village committees and districts ensured that there was a decision without opposition. 'Bhagbanda' or distribution became a term of the new popular lexicon. Positions in bureaucracy, ambassadorship, insurance company licences, government land lease and construction contracts, amongst others, became distributed between the parties. The oligarchy of the key party leaders in Nepal being referred to in Nepali as 'Shirsh Neta' or top leaders became the undisputed autocratic decision-making machine that had neither transparency nor accountability. The focus of these leaders was on keeping the power equation ticking, while they did not have any serious interest in promulgating the Constitution. At the personal level, they did not believe in a federal, secular or inclusive Nepal. If not for the earthquake of April 2015, which led to an outpouring of protests against the political parties, they would not have pushed for the completion of the writing of the Constitution.

## Constitution Mania

The Constituent Assembly created to draft a new Constitution has been historically thought of as being a panacea to all of Nepal's ills. Nepal in the past sixty-seven years had seen seven constitutions. Post 2008, a new Constitution that had the fundamentals of secularism, federalism and social inclusion was seen as the key foundation on which the future of New Nepal would be built. However, the first Constituent Assembly was dissolved in 2012 and the second one was promulgated on 20 September 2016, only to be rejected by the agitated Madhesi parties comprising the people living in the southern plains of

Nepal—dominated by Nepalis of Indian origin, thus inviting an economic blockade from India. This blockade since September 2015 lasted till February 2016, paralysing an already flailing economy that was hit by the earthquake of April 2015. The local elections to be conducted under the new Constitution could only be completed in phases.

Constitutions are never meant to be used as a one-stop solution. Nepal and Nepalis have never grappled with the idea that a strong legal framework, effective implementation and an ethical approach towards being law-abiding citizens are key for growth, while a document that is put away like a religious scripture is not. The quest to finding solutions to each and every problem in the Constitution has led to it becoming a document with much room for misinterpretation.

## Constitution: Political Document

When one reads the preamble to the Constitution,[3] it is very easy to interpret it is as a political document of settlement with a list of aspirations, without any indication of implementation. It guarantees every right and freedom one can think of. It is vague, to say the least. For instance, it says that Nepal will pursue socialism, but nowhere has this term been defined. Hence, it could mean anything between the kind of socialism in the Nordic countries to the kind practised in North Korea. Further, the word 'prosperity' has been depicted as the outcome of Constitution implementation and was used extensively by the government in 2018. They have abused the word. A good reading of the Constitution can find holes in it as it was implemented in a rush. It is also understood that the Constitution is not a sacrosanct document and amendments can be made. However, since it was promulgated, doubts remain on how many lawmakers have actually read it and have the capacity to work on the gaping holes that have to be filled.

## Left-leaning Distributive Economy

From my analysis, the 2015 Constitution has five major flaws. First, it pushes for unplanned distributive economics. While all promises by the state have a cost, it is unclear how it is going to raise the money to pay for social security benefits or the other sops it promises. Second, it undermines the role of the private sector. Having provisions like mandatory participation of labour in management sends a clear signal that political forces would like to continue making labour a tool to negotiate their agenda with business owners. Third, it does not take into account international practices. It mandates the Nepali language, Nepali calendar year and the Nepali fiscal year, which are all impediments to global business practices. Fourth, it pushes for domestic investment and capital formation and does not accept the reality that for the economic growth of countries like Nepal, it is only foreign investment that can bridge the investment gap. Finally, it says cooperatives are to lead the economy. The unregulated sector of cooperatives is being promoted as an alternative to capitalism.

## The Business of Conflict Resolution

The rapid and rather unexpected conclusion of the insurgency through the non-violent uprising of April 2006 and the eventual peace accord of 2006 also came as a trump card for the donors. It became a means for them to immediately get their hands dirty and prove that their involvement in Nepal for the past few years in their newly touted subjects of conflict resolution and peace studies were coming to fruition. This proved an ideal platform for the development community overall to vindicate itself and justify its work. The streets of Kathmandu started being flooded with people of various nationalities while eating places and watering holes started buzzing with people working for the United Nations Mission for Nepal (UNMIN). Nepali development workers found a new Mecca for high-paying jobs while rhino-horned SUVs started being seen in parking lots. Media guesstimates of expenses of the UNMIN range from $70 million to $100 million in the first year of operations in 2007.

Multiple countries proposed multiple ways for Nepal to transition towards a Federal Democratic Republic. The Swiss had their own model of grass-roots democracies while the concept of committees was borrowed from the United States. Different agencies brought in different concepts, but in the end, these were executed by consultants mostly coming from India (due to lower costs), which created a South Asian concoction of ideas. The conflict resolution business kept the hotel cash box ringing with an endless number of seminars, conferences and meetings. Many of the folks who specialized in making reports during the early nineties on environment issues fully turned into conflict resolution specialists. Old sector experts turned into a new breed of gender, social equity and inclusion specialists. It was a time for romantic perusal of ideals and utopian thoughts. Little effort was made to answer key questions like how the new framework would be implemented, what was the economic side of the issues, where the investments would come from, how the size of the army could be reduced, amongst others. Accompanying supposed political leaders for training, exposure visits and meetings abroad became a good opportunity to visit countries and increase one's bank balance from saving daily allowances and expenses. Most Nepali students aspired to get into this profession, leaving the private sector and businesses to hire people who could not make it to these cash-ridden projects. Many reports and books got written and published, billions got spent, and when it came to the actual point of making the Constitution work, many of these people took this Nepal expertise to other countries and ensured the cycle was perfectly repeated there.

## Federal Nepal: No Champion

When the Constitution was promulgated, no one even fathomed the effort that would be required to make the concept of federal Nepal work. It will take a long time to either make it work—perhaps ten years or two electoral cycles—and to reverse the decision and get back to central control will take three electoral cycles or fifteen years.

The primary structure of the Federal Democratic Republic of Nepal consists of three levels, namely, the federation, the state and the local level. The federation comprises seven states and the states are made up of districts. With the readjustment of two districts from the seventy-five under the previous system, Nepal now has seventy-seven districts. The local level consists of village institutions, municipalities and district assemblies. Currently, there are six metropolitan cities, eleven sub-metropolitan cities, 276 municipalities and 460 district assemblies. A total of 6743 wards make up these 753 local-level units.

The issue of federalism is so complicated that the name of the province and its capital were left for the provinces to decide, and the seven provinces are still referred to by their province number, apart from Province 4 which was named Gandak. So, Province 3, which houses the capital city of Kathmandu, and Province 4, where Pokhara is located, are the only two provinces with revenue surplus while the others have to depend on federal grants. The concept of federalism has now been understood as the distribution of money for local politicians to spend, unlike the earlier concept of resources being abused by politicians sitting in Kathmandu. The installation of local governments meant that opportunities were localized 753 times. With a third of locally elected people being business people, they saw opportunities everywhere. However, their focus remained on land-grabbing. Forcing public schools to close or merge, they could land deals at low lease rentals. Construction projects are always lucrative for grafts, and that is what they pursued. Haphazard constructions dotted every city, town and village of Nepal.

The biggest challenge has been the lack of champions or ownership in making federalism work. In the absence of strong proponents of this big transformation, issues of its potential failure were discussed across the spectrum of society, rather than ensuring it works. The delay in getting laws promulgated and the absence of preparedness for something that was decided three years ago reflected the attitude of the political leadership. For instance, the necessity of a new Parliament building was clear once the Constitution-writing process started, but till the end of 2018, the Parliament building was not even close to being completed.

## Election Processes Remain Unchanged

Political parties have been able to manage the business of lies very well. Members lie with regard to their strength to get nominated as candidates. They prepare manifestos that are comparable to the ridiculous claims made by clinics boasting of tackling hair loss or weight loss. Subsequently, they fight elections based on lies. Further, with political parties owning the media, the matter gets more complicated. They also lie about the sources of funds used to fight elections, as well as when submitting expense statements on elections. Consequently, lying becomes a way of political life as they continue to get away with it. Furthermore, money enforces the lies and ensures that the business of lies is managed in a superb manner.

Democracy in South Asia therefore sees elections as a festival with the voter as the consumer of lies sold like many FMCG (fast-moving consumer goods) products. It is about the selling of perceptions. The voter as a consumer of democracy in this festival sees this as an opportunity to get goodies, and the political parties meet their expectations by providing money, gifts, wining and dining. The relationship therefore has been legitimized in people's minds as the consumers and wholesale dealers of democracy, with voters and political parties looking at it from a transactional perspective and not a transformational one. Many wholesale dealers then compete with counter-offers, cash incentives and other tools. Subsequently, the oligarchs of democracy, the political parties, are able to cartelize against rules pushing for accountability and transparency. Further, with the conflict of interest of them being both regulators and service providers of the 'democracy industry', all parties work together beautifully to thwart any moves that will change the rules of the game. For instance, all parties are in unison when it comes to opposing legislation to improve transparency in election funding or disclosing the wealth of candidates, whether elected or not.

Politics in Nepal, like elsewhere in South Asia, has been directly seen as a way of being able to make money and secure one's own future rather than to contribute to nation-building and economic development. A vicious cycle erupts whereby once a political leader is in power, he or she can make money, which is then spent to win the next elections that will subsequently ensure that more money is made. The fact that former politicians do not want to vacate government residencies once they are out of power, and the cabinet votes to provide lifelong benefits to people who come to power, is a testimony of how the relationship between power and money gets cemented.

## Earthquake

It only lasted for twenty seconds, but the 7.8 magnitude earthquake that rocked Nepal at midday on 25 April 2015 has impacted the country on an unprecedented scale. More than 8000 Nepalese lost their lives. Twice as many were injured. Although the initial quake also hit the capital city of Kathmandu, the worst affected areas were the adjoining districts—some so remote that it took a week for the first batch of relief materials to arrive. In the capital, the heritage sites of centuries-old temples and palaces were razed to the ground, and many houses—both old and new—collapsed. Pictures of cracked high-rise apartment buildings, the icons of Nepal's economic progress, flooded social media. Many people believe that the impact would have been a lot more devastating had the earthquake not taken place on a Saturday, when offices and schools were closed or the earthquake was at night instead of midday.

While the responses from the army, police and Nepal's friendly neighbours were immediate, key government officials, political parties and political civil society failed in getting their act together. The prime minister of Bhutan, Tshering Tobgay, personally delivered a cheque of $1 million and a team of sixty-eight people, comprising doctors and paramedics. Air traffic controllers worked overtime and managed 450 flights on a single day at Nepal's only international airport. Many arms of the government worked well. The state-owned Nepal Telecom provided free text and phone calls as more international service providers like Skype and Viber joined in to make calls to Nepal free. The electricity grid was restored quickly and some key officials in the government worked non-stop on coordinating relief work.

But the major political parties were completely absent from the scene. These parties, which boast of raising hundreds of volunteers at political rallies and enforcing nationwide strikes, could not garner the support needed to deliver relief to the very people who voted them into power. The absence of a national mechanism amongst the coalition government hampered coordination and impacted relief efforts. It took the government a week to clarify its position on whether NGOs could receive charity money and goods for relief or be given customs waivers. This lack of clear-cut directives and strategic thinking comes at the cost of forgone donations.

The initial relief efforts were conducted by volunteers who spontaneously gathered to start delivering tents, food and medicines to affected people. These groups were organized through social media to meet demand and supply. They delivered relief at zero cost, paying for their own food, water and fuel.

The credibility of the prime minister's relief fund was continuously being questioned. International donors preferred to work through international agencies rather than give cash to the government. The absence of local governments since 2002 in the villages and towns had resulted in powerful political syndicates known as the APM. These APMs disbursed money to party workers in a system that was ridden with corruption. The relief efforts being caught up in the political and bureaucratic system continue to be reported by the media.

There are six observations and lessons. First, the earthquake woke up the politicians who were completely absent from the scene in the most trying times. They had to push the Constitution-writing process, which eventually led to promulgation and invited the Indian blockade. Second, it tested the disaster preparedness programmes. In one of my columns in 2014 I had mentioned an organization that boasted of being pioneers in disaster preparedness while taking months to decide on a consultant. I had written that if they took months to choose a consultant, what would they do if disaster really struck? The earthquake had given an opportunity for people who put in millions to organizations in the disaster preparedness business to gauge whether the buck had travelled the final mile. During the chaos, there was a realization that people who could perform well at conferences, report writing and junkets could not deliver when push came to shove.

Third, the earthquake saw relief workers divided into categories. The first were the silent crusaders, who took long leaves from their jobs or business. Another kind flew in to help Nepal during the difficult time. Next, there were those who raised funds on their own and worked hard without posting pictures on social media. Finally, there were the people who used the opportunity for their own political agenda; this included the diaspora community, which wanted to be there to hand over a cheque to the ambassador and quickly post pictures on social media.

Fourth, the saddest part was to meet people who would tell you with a big smile that they decided to stay back in the US using the Temporary Protection Status (TPS) that let Nepalis do so, citing the problems the earthquake had created in their home country. The range of people who decided to leverage this status included people who had gone on fellowships to people working in multilateral agencies. This again reflects our culture of rent-seeking on any opportunity that comes by. The society, on the other hand, rather than decrying such people, felt sad about why they were not lucky enough to have the same opportunity to rent-seek!

Fifth, Nepal could ensure it was tapping into the new-age philanthropy. One of the international agencies was reported to have been selling the 'One million people face food insecurity risk in Nepal' story and raising $3 million out of the pledged $23 million. Meanwhile, Facebook raised $18 million, and companies like Google spent more than some of the international agencies in Nepal. These new-age institutions and foundations that included technology companies have different ways of looking at engagement and impact. They are not interested in the seminar/conference, media-hogging ways of doing things. They like to get things done with impact.

Finally, the earthquake showed a hopeful side of Nepal's future. Young people rose to the occasion. The silver lining of the earthquake was an increase in the social capital. There was a volunteerism, community spirit and social consciousness that was unlike anything that had been seen before.

## PDNA: Post Disaster Nothing Achievable

The earthquake drew tremendous international attention towards Nepal. Nepalis in every part of the world could garner support from their sphere of influence. Never before had the country experienced such heart-warming support from people around the world. However, like any religious function, these feelings were short-lived. Nepal could not capitalize on the generosity the world had to offer. A Post Disaster Need Assessment (PDNA) Conference was conducted in Nepal where pledges of $4 billion were made but Nepal could never draw upon these pledges as it got back to its traditional style of functioning.

A Nepal Reconstruction Authority (NRA) was created but it started being referred to as the No Reconstruction Authority as political wrangling peaked. Two people got appointed to the position of CEO twice, therefore there were four sets of tenures in as many years. The way Nepalis handled immediate relief through volunteerism showed the world what it could do when the need arose. At the same time, the politicians and their cadres demonstrated that there could be $4 billion available, but Nepalis would choose to fight over it and ensure it would never get utilized. This again proved that in Nepal, the challenge was not the lack of resources but rather their management.

## Blockade

When India merely noted the completion of Nepal's Constitution in a press statement, it was clear that New Delhi was not satisfied with the end product. Although a big achievement, contentious provisions in the new Constitution triggered a controversy within Nepal and attracted criticism from India. The most critical issue concerned citizenship rights. The Constitution does not treat Nepali women and men equally when it comes to passing on citizenship to their children. Questions also remain over whether a foreigner naturalized as a Nepali citizen can hold political positions. Additionally, some—especially the Madhesi communities living along the border with India—were dissatisfied with the way the Constitution demarcated provinces.

The Madhesis, many of whom are of Indian origin and live in the plains near the Nepal–India border, launched protests against the Constitution before its adoption, as they felt their interests were not well represented in the process. Historically, Nepal has been ruled by members of what are called 'the hill community' in Kathmandu. Since Nepal's transition from monarchy to federal republic, the Madhesis have been pushing for greater representation in the political processes. Following the official release of the Constitution, activists of the Madhesi community took out protests at the border and appealed to the Indian government for an intervention. From Nepal's perspective, India obliged by tightening the border points, effectively imposing an 'informal blockade' in order to pressure Nepal into making changes to the Constitution.

Nepal, a landlocked country, depends on Indian ports and transit routes, formalized through a bilateral transit agreement. Nepal's biggest import is petroleum products that come through India.

The choking of petroleum products and other supplies took a massive toll on Nepal, especially since the country was just recovering from the devastating earthquake. In the cold winter months, the largely hydropower-generated electricity supply experienced up to one hundred hours of disruption per week. The blockade only ended after Nepali leaders announced plans to amend the Constitution to address Madhesi concerns.

The blockade had three major impacts. First, Indian Prime Minister Narendra Modi, after becoming popular in Nepal following two visits in 2014, became hated by the public overnight. This changed the direction of Nepali politics and geopolitics forever. K.P. Oli was the biggest beneficiary as he whipped up nationalism to win elections and Nepal opened up to China like never before. Second, the blockade made the Madhesi politicians even more unpopular in their own constituencies as well as in neighbouring states in India. They went on to lose a significant chunk in the 2017 elections. Third, the blockade alienated an entire generation of Nepalis. Young Nepalis who were looking up to India for opportunities and personal growth could not believe that India had imposed a blockade in the twenty-first century and thought it could get away from it. This has led to a complete shift in the way young Nepalis think of India and Indians.

## Not Reaping Peace Dividends

Many countries have catapulted their economic growth on the foundations of conflict resolution and the establishment of peace. Historically, after the World Wars, Germany and Japan are used as the best examples of countries that leveraged peace dividends. In the past couple of decades, Rwanda and Cambodia are often cited as countries that went through unprecedented troubled times, emerged from war and then pushed economic development to become the most attractive investment destinations in the world. Generally, it only requires about a decade for a nation to put its house in order post a conflict and start building its economy around reaping peace dividends. If a nation fails to do that, it continues to be embroiled in a fresh series of conflicts, as we have seen in the case of countries like Sudan, South Sudan and Congo. Nepal managed the peace process well—integrating armies, allowing space to insurgents and finding home-grown solutions to conflicts. However, there are three reasons that can be attributed to why Nepal could not reap peace dividends.

First, the political syndicate in the garb of the APM became larger than the political system itself, dragging everyone into the game of politics. The Commission for the Investigation of Abuse of Authority (CIAA) became so powerful at one time that its chief only got removed after a citizens' movement in January 2017. The appointment of judges became a constant bone of contention. A no-confidence motion was moved against Nepal's first woman chief justice, Sushila Karki, and she was replaced by a tainted judge, only to be removed after citizen protests. The army was dragged into controversy many times and put in a spot when it was decided that the Fast Track Road from Kathmandu to Nijgadh (in the Terai) would be built by the army. Every institution was dragged into controversy, none were spared.

Second, the government could not spend. Till 2006, funds were an issue for Nepal. Low government revenues ensured that there was little money for spending. Most of the annual budget was for regular government expenditure and very little for capital expenditure. Loans, grants and doles from foreign governments have been the focus of successive Nepali governments, which beg for money without realizing that they have not been able to spend what they got. Nepal as an economy grew from $15 billion to $34 billion over 2006 to 2018, but the mechanisms were still archaic. Billons of rupees went into buying goods and services from folks who either paid their way to politicians or were controlled by politicians themselves.

'Asare Bikas' is the term given to development in the month of Asar, the last month in the Nepali fiscal year. There are stories of how during the last few nights of the fiscal year, staff go to the office with torchlights to figure out which budget heads have money left and next morning use their political clout to ensure that projects are sanctioned. Blacktopping on top of muddy soil which lasts only for days or digging to lay water pipes or sewerage pipes haphazardly or just laying bricks in an inner-city square, all are vivid images that people carry these days, courtesy of social media. The government cannot spend the allocated money either from its own coffers or from the donors they agreed to get loans or grants from. Because of corruption and the structuring of procurement rules, good companies are not interested in working in Nepal. There are mediocre global companies tying up with rent-seeking Nepali businesses to deliver poor results. The procurement system is not transparent, and it has been designed to benefit a few individuals at the cost of the nation. Further, the capacity gaps due to the low quality of human resources and logistics makes it worse. Meanwhile, transport cartels ensure that global logistics companies cannot do business in Nepal the way they do in other countries by not allowing international firms to set up operations in Nepal. The successive patronage of labour by political forces has made labour productivity low with little investment in training and development. Building infrastructure needs good engineers with world-class training. While Nepalis are building good infrastructure elsewhere in the world, the government has not been able to attract the same people for our infrastructure development as our reward system is flawed. Productivity is not rewarded, while rent-seeking is.

The third and final factor is that Nepal did not stop being inward-looking. A major news event[4] which included the Norwegian company Statkraft pulling out of the 650 MW Tamakoshi III Hydropower project, after not being able to make any major breakthrough with the government even after a decade, went unnoticed. Over the years, the company spent more than $20 million trying to figure out the planning for the proposed $1.5 billion investment. If this had happened in another country that takes foreign investment seriously, the prime minister would have flown to Norway to persuade officials not to withdraw. Perhaps Nepal is unique. Perhaps in Nepal, the private sector and folks in government and politics opened a couple of whisky bottles to celebrate yet another departure of a foreign investor. Yet another project that could be done the Nepali way. Yet another opportunity to create a trust with the shareholders, comprising parliamentarians, politicians and crony capitalists, like in several other ventures, against the spirit of company law, ownership, management and government structure. Perhaps the people in power were happy that they would not have to review large sets of documents done in English by global law firms and could instead create documents in Nepali that would never have to adhere to global standards. Perhaps they were happy with yet another project where negotiations would not have to be done in English, ensuring that speech-makers who like to make speeches in Nepali could align a project according to their whims and fancies. Perhaps they were happy that Nepal would not be under global scrutiny for adherence to contracts, 'change of law' clauses and international norms. The fact that foreign direct investment is critical for growth and an ecosystem for attracting global capital and human resources is essential has never been understood.

## It Could Have Been Worse

When we look back at the events of the past decade, we should be happy that things are not worse. There were many times when people had given up hope that the problems would be solved. No one was clear about what the Maoists would do in 2009, as their use of force had not ceased. The Maoist factional infighting could have become violent, and killings could have taken place, as has often happened in the fight for leadership in other parts of the world. The former king who continues to surface now and then could have aroused a lot of religious sentiments by beginning a movement that could have made the situation more chaotic. The heightening debate and volatile temper of the people who wanted ethnicity-based federalism against those who opposed it could have led to violent clashes resulting in bloodshed. The intra- and inter-party fights between the Madhesi parties could have followed the pattern of fights in Bihar and Uttar Pradesh that would have not only led to bloodshed but also made the Terai a difficult place for the hill-dwelling Nepalis to live in. The integration of the ex-Maoist combatants could have taken a prolonged route, similar to what happened in a few countries in Africa, like Sudan and Sierra Leone. The army stayed away from politics during a tempting time. International agencies slowly retreated from the discourse around ethnicity-based federalism, a fire they lit but could not douse. There were points when the conclusion was that the elections would not take place for the Constituent Assembly and later for the federal, provincial and local governments. The rumour-brokers and those who lived off selling Nepal's problems got sidelined due to the rise in social media, and younger people who were hungry for success started alienating those who peddled doomsday prophecies.

Whenever the situation seemed to be getting out of hand, a sudden sense of order came in. Sense prevailed on India as it lifted the blockade without creating further damage and tried to mend fences with the power equation in Kathmandu. Overall, it was a tightrope walk for Nepal, but it got to the other side with another open moment to rebuild Nepal's economic and development narrative.

# 7

# The Leap: The 'Unleashing Nepal' Journey, 2006–18

In June 2017, when the World Economic Forum reported[1] that Nepal was the third fastest growing economy in the world after Ethiopia and Uzbekistan, international media outlets did not know how to react. For the first time in recent memory, Nepal was in the news for positive reasons. A 7.5 per cent economic growth rate verified by the World Bank, the IMF and the Asian Development Bank (ADB) prompted global investors to pause and reconsider their impression of Nepal.

## The Business of Selling Uncertainty

It is very difficult to say that Nepal is worse off than it was twelve years ago. In rural Nepal, people find that the agenda of political discourse is only for people in Kathmandu and some other cities. They are busy constructing new roads and new houses, buying motorcycles and talking about what schools their children should go to. Those at home are busy receiving remittances from money transfer centres. The others, who remain fatalistic about Nepal, are busy pursuing options to go abroad. Mobile phones and social media have provided new tools for the youth to indulge in, as they discover the world beyond Nepal and connect with a world that was closed to them for decades. Families feel closer as they connect through mobile phones and free Internet platforms like Skype, Viber, WhatsApp and others through which they are able to stay in touch with their near and dear ones. Grandparents in Kathmandu enjoy hearing their grandchildren speaking in Nepali on the Internet, something that could not have happened ten years ago. Despite all the perceptions of uncertainty fuelled by a media feeding negative political news to a news-hungry population, and a complete lack of analysis of Nepal's economic growth, Nepal did make big strides, supported by the expansion of communication networks and the building of road networks. Communities started empowering themselves by taking their own decisions, no longer waiting for the political masters in Kathmandu to make the move. The gross disposable income increased manifold, as did Nepal's performance in the Human Development Index.

Nepalis suffer from mass Alzheimer's, and people tend to forget many things very easily. The ten years of insurgency that left 15,000 dead has already been forgotten, as has the fact that at that time it was almost impossible to travel within Nepal due to several blockades put up by the state as well as the insurgents. The Maoists had actually threatened to capture many places many times, but still Nepalis were very happy to invite them as chief guests at their functions and show off how close they were to the same folks they had once protested against. For the forgiving, resilient and forgetful Nepalis, life moved on.

If you stand at a street junction in Kathmandu for ten minutes and observe the traffic and people, you suddenly wonder where all these women driving cars and bikes came from. You notice that there are no barefoot Nepalis or people clad in tattered clothing to the extent depicted in reports produced by development organizations.

You then realize that perhaps the poster boys and girls of poverty projects are slowly vanishing. You start seeing teenagers sporting

South Korean fashion, emulating the stars they watch on Korean soap operas. Walk and drive around and see the numerous party palaces, day-care centres and beauty salons that have opened not only in Kathmandu and major cities but even in smaller towns. The collages of signage seek the attention of the customer, who now has some money to spend.

## The Complaining Nepali

Every time a friend complains about life in Nepal, my simple question to him or her will be: Can you name five people in your circle of influence who are worse off now than they were ten or twenty years ago? I have yet to get a name on the list! Perhaps complaining has become the very way of life. Nepalis in the diaspora community do it too; it is not only about Nepal, it is perhaps about Nepalis.

Haven't people fared better? In the cocktail circuits of Kathmandu, I listen to business people complaining about the situation. They would have bought better cars, land, apartments and gone on multiple international trips but they are still not happy. I listen to the complaints of people who have raked in a lot of money on the stock market. People who invested a few hundred thousand dollars when starting a bank are now worth hundreds of millions but they still complain. Banks that have over half a billion dollars of market capitalization are complaining about not being able to find some free money from a donor to start a bank product. People who throw parties worth millions for their kids coming-of-age ceremonies talk about the problems in Nepal. My simple question has continuously been: Are you not better off than you were ten or twenty years ago?

I look around and see my friends, relatives and business acquaintances and how their lives have changed. Apart from a few I know who are selling inherited land to eke out a living, most of them have leveraged their ancestral properties, earned well and transformed their lifestyle. This is not only true for people in Kathmandu and urban centres in Nepal, but also in rural Nepal. People who rent-seek find ways to make a living around selling poverty. Be it finding the only poor neighbourhood in some parts of far western Nepal and showing Nepal's poverty or telling people to remove their motorcycles and refrigerators during the visit of a senior person from development partners. In the handicraft shops in Patan, I notice folks who keep telling tourists they cannot lower prices as they have to feed many mouths. Little does the tourist know that this shabbily dressed man in slippers with a rickety bike parked outside would actually be earning a million rupees a month on rent and in the evening be driving home in an expensive car while sipping on nothing less than Black Label.

## Of Single Malt Whisky

Opportunities have changed Nepal. After multiparty democracy, schoolteachers have become rich politicians in a few decades. Bureaucrats earlier had to wait for a royal blessing to find post-retirement engagements. Today, retired bureaucrats are more powerful and financially stronger as they lead NGOs and consulting assignments in Nepal and abroad. They can make a living by criticizing the government and the system they spent decades in, failing to transform the very problems they cite after retirement. During my trips in India, bureaucrats there asked me how bureaucrats in Nepal afford expensive international education for their children. When I tell them there are 10,000 students going to the US alone each year, they are shocked. Of course, there is ancestral land to leverage, some firms to subsidize costs, or/and graft money to be used. They wonder how a supposedly poor country manages this.

People in far-flung villages can get a passport and work anywhere in the world and send money back home. That was not possible before the democratization of the passport system. With millions of people from India coming and working in the construction, building, tertiary and microenterprises segment, the opportunities are immense in Nepal for workers. Farmworkers in far-flung areas are earning NPR 800 a day, which is far above the minimum wage. Now if they blow it on a bottle of beer or half a bottle of whisky each day, then that is not the state's problem!

All around, we see professions that were not previously looked upon as being money-making starting to transform the lives of people. Musicians are building homes with royalties from music albums or online downloads and participating in shows. Journalists have been able to fund their own media businesses. Artists and writers are able to pursue their professions full-time. You don't need to be a doctor or an engineer any more to be able to make it big.

## The Big Leap

The discourse around the Nepali economy, especially in the Kathmandu valley, was all about it being a small, landlocked, poor country in between two large neighbours. However, there were people who started rethinking this and agreed with the perspectives in my previous book, *Unleashing Nepal*,[2] which looked at Nepal as the fortieth largest populated country in the world in 2008. In 2018 it was the forty-eighth.

When we travel through the length and breadth of Nepal, it is hard to think how Nepal is different than those countries which have a higher per capita income. With 86 per cent of the people owning land, the increase in land prices led to increased disposable and rental income. As people invested the surplus in more land, more rent was received. The construction industry boomed like never before, with more cement factories being established, more plants churning out steel beams, more imports of furniture from China and more workers coming from India to work in Nepal.

People spend more on social events and functions. A child's birthday in a faraway village has to be celebrated by cutting a birthday cake, only so it can be posted on social media. Banquet halls, popularly and strangely called 'party palaces', have started to mushroom all over the country along with an increase in jewellery stores and fashion boutiques. As the price of gold went up, the number of jewellery stores has increased, with people buying more and making everyone wonder where the money is coming from. Despite no official e-commerce laws and platforms, people can buy things from anywhere in Nepal and also from India, getting them delivered to one's doorstep by a courier company which accepts cash. This has been possible due to platforms like Instagram, Viber, WhatsApp and Facebook. Smartphones provided Nepalis with a window to the world, and people want their homes, bedrooms, kitchens and bathrooms to look like what they see on YouTube and other channels, creating demand for goods and services which Nepal neither bothered to produce nor serve.

The end of the conflict and open extortion ensured that people were willing to display the wealth they had. They were not scared to build new houses as there were no levies to be paid to Maoists or other extortionists. Nepal suddenly started looking beautiful and domestic tourism started to boom. Hotels cropped up in every city and town catering to the new Nepali middle class that wanted to discover their country as pilgrims, adventure seekers or visiting friends and families. The fact that one could go to Butwal in west Nepal from Dharan in east Nepal, either via ten hours on the road or through a connecting flight in Kathmandu, created a market for air and road transport. People found it safer to travel, especially after the CPN (Maoist) were defeated in the Constituent Assembly of 2013, as the terrifying image of the Maoists had been shed. With a high potential of resurgence, people took five years to come to terms with the Maoists' intent and behaviour. It had been proven that they were just like any other political party in Nepal looking to grab power, the only difference being the 13,326 lives[3] and the decade lost for their cause.

Nepal was connected like never before as people started demanding roads, and the government started building them, albeit in a haphazard way. These construction projects got a go-ahead as they benefited various businesses that funded political parties. Places where one could hardly find a hotel with a toilet within walking distance now had hotels with good amenities and coffee shops that could rival those in Kathmandu. While international food entered dining rooms, there was also renewed demand for the diverse variety of local food available in the country. Thakali restaurants serving good dal bhat (rice and lentils with meat and vegetables) dotted the highways, even though Thakalis belonged to an area where no rice is cultivated. The demand for meat increased, and interestingly, buffalo meat, which was considered poor people's meat, became more expensive than chicken as traditional buffalo dishes and items such as dried meat started to be exported. There was a renewed appreciation of the variety of food found in the country. The price of Himalayan peppercorn, timmur, soared as tons started getting exported to wherever the Nepali diaspora lived. Traditional Newa dishes like yomari started gaining popularity with more restaurants putting it on their menu. The production and consumption of Nepali coffee and tea also increased to unprecedented levels.

## Changed Numbers

GDP rose from $10 billion in 2006 to $34 billion in 2018, a threefold jump in twelve years. The Nepal government's finances changed from it having a revenue of $1.24 billion to $7.68 billion, and expenses soared from $2 billion to $8 billion. So, even if by popular estimate, 10 per cent of expenses was siphoned away through graft, the pot increased from $200 million to $800 million, which explains the increase in spending on non-essential items, luxury goods and soaring real estate prices.[4]

Tax revenues increased from 9.8 per cent of GDP to 14.45 per cent. Nepal today has the highest revenue collections in South Asia as a percentage of GDP. This has been attributed to taxes on petroleum products, the demand for which continues to grow, and high taxes on vehicles that keep getting imported in big numbers. Motorbikes worth $1500 in other markets cost $5000 in Nepal due to high taxes and dealer margins. Similarly, a vehicle worth around $20,000 to $30,000 in other markets sells at around $1,00,000 to $1,50,000. The volume of sales makes the principal manufacturers in offices across the world wonder where the money is coming from as they flip through reports written about Nepal's dismal poverty by some poverty-brokering institution or individual, as there are few other publications people can get their hands on that have this analysis.

In terms of social indicators, from a 66.32 per cent net enrolment rate (both sexes) in schools in 1999, the enrolment figures have jumped to 96.96 per cent in 2016. There are 4,49,642[5] people who appeared for the Secondary Education Examination (SEE) in 2017 compared to about 33 per cent of that figure in 1999.[6] From just a few government education institutions in 1990, today, with the help of private institutions, Nepal is producing hundreds of doctors, engineers, management graduates, PhD researchers, accountants and other professionals each year.

## Changed Quality of Life

Nepal reported the achievement of Millennium Development Goals (MDGs) in 2015. The MDGs consist of eight parameters with measurable targets and clear deadlines for improving the lives of the world's poorest people. To meet these goals and eradicate poverty, leaders of 189 countries signed the historic declaration at the United Nations Millennium Summit in 2000. At that time, eight goals ranging from providing universal primary education to avoiding child and maternal mortality were set with a target achievement date of 2015.[7] Nepal's extreme poverty, with people living on less than $1.25 a day at 2005 prices, came down to half, from 33.5 per cent to 13 per cent, by 2015. Similarly, the goal of halving the population living below normal dietary requirements was met. Maternal health goals were met as infant mortality reduced dramatically and so did the maternal mortality ratio.

Life expectancy increased from fifty-five years in 1990 to sixty-eight years in 2006 and seventy-two years in 2018. This meant that there were more healthcare services required; at the same time people started looking for second careers after retirement. The society saw more celebrations among the Newa community—of 1000 full moons, eighty-fourth and eighty-eighth birthdays—and of milestones in other communities. People living into their nineties became a common thing and people in their eighties being active did not come as a surprise. Nepal also did well to increase access to primary education.[8] Access to education changed, with more schools, colleges and universities coming up, and people did not have to travel much outside the place they lived, unlike till the nineties where students had to come to Kathmandu or go to India. However, more Nepalis started going abroad for studies as educational consulting companies mushroomed across the country. The power of the Internet ensured that people living in far-flung regions of Nepal learnt through online programmes with videos and access materials.

Access to healthcare changed, with private providers proliferating as well as multiple donor-supported government projects being undertaken. World-class hospitals were built in Kathmandu and people from Nepal could get the bulk of healthcare services in the country. A new social status was created in villages as people got airlifted by 'heli' (helicopters)[9] to be brought to the swanky hospitals of Kathmandu that were equipped with helipads. When I spoke with Upendra Mahato and his team at Mediciti hospital, which opened in 2017 in Kathmandu, he said that 90 per cent of patients that came in helicopters were not foreign tourists but Nepalis from different parts of Nepal.

The establishment of world-class health centres in Nepal set the benchmark for what people expect. Some of the private ventures have been resounding successes and made a massive difference to Nepali society at large. Hospitals like Dhulikhel Hospital and Tilganga Eye Hospital, and doctors like Dr Sanduk Ruit, a Magsaysay Award winner who made corneal transplantation affordable and accessible, and Dr Ram Shrestha, a surgeon who returned to Nepal after working for fifteen years in Europe to start a world-class affordable hospital for the masses in Dhulikhel, have shown what can happen when efforts are undertaken thoroughly with a worthwhile intention.

## Role of Women

One of the major transformations of these times is how the role of women has increased. The Constitution did mandate reservations for women in different legislative bodies and government agencies, and there were marked transitions in the roles and acceptability of women taking them on. In 1990, only a fraction of people who graduated from their SEEs were girls and only a few were seen applying for government jobs. In 2019, more than half the students who graduated from SEE were girls, and women outnumbered men in terms of people appearing for the civil services exams. With more than 40 per cent of locally elected leaders being women, the seeds of change have been sown. Visitors, especially from northern India, where women face multiple challenges, are surprised when they see women cops checking male drunk drivers and taking them to task at ten in the night. This can perhaps not be seen in any other South Asian city. When a Nepali minister in 2018 made derogatory remarks about women in a speech he delivered to a mass of girl students in Bangladesh, public pressure forced him to resign.

With the migration of men outside their homes within the country or outside, women took on stronger roles. From village markets to banks to government services, more women can be seen today. Women going out to eat and drink or travel for holidays has become socially acceptable. With mobility through driving two-wheelers and cars and security through mobile phones, women in Nepal are behind the transformation of society in a big way. They are no longer dependent on men and feel more secure now than they did a decade ago. Acts of abusing women like throwing water-filled balloons during Fagu[10] are now history. Women feel safer in Nepal than in the neighbouring countries and this has changed business fortunes as more than half of the population started to get integrated with the economy.

Many countries that have made major transformations in a short period of time have relied on women to lead the change. This change is not based on the lip service of gender mainstreaming or empowerment that gets limited to reports and tokenism, but inner changes in society. The hill societies of Nepal have comparatively more respect for women, and as communities in the capital region and the southern plains transform, Nepal will be able to leapfrog its development and economic growth ambitions.

## The Youth and the Market

When talking about markets in Nepal, there is a complete lack of understanding that the country's population comprises 50 per cent or 15 million people who are under the age of twenty-five. Even if we assume that 3 million of them are already outside Nepal, there are still 12 million who are looking at starting their careers and being trendsetters in the community. This has opened major opportunities in skills that were earlier never thought to be commercially possible or viable.

Today, someone who is not in a mainstream profession but is associated with arts and culture can make not only a decent living, but a good one. Nepali films are produced in record numbers as actors who have a good fan following can make around $5000 inaugurating a store or get money peddling brands on Instagram. Movies are grossing $2 million. Cartoonz Crew, a YouTube channel with 1 million subscribers, makes close to $1000 a month. Slam poetry artists charge $150 for a six-minute gig. The way music is curated and delivered has changed forever. Today, an artist is judged by YouTube downloads, and crossing 1 million has become the benchmark. For instance, bands are not only performing in concerts in Nepal but are also going global, following the Nepali diaspora. Thirty years ago, a performance in Darjeeling and Guwahati was the maximum one could think of.

In November 2018, I travelled to eastern Nepal along with the band Nepathya for their silver jubilee concert. In the small town of Birtamod, 5000 people turned up, paying NPR 1000 ($10) per ticket, and the show was sold out. It began on time and ended on time, and the crowd enjoyed it without alcohol being allowed or served. Groups of young women found it safe to attend. With six trucks, nine vans and a crew of sixty-five people that formed the backup team, this band performed in a manner that could have been a success anywhere in the world.

Reality shows also started becoming big in Nepal. *Nepal Idol*, an international franchise, had a fan following and interaction on social media just behind *Indian Idol*, a show in a country of 1.3 billion people. In the second edition of the show in Nepal, the prize money given out was higher than in the tenth edition of the Indian version. Telecom companies had a field day as there were 93 million votes in *Nepal Idol* when there were 27 million votes in India. When the finale of the second edition was held in December 2018, people bought tickets that cost up to NPR 5000 ($42) to attend. In the meantime, a rival show, *Voice of Nepal*, held its finals in Dubai, spending more than half a million dollars on production. Meanwhile, Rajeeb Jain became the first Nepali to win the Nepali franchise of *Who Wants to Be a Millionaire*.

The world of Nepali sports was going through its own positive upswing. Despite a chequered history of sports associations and strong links with politics, there has been significant development in Nepali sports. It was hard to believe that Nepal actually had a national hockey team which was pretty good. Football was popular but the politics around the association, including suspension of the association and criminal action against players and officials for match-fixing, cost the sport dearly, with only a few players being able to play for international clubs. However, there is massive interest in the game in Nepal and fans flock to any opportunity to watch the national team play. For instance, when Nepal played Afghanistan in an Asian Cup semi-final match in 2013, the gate proceeds from the match alone exceeded $1,00,000.

In cricket, Nepal climbed up the ladder, winning lower-division tournaments and finally qualifying for the T20 World Cup in Dhaka in 2014. It was also able to get One Day International Status in 2018. The big break in sports at the individual level came when Sandeep Lamichhane was selected for Delhi Daredevils, a franchise in the cash-rich Indian Premier League. He also went on to play for Melbourne Stars in the Big Bash League, the premier T20 competition of Australia. In May 2018, he signed for Barbados Tridents in the West Indies for $70,000. At home, the craze for cricket increased, with multiple tournaments being hosted and prize money increasing each year. These tournaments also had Nepali teams featuring foreign players, something we had not seen earlier.

The Nepali art scene underwent tremendous transformation, with Nepali art getting better access to global markets. More art galleries sprung up, and more Nepali artists started to globe-trot. Events like Photo Kathmandu and Kathmandu Triennale brought world-class artists to Nepal. With an exciting commercial future in the historical and cultural arts, many young Nepalis went back to understand their heritage and culture to be able to interpret it to the world in modern formats.

Nepali publishing has been one of the surprise successes of recent times. With multiple publishing houses, the Nepali language market has expanded like never before. While *Palpasa Café* crossed the mark of 50,000 sales for the first time in 2011 for a Nepali book, many others have crossed the mark since then. Today, a Nepali-language author can make a living by writing, getting published and attending events related to the book.

The restaurant and coffee shop business has exploded, with young Nepalis across Nepal embracing the culture of going out. A newly opened popular youth hang-out in Kathmandu made $50,000 on Nepali New Year day within a period of twenty-four hours. Similarly, when DJ Marshmellow scheduled a show in Kathmandu, people dished out NPR 1,00,000 ($1000) for the front tables. (Unfortunately, the event was cancelled.) It's not uncommon to hear of clubs crossing $1,00,000 in sales on a Friday night. Even in smaller towns and cities, clubs and lounges requiring half a million dollars' worth of investments opened.

The youth had found the market and vice versa, but there was also the other side of this phenomenon, which brought many new problems and challenges.

## Some Things Did Not Change

A favourite pastime for Nepalis has been lambasting politicians on social media. However, we tend to forget that politicians do not drop from Mars or Venus; they are the products of our society. Nepalis have become very good at making big statements and commenting on big issues that haunt them, while completely forgetting the little ones. It is these little things that matter, that build habits and perhaps institutionalize a system that people follow. Perhaps the habits of people who reach key positions define or shape the habits of the people who work for them. Followers of Gandhi became strong believers in conscientious consumption. Followers of Mao wore the same set of clothes throughout their lives. In Nepal, during the autocratic Rana and Shah regimes, order was created on the basis of a set of rules for the subjects that did not apply to the rulers. Perhaps this trend has continued, with people in power feeling they are outside the purview of the law. Perhaps people fight hard and spend a lot of money to get to key positions so that they can get impunity from the law.

If we look around us, we see the flouting of basic civic behaviour norms. Be it throwing trash out of the windows of SUVs, letting garbage pile up in courtyards, speaking on the phone continuously inside a cinema hall while disturbing others, occupying the footpath to run one's business, encroaching on public space, parking where it is not allowed, students blocking streets while they walk out of their colleges, having minimal parking space in establishments where hundreds of cars turn up for events, breaking queues, turning up late, speaking ill of people without evidence—the list goes on. Without a major transformation in societal behaviour, it is difficult for politics to change. Rent-seeking by blaming politicians for everything becomes the biggest lucrative business, as one can pass any personal or communal deficiencies or inefficiencies on to the politicians.

With the liberalization of the markets after the 1990 Jana Andolan, the government put all its emphasis on the private sector as the primary vehicle for growth. Market-oriented reforms and deregulation brought a flow of foreign direct investment in Nepal with manufacturing companies, foreign banks and insurance companies entering the Nepali market. Yet, the Nepali private sector, which was initially excited at the opening of the economy, slowly realized that liberalization and globalization would mean that they would have to compete in global markets. Despite government efforts to open up the economy, the nexus of the small business elite continued to utilize their political and government patrons to frustrate reforms. For instance, since 2002, no new global or regional firms have entered Nepal in the banking and insurance sector. Nepali business houses that own these businesses created a Nepali structure of institutions. When the Nepal Rasta Bank issued orders for the consolidation of banks by putting in a requirement for additional capital, it expected financial institutions to merge, thereby reducing the number of A-class commercial banks. However, with a burgeoning speculation-filled capital market dominated by financial institutions, bank promoters saw this as a moment to add value to their wealth. New shares were issued, and people queued to buy them. People liquidated deposits or took loans from one bank to buy the shares of other banks. This incestuous way in which money moved from one part of one bank's balance sheet to another part of another bank's balance sheet became a unique example of how closed minds create self-destructing structures.

In many countries like Cambodia, Rwanda and South Africa, the opening up of foreign direct investment post-conflict resolution and the activities of global business leaders changed the fate of the economy. Unfortunately, for Nepal, like its rituals, it was the closing rather than opening of doors that was found to be more lucrative for businesses. The perpetuation of the rent-seeking culture through forming cartels in the guise of associations and the politics within these associations worked very well with and for the political syndicates. This also pushed real entrepreneurs, especially young ones, to the fringes, leaving them with the choice of either joining the Nepali way of doing things or seeking opportunities in greener pastures outside Nepal.

## Some Things Got Worse

While people clamoured for more money and power, some age-old traditions got revived. While Nepal transitioned from a monarchy to a federal democratic republic, multiple kings and royals seem to have been created. On the one hand, there was the challenge of a lack of civic sense; on the other, there was pomp and grandeur in terms of spending money, with no emphasis on changing conservative traditions and rituals. For instance, while the major imports from all over the world came in terms of culture—lavish destination weddings, wedding photography and Bollywood-style rituals were adopted—the rituals for death did not look any different from a century ago. No efforts were made to reform rituals or push for better facilities like electric crematoriums and key messaging on organ donations.

The biggest eyesore was the increase in the ridiculous ceremonial functions and rituals in Nepal and amongst the Nepalis outside Nepal.

Among the many things that got worse during this period, I pick out five. First, the proliferation of messages. Newspapers were filled with messages of congratulations. This is a practice that supposedly began by sending greetings to the king and queen and letting the whole world know of your loyalty. The practice continued for all democratic leaders under the constitutional monarchy as well as the republic. Random people put up advertisements felicitating the political leaders with whom they had no connection to give the impression that they knew the person in power and could get work done. In business circles, people would ask their friends/colleagues to print congratulatory messages when they become directors of banks and other institutions to let the world know that they were the folks to contact if someone wanted a contract with these institutions. This entire behaviour stems from the 'sycophancy' traits of a feudal society which have been institutionalized as chakari and propagated during the autocratic Rana regime. I got messages about the death of a chartered accountant colleague's parent on my phone at 6 a.m. What a bad way to begin a day, and why should I be alerted about the death of people I don't know? Similarly, Facebook pages got filled with RIP messages, pictures of cremation ceremonies, visits to grieving families and people in their deathbeds in hospitals.

Second, the garland, khada and scarf culture with the smearing of red vermilion all over the face became a part of Nepali identity. The more the garlands and the more painted the face, the better. The fact that non-Nepalis saw this as a sign of tradition was unfortunate as so much time, resources and money were wasted.

Third was the sense of entitlement or the prevalence of VIP culture. The segregation of people continued, despite the caste system being abolished. During a function or a ceremony, self-entitled people sat in the first rows on sofas, and other 'special' guests sat in distinct chairs of a different design and colour than the ones for the general audience. The long ritual of 'ashan grahan' or taking seats became something people loved, and at times, in functions that I have attended, by the time everyone was called to the stage, there were more members on the stage than in the audience. I still cannot figure out why so many people had to sit on the dais donning those ugly badges while their names were called out by each speaker.

Fourth, the token of love. Many functions ended with a vote of thanks speech that was longer than the keynote address. At the end, a 'token of love' was provided. When I burnt down three boxes of such tokens of love, I kept wondering about its use. But people loved to display them in their homes and offices.

Finally, the lack of respect for time. Events began way later than the scheduled time and no one apologized for the delay. The culture of the most important person arriving late became popular. In events I attended outside Kathmandu, it was common for people to be invited an hour or two before the main event if there was an important person attending or speaking—the more important a person, the more late s/he should be.

Fighting all this has been a tough task, but it is perhaps important to pass on the right message. Over the years it became more challenging as the president started reminding people of the king and the Rana prime ministers. The second president, Bidya Devi Bhandari, received tremendous criticism on social media when she started to behave like the former king in various ways: attending various religious functions, obstructing traffic for her travels, demanding various luxury vehicles, shifting the Police Academy to accommodate a helipad, even demanding helicopters dedicated to her service.

Similarly, Prime Minister Oli started drawing much criticism for making people wait. At a function that I attended on inaugurating an electric vehicle project, he turned up more than an hour late, keeping more than 500 important civic figures waiting. His view on being late interpreted as being important made people mimic him and every event started late from then on. Suddenly, people who began programmes on time and ended on time were seen as being non-nationalistic and influenced by foreign culture.

## Towards a Litigious Society

One of the key developments in the last decade is that Nepali society has become increasingly litigious. All major decisions are sent to the court so it can put forth a verdict. However, while this is happening, the credibility of the judiciary has also gradually eroded, as there are a number of ways that decisions are being influenced. On 2 June 2017, the CIAA arrested the director general of the Inland Revenue Department, Chudamani Sharma, for misappropriating revenue while settling taxes in a tax tribunal. He was later acquitted in November 2017 when he submitted bail and a bank guarantee of NPR 10 million. This case involved billions of dollars of a tax scam but then, as alleged in the media, he got away by fixing the judiciary. Many such cases started to become prominent. Every government decision started being challenged in court. If someone did not get a contract, they went to court. The courts became powerful and they could let off people who had committed fraud and scams by taking deposits.

The appointment of judges became more politicized as money changed hands. In the absence of international law firms, and local legal firms functioning under a Bar Association whose leaders openly towed party lines, the certainty of law in Nepal became a big challenge. The court was deciding on a variety of issues, including who should be appointed to the boards of banks and to positions in business associations. The excessive engagement of the judiciary in every aspect of society is alarming as businesses and investors do not like to be caught up in judicial webs, especially when one hears of all these allegations.

## Replicating the Ills of Kathmandu

One big challenge that Nepal will find almost impossible to reverse is the exploitation of resources through bulldozer terrorism undermining aesthetics and replicating all the bad things about Kathmandu all over Nepal. The rapid urbanization catalysed by road development was a South Asian phenomenon which led to villages being converted to towns and towns to cities. The absence of governance and the strong nexus between political forces and real estate developers ensured cities came up overnight.

The rampant construction meant that for developers, open spaces became an eyesore, and they figured out different permutations and combinations to come up with real estate development plans. Aesthetics did not matter and neither did the existence of utilities. Electricity connections were available for those who could grease palms, and water was something that people were made to believe would come in tankers and not on their pipes connected by the water utility. Sewage and garbage was a caste issue, so no one even wanted to think about it. As in many other major cities of the world, we managed to convert the Kathmandu valley into a concrete dumping site. The views of the Himalayan range, the fresh air and open space became a luxury. The education system, the sudden myopia on the price of land per anna,[11] and wealth spiralling due to asset-price increase did not promote the larger sense of need of open space and greenery. Now, people can only dream about the majestic views which was once one of the city's crown jewels. When the royal family members themselves started to lease out open spaces for ugly constructions, everyone started to think that it was the way to go. Future political masters ensured this legacy continued. When one watches how Tudhikhel, the central open space in Kathmandu, is being encroached with structures by the Nepal army, one tends to believe that development means no open spaces but only constructions! With some of the big real estate folks entering Parliament and lawmaking bodies, more construction-friendly laws emerged with complete disregard to open spaces, architecture, safety and potential hazards.

Now, there is strong competition among the oligarchs in this business to see that every open space becomes real estate booty to encash. It does not matter whether it belongs to a school or is an existing heritage space. Folks who lack aesthetic sense put up structures that are built replicating the worst structures in the worst cities of South Asia. The capital city's problems of traffic jams, poor air quality, garbage heaps, parking issues and the lack of open spaces are becoming the bane of every city or town in Nepal.

Our hate for trees was another challenge as a project was undertaken to fell trees which had high timber value. So, with a bulldozer, political agents garbed under a certain company cleared heaps of forest land for timber with the excuse of construction, going on to extract sand, stone, slate and every natural resource possible. People were oblivious to the issue as this was the image of development sold to them. Thereafter, tippers would transport the extracted natural resources to feed the ever-growing demand for construction project materials. The knocking down of trees impacted watershed management and triggered natural disasters in the form of floods and landslides. Caring for trees and environment got relegated to Environment Day speeches.

## The Business of the Environment

In the early 1990s, just after the restoration of democracy, environmental issues became the most lucrative business. The Shah kings established the King Mahendra Trust for Nature Conservation to apparently wash off their sins of hunting prized animals. This trust became one of the most influential ones as it started the Annapurna Conservation Area Project (ACAP) which brought Nepal on to the global map of managing conservation. One of the first journalist associations that began was the Nepal Forum of Environmental Journalists (NEFEJ) which focused on journalism pertaining to environmental issues. Many big-name journalists of that time were associated with this.

The Earth Summit in Rio de Janeiro was one of the first events where people not connected to the palace could embark on junkets. As Nepal opened up to international agencies, lots of money started pouring in. There was more money available to work on stopping projects like Arun III than to build a project like it. Globally, there was a big movement post the Earth Summit. If you were an educated Nepali in the Kathmandu valley in the early 1990s, it was rare if you were not associated with an organization dealing with the environment or conservation. I was involved with many too!

However, with international attention on this subject drying up, and the business around the conflict emerging after the insurgency in 1996, dealing with the environment started increasingly becoming about tokenism devoid of intent. The first set of tipper trucks started to arrive in the mid-1990s, and heavy earth-moving equipment came along with it. The picture and perception around development started to become raging 'bulldozer terrorism' in the name of delivering development through road construction. With India's insatiable need for timber, sand and natural materials for urban development, transporting these resources to India from Nepal became a big business. The ten years of insurgency and the twelve years of transition which followed provided the perfect political platform to conduct such businesses. With the blurring of lines between business and politics, the earnings from rampant destruction became the easiest way of wealth creation.

In a rent-seeking society, open spaces are always hated as they provide the best rent-seeking opportunity. From schools to trusts to the Nepal army, everyone has abused open spaces to create business opportunities, be it building commercial spaces or banquet halls. Business folks have always seen environment-related issues as an impediment to manage rather than a responsibility to fulfil. Therefore, in about three decades, we have been able to convert the beautiful Kathmandu valley and other smaller cities and towns into an urban menace that we can complain about but do little to fix.

## Looking Ahead

Despite the challenges in unleashing the potential, the twelve-year journey would have more positive stories than negative ones. The foundations for building an economy have been laid, and we will continue to examine how we can leverage this for Nepal's future economic growth and development. The unleashing of potential at individual levels has taken place; it is now time to harness this collectively to bring about major transformations. We will discuss this in Chapter 15.

# II

# Context

It is important to understand the context of a country to comprehend the journey of its economy. In Nepal, a lot is written about politics and political instability, and many books have been devoted to criticize the government and its policies, highlighting the failure of the bureaucracy and judiciary. But this is where the discussions end.

In the following five chapters, issues that are little talked about, discussed or written are examined. This includes the importance of the private sector and the world of development partners in shaping the current state of the Nepali economy. Another critical point of discussion is the spread of Nepalis around the world; they are no longer limited to Nepal. The world of migration and remittances has always been looked at from the lens of poverty, with the popular narrative being that it is the reason Nepalis migrate. But there is more to the world of global Nepalis that has emerged in the past two decades.

Meanwhile, there is a fair bit of literature on Nepal and India, but little on Nepal and China, and it is altogether difficult to find an exploration of what it means for Nepal to be between India and China. This is discussed in detail.

Finally, Nepal has debated enough on capitalism versus socialism but achieved little in terms of changing the status quo. It is important to understand why it must change, and why an opinion on the capitalist welfare state must be formed.

8

# Cartelpreneurs: The World of the Nepali Private Sector

With the opening up of the Nepali economy in the 1950s and further liberalization in 1990, the Nepali private sector today leads the economy with 58 per cent contribution to GDP. The small formal private sector is dominated by large business houses while the informal ones across the country provide much-needed goods and services to the people of Nepal. However, the growth of the private sector has its own challenges; among these is an image issue. Cartels rule the roost, and the sector is identified with low-quality products and services offered at high prices.

In this chapter, we will explore the evolution of the Nepali private sector, understand the cartel economy, get a perspective on the challenges, and learn from some success stories.

## History of the Nepali Private Sector

The private sector is largely understood as being run by individuals or companies who operate in an environment which has the freedom of ownership of assets, including land, and where knowledge and

networks are allowed to be leveraged for profit, unlike the public
sector that is owned and controlled by the government. The private
sector is not controlled by the state but is regulated by it. The history
of Nepal's private sector has to be considered from this perspective,
but that becomes complicated for the following reasons.

First, during the rule of the Shahs and Ranas, who does business
with whom was determined by one's caste and not by one's ability.
So typically, the ruler decided who could do business and who could
not. Second, since the ownership of land under the feudal system
rested with the rulers, there was no private ownership of land.
Therefore, the concept of free enterprise did not exist. Finally, the
government could intervene in multiple ways—raise taxes, create
laws like labour laws that could be unfavourable for businesses, decide
on what business they could do, decide on how much they could buy
or sell through licensing requirements, decide on how much foreign
exchange they could get or keep, and decide on many other things
to the extent that the state could either create a public-sector entity
to compete with the private sector or nationalize the private-sector
entity. This meant that till about 1950, the private sector in Nepal
was practically non-existent.

In understanding the history of the Nepali private and business
sector, it is important to understand the evolution of the various
communities that are identified with business, like the Newa,
Marwari, Bahun and other communities. A further new dimension
was added when non-resident Nepalis (NRN) who had made fortunes
in other countries returned to invest and do business in Nepal.

## Rise and Fall of the Newas

The caste system mandated a certain caste to have designated duties.
The Newas of the valley were grouped as a single caste despite having
their own divisions within their culture—they were the ones who
could do business. However, the Newa family and community
structures proved to be a significant challenge in adapting to the new

business environment that was created in Nepal after the fall of the Rana regime and the liberalization of markets, both in the 1950s and 1990s. A fatal flaw in traditional Newa and most Nepali business models was the intimate link between business activity on the one hand and caste, ethnicity and gender on the other. Historically, the caste system had designated particular ethnicities and castes as the administrators and managers of trade and business. Additionally, these businesses were family-run and were passed down through the eldest male descendant of the family, who then took on the responsibility of heading the business with other family members acting to support him.

With the corporatization of businesses in Nepal, few Newa businesses were able to switch from this traditional family-based operational modality. The Newa merchants, who were seen as pioneers in business and entrepreneurship, slowly lost out as the newer generation of Newa business people did not change with the times, be it in corporatizing, hiring professional management, or tying up with international firms to further their business. Internal family feuds that were unresolved due to the lack of openness in adapting to newer ideas were another hindrance. The general observation has been that the Newas outside the valley were more hard-working and entrepreneurial as they had lesser access to power centres. They were responsible for establishing the trade hubs of Tansen in Palpa, Bandipur, Dhankuta, Bhojpur, Chainpur and Bahrabise in the earlier days. They went on to create hubs in Banepa, Butwal and Narayanghat. They controlled most of the entry ports to Kathmandu, be it Bhainse near Hetauda when the new highway was built, or the old routes of Bhadrapur in east Nepal.

## The Advent of Marwaris

The Shahs and Ranas looked upon the Newa community as one they had conquered and always wanted to ensure that it was kept subdued. To ensure that it had competition, the Ranas decided to invite the

Marwari community to do business in Nepal. A 'Prajapatra'[1] to this effect was issued in 1875 by Jung Bahadur. Hailing from the hot, humid and arid desert lands of Rajasthan in western India, the Marwaris were entrepreneurial people who had already tried their hand at competing with the Newa people for trade with Tibet when the Chumbi valley route through British India opened up. From being small-time traders in villages they suddenly found themselves hobnobbing with the rulers of a country that their colonial masters, the British, treated as close friends. The 1936 Nepal Companies Act was largely created to facilitate Rana interests in establishing industries in Nepal in partnership with Marwari businessmen from present-day Kolkata. The Marwaris provided the bulk of capital for investment while their Rana partners ensured smooth operations in Nepal. However, the Rana regime's unwillingness to invest in infrastructure, transportation and communication, along with a strong opposition to market and social liberalization, acted as significant barriers to industrial growth. These initial ventures met with limited success, partly due to the business environment, which was entirely dependent on knowing, befriending and working with the Ranas. Success was hampered primarily due to a shortage in materials caused by the outbreak of World War II. Yet, even after the fall of the Rana regime, the Marwari community's acumen for business allowed it to continue thriving in Nepal. Further waves of Marwaris were noticed in 1962 after the closure of the Tibet border with India, during the annexation of Sikkim in 1975 and the Gorkhaland[2] movement in 1985. Hordes of them moved from Darjeeling, Kalimpong and Sikkim to Nepal. After 1990 and 2006, two distinct waves were noticed, this time from small towns in Bihar and Uttar Pradesh, mostly in informal sectors, in contrast to the larger trading families in the earlier ones.

Among the few entrepreneurial communities in Nepal, the Marwari community has by far been the most successful in establishing and expanding Nepal's private sector. It continues to control the formal as well as informal sectors, and many Marwaris have become well-entrenched in Nepali society even though many Nepalis treat them as outsiders. Therefore, during times of political tensions between Nepal and India over the past hundred years, they have had to bear the brunt. Any connection with India, whether through marital relationships or by having a male child born in that country, becomes a cause of nationalist conflict.

## Rise of the Bahun Business Barons

More and more people from the Bahun community were seen doing business post-1990; earlier, they were largely involved in bureaucratic jobs. Politics in Nepal is dominated by Bahuns, with all the top leaders of parties being Bahun men. Even in the parties of the Terai, which tried to distinguish itself as a separate ethnic group, it was the Brahmins (Bahuns) or upper-caste men who dominated. Having taken the lead in bureaucracy and politics, naturally, they were a strong presence in business circles as well. If Newa business people had flourished during Newa rule, it was quite natural that Bahuns led in the business world at a time when they were at the forefront of all other spheres as well. They put to use the same networks and signature style of operating as they did in politics and the bureaucracy, engaging not only in trading but also in industry, media and financial institutions. They were also instrumental in providing an 'alternative' to capitalism and starting the 'cooperative' movement. If a survey was to be conducted to find out which ethnic group was promoting the cooperatives, it would be very clear where the leadership lay. The Bahuns basically followed the same models as the Chhetris and Newas, that is, hiring their kith and kin in the business they got engaged in, especially as promoters. However, the Bahuns were a shade more hard-working, and this, combined with heavy networking, led to them acquiring a number of key positions in publicly listed companies as well as business associations. However, like the Newa business people, their reliance on male members of the family, respecting age over talent, isolating women members, and their inability to globalize in their thought processes will become an impediment in future. Only time will tell how they respond to those situations.

Although a few other communities including the Thakalis, Gurungs, Rais, Tamangs, Limbus, Sherpas, and Tibetans were involved in entrepreneurial activities, there are precious few examples of truly great successes. The Sherpas dominated the climbing businesses, while the Gurungs from Manang had business in their genes, as discussed in the earlier chapter. The Thakalis made their mark through close-knit investment groups which functioned like village groups under a community leader rather than a corporate entity. Nepal's fatalistic and deterministic social structures are perhaps major factors in discouraging and suppressing the entrepreneurial instincts of other community groups.

## Level Playing Field

It was only post-1990 that a liberal way of life and economy along with professionalization of business emerged. People of lower castes, for whom the caste system was a barrier in unleashing their potential, discovered that they could move beyond it and no profession was looked down upon if it made money. Those belonging to untouchable classes like tailors emerged to open dress boutiques and designer stores, barbers started being respected as hairdressers, and higher-caste people also joined the bandwagon to open beauty parlours. With the popularization of refrigeration technologies, butchers were not looked upon demeaningly, but rather had to face competition as others joined the business. Similarly, people who operated tea houses, cooked food or simply cleaned homes suddenly got respect as English words brought respectability to jobs which were previously considered to be demeaning. The 'dhobi' or laundryman became the 'drycleaner', the *bhanse* or cook became the 'chef' and blacksmiths graduated to studio artists. Plumbers, mechanics, carpenters, masons and similar folks who had been divided through the caste system were sought after and now carried business cards and made house visits, scheduling appointments and charging like doctors, or went for plum jobs outside Nepal.

## Arrival of the Non-Resident Nepalis

When Nepal opened its door to the world in the 1950s and aid poured in, opportunities to study abroad burgeoned. With the Cold War at its peak, the USSR and the US competed in taking young people into their countries to indoctrinate them with their ideologies—communist socialism by the USSR and democracy and free enterprise by the US. Many Nepalis went to these countries during the 1950s and 1960s and became established in trade and business. Thereafter, the second wave of people migrating to the US, Australia and the UK began in the 1990s via student visas—their objective would usually be to actually stay back, work or do business.

During the 2000s, and especially after the civil war ended in 2006, many people returned to start businesses in Nepal. This did not follow an ethnic pattern but was instead determined by the countries people had returned from. People from the former USSR countries grouped together to start banks and hydropower projects, while people from the US invested in hotels and technology firms, and people from Australia started process outsourcing businesses. Many of them leveraged the networks they had established during their student and work years along with cultivating political connections back in Nepal to get all kinds of businesses running.

## Journey of Nepal's Private Sector

Nepal traditionally possessed a feudalistic system that limited the rights of ownership to elites—the granting of property to the aristocratic elite was prevalent. It was only after the fall of the Rana regime and the establishment of the interim Constitution in 1951 that a legal and constitutional structure was created for a formal private sector in Nepal. Although Nepal's first Companies Act was coded in 1936, it only allowed for the formation of public companies on a joint stock model that was based on people contributing to business in terms of shares with limited liability. It was only through the Companies Act of 1951 that individuals were authorized to register private limited companies. The Panchayat government also introduced the Industrial Enterprises Act of 1962, encouraging foreign and direct investment and providing a number of sops to these enterprises, which included a ten-year tax holiday. However, Nepal's landowning elite, since the time of the Ranas, had found it safer to invest in India rather than in Nepal. This was a purely market-driven rationale as industries in Nepal, lacking energy and resources, were poorly equipped to compete with the established industries of India. For the Ranas in particular, investing in India remained a hedge against potential political turmoil in Nepal.

During much of the Panchayat era that lasted from 1960 to 1990 the growth of the private sector remained sluggish. Although starting a business in Nepal during this time was a lot easier than during the early half of the twentieth century under the Rana regime, significant barriers to entry remained. The deep trade links between India and Nepal were also a problem. The Panchayat government, aware of the dangers of this situation, sought to build up its trade networks with other countries as well. This proved a challenging task, since trade with any other country had to pass through India as the only allowed port for Nepal—as per Nepal's transit agreement with India—was Kolkata. Given India's protectionist policies which targeted import substitution, New Delhi did not look upon the import of third-country goods into Nepal with much pleasure—since these goods were often sold back to Indian consumers at prices that were favourable compared to Indian products. Nepal's position as the provider of top-end luxury goods and electronics for the Indian market was demonstrated by the establishment of Bishal Bazaar, a massive mall in the heart of Kathmandu city, in 1976. Aside from drawing an increasing number of Indian shoppers, Nepali businesses were also able to re-export goods into India through unofficial routes. However, the problem of re-exporting to India has remained a major bone of contention for Nepal–India trade relations ever since. A significant number of industries, such as steel utensils and yarn-producing factories, has flourished in Nepal, taking advantage of export duty differences between the two countries, only to be shut down in a few years due to India's reaction.

Nepal's only private sector outside the country in Tibet also started to wane during this period. For the greater part of the 1950s and 1960s, Nepali traders in Tibet were displaced by Chinese business people as they consolidated power in Tibet. The 1962 Sino-Indian war between India and China led to virtually all Nepali businesses shutting down their operations in Tibet. Nepal could not link up to the various trade points in Tibet with roads, as India continuously expressed concerns about the land link between Nepal and Tibet. The strained political relationship between China and India after the 1962 war meant that all issues related to Nepal were examined by India from a geopolitical perspective. The absence of a good road link with China meant that Nepali imports from China had to come all the way through the ports of Kolkata, consequently costing more and being subject to constant Indian interference.

With the liberalization of markets after the 1990 Jana Andolan, the government put all its emphasis on the private sector as the primary vehicle for economic growth. With this intention, waves of market-oriented reforms were carried out. The financial sector was deregulated along with the tourism, aviation, insurance and power development sectors, and industrial licensing was scrapped. As a result, during the early 1990s, foreign direct investment started flowing into Nepal, and Unilever, Dabur, Asian Paints, Coke, Pepsi as well as foreign banks and insurance companies entered the Nepali market. However, the Nepali private sector, which was initially excited at the opening up of the economy, slowly realized that liberalization was the first step to globalization, and that soon they would have to compete in global markets. Despite government efforts to open up the economy, the nexus of the small business elite continued to utilize their political and governmental patrons to frustrate reforms.

Without a vibrant industrial component and any major comparative or competitive advantage, business within Nepal has historically been confined to trade. Trading makes arbitrage a core business strategy, whether in the form of working around duties, taxes or the demand–supply gap. As with mobile phones, arbitrage grew into a major industry in its own right with the objective of working the system and making it play to one's favour. This made it essential for businessmen to hobnob with government officials and politicians. Duties and taxes were negotiated over glasses of whisky, and loans were handed out for a commission. This form of myopic lobbying carried out by the private sector with the objective of securing immediate profitability rather than long-term economic prosperity created a business environment that thrived on corruption. The reach of these lobby groups was such that at times it created distortions in the government's annual budget to the extent of being completely contrary to its long-term five-year plans. The budget started to reflect private interests and accommodate provisions at the behest of private-sector individuals or groups. Therefore, customs duties were reduced or increased based on the 'briefcases' that were traded rather than on economic fundamentals.

This shift from market growth to protectionist ploys was the direct result of an increasing realization among local small businesses of the threat international players posed. As a result, the nexus of small business elites used political and governmental patrons to leverage their position and frustrate reforms. For instance, when J. Walter Thompson, a multinational advertising agency, sought to enter the Nepali market and establish a subsidiary in Nepal, it took them over one and a half years of haggling and bargaining with the government, due to a strong local lobby group that tried to block and discourage their entry into Nepal. Similarly, Maersk, an international shipping, freight and logistics company, took a long time to be registered as the government was under immense pressure from smaller local businesses, stalling registration for more than a year and a half. They saw the entry of Maersk as the biggest challenge to their way of doing business. It was the same case when DHL, an international cargo company, tried to establish a fully owned subsidiary in Nepal. Local courier companies ganged up in an attempt to stop the registration process even though legally there were no issues for contention. Similarly, not allowing international travel companies to operate in Nepal at the behest of the strong local lobby made tourist development a fraction of what it could potentially be. In 2019, in the new Foreign Investment and Technology Transfer Act, new items were added to the negative list. The milk cartels ensured that Indian dairy giant Amul stayed away from Nepal and no international agriculture companies could enter Nepal.

## Politics of Business Associations

Fearing international competition, many Nepali enterprise owners preferred to adopt protectionist policies, fighting for positions in their respective trade associations rather than making an effort to take their business to a regional or global level. Unlike in India, where business associations took on the onus of transforming policy and furthering the reform agenda, private-sector associations in Nepal have had very little role in making their members ready for the global marketplace. Like the worker stuck in a union where upward mobility meant becoming a union leader rather than increasing productivity or moving up the organizational hierarchy, the businessman was stuck in the quagmire of politics in business associations. Starting trade associations and reaching coveted positions in the associations and chambers of federations, along with a strong presence in the media, had overtaken the hunger for building competencies and expanding. In one of the bilateral chambers of commerce, the agenda always remained the gaining of duty concessions on certain products produced by members who were in the executive committee.

The biggest deficiency in Nepal's political and business community has been leadership. Although there have been plenty who have taken on the mantle of leadership, most have sadly been lacking in charisma,

integrity and drive. The inadequacy of leadership is apparent when the
president of the Federation of the Nepalese Chambers of Commerce
and Industry (FNCCI) in 2006 decided not to step down despite his
name being widely published as a defaulter of bank loans and his firms
booked under tax evasion. Between 2011 and 2014, the FNCCI was
mired in controversy, with court cases being fought on the subject
of its presidentship. The same people had been at the helm for over
two decades. In 2014, the FNCCI elections were fought in a manner
no different than those that involve political parties, featuring mud-
slinging in public and buying of votes through endless wining and
dining. The media followed candidates with rumours and gossip as it
is easier to pursue politics than in-depth stories on economic issues and
the business environment. In 2016, the infighting in the FNCCI led
to court intervention.

There is a vacuum of role models for young entrepreneurs. The
lack of success stories of people who made it big without taking
advantage of political linkages or unscrupulous business practices
speaks for itself. The selection of leadership in the association has
always been political in nature and has isolated the few successful
businesses and business people who are not keen to join the political
bandwagon. There is a distinct lack of correlation between the size
of a business and the quality of leadership. If we were to take the top
twenty-five companies in Nepal today in terms of turnover, profits,
number of employees and taxes paid, then it would be surprising that
only a few of the companies are actually involved in the leadership of
various business associations. Since 1990 till the present day, the fact
that the leadership of such organizations excludes formidable business
enterprises has also limited the efforts of multilateral and bilateral
agencies working with them, as these agencies see little credibility in
the existing leadership.

Business associations increasingly started to be used as a means to
further individual agendas. People who did not have good meeting rooms
in their own offices suddenly found spaces for free at these association
premises. With donors focused on working with such associations,

money for junkets became easy to come by, and association positions became lucrative as they entailed the benefits of travel and hospitality. People who led the associations continued to find opportunities for themselves as they got to hobnob with the politicians.

The lackadaisical attitude of the business associations did not improve and they failed to bring in a sense of professionalism. They did not hand over the management of associations to the professionals; instead, these were run by political leaders who canvassed and spent donor money on election after election. The rivalry between various factions within the associations as well as with other associations continued. For instance, a powerful programme of the Nepal Business Forum, sponsored by the International Finance Corporation (IFC), lost a lot of time on deciding on the location of the secretariat, as the FNCCI and the Confederation of Nepalese Industries (CNI) continued to fight rather than cooperate. A private-public dialogue forum successful in many countries could never take off in Nepal. As chair of the Nepal Economic Forum, I had offered IFC to host the secretariat temporarily, but IFC being a bureaucratic organization was not willing to think out of the box.

The objectives of the average businessperson continued to be status and power rather than taking the business to the next level. Many more business people became consuls general of countries ranging from Malta to Togo due to their political connections. With special blue licence plates on their vehicles, and special treatment at airports, they felt a great sense of arrival. There are more blue-number-plated vehicles that business people drive in than the number of vehicles foreign diplomats drive in. The ultimate goal of the Nepali entrepreneur was to pull out a multifold business card that carried the list of institutions he was affiliated with, drive a blue-number-plated vehicle, get felicitation notices printed in newspapers and constantly be covered by the print, online and social media and television. Such markers were seen to be prestigious, enabling them to gain access to offices of government, development partners and civil society organizations easily.

In Nepal, while individual businesses and entrepreneurs had their own identity, they derived more clout through taking leadership positions in the different business associations they belonged to. These could be associations based on the sector they worked in or they could be some trade-specific associations, or it could be the larger umbrella organizations that are super-associations.

## Cartels in the Nepali Context

After the end of monarchy in 2006, following a decade-long conflict, multiparty democracy was introduced and free-market norms were embraced. The private sector burgeoned in the economy then, unlike in any earlier period, and socio-economic growth thereafter was mostly private-sector–led. However, this growth came at a seemingly heavy cost.

A new lexicon entered the Nepali language. 'Setting', an English word, became a Nepali word meaning the nexus you built through connections acquired through political power or financial power. 'Syndicate' in Nepali started to have a negative meaning of businesses ganging up to profiteer. 'Bhagbanda', a Nepali word meaning split, became synonymous with the sharing of contracts, business and positions by political parties.

Just like any 'Fragile to Frontier (F2F)'[3] country—a nation that turned into an investment destination after conflict—corruption became a widespread issue in Nepal. Some similar post-conflict countries like Rwanda tried to overcome this and pushed their economies forward by opening themselves for international investors and global firms, thereby making a sustainable march towards economic development. On the contrary, Nepal chose to build platforms for crony capitalism and protectionism, as seen by the proliferation of syndicates and cartels. In fact, corruption and cartels seemed to have been feeding off each other, subsequently reinforcing the other and landing the country in a quagmire that was proving difficult to get out from. These business cartels exploited the political transition phase and spread their roots in such a way that a decade later they were entrenched in the whole of the economy. And this was only possible because political parties, supposedly the guardians of the new-found democracy, themselves became perpetrators. In the name of transition, these two groups were able to develop a nexus with each other and reap super profits and benefits for their members at the expense of the consumers and the nation. They were also able to misuse the media through misleading advertorials and government agencies like Commission for the Abuse of Authority further their own interests.

Consequently, further growth and development of the country were choked and it is now mired in several economic inefficiencies. Moreover, consumers are bearing the burden and brunt of this cartel economy; they are made to pay higher amounts for substandard services and uncompetitive products and to live a lower quality of life than would otherwise have been possible.

So what do we mean by cartels? There are many ways in which a cartel is defined, but it is understood as any monopolistic union between independent business firms in an industry or sector to influence prices, fix the quantity of products, deter the entry of new producers or restrict the market share of existing ones. Cartels are formed with the objective of eliminating market competition and creating monopoly profits for the colluding parties. These cartels were protected by supercartels, or umbrella bodies like FNCCI that gave the cartel legal legitimacy and ensured that they were not dismantled.

In Nepal, a cartel is loosely called a 'syndicate', an English word used in the Nepali language. Syndicates are groups that pursue business interests towards super profits by not adhering to quality and by fixing prices, prohibiting entry and influencing regulations very much like the guilds of medieval Europe. More importantly, these cartels under the veil of nationalism have been successful in keeping efficient and foreign firms at bay, thereby not necessitating them to compete with world-class products or services. These cartels are either formally organized under the garb of business associations and federations of such associations or operating informally.

After the imposition of the autocratic Panchayat system by King Mahendra in 1960, the need for patronage further went up. Like jobs in government offices, private businesses only survived if there was patronage. This feudal system of patronage created business associations that lived on the basis of protection bestowed by the king and royal family.

Further, the leaders of the associations were elected based on the support they had from the palace. This ensured that positions in the leadership of business associations provided access to the rulers and the government. This relationship continued post-1990 after the restoration of multiparty democracy. However, after Nepal was declared a republic in 2008, the patronage and nexus of these associations shifted from the palace to the different palaces of the multiple rulers that the political system had created.

## Control under the Guise of Associations

An interesting phenomenon peculiar to the Nepali economy is that cartels here most often operate under the garb of business associations and committees. Forming associations is not illegal per se under the legal framework of Nepal, and while they were initially formed to help their members, over the years they have evolved as a tool to profiteer and rent-seek. They have been able to increase their clout and ensure super profits either through fixing prices, quantities or the rules of business. These associations are now seen as cartels in disguise that have had long-lasting impacts, impeding the development of a healthy entrepreneurial ecosystem. Currently, there are more than 250 business associations registered under the FNCCI and the CNI, while under the Federation of Nepalese National Transport Entrepreneurs (FNNTE) there are more than 200 smaller transport associations. Apart from these, there are bilateral chambers of commerce that influence how investments from countries are made.

For instance, in case a Nepali would like to apply for a business visa to Thailand, it has to be endorsed by the Nepal–Thai Chamber of Commerce and Industry. Such-rent seeking behaviour, with the help of the government, has ensured that people in key positions in these organizations derive power and opportunity to leverage it for personal gains. These associations sometimes dominate the entirety of their respective sectors and determine the quantity and quality of products and services to be made available to the public. The most notorious of such associations in Nepal are in the transportation sector. They have a monopoly over various routes and bar new producers from plying vehicles on the road. In fact, the government is said to give route permits to new transport suppliers only under the recommendation of these associations, which often resort to threats and vandalism.

An example of this is a letter sent by the Tokha Chhahare Minibus Enterprise Association, which has a monopoly on the Tokha route, warning the Department of Transport Management not to issue new permits without its consent.[4] Another example is that of the NEGOSIDA (Federation of Nepal Gold and Silver Dealers' Association), which plays a crucial role in the functioning of the country's entire gold economy, i.e., the buying and selling of gold. In a country where gold imports through official channels total $220 million a year,[5] the business of gold is one of the most lucrative ones. There are individual quotas set for imports.[6] Individual gold dealers, however, can only buy gold from commercial banks if they are members of the NEGOSIDA.

One can see cartels omnipresent throughout Nepal and they have proliferated to grass-roots levels as well. For instance, the operation of boats in the Fewa Lake in Pokhara is controlled fully by the Fewa Boat Association. Independent boat owners cannot provide their services to willing customers without becoming a member of the boat association; in fact, the association decides specific boats and the number of times they can make rounds of the lake in a day. Similarly, there are multiple associations of eateries on highways that sell the same menu items for the same price, leading to travellers having to pay high prices for low-quality food and service. These highway eateries gang up under the banner of the association to stop any proliferation of organized business operations of food chains that are run in a professional manner.

## How Nepali Cartels Are Different from Global Ones

The presence of cartels and syndicates in Nepal is not an uncommon issue. One crucial difference between Nepal and other countries, however, is that in other economies, there are strong anti-trust regulations, and governments scrutinize such activities closely. Moreover, heavy sanctions and penalties are decreed on parties involved in cartels if they are busted. For instance, the four producers under the Spanish sugar cartels in 1995–96 were fined 8.7 million euros.[7] This is not so in the case of cartels in Nepal, which function openly and nonchalantly; no government body has taken any strict action against them even though they were made illegal by the Supreme Court through the Competition Promotion and Market Protection Act, 2006.

Globally, cartels often tend to disband within some period of their formation, either by themselves or by government decree. The peculiarity of cartels in Nepal is their pervasiveness, longevity and stability. This is the biggest challenge to Nepal's economic growth, development and to its integration into the global economy. The proliferation of businesses relying on cartel networks make them insular from foreign firms and competition, and thereby unwilling to compete with global products and services. Further, the myopia of doing business through policies based on protectionism make firms weak and unable to compete with companies in other regional and global markets. In Nepal, due to the political parties and governments supporting cartels, they have integrated into the government system and processes. An example of this would be the transport cartels. For instance, in Nepal one has to get an approval from the transport syndicate before getting a government licence to run commercial vehicles. This reflects how cartels have become part of government processes, therefore making them very difficult to disband.

## Cartelpreneurs Thrive on Rent-seeking

The history of Nepali economic growth has been based on rent-seeking being preferred over entrepreneurship. Cartels further encourage this, which is evident in Nepali society. There are frequent news stories about syndicates disrupting the regular supply of products and services because of certain government rules and regulations that are unfavourable to them. For instance, petroleum dealers continuously engage in shutting down fuel stations whenever the government starts conducting quality checks because they want to benefit at the expense of the consumers and the nation.

One example of such rent-seeking behaviour was when petroleum dealers under the Nepal Petroleum Dealers' Association protested against the Nepal Oil Corporation to increase shrinkage and evaporation loss[8] compensation. The Essential Goods Protection Act, 1955, has considered petroleum products a basic necessary commodity; as such, the Act has barred fuel sellers from launching protests and disrupting supplies. However, dealers under the association stopped regular supplies of petrol and diesel nonchalantly.[9] Similarly, in 2013, four water associations in the valley announced a strike and halted the supply of both tankers and bottled water, which affected the lives of millions of people, indefinitely asking the government to fulfil their demands.[10] In March 2018, the Bankers' Association decided to punish NIC Asia Bank by not allowing transactions with twenty-seven other banks as they decided not to adhere to the banker cartels' diktat of capping deposit rates.[11]

Likewise, shopkeepers in Dhading went on a strike in September 2017 and closed their shops to protest against the sealing of a number of stores on the charge of overpricing by the government market monitoring team led by the then state minister for supply,

Karna Bahadur Bishwakarma. In the same way, when four branded stores
in Durbarmarg, Kathmandu, were sealed by the ministry for charging
exorbitant prices, other suppliers led by the Durbarmarg Development
Board closed their own stores in protest of the government's move.[12]
Similar stories are often heard in the media about gold dealers shutting
their shops against government charges when they were found to have
rigged weighing machines or taxi cabs halting their services when meter
boxes were found to be tampered with.

Moreover, rent-seeking behaviour is contagious; such activities
in one sector have induced suppliers in other sectors to be involved
in similar activities as the government doesn't take any firm to task,
or easily gives in to their demands when it does.

A matter of grave concern for the economy is that such cartels
have alienated the actual competent entrepreneurs who are from
business association leaderships while rent-seekers pay a lot to make
their way into those positions. The new breed of 'cartelpreneurs'
have devised ways to multiply their business assets with little
accountability while influencing every aspect of business from hiring
people to regulating service standards. This has led to a change in the
perception of businesses in the eyes of the youth.

## Cartels Cost the Economy Dear

Cartels cost the economy about $4.5 billion, which is around 15 per
cent of the GDP as per a study conducted by the Nepal Economic
Forum that I chair.[13] This is a simple computation, but its impacts
are far-reaching in terms of throttling economic growth and
development. Cartels in Nepal have three key characteristics.

First, they are all-pervasive. Under the guise of associations,
cartels are present in almost all sectors of the economy. Some of
them are blatantly present, like in the transport sector, while others
are hidden from public purview, as in the education, agriculture
and health sectors. Others crop up in the news time and again; they
include construction companies, water suppliers, taxi cabs, truck

carriers, tourism professionals, petroleum dealers, sugar companies, banks, LPG suppliers and so on. Hence, cartels have a grip over pretty much the whole economy.

The brunt of the cartel economy is directly borne by the consumers. Cartels have become a way of life for the average Nepali, impacting every element of their life from the time they wake up to the time they go to bed. They are forced to pay higher prices for goods and services of subpar quality, which means their quality of life has been compromised and their purchasing power has decreased, even more so for luxury goods. Moreover, very limited options of goods and services are available to them.

Further, along with some of the private media houses, cartels have exploited social media to create the perception of being synonymous with the private sector. They have been able to leave an impression with the general public that they represent the best interests of a business and its consumers while working to perpetuate questionable business practices. Therefore, elections to business associations have become more important than the businesses themselves with more media attention paid in that direction.

Second, cartels ensure businesses get away with providing substandard goods and services. For instance, when Sajha Yatayat, a public cooperative, started to operate buses in Kathmandu in January 2017 with better amenities, associations went out and caused physical damage to the buses.[14] In private schools, fees are charged way above the norm, flouting the education directive of the Ministry of Education. However, a powerful association of private schools whose founder president became a parliamentarian and went on to be part of house committees ensured that these violations were not penalized. These are the ways that consumers are being cheated. To cite another example, in the jewellery business, either underweighted gold is being sold as measuring balances are rigged or the gold is impure as there aren't regular quality checks from the government, but sellers get away with it as they have protection from their respective associations. Nepal is one of the very few countries in the world where a citizen cannot walk into a bank and buy gold or ensure that they get hallmark certified gold.

Using taxi cabs is an equally nightmarish experience. Drivers more often than not refuse to use meters. Even if they do, the meters are rigged; a 3 km ride might cost one NPR 200, double of what the meter would have shown. Customers have to continuously haggle with taxi drivers for fares, and they usually end up getting cheated. The existence of these cab services has ensured that companies with ride-hailing apps like Uber have been kept at bay. When Pathao, a Bangladesh-based company, started its ride-hailing app in August 2019, it met with tremendous resistance. Further, taxi associations do not blink an eyelid when it comes to collectively going on strike whenever the government tries to enforce regulations.[15]

For those who use their own vehicles, adulterated petrol and diesel is another issue. Using contaminated fuel damages the engines of vehicles. Moreover, the supply of petrol and diesel is frequently disrupted by petroleum dealer associations, sometimes through artificial shortages, and other times due to protests against the government to fulfil their ridiculous demands.[16]

Meanwhile, there are barber associations which determine the prices of haircuts, paragliding associations which determine the charges for paragliding, and banks which gang up with each other for interest rate cartels. Cartels are omnipresent, omnipotent and omniscient in Nepali society.

Third, the vicious circle when it comes to cartels means that no one opposes them. People do not raise their voice because they are themselves part of other cartels. Moreover, increased costs due to the presence of cartels in one sector seeps into the cost of other sectors. For instance, transportation costs, if higher, tend to reflect on the cost of other sectors which require transport services in any way.

So, a vegetable vendor uses cabs from a particular cartel, the cabbie goes to a doctor whose prices are determined by another cartel and is recommended to a polyclinic that is also running on cartel pricing. The doctor pays his children's fees that are determined by school cartels while school transport is run by the transport cartel.

There isn't any part of the economy that remains untouched by cartels. They are everywhere, and they dictate a consumer's everyday life. This has led to mounting frustration amongst the public which is made to live a low-quality life and would rather move abroad; when even the basics aren't right, it is very difficult to sustain a life.

Fourth is the issue of conflict of interest. The biggest challenge is that the state has become part of the strong machinery that helps cartels to proliferate by giving associations a role in making regulations or drafting laws. In the international arena, when businessmen become part of the government, they are required to forfeit their business involvements. For example, when business leaders become involved in government positions either through political process or appointments, they must make the appropriate disclosures. However, this does not happen in Nepal. Politicians, party members and members of Parliament (MPs) have business investments in various sectors, and sometimes in the very sectors they are supposed to be regulating. This creates a conflict of interest as lawmakers then tend to formulate policies that are beneficial for business cronies and are inimical to the upliftment of the entire sector. The fact that many business people contest in the federal, provincial and local elections reflects the close relationship between business and politics. Binod Chaudhary, Nepal's only billionaire in the Forbes list since 2013, has felt it necessary to be in Parliament through different political parties at different times. In his autobiography, he reflects on how it is important to be part of the political system to further one's entrepreneurial pursuits. He earlier represented the Nepal Communist Party (UML) and in 2018 switched to being a member of Parliament through the Nepali Congress.

A very good example is the strong contestation of the implementation of the Health Profession Education (HPE) Bill by several NCP lawmakers who have made investments in the Manmohan Memorial Academy of Health Sciences.[17] The HPE bill is supposed to bar any medical college from getting affiliated with Tribhuvan University. If this bill finally becomes a law, their institutions would be precluded from getting affiliation to the university, therefore making their investments lose value.

There are MPs who own manpower agencies and are members of the Industrial Relations and Labour Committee of Parliament, one of the lawmaking bodies for foreign employment. The Private and Boarding Schools Organisation (PABSON) and the National Private and Boarding Schools Organisation (NPABSON) members who themselves own schools sit in the fee determination committee at the Department of Education and are MPs as well.[18] The vice president of the Institute of Chartered Accountants of Nepal and the vice president of the FNCCI sit on the Securities Board of Nepal. Chairmen of private commercial banks sit on the parliamentary finance committee responsible for formulating the Banks and Financial Institutions Act.

The rise of cartels that have a nexus with political parties and bureaucracy makes it difficult to understand who is playing politics and who is doing business as entrepreneurs engage in cartel politics and politicians engage in business through cartels. Political appointments are made to benefit cartels while cartel leaders become parliamentarians and push for law changes.

Finally, it is important to understand the politics of cartels. Studies have revealed that the major business houses that have emerged since 2006 are the ones alleged to have strong connections with the political parties and government.[19] Further, the elections to business associations have been fought on the lines of political parties. For instance, in the case of the manpower business, the Nepal Association of Foreign Employment Agencies has been a powerful body that controls the foreign employment business that sends half a million workers abroad each year. Even if a person spends $1000, these agencies make $500 million a year! To ensure that this sector is least regulated and erring firms not penalized, it is ensured that the lines between the government and these agencies are blurred. In an attempt to control the entire value chain, the leaders of this association also push for being appointed as ambassadors.[20]

## Cartels and Election Funding

Many argue that due to the absence of a mechanism for political parties to raise funds in a legitimate manner, they are compelled to work with businesses to fund the ever-increasing costs of elections and operating a political party. It becomes easier to negotiate with business associations rather than individual businesses. Therefore, political parties who come to power funded by such associations find it hard to act against them, forget about making attempts to disband them.

There is also the issue of ethical business practices. International firms which are governed by an ever-increasing stringent code of conduct on political contributions and graft are never able to pay political parties. Therefore, the opening up of foreign investments actually dries up the coffers of political parties in a significant way. Even if there are some cases of graft, international media attention is drawn that is detrimental to the image of the party and government. Therefore, keeping foreign investments at bay helps the interests of local business associations and also protects the funding relationships for political parties.

Political parties and government officials generally comprising people with a lack of understanding of the functioning of the global economy enjoy dealing with similar-minded folks that lead cartels— or cartelpreneurs. The increase in internationally competitive firms that are led by professionals and people who abide by different practices and ethics, unlike political leaders, threatens the people who have survived through cartels. If the government pursues reforms and brings in a business environment based on openness, competition and adhering to the global mindset, it fears the erosion of the base of sycophants and power-brokers.

## Challenges of the Nepali Private Sector

It is now evident that the presence of cartels under the garb of business associations or informal groups has been one of the biggest external challenges to the Nepali economy and Nepali businesses. However, internal behavioural challenges within firms and sectors also compound the impact of cartels. Following are the key challenges faced by the Nepali private sector, which is more than the challenge of access to finance or the lack of capital—it hinges on mindsets.

## Globalization and Professional Competencies

In the long run, the entry of multinationals into Nepal has been a huge boost to the national economy. They have brought with them a new way of doing business—in operating procedures, professionalism and service-oriented delivery. Small businesses in Nepal were well aware of the lack of professionalism in their organizations—they knew that their service delivery was mediocre at best and they also knew that they faced serious gaps in management ability. However, instead of seeking solutions to create a more dynamic and efficient organization, most companies took the easier way out by simply blocking all competition. Their lack of ambition has had a significant detrimental impact on the Nepali economy by discouraging the entry of international companies and foreign investment. It has also prevented most industries in Nepal from fulfilling their potential and competing in the global market.

The building of competencies and capabilities can be explained by contrasting Nepal's hotel industry, in which international hotel companies are allowed to operate, to Nepal's travel industry, in which international travel companies are not allowed to operate. Thus, we have competent hotel staff, systems and processes, but due to the absence of international competencies in travel agencies there is a lack of ability in scaling up the tourism business. In areas where foreign firms have been allowed, be it consumer product companies, marketing, banking, courier services, advertising or market research, Nepali competencies have developed to international quality and standards, while in areas where foreign firms were restricted—

accounting services and legal firms, for instance—the service is way below international standards.

Succession planning and execution is one of the hallmarks of success in business, but, like in politics, the older generation did not want to hand over the enterprise to the new generation as family business scions wanted to operate even after they had to be kept on life support. It was not unusual for the family patriarch to be seen coming to the office with oxygen cylinders and attendants in tow to sign cheques. The 'younger generation' only got the opportunity to take over the mantle when they were way beyond their productive phase, and again, like the previous generation, they too held on and did not transfer the leadership to the next generation.

The best example of the advantages of an international player being part of the local market is exemplified by the entry of Grindlays Bank (now Standard Chartered Bank) into Nepal in 1988 and its impact on the banking sector. While most banks remained identified with their owners (either the state or private business houses), Standard Chartered focused on building a management team that was distinct from ownership. They brought in international standard operating procedures, a checks-and-balances system, and a logistical framework with a sharp focus on service delivery. They not only compelled other banks to develop their own business structures in order to be able to compete with them, but also taught other banks what they had to do. For instance, a major problem banks faced was their inability to retain skilled professional staff, which hopped banks as and when better offers for their services came from other banks.

One of the biggest hindrances to the acceptance of corporate culture in Nepal has been the resistance to the independent management of companies by their owners. Owners just could not keep from interfering with management, which posed real problems for professional management companies. This lack of corporate culture and professionalism has deterred foreign companies as it poses a significant hurdle to competent management, accountability and transparency. It has also restricted foreign brands from ensuring the quality of service that is associated with their brands.

## Myopia in the Face of Opportunity

Even when Nepali business enterprises banded together and worked positively towards market reforms, certain sections of the business community have always been successful in abusing reforms for their short-term benefit. For instance, when the Indo-Nepal Trade and Transit Treaty came up for renewal in 1996, a group of businessmen from Nepal's FNCCI and India's Confederation of Indian Industries (CII) came together before official government talks were held, and came up with a list of recommendations for their respective governments. The treaty remains one of the few times private-sector groups got together and worked out the terms and conditions they would like to see in a treaty that would govern trade between their two countries. The governments were very receptive to the ideas they proposed and adopted the recommendations of the private sector. With the ink just drying on the treaty, opportunistic businessmen in Nepal started to export vegetable ghee, acrylic yarn, zinc oxide and copper products from Nepal to India. However, all these products were essentially taking advantage of the reduced customs duty between Nepal and India. It harked back to the trade problem India and Nepal have had from the time of the Panchayat regime—where differences in customs duty unduly dictated the nature of not just trade but even enterprise in Nepal, but only for a short while, until India, realizing its loss, put a stop to it. For instance, the vegetable ghee industry suddenly boomed by taking advantage of a difference in price caused by duties.

India does not levy import duty on Nepali imports, and Nepali import duties on palm oils from South East Asia happen to be considerably cheaper than those levied in India. Simultaneously, the 1996 treaty had imposed a relatively low duty on import and export costs between Nepal and India. This made it possible for opportunistic businessmen in Nepal to import truckloads of palm oil from South East Asia, repackage it into smaller packs, and re-export it to India as vegetable ghee at a price that was still cheaper than what was available in the Indian market. This arbitrage, conducted by Nepali businessmen, did not last long, and ended with an amendment to the treaty, with specific clauses on the certification of origin and value addition in 2002. In another example, vitamins used in imported animal feed products were repackaged into smaller packages and exported as Made in Nepal products. Time and again, Nepal has been unsuccessful in appropriately utilizing a treaty that benefited exporting to India in the long run and instead took advantage of it to capture immediate gains. In 2017–18, palm oil exports to India jumped from zero to Rs 10.1 billion because of higher import tariffs in India and ease of repackaging the product. The certificate of origin is provided by the concerned private-sector bodies.[21]

The myopia of Nepali enterprise towards the fundamentals of doing business may be understood as a product of the complicated political and cultural history described so far. Yet, it is the customers and end users of any good or service who ultimately pay the price. For instance, the private sector is yet to implement a comprehensive consumer protection law that would set a standard for goods and services. Most businesses in Nepal see more benefit in ripping the customer off and making an extra buck than in being concerned about, say, customer relations and ethical practices. A striking example of the lack of concern for the customer, combined with the increasing pressure business faces from labour, is the implementation of the service charge in most labour-dominated service industries. In most countries, the service charge is for the quality that is guaranteed by the business, and if this quality is not met, service charges are waived. Without a regulatory framework to ensure quality, service charges are essentially taxes on the consumer. They not only increase the cost to the customer, but also fail to result in improvements to the service rendered. For a country that is heavily dependent on tourism from budget travellers, a 10 per cent service charge can define a better experience in Nepal relative to other countries. The myopia of businesses agreeing to a service charge, a portion of which comes to them, has impacted the tourism service industry wherein hotel and restaurant owners and labourers are living off that additional 10 per cent from the consumer without providing the added edge in service.

However, it is important to realize that the lack of quality services in Nepal is as much a fault of the consumer as it is of business and labour. For instance, over 300 brands of bottled water are available in Nepal. The consumer clearly does not care about the brand or quality of water being provided as long as he/she believes that any water poured from a sealed bottle is good, clean and natural. The lack of value the consumer associates with the brand is a telling sign of an economy that has not fully matured and is not aware of the choices it makes. This could partly be the fault of manufacturers and service providers in failing to promote a quality brand, but also at fault is the end user's lack of interest or awareness of the quality of the good or service he or she buys.

The service providers don't train their staff for effective service, and the staff takes their job as a mere jagir or lifetime grant—they don't believe that they have to serve the customer even though customers are actually the ones who, in the end, are paying their salaries. For instance, at a food court, the staff is keen to close operations before the scheduled time, just like the staff at government offices. The treatment of customer-oriented work as a mere jagir position is part of a culture of work that has crossed over into the private sector, making it difficult to distinguish the attitude of a worker at a government utility and the staff at a private-sector–owned Internet company or cable operator.

Another example of the lack of ethical standards and awareness of Nepali businesses is the close proximity of alcohol shops to schools, and clubs making loud noises in residential areas. The former is a clear-cut example of a business that does not extend its ethical practices beyond its immediate interests while the latter is an example of a business that is completely out of tune with the sociocultural norms that many still practise. Any event that involves the youth is sponsored by alcohol companies, and their advertisements as sponsors make one wonder if Nepal has no other business that needs advertisement or can afford advertisements. Indeed, the fact that many a business has thrived on selling alcohol and cigarettes to minors is a clear indication of a business community that simply does not care for anything other than the immediate acquisition of profits. It is also a telling sign of the lack of concern among big business houses about how or to whom their products are being sold and how it affects society. But, most importantly, it gives a clear indication of a government that does not know its responsibilities and cannot institute the basic rules and regulations that any parent would be instituting among their children.

## Lack of Respect for Knowledge

During the autumn, the festival of lights, Tihar (Diwali or Deepawali in India and other countries) is celebrated with dedication to Goddess Laxmi, the goddess of wealth. However, the pictures and images of Laxmi are never in isolation; there are two other images that accompany them: of Saraswati, the goddess of knowledge, and Ganesh, the elephant-headed god known for his power to remove obstacles. The Nepali private sector was focused on Laxmi and it ignored the other two. The understanding that systems and processes, good insurance and risk management along with doing things the right way is as important as having financial resources was ignored. Further, it worked for financial gains only. Therefore, despite a huge leap in private-sector earnings, no art centre, library or other cultural centre got built, nor were any schemes to contribute towards reducing income and economic inequality pursued.

Despite having billion-dollar businesses and institutions with billion-dollar market capitalization, there were no organizations that employed an economist or had a research department. There were no think tanks or research organizations supported by the business associations or cartels. So, despite growing in size, things did not change much in how business plans were made, board meetings conducted, or employee performance appraised. Bank managers that sold online banking or mobile banking to customers did not use these services themselves, nor did hotel owners and managers know the ingredient of dishes they sold in their outlets. Real estate and hotel developers had no understanding of eco-friendly ways of building or operating properties. Like one hires a priest to conduct a ritual, business processes were outsourced to fixers. Despite the private sector being worth $21 billion in 2018, the business consulting market was minuscule as hiring of consulting firms to help in process, vision and growth was practically non-existent. This allowed many people and firms to have a field day as their services were never benchmarked to global norms while they got away with unimaginable ethical practices.

## Cooperatives: The Unregulated Sector

In Nepal, where the definition of the private and public sectors is fluid and the private sector just consists of businesses owned by people from the public sector or fronts for political party investments, the promotion of cooperatives has become a major challenge in Nepal's quest for integrating into the global economy. Cooperatives in Nepal are organizations that are built with contributions from members for the members to organize themselves, avail loans and get better deals. The world over, cooperatives have been successful in different forms but only for small businesses or to aggregate farmers, artisans and small producers. In Nepal, they have given rise to mighty groups that own banks, real estate and other businesses without having to comply with any of the regulations a private-sector company has to face or the regulation of the Central Bank on financial transactions. The cooperative movement created powerful people, who then went on to become noted business people and later influential politicians. Similarly, politicians and people in politics found the cooperative to be a good veil to hide informal businesses and get away from regulating authorities for revenue and foreign exchange. It is now rare to find business people not involved in cooperatives. A thriving banking business following global standards became embroiled in cartel-like behaviour, fixing exchange rates and ensuring the regulator remains conservative. Bank owners invested in cooperatives and cooperatives invested in banks. Some of the cooperatives were bigger than the banks and many of them failed miserably, but the cooperative promoters got off scot-free or spent five years in prison to legitimize money made through fraud and embezzlement.

Families and friends got together to set up organizations that could take public money to be spent at the will of the cooperative board. People, especially traditional business people, found a new way of depositing money for higher returns, which was never under the scanner of the tax man or government regulator. The promoters of these cooperatives would form a board of their choice and start investing money at their own discretion and also pay themselves fat perks and benefits. A large set of investments was made in real estate, where, like in a monarchy, the principle was that the gain was personal, the loss cooperative. By June 2018, the Department of Cooperatives listed that 34,512 cooperatives had been registered with an outlay of NPR 274 billion ($2.6 billion) that involved 6.3 million members or 20 per cent of the population. However, increased investments in real estate made many of them go bankrupt. With the courts staying away from the recovery process, many Nepalis who believed they did not have enough money or were scared of the processes of the banking system lost their hard-earned savings. The desire among Nepalis for high returns coupled with the lack of innovation within the banking system to reach the bottom of the pyramid was also responsible for this.

## Learning from Examples of Success

Despite these challenges, there are many successful stories that people have gone all out to replicate.

Himalayan Java, a coffee shop that began its journey in 1999 with its first outlet in Thamel selling handcrafted coffee and bakery goods, had thirty outlets in Nepal, Bhutan, India and the US in 2018. They changed the way young people hung out and brought about a coffee culture that has benefited Nepali coffee farmers in a big way. They also set a benchmark in terms of design, layout, ambience and clean toilets. Today, there are hundreds of coffee shops that have been inspired by them dotting the country.

Bhatbhateni Supermarket is a classic example of a successfully leveraged growth model. Starting in 1992 as a small mom-and-pop cold store in a 300-square-foot area with NPR 1,00,000, Min Bahadur Gurung reinvested in and expanded the business gradually. Leveraging his position along the way, he expanded the small cold store into the biggest retail outlet in the nation. Gurung, who is founder–chairman of the company, believes in hard work and positive thinking. He quotes a Nepali proverb on how if one works hard consistently, one can extract oil out of stone. In 2018, he proudly reported that Bhatbhateni had 1 million square feet of commercial area in twelve locations with 4500 people working directly under it, and thousands more indirectly.

The post-1990 period did bring about many business success stories but the story of Kantipur Publications, a private media house, stands out. A company that had a humble beginning in 1993 with a broadsheet newspaper, it had expanded into magazines, radio, television and an online portal by the year 2000. It took advantage of the free media policies and filled the vacuum created by the inefficient Gorkhapatra Sansthan, the state-owned media publication house. By the time the two partners who founded Kantipur Publications decided to part ways in 2008, media reports indicated that the company was already valued at NPR 1.5 billion. Informal valuations put the group at a value of $100 million in 2018.[22] By 2018, it had a presence in all platforms, including digital, and had set up an investment arm for start-ups.

In 2018, Nepal's private sector was valued at around $21 billion, a two and a half fold jump from $8 billion in 2008.[23] It is by far the most active sector of the economy and its biggest employment provider. Some of the key sectors that have significant contributions from the private sector are financial services, hospitality, media, education, healthcare, aviation, communications, IT and energy. For instance, business houses brought in international-partnered banks to Nepal, which changed the way the banking sector operated. Today, it is one of the most vibrant and competitive sectors in the private sector. Likewise, private-sector–led power producers contribute more than 30 per cent of the total electricity supply.[24]

The bulk of the private sector, up to 90 per cent by some estimates, is composed of enterprises which can only be classified as small or micro-enterprises. Although these enterprises are Nepal's largest employers, generating more than 90 per cent of the entire country's employment opportunities, they account for a mere 4 per cent of national GDP.[25, 26] For the creation of an employment-intensive economy, these small and medium enterprises must be fostered and encouraged. Compared to large industrial enterprises which, on average, create one job for every $5000 invested, these small enterprises create a job on no more than $150.[27] However, a major reason for stagnation in the Nepali private sector is the inability of these small enterprises to scale up, expand and grow. For instance, a successful restaurant or a store selling handicrafts does not open a second branch or spread over different cities in the country, thereby not leveraging the competencies it has successfully created. While some of this is due to a surprising lack of ambition among enterprise owners, the bulk of the problem remains an inefficient and unregulated market that is unable to deliver easy access to finance, markets, technology and skills.

The journey of the Nepali private sector has been an interesting one. While the informal sectors continue to provide impetus to

economic growth, especially outside Kathmandu, the successful
formal sectors tend to hide under the garb of associations that are
generally a front for cartels. The private sector has been able to fill the
void where the government has not been able to deliver, especially
in the supply of essentials like healthcare, education and social
infrastructure. However, there have been issues in terms of quality
and price that have impacted the Nepali consumer in a big way,
making Nepal expensive compared to its regional neighbours. It is
also heartening to see more young people take on entrepreneurship
and leadership in traditional business houses. Challenges are always
there, but if Nepal is to transform and unleash its potential, it has to
be led by the private sector. We will discuss how the private sector
can be transformed in the third part of the book.

# Donorpreneurs and the Business of Development

The Nepali economic system, until the abolition of the caste system, revolved around the Hindu philosophy and way of life. One's current life was defined by deeds in past lives, and the deeds of the current life defined the deeds of future life. Life revolved around fate. A person could be born into the ruling class and by fate be designated a general before birth—as in the Rana tradition—and grow up in the lap of luxury. In contrast, someone who is brilliantly curious and knowledgeable and in possession of tremendous memory power could live the life of a scavenger because s/he was born into the untouchable class. Fate ruled, and still rules, for many in Nepal.

In this context, the word 'development' is alien as it does not exist in religious scripts or cultural nuances. In life, there is poverty and wealth—both destined before one is born—while there are also essentials and luxury, the two extremes. So in such a society the discourse around development and the role of development partners popularly known as donors becomes very complicated. In this chapter, efforts have been made to provide a perspective on the world of development, development partners, the aid community and

NGOs, with examples of hands-on engagement as well as friendly, advisory roles with development partners at different stages of operations. We will discuss the history of development aid in Nepal, the complications due to lack of contextualizing the understanding of aid in Nepal and the dependency and cultural influences of aid that have impacted the economic development of Nepal.

## The Concept of Development

The concept of development as part of a linear economic growth model became popular during the implementation of the Marshall Plan. The common understanding was that investment in development activities would further economic growth, which would in turn take people out of poverty in a world that had high disparities in levels of income and quality of life. It also brought about the concept of donors and recipients of aid. However, in the context of talking about development in Nepal, it is important to understand the significance of its history as a nation that never came under direct colonial rule, even though it did pay annual taxes to China as part of a treaty. It would also be naive to assume that Nepal and the British empire were on equal terms. The Rana regime was aware that any direct conflict with the British would mean compromising its most productive lands in the Terai while the British saw sense in using Nepal as a buffer state whose foreign and trade policy were entirely through British India control. Thus, although not a colony, Nepal found itself in a position of dependency in relation to the British empire. Nevertheless, there was no concept of aid back then.

## 1950s: Aid Arrives

Following World War II and the demise of colonialism, Nepal entered into a new world order in which the former colonial powers of Western Europe and the United States became collectively known as the 'First World'. The communist industrial countries comprised the 'Second World'. Nepal, along with the least developed of the former colonies—those lacking in industrialization, capitalist institutions and democratic governance—became eligible for foreign aid as members of the 'Third World'.

The first aid package Nepal received was part of the US-led Marshall Plan. This was the first international development plan which combined humanitarian aims with political stability and economic growth in Western Europe after World War II. It was also an attempt to directly challenge and restrict the expansion of communism into Western Europe.

The aid package from the US arrived in Nepal in January 1951, a month before the Rana regime was toppled. Given the strategic importance of Nepal due to its geopolitical location, sandwiched as it was between an expansionist Maoist China and socialist India, the Americans were keen to maintain some influence in the region. Nepal was also an important buffer zone for India against an expanding China. it had traditionally been under the sphere of influence of its southern neighbour, and so it came as no surprise when in 1952 India reasserted this influence by starting to provide aid and assistance to Nepal, even though India was itself an aid recipient.

This was a time when the US made its entry on the world stage as the power of the older European nations was waning and its own rising. It heralded the beginning of the development era, with development being propagated not only as the expansion of capitalism, but as the moral, just and indeed necessary exercise of liberating nations from poverty and deprivation. Nepal entered this world as an underdeveloped country, a third-world country defined as being between the two battling superpowers of that time, a country that because of its underdevelopment would be an aid recipient. The nature and identity with which Nepal entered the international arena and the way development was talked about and understood at the international level has defined how it has understood and experienced development.

## Understanding Development

In Nepal, development has always been understood as an attempt to reach a standard of living prevalent in the US and Europe. It meant the building of schools, hospitals and infrastructure along with the development of the public sector, land reforms, mass mobilization, improved manpower and the creation of administrative organizations. In this understanding, the justification for development was the primitive state of the Nepali economy in comparison to the global capitalist economies of the West. The goal was always exterior to Nepal, and the task of development frequently suffered from an amnesia about the past. Nepal was unable to reconcile with its feudal past and often completely ignored the ground realities of its historical, cultural and traditional legacy. So people who grew organic rice, for instance, and fed themselves well (what would today be defined as a good minimalistic way of life) were dragged out for Food for Work programmes and given enough money to buy fertilizer-treated rice. The lack of any relation between the Nepali people and the project of development perhaps most strikingly reflects the state's failure to garner local support and ownership in this initiative.

## Imported Bikas and Original Bikas

The people who were supposed to benefit from development to this day associate and identify it with the government and foreigners. Development to the average Nepali is something they lack, something that is not present at the local level—a notion that has been well-honed and nurtured by the development industry over the past seventy years. The onus of development lies with the state, for it is something conducted by the state and by others who are not locals. It is an external factor; something imported into the country and distributed by the government. Thus, the concept of development as introduced to the Nepali people was not something they ever identified with. It was never internalized by them and they never saw it as something that involved them personally. This understanding is clearly demonstrated by the use of the word bikas to describe things ranging from imported apple varieties (*bikase shyau*) to character, education, infrastructure development and employment. The Nepali dictionary understanding of bikas is very close to that of the English word development, but it can be used in colloquial speech in reference to anything foreign or imported. This has created further stratification in the Nepali society, with an almost racial distinction between those who were 'developed' and those who received the 'development'.

## Donor Is *Daata*

In the Nepali language, a donor is referred to as daata and a donor organization as *datrisansthan* which is basically understood in the colloquial sense of a person or an organization making an offering, giving alms or distributing resources. These words come from the concept of giving donations, which in the Nepali language is a derivative of the word *daan*. So a donor making a donation in Nepal has a different religious and cultural connotation from the Western meaning of aid, recipients and development partners. While aid can demand accountability, a donation may not. For instance, when we make offerings to temples or to priests, we never ask where the money is going or question the transparency of the system. We do not question if the temple money is spent on a personal party hosted by the priest or is used to finance alcohol or marijuana consumption! Likewise, in feudal society, there is the feudal lord who can give '*bakas*' to someone, which loosely translated in English means a grant. In Nepal, money from donors has many times been seen as bakas or grant. Though the culture of India and China have influenced Nepal through practices surrounding Hinduism and Buddhism, they have different perspectives on the concept of aid, development, donors and recipients than Nepal. This makes the Nepali challenge of understanding aid and development even more complicated.

For a beggar, it is his or her right to receive alms even if s/he is capable physically and mentally of earning a living. As per the caste system, even if someone could perform duties beyond his or her caste or vocation, they did not have any opportunity to do so. Especially if s/he belonged to the lower caste, there was no option but to beg. Similarly, it was not wrong for someone to go to a richer person's house to beg for money, food or other stuff as bakas/bakshish.

These days, it is common for people to engage in donation campaigns or beg for contributions when they have to go on a picnic or holiday or study tour or undertake medical expenses. Such a practice plays a big role in how Nepal perceives the development discourse and the players in development. Therefore, successive governments have felt it is okay to ask development partners to fund government projects that could have been funded by government coffers—whether it is an official trip, a hydropower plant or the printing of driving licences. The right to beg and the societal acceptance of begging has ensured that the idea of the government 'putting out the begging bowl' is well-accepted by society in the development discourse.

## Free-for-All: Evolution of Donor Assistance in Nepal

During the 1950s and 1960s, the US remained the most significant donor in the world, and following the success of the Marshall Plan in Europe, it adopted a similar model in Nepal. Its development work, carried out on the basis of the modernization theory—a theory propounded by Walt Rostow which outlines the stages a 'traditional' economy goes through to become 'modern'—failed for a number of reasons.

One, Nepal did not possess an educated population that was accustomed to industrialized society, while Europe did. Two, there was a lack of willingness to implement major land and agricultural reforms as the Americans had advised. They had emphasized documentation of landholdings, stronger security for smaller farmers and a ceiling on individual landholdings. Of the reforms that were implemented, there was limited success due to problems in the implementation model itself. The primary reason was that there were too many loopholes in the Act which allowed large landholders to maintain control of the land, and thus there was hardly any success in land redistribution.

The Americans also faced considerable problems in transferring knowledge to the local level when carrying out projects. For instance, a 1958–63 programme for constructing suspension bridges was meant to be carried out by an all-Nepali team with American equipment under American supervision, but the training turned out to be a complete failure. Of the targeted seventy bridges in two years, only one bridge was constructed in five years.[1] The reason for this failure has been pinpointed as the American inability to transfer technology and technical skills. Further, the rivalry between the US, the USSR and India in securing a strong foothold in Nepal often impacted which way aid flowed. For instance, funds from the above-mentioned suspension bridge programme were temporarily diverted to fund the purchase of three DC-3 aircraft for Royal Nepal Airlines. This was to prevent the entry of the Soviets, who were interested in setting up Nepal's aviation industry. Finally, political turmoil and instability in Nepal also caused problems for donors in the effective implementation of programmes.

From the mid-1960s, following a decline in the regional importance placed on Nepal by the US, India stepped up to become Nepal's largest aid provider until the early 1980s. While the Americans were drawn into Vietnam, a more cautious India sought to maintain its power balance against China. Unlike the American aid policy, Indian aid was mostly tied to its own strategic interests of promoting trade flow. With this intention, it initially focused most of its aid money on financing infrastructure developments and the construction of roads. It also diversified its aid portfolio into sectors like education, health, agriculture and power. However, there were considerable disagreements between the two countries over a number of infrastructure and power development projects, with many in Nepal identifying India as taking an excessive share of the resources. This was particularly the case with Nepal's river sources; for instance, there was heavy opposition when in 1959, the Nepali Congress negotiated the Gandaki scheme which allowed India to construct irrigation canals to irrigate 5 million acres in India, while Nepal would get enough water to irrigate a mere 3,43,000 acres and operate a 10 MW power plant. Disagreements on the sharing of resources have since then resulted in limitations on the use and development of Nepal's significant water resources.

It was only after 1990 that the floodgates opened and Nepal became a fertile land for people to experiment with ideas and quick-fix solutions in the quest of solving its problem of poverty.

## Lack of Coordination between Development Partners

Exhibiting an attitude of dependence, Nepal did not bother to have a comprehensive foreign aid policy until 2002. The lack of a national body directing and coordinating aid was a considerable drawback—not only did it compromise the sovereignty of the nation, it often directly challenged the will and intentions of the government. Without any regulatory framework, donors and aid agencies were at liberty to work out their own strategies based on their own priorities. Predictably, the priority of donors and aid agencies sometimes even came into direct conflict with the Nepali government's own priorities, directions and policies. To put it mildly, there was a significant lack of coordination and cooperation between the two parties. This led to some priority areas defined by donors getting excess aid, at the cost of other areas getting little to no attention. To compound things, an appalling lack of communication and coordination between different ministries and departments within the Nepali government itself caused significant confusion. As a result, there was considerable leakage and wastage of aid money, combined with an increasingly complicated bureaucratic structure to be negotiated for the disbursement of funds.

In 1976, in an attempt to coordinate aid from Western Europe, the US, Japan and the United Nations, the World Bank established the Nepal Aid Group. However, during the early years of donor assistance, the Nepali government's strategy was to get donors to compete with each other rather than establishing an integrated framework for aid that would best meet both Nepal's development needs and the donors' criteria. The government was of the view that getting donors to compete with one another was the best way to get the best deal. In the long run, the entrenchment of this attitude in the bureaucratic environment has made coordination with the Nepal government a difficult task for anyone. As a result of the geopolitical situation that Nepal found itself in, India, China and the USSR chose to remain outside the Nepal Aid Group while still providing aid to Nepal, which further reduced the coordination capabilities of the group.

In the 1980s, largely due to World Bank and IMF policy changes, the Nepal Aid Group had to adopt a conditional approach to releasing foreign aid and loans. These conditions included neo-liberal policy reforms and structural adjustments within a time-bound frame to ensure the release of funds. These measures were taken to ensure better accountability but also to enforce what the IMF and World Bank saw as necessary economic reforms. However, both the approach and its effectiveness came under increasing criticism and directly challenged the sovereignty of the nation that was coerced into enacting reforms. Critics argued that such reforms and impositions never took into account the actual capabilities of the bureaucracy and institutional capacity in being able to successfully implement them. As these reforms were not home-grown out of a need identified by the government and country, but were instead imposed by aid groups, there was a lack of a sense of ownership in Nepal with regard to them. Since the reforms were imposed on the government, the lack of interest in ensuring implementation meant that most of them were doomed to fail in practice. Madhukar Rana, an economist and a former finance minister, argues that the failure was because local data was fitted into an existing model, whereas for real success a local model should have been created from scratch. For instance, planning processes began with templates taken from other countries rather than trying to look at whether the information was relevant to Nepal.

For example, the World Bank poured in money during the late 1990s to revive the Nepal Bank and Rastriya Banijya Bank, which had half the deposits of commercial banks but were technically insolvent, which meant they did not have resources to repay loans. Despite this infusion of funds, the management teams could not deliver the desired results in terms of loan recovery. What was imposed at that time were guidelines on loan recovery practised elsewhere in the world, while in Nepal, in practice, no bank officer would have the guts to take on an existing business head, as there were definitely linkages with political powers to reckon with. Ken Ohashi, country director for the World Bank from 2000 to 2007, admitted that 'recovery of loans is more of an issue of political governance and cannot be resolved technically'. He also asked government, political and business leaders to use their influence in helping new management recover loans. Rather than getting into management contracts, if these banks were sold to international banks, the results would have been better. Since people in these management-contracted firms worked in positions for just a few years, the goals of turnaround could not be achieved. Given that the nature of such decisions of contracting is outside the control of the people leading the country offices of institutions like the World Bank, it may be that the same failed prescription is prescribed sometime in the future.

## Who Is a Donor?

The word donor or daata in Nepali is used very loosely to mean anyone who has anything to do with development or money.

It is not uncommon for people to refer to institutions like Save the Children or even CARE as donors. There is little understanding of how they function. In Nepal, there are five types of institutions that we see functioning. First, there are the multilateral agencies like the World Bank and ADB. Second, there are the UN agencies with their multiple theme-specific roles. Third are the bilaterals like DFID, USAID, SDC, etc., who sign bilateral agreements with the government and operate. Fourth, there are the INGOs who are basically not-for-profit organizations that implement projects and programmes on behalf of multilaterals or bilaterals with the objective of also making surpluses. Many of these entities have their for-profit arm also; therefore, profits rather than Nepal's development is their agenda. Finally, there are the NGOs that are registered in Nepal, which can range from family trusts to local sports clubs to religious institutions to large consulting firms to political bodies to cartels in the guise of associations. Apart from these NGOs, there are thousands that operate without registration.[2] So there is an NGO for every 600 Nepalis—nearly three times the number of doctors in the country. In 2018, a country like India with 1.3 billion had 13,000 (down from 33,000 just a few years ago), making one ask the big question: Why does Nepal need so many NGOs? What do these organizations do? Why is there a sort of mania in Nepal of wanting to be part of NGOs and taking on their leadership position? Why are Nepalis hell-bent on volunteering so much, as NGOs are supposed to be platforms to volunteer and are technically not a platform to rent-seek or earn money?

The entire development sector is not self-sufficient and self-sustaining. It is entirely dependent on and caters to the direction in which aid flows. At the top, INGOs, despite having their own sources of funds, play the role of effective managers for a large chunk of the money released by bilateral and multilateral organizations. Some scholars have accused the development sector of being too top-heavy, with a large chunk of the money entering the country being used up along the way as it trickles down to its intended targets. Further, the overheads of these institutions can be as high as 35 per cent, as noticed in some of the post-earthquake crowding of institutions.

It is very difficult to understand why, for instance, a multilateral like the World Bank or ADB that can work with the government or private sector directly will channel money through a bilateral agency, which in turn will hire a UN agency or an INGO that will then hire a local firm, which will body-shop people to get the task done. No convincing arguments have been made in support of why such a structure is required that eats up the bulk of the money intended for the betterment of the lives of the Nepali people.

Beyond consultation and overhead fees, there remains a fundamental Catch-22 with all development work. All development organizations are, as *development* organizations, working, on paper, towards their own redundancy and unemployment. To forestall such an outcome, mediocrity is built into the system—too much success threatens their own employment, too little threatens loss of funds. The donors themselves seem to emphasize this through the relatively quick rate at which they keep changing their leadership. Every three years or so, a new director enters the organization with his or her own set of agendas, working styles and preferences. On one hand, there is the Nepali staff which have to accommodate the whims of every new leader, while others perpetuate their own existence and drive the organization, knowing very well that the boss is only there for a short period of time. The insurgency allowed the development sector to hide all its inefficiencies and failures. The conflict became the golden ticket to not only excuse past failures but also to shift gears from the largely unsuccessful campaigns of poverty alleviation to that of conflict resolution and human rights. It also provided an excuse to hold lavish workshops and seminars in high-end hotels (rather than out in the field) to discuss the problem of poverty and the means to contain the insurgency. It is only in 2019, as Nepal is to graduate to a middle-income country by 2030, that the discourse around making development aid redundant has begun. Institutions like USAID are planning to make their exit plans, and some agencies have changed their mandate to work towards private-sector growth rather than working with the government.

## What Is Happening with Aid Around the World

There are many people who question this form of development through intermediaries who rent-seek on poverty brokering, and there is much written on the failure of aid. However, it is also important to understand how the landscape is changing. There are now foundations that have different ways of working and which look for results in a different manner. The Bill and Melinda Gates Foundation and other new-age philanthropists who make their money in the technology and innovation sector have been able to think differently. The other realization has been that the transformations that are required are long-term and no donor across the spectrum can look beyond three to five years. Further, the entry of China with its massive corpus of money will change how development partners operate and how the development sector will evolve. Already in the financing sector the China Development Bank (CDB) alone has significantly more assets under management than the multilateral development banks (MDBs) as a group.[3] Similarly, the Belt and Road Initiative (BRI) of China signed up $390 billion of deals in the first four months of 2018—that would be three times the Marshall Plan outlay of $13 billion or $130 billion in 2018 prices in four years.[4]

Strangely for Nepal, where most of the policies, laws and institutional structures are influenced by India and now also looking north to China, the realization never struck that both China and India did not push economic growth and development through aid money. It is very strange how Nepal believes it will be able to do great things through aid. While China pursued the state-controlled expansion of markets and the opening up of the economy, India pursued private-sector–led and public-sector–supplemented democratic systems. Both being aid recipients in the early 1960s, they have now been able to reduce their aid to GDP to negligible levels. Perhaps the absence of the feudal relationship of give and take in both countries, unlike in Nepal, prompted them not to be dependent on aid.

## AIDS or Acute Immune Dependency Syndrome

Ever since its first aid grant, and perhaps even before that, the Nepali psyche has adopted a mode of dependency. It has made itself believe that the country is entirely dependent on the goodwill of foreigners and will face major problems without foreign aid. It is here that the omnipresent and omniscient nature of the Nepali understanding of foreign aid is revealed. This rather nebulous understanding of foreign aid makes it seem as if it encompasses everything, while in essence it remains ambiguous and confusing. However, what remains consistent is the perception that foreign aid is a gift or favour bestowed upon Nepal. Ironically, this view echoes the view of the Panchayat government, which saw its works in national welfare as a gift or favour from the crown bequeathed upon the loyal subjects of the nation. In both cases, there is the creation of a hierarchy of supplicant and provider in the relationship, which precipitates an enduring dependency.

Ever since Nepal received its first shot of foreign aid, it became an aid junkie. It was entirely dependent on foreign aid to carry out development work for the first couple of decades after the Rana regime fell. Thus, the belief that Nepal has always been aid dependent is to some extent valid and justified. For instance, the First Five-Year Plan (1956–60) was completely reliant on foreign aid and almost all infrastructure projects since then have been financed through foreign aid. To its credit, Nepal has successfully tapped into aid money from a variety of sources and diversified its aid portfolio of countries and organizations representing the first world. This has made Nepal the most aid-dependent country in South Asia with the highest foreign aid to GDP ratio in the region. The haphazard and ambiguous way the government has carried out development can in part be explained by this cross-cutting of agendas. It was strange that even post-liberalization economies like the UK tried to provide aid rather than trade. As Dr Singha Bahadur Basnyat, former ambassador to the UK, remarked in a conversation with the author,[5] 'It is strange that a 200-year relationship with Nepal has not seen a single UK prime minister on an official visit to Nepal and no large investments or trade relations with the country.'

## Key Challenges with Development Assistance

While billions of dollars have been poured into projects, I always ask the people who are working on them whether they can look in the mirror and ask themselves if they have achieved what they wanted to and whether they have taken the dollar to the last mile. There are few who can then look me in the eye. For instance, someone who worked in a project that had spent over $80 million in twenty years on entrepreneurship development could not answer a basic question about the benefit of such a project. If that money had been distributed to the people it was meant to benefit, and they put the money in the bank and earned interest, they would have been better off. Another person who worked in the development agency for decades explained that perhaps the aid has helped the livelihood of a few Nepali employees, consultants and vendors to improve. Aid cannot do more than that!

The major challenges often discussed on the issue of aid can be grouped into four categories.

First is the issue of coordination. Both, donors and the government, are aware that development in Nepal has been significantly hampered due to a lack of collaboration and coordination. The first step in resolving this problem is for the government to know what it needs and to identify a long-term vision, which successive governments can pursue irrespective of their political and ideological standpoint. The Foreign Aid Policy in 2002 was the first step taken by the government towards creating a framework for the direction of foreign aid based on the needs and priorities of the nation, rather than that of individual donors.

Second is the issue of transparency. Fundamentally, all foreign aid that comes into Nepal is for the people of Nepal. This makes foreign aid a public good. Further, it also burdens Nepalis with foreign debt. Transparency and accountability on all foreign aid is not only justified but required. Irrespective of where the aid comes from or how it is used, disclosure of its source and maintaining an account of its spending is essential. Whether it is money donated by individuals for orphans in Nepal or big money grants for hydropower projects, both have to be transparent and accountable. As a public good, the lack of transparency is a violation of the right to information and raises questions of public accountability, fraud and corruption. Further, the awarding of contracts to implement aid programmes has been questioned, and the processes are still seen as opaque, with domestic firms forced to partner with selected shortlisted international vendors. The selection of local firms has always been questionable due to procurement processes that are interpreted in different ways.

The Nepali government at present does not have accurate information on all the aid that is flowing into the country. Although the bulk of it is recorded in the Red Book, the government's revenue record, there is a considerable portion of aid that remains undisclosed. For instance, a number of schools are directly funded by the Indian embassy without having to go through the government. Similarly, there are no records of Chinese assistance to school language programmes or exchange visits. The 1990s began a culture of misguided, unwarranted flooding of foreign money, totally unregulated and outside the budgetary framework. Without any regulatory frameworks or requirements to control and record such funding, donors and aid agencies are at liberty to intervene in Nepali society based on their own priorities, without consulting the government.

Third, as Madhukar Rana argues,[6] aid has a built-in incentive for corruption—constantly spending on the same thing provides more incentives for corruption and when this happens over successive short-term governments, the incentives only grow. He cites the example of the Middle Marsyangdi hydropower project, built with aid, which is being completed at many times the original cost and time, benefiting all the people making money from the project, be it in the form of salaries for the months of delay or hiring charges paid for vehicles and equipment. The golden rule being: the longer the delay, the greater the opportunity for self-enrichment. The lack of regulations, transparency and accountability placed on foreign aid is a direct result of a weak government.

Finally, there is the issue of creating threshold levels. For the government, managing multiple players in the arena of development assistance has been a difficult one. It is now important to categorize development assistance into different areas and have some laser-focused strategies for each. The current president of Afghanistan, Ashraf Ghani, during his tenure as finance minister, relates stories on how he created a threshold level for development assistance into Afghanistan. Some other countries follow similar strategies. Therefore, for engagement in Nepal a certain minimum limit has to be set to ensure that the government does not treat institutions that are putting in large amounts of money identically to those that provide negligible assistance. Former UN assistant secretary Kul Chandra Gautam calls on the 'cottage industry of development' to end, meaning that the government should work with the big ones in a more meaningful manner. Further, the time has come to also distinguish between agencies that bring money and those who execute projects. Understanding relationships between these different types of agencies will also help the dollar to go the last mile.

## Influencing Culture and Long-term Negative Impacts

In a country where the culture suggests that skin colour matters, the word 'gora' or 'white skin' is used to denote supremacy—a notion that goes back to the times when Nepalis served in the British army under British officers. Therefore, the acceptance of the gora supremacy infiltrated Nepal as it opened up. Further, the initial tourists who came to Nepal were rich people who could afford to spend a lot to be accompanied by staff carrying food and other amenities for their travels. The initial people who came to Nepal as risk-takers trying to help Nepal also included genuine people from Europe and the US who wanted to help Nepal and did not just intend to do a job. For instance, the US Peace Corps members made great contributions and continued to stay connected with Nepal. They also invested their personal resources in the country. Therefore, the imagery of the Western donor and his/her staff was of the real benevolent giver (daata); therefore, whatever they said was strongly believed. However, post-1990s, as Nepal opened up and the development business people in the garb of different institutions got into the mix, it left some marks and societal norms that will take a long time to reverse. In the following paragraphs we will discuss nine key ones.

First is the non-declaration of conflict of interest. Some INGOs and many NGOs have got a reputation of being an arm of power-brokers and political forces for furthering the goals of power and money. It is common in Nepal for NGOs to rent the house of the relative of a government official or political person or to give an NGO job to one of their family members. Everyone knows that to appease a politician, even a prime minister, it would not be wrong to work through his wife's NGO. It will be interesting to see a list of the sources of funding for such organizations run by 'politically affiliated' family members! This challenge is similar to the one in the corporate world on insider trading as to what is tantamount to conflict of interest when it comes to the Nepali stock market. So the argument thrown around is that if a director/shareholder of a company can indirectly operate a stock-brokering outfit that advises clients against the directive of the regulator, it is not surprising that the same happens in the NGO world.

Second is the institutionalization of bad practices. There are many that Nepalis have learnt. For instance, alcohol consumed at programmes gets billed as chilli chicken or some other food item to circumvent the rules. Meetings start to be held after office hours to facilitate payments to government officials and buy them dinner (again, alcohol will be billed as chilli chicken). The concept of per diems is widely used more as compensations. Air routes are reworked to accommodate visits of government and other officials to their relatives or get in some fun time at transit cities. This tradition of giving out allowances for attendance, popularly called *bhatta pratha*, was initiated by aid agencies in villages to compensate daily wage workers but it became even more popular in the cities. The donors started a tradition of compromising with transparency. For instance, in a governance project, a consultant is told to reduce rates but increase the number of days of involvement just to adhere to the rules. Thus, Nepalis have learnt to tweak many rules because they thought that was the way of life.

Third is the distortion of markets. With questionable accountability and the use of methods like showing alcohol in bills as chilli chicken, many distortions have been created in the market. Translation costs based on pages, designers billing in hours, the cost of hall rentals in hotels, paying high stipends to interns; the list goes on. Vendors for certain services and people working for these vendors have mastered the process of service provision in Nepal. They have captured the market and are now providing mediocre services at unaffordable rates. Now, private-sector firms are finding it more cost-effective to work with vendors from outside Nepal, where they at least know that they are getting their money's worth. Books by Nepali publishing houses are now being printed in India. Websites are designed in India for one-third the cost.

Foreign aid has also had a significant impact on the real estate market in the Kathmandu valley and other cities. Houses are often rented from people who are close to the renting agency's staff, while vehicles are rented from influential individuals at rates higher than the going market rate. These provide nice commissioning counters for development agency staff workers and a secondary source of income for well-placed and high-ranking officials. For instance, a politician or government official can request a particular aid agency to rent a vehicle or a house for office or residence premises from his or her relative. With no definitive procurement policies, these contracts are made at higher than market prices, thus allowing an indirect source of income for the concerned politician or government official.

Fourth is the distortion of the value of knowledge. In Nepal, when you ask people to go for training, the question that is asked is how much s/he will be paid. While this is a problem in many other developing countries where aid is pervasive, in Nepal, where literacy and comprehension levels are a challenge, this has created a perception across the country that one does not have to pay to gain knowledge, but has to get paid. This practice exists because training is a budget head that has to be spent by the organization that is conducting it.

Similarly, development agencies hire retired government officials who seem to have suddenly acquired the skill, competence and knowledge to perform miraculously better than when they were in a position of power. Such lopsided views have impacted project planning and implementation. The importance of issues like knowledge and competencies have been completely sidelined.

Fifth is the way that NGOs demean Nepalis by having different pay scales for Nepalis and non-Nepalis. This is not unlike Qatar, where, irrespective of your passport and country of residence, you are paid according to the colour of your skin. So even if you are an international Nepali consultant based out of Kathmandu and you command international rates in other markets, you will be paid Nepali rates as it is assumed that the cost of living for a Nepali is lower than that of an expatriate. I have personally faced this problem. This distinction in the workplace is made by addressing people who are paid in local rates with the suffix 'jee', denoting that they are different from those who are paid in US dollars and called by their first name.

Sixth, the development sector has perhaps impacted the private sector the most through the loss of some of the best people to development organizations. It remains an unfortunate feature of work in Nepal that people, during their most productive years, spend most of their time churning out reports, sitting through seminars and moving from one project to another. At the end of over fifteen to twenty years of work in the development field, many begin to question their work and its actual significance and impact. Having worked for over twenty years in a development organization, a senior development worker reflects that perhaps it has been a waste of time. He finds himself frustrated and the victim of a false dream. Perhaps what is most telling about his predicament is the feeling that he is stuck in a system that at his level becomes a tangible representation of imperialism.

Seventh are the major dichotomies that exist. People who work in a secure job are undertaking entrepreneurship development programmes to become entrepreneurs and strengthen the private sector. Similarly, people with entrepreneurial pursuits in villages have been brainwashed to become social mobilizers, tapping away on laptops and telling people how to run self-help groups rather than run businesses and employ people.

Eighth is the problem of emphasis on reports more than the work itself. Yet, the reporting demands placed on NGO workers are grossly overbearing. The success of their work in most cases depends on the quality of the report written about them rather than on their work. For instance, a water and sanitation project in the 1990s in the northern hills close to Manang was considered successful in building the targeted number of toilets. However, six months down the line, none of the toilets were usable as they were full of stones. The project implementers had failed to understand local customs and to realize that stones were a substitute for water or toilet paper in the region. A success story on paper, the work remained of poor quality. The heavy emphasis on reports makes it necessary for small NGOs to divert an excessive amount of funding towards report-writing by hiring expensive consultants with a good command over English. With what some claim to be the highest per capita number of reports, Nepal suffers from the 'project mentality'. This syndrome makes the report more important than the actual work. This mentality is prevalent not just in the development sector but is also well-entrenched in state-owned enterprises and government bureaucracy. Those infected with it will often propagate a problem so that the necessary reports justifying the continuation of a programme to solve it can be created. This helps them secure their seats. The logic is that the more problems that are identified, the more time is taken to find a solution, which will require more reports, all correlating to the minimization of work with maximization of income through salary. Passive until absolutely necessary, they act only when projects need to be displayed or inspected and when the possibility of funding increases.

Finally, there is the issue of the creation of a class of donorpreneurs. There are people who know how much money to take from which donor and how to do it. In this regard they are very entrepreneurial. In villages people know how to describe their village in the right lingo, explaining gender demographics and the number of Dalits, for instance.[7] Not only at a family level, but even big banks have been able to figure out which part of their expenses can be paid by a donor programme. These donorpreneurs move from one sector to the other, one programme to another, knowing very well what the next flavour of the month will be; it could range from an environmental study to Constitution-building to conflict resolution to climate change to gender mainstreaming to social inclusion to culture to agriculture. They will fight tooth and nail to keep the concept of free market and foreign investments away, as a better marketplace will endanger donorpreneurship. Such people never want to see Nepal graduate from the tag of a poverty-stricken country and will sell doomsday stories of disparity. They want to build houses to rent to the plethora of NGOs they would have founded, with friends and family, ensuring that there would be a steady income for their whole lives. They invest in cooperatives and promote Ponzi schemes but stay away from paying taxes. They oppose the payment of value-added tax (VAT) on consulting services or the shifting of a mandate of operations from the Social Welfare Council (SWC) to the office of the company registrar (OCR) as it will increase transparency and disclosure. They know how to get work and operate 'body shops' to ensure they hire people by paying less and making them work more, but charge more by billing more work days to the client. Of course, they are learning a lot from the international donorpreneurs who have mastered this craft in a big way.

## Of Course There Are Success Stories

Although this chapter focuses on the largely negative impact of the development sector, the success stories also warrant a critical analysis. The billions of dollars in foreign aid from the 1950s had a limited impact on poverty, education, health, gender disparity and the environment. However, there have been a few outcomes that highlight the potential of foreign aid when applied to the local context within the existing social structures, through the community, and with the intention of divesting ownership and rights to the local population. Within such a framework, sustainable living, entrepreneurship and ultimately the growth of a strong private sector is promoted.

In 2000, the Forestry Sector Policy, an updated version of the Forestry Master Plan Policy and subsequent amendments to that document, was released. This policy statement for the forests of the Terai, Churia hills and Inner Terai provided explicit management options for the forests in the hills and mountains of these regions. This gave rise to the increasing local management of community forests, which significantly benefited the livelihood of people. For instance, a community forest was established amongst the families using the forests, who then become members of forest user groups. They elect executive committee members for the management of forests, who initiate many income-generating programmes like handicraft-making, sawing, making agricultural tools, etc. The executive committee also decides on whether or not to provide loans, with the loan money mostly coming from taxes and fees levied upon the users of community forests in return for the proper management of these programmes. This became a seminal part of the work of Elinor Ostrom, the first lady to win the Nobel Prize in Economics in 2009.

Nepal's community forest success story is premised on participation and consensus, transparency, local decision-making, management and ownership. That is why there are provisions for the marginalized to also benefit from the local governance of community forests. The Forestry Master Plan of 1990 laid out these principles, and they are being followed till date.

A good example of the advantages of an effective assistance programme is the Nick Simons Institute (NSI) which was established as a philanthropic project of James and Marilyn Simons from the US in memory of their son, Nick, who had worked in Nepal as a volunteer and was concerned about the standard of healthcare in rural areas. The institute's mission is to train and support skilled and compassionate rural healthcare workers. Dr Bhekh Bahadur Thapa, chairperson of the NSI, says that it is an institute that runs under Nepali leadership and Nepali management, receiving only temporary input from abroad for the sole purpose of enhancing local capabilities and capacities. Such institutes that work on becoming genuinely Nepali institutions while receiving only endowments from foundations can pave the way for new aid architectures for Nepal.

Across the world, the development industry has been identified as being poverty-brokers that have built such monolithic institutions where only a fraction of the resources reaches the real people in need. The cost of the layers of bureaucracy and the fund-raising to manage overheads and other allied activities keep them occupied for most of the time. In Nepal, the discourse on poverty has been one that creates jobs for people other than those who are really poor. The mushrooming of NGOs and various organizations became vehicles of consumption, but even with investments of billions of dollars they could not get the desired results. Now the realization is that a $30 billion-plus economy with high asset valuation and remittance may not be seen in the same light as a $6 billion economy a few decades ago. Therefore, Nepal's future pace of economic growth will also depend on how the poverty-brokers can transform themselves into prosperity catalysts. In the long run, aid has to make itself redundant.

# 10

# Global Nepalis: Migration, Diaspora and Remittance

The concept of migration in Nepal is not viewed in a positive manner but is associated with hardships, challenges and separation from family. Popular writings and literature have mostly portrayed migration as a curse. In conservative Hinduism, crossing the oceans is actually said to make one impure. The proponents of nationalism treat people who migrate as people who don't have a sense of nationalism. There are thus multiple ways in which this issue can be viewed.

However, we need to understand that migration has existed throughout history, starting from when the first set of humans moved out of Africa. In Nepal, people came from the west, the north and the south, and this can be seen in the Kathmandu valley, which is itself a melting pot of migrants. The Shakyas migrated from Kapilvastu, the Kiraats migrated from the east, the Mongoloid tribes migrated from the north, and the set of rulers who ruled Nepal migrated from the south.

Until the advent of passports and strict travel processes after the World Wars, human movement was not curtailed. People travelled to faraway lands in search of economic opportunities or to escape wars and natural calamities or to get away from social problems. It was only after the restriction of human travel because of visas, passports and travel documents that the world of travel became complicated. The concept of viewing human migration in a way that links it with socio-economic issues and development is only a recent one, like the discourse on economic reform.

Therefore, in the context of Nepal, it is important to understand how society views human movement, how the discourse has changed over the years, how the development actors with a project mindset interpret it, how the movements have taken place till now, how the concept of diaspora has emerged and what all this has done to the economy in terms of financial remittances, exchange of cultures, changes in social behaviour and the overall impact on society. This chapter will weave perspectives into this discourse to contextualize migration to understand the past and look at the future. We will counter some of the major misconceptions around migration and discuss why Nepalis migrate while explaining the historical and cultural context. We will then understand the world of remittances and the Nepali diaspora, popularly known as non-resident Nepalis or NRNs.

## Migration Timeline

The first batch of migrants that went out of the Kathmandu valley would perhaps be the one that left with Princess Bhrikuti in the seventh century. Thereafter, in the twelfth century, Arniko triggered the culture of migrating for work and later for business too. With Tibetan Buddhism flourishing, craftsmen from Nepal found work building monasteries and furthering their craft in the Himalayan kingdoms.

However, the big exodus of people began after Rana rule was established in 1846 as a result of hardships faced under the regime and simultaneously to take advantage of growth in the region. It began with the cropping up of tea plantations in Assam and Darjeeling, which were labour-intensive, and their spreading further to Malaysia and Burma, which was then part of the same British empire and not different countries with borders.

The perception of migration as being bad perhaps stems from the enduring benchmark of success for all Nepali migrant workers: mercenaries in the service of the British and Indian armies. Sanctioned by the state in most cases, but equally a choice made by many young Nepali men, the exporting of mercenary soldiers or lahures has been a lucrative business in Nepal since the conclusion of the Anglo-Nepali war in 1816. The biggest deployment of Nepali soldiers was in the suppression of the Indian Rebellion in 1857, with many of them going on to settle in India. The ones in eastern Nepal in particular started looking eastward to settle in Bhutan, Darjeeling, Duars and Sikkim.

When rituals change, the migration floodgates open. There was a caste purification ritual called *pani patia*[1] that had to be performed on people who went outside Nepal. While it was waived for crossing the border to India in 1900, it was only in 1920 that it was completely abandoned for soldiers as well as others. This is seen as a key event in terms of migration being accepted within the society.

It is also important to understand the issue of internal migration within Nepal. Till the end of Rana rule, Nepalis from outside the Kathmandu valley, especially the Terai, needed a travel document to visit Kathmandu. With the Ranas in control of the valley through their army, business associates and administration, it was difficult to enter it. Further, due to caste issues that impacted daily life, including access to basics like water, there were challenges in terms of renting and finding places to stay in Kathmandu. It was generally people from the valley, especially the Newas, who had fewer travel restrictions, which resulted in them going to other parts of Nepal. It was only after 1950 that the travel floodgates opened, and Nepalis were free to move to any part of their own country. After 1990, with better road connectivity, people started moving to the Kathmandu valley and other urban centres. The valley's population grew from just half a million in 1980 to 5 million in 2018, a tenfold jump in less than forty years! Similarly, all urban centres saw massive migration from rural areas, like in other parts of the world. However, the ten years of conflict accelerated the process and the internal migration continued during the Terai movement that took place in the southern plains.

## World War I: Gorkhas Start the Remittance Economy

During World War I, the then prime minister of Nepal, Chandra Shumsher, had sent over 55,000 recruits to serve in the Gorkha regiments of the Indian army. On top of this, he had also sent around 18,000 Nepali soldiers into India to take over garrison duties. In total, including Nepali soldiers in the British army and those working for the British-controlled military police in Burma, it is estimated that over 2,00,000 Nepali men were involved in the war. Of this, over 10,000 were killed in action while another 14,000 were wounded or were missing in action. For his contribution to the war, the British provided Chandra Shumsher an annual subsidy of NPR 1 million, instead of the proposal of the Rana rulers returning some of the territories Nepal lost to the British in the Sugauli Treaty of 1816. The Rana rulers' unquestioning loyalty to the British was again demonstrated in their support for the British during World War II, in which over 2,50,000 Nepali recruits and soldiers are estimated to have played a role in the victory of the Allied forces.[2]

In the process of fighting for other countries, for causes that have never been their own, Nepali soldiers have earned a reputation for unparalleled ferociousness, loyalty and bravery in the face of insurmountable adversity. The Gorkhas have fought on the side of the British in almost every military campaign from 1816 to the present day. Conservative estimates place Gorkha casualty figures at 1,50,000 wounded and 45,000 killed in action in the two World Wars and other conflicts. More than 6500 decorations for bravery, including thirteen Victoria Cross awards and two George Cross medals, have been awarded to British Gorkha soldiers.[3]

## Migration Proliferates

In Burma before its independence, Nepalis were part of the British military police, and many Nepalis had settled there, especially those who had relatives and family in Assam, which was part of British India. After India became independent, north-east India started becoming a conflict zone, and with Burma gaining independence in 1951, the equations changed. With Rana rule ending in Nepal, those who were exiled felt it safe to return, and many others returned in the hope of being part of a prosperous New Nepal. The eradication of malaria in the Terai made large tracts of farmland available and migration lucrative. Many people from India and Nepal went on to settle there. We need to continuously remind ourselves that in those days no documentation was required to travel between India and Nepal.

Nepal also hosted around 16,000 Tibetan refugees who fled the conflict in their land. Another wave of Nepalis from Burma came to Nepal after the Burmese Citizenship Act of 1964. This was one of the biggest ethnic exoduses from Burma of people that were originally Indian and Nepali. In the late 1960s, many Nepalis fled north-east India after it became difficult for them to live in Mizoram and Meghalaya, and such trends continued till the 1980s in spurts. In 1970 it was recorded that 10,000 Muslims who fled the India–Pakistan war in East Pakistan (now Bangladesh) settled in the Terai district of Jhapa.

The demand for Gorkhaland, comprising the hills of Darjeeling and Duars in West Bengal in India, gained momentum in 1985, and many Nepalis left to save themselves from the brutality of the Indian security forces. In 1990, Nepal hosted the biggest flow of Nepali refugees from Bhutan, that at its peak numbered 1,07,000. These refugees later settled in the US, Europe and Australia, adding a new dimension to the composition of the Nepali diaspora, with around 10,000 remaining in Jhapa in 2018, waiting either to go back to Bhutan or receive Nepali citizenship.

# For Nepalis, Migration Is a Way of Life

Despite being in the business of exporting its human resources, Nepal showed little interest in capitalizing on a niche labour market in the global economy. Other than during the World Wars, when the ruling Rana aristocracy made a considerable profit exporting Nepali soldiers to the British army, there has hardly been any government interest in the area. However, the lack of government interest did not stop Nepali workers from dreaming of the riches to be earned in foreign lands. Taking full advantage of the porous and deregulated border it shares with its southern neighbour, India, a steady stream of Nepali workers set out into the world to pursue their dreams. Given the similarities in language, culture and tradition, India was easily the preferred choice for Nepali workers. In the 1952–54 census, around 1,57,000 Nepali workers were estimated to be working in India out of an estimated population of 8.25 million, accounting for around 2 per cent of the total population.

A tradition to go work in India as seasonal workers in the 1950s and 1960s intensified and an increasing number of Nepali youth made their way south. Part of the reason that these workers chose to go to India rather than Kathmandu was because the big Indian cities remained considerably more accessible, due to road linkages, than Kathmandu and also held more opportunities.

During the 1960s, it was estimated that at any point in time, around 25 per cent of the entire population was on the move, either going home after working or seeking work elsewhere. Of this, as many as 87 per cent of those travelling were male workers. This trend of overseas migration also encouraged internal migration and resettlement, with the bulk of the migration happening from the hills to the Terai as well as to urban centres. By the 1980s, the bulk of the population had shifted from the hills to the Terai, with the hill population decreasing through migration by 20 per cent in twenty years.[4] Migration to the Terai was made more attractive by the availability of land there in the 1960s, through deforestation and the proximity of the Terai to India as a destination for seasonal work. The preferred destination of most Nepali workers before the 1990s, India still accounts for a substantial portion of the migrant workforce, with estimates as high as a couple of million Nepali citizens being there. India also provides a considerable market for seasonal migrant workers from Nepal who spend a few months working in India during the non-farming months and then return home during the farming season. By 2018, interestingly, many Indian workers were coming to Nepal during the harvest season because of the shortage of male agricultural workers.

The Gorkhas have effectively carved out a name for themselves at home and abroad with their khukris,[5] a utility knife that has become a symbol of bravery. As Nepal entered the modern era in the 1950s, the legendary success of the Gorkhas in foreign armies in foreign lands was already well known. The Nepali economy had defined its comparative advantage and its primary export: its loyal, trustworthy and brave youth. Simultaneously, the Gorkhas who came back home brought with them tales of technology and progress that were unheard of, and a world richer than their wildest dreams. Most importantly, the Gorkhas who returned were richer than anyone else in the village. This was the myth of the money and success nurtured by the bideshi (foreign) Nepali workers or *bipali*s.[6]

When the Indian prime minister, Indira Gandhi, declared a state of emergency and invoked autocratic powers in the 1970s, India started reeling under an economic and political crisis. Then a large number of young Nepalis who traditionally went to India started to look farther afield. The oil boom in the Middle East during the 1970s provided the perfect destination for such aspiring youths. By the 1980s, the opening up of labour markets in Korea, Japan and the Middle East provided the opportunity to work for greater rewards than the stagnating state-controlled economy back home. However, restrictions on passport issuance in Nepal encouraged many Nepali citizens to go through India as Indian citizens or through illegal channels. Even those who could get their hands on passports often found it easier to transit to their destination countries through India due to limited air links from India and tardy visa processes. Additionally, given Nepal's weak financial system, these workers had to take loans either from their immediate family or from moneylenders. All this—loans, illegal transit through India, etc.—was part of the risk of going abroad. Much like the mercenary lahure of old who put his life on the line for his money, this new breed put everything, including their integrity and property, up for sale for the opportunity to make a living. These workers became the tragic heroes of contemporary Nepal.

## Understanding Migration in Nepal

While there are different types of migration, the primary reasons for taking it up can be multiple: first, to migrate and not return; second, to migrate and work for a long period of time and return; and third, comprising the biggest segment of people, to work for a short period of time and return.

With over 5,00,000 people coming into the job market in Nepal each year, and only 50,000 jobs added, the only option for people is to migrate. We therefore need to understand that migration has acted as a safety valve against the accumulation of a large number of unemployed and disenchanted youth in the country. We need to imagine the dreadful situation when the country has to deal with millions of unemployed youth.

The categories of those who migrate can be divided into people with high skills, medium skills, low levels of skill and no skills. Like in any volume and value game, the bottom two categories have the highest numbers but may not necessarily add the highest value.

The Nepal government's laws mandate that people who leave the country as students need to get a No Objection Certificate from the Department of Education, and those who leave for work need to get a permit from the Department of Foreign Employment (DoFE).[7]

In the 2017–18 fiscal, DoFE issued 3,54,082 permits to people going to 142 different countries. It is interesting to see the list of countries as one wonders what people do there—808 to Algeria, 316 to Romania and 3620 to Poland. Also interesting to note is that 22,417 of these permit applicants are women. 3,23,877 of these permits were issued through different agencies registered with DoFE. The fact that 1072 agencies were in business that year, with the highest one sending just 5804 people, or less than 2 per cent, explains how fragmented the businesses are.[8] It is now estimated that more than 3 million Nepalis are working outside Nepal. This means one person in every third household has someone working outside Nepal.

## In Search of Migration

From migrating only for work, the tendency now has been to look for permanent migration. This trend has been visible especially after the advent of the Internet as agencies can use search engines to fetch information and sell dreams to different parts of the world. Nepalis are currently settled in 130 countries with seventy-five of these countries having a chapter of the Non-resident Nepali Association (NRNA) that was just established in 2004. There are different ways in which such migration has taken place, and we now discuss three prominent ones.

Hong Kong ID: There are many Nepali songs and stories about the Hong Kong settlement scheme popularly known as 'Hong Kong ID'. There were many people who purchased fake birth certificates and submitted them to British Overseas National Passport (BONP) agents, allowing them visa-free entry to the UK as well as access to many other countries.[9] This was one of the biggest scams people used to discuss in 1996, the window year before Hong Kong was returned to China. Stories of people changing names, caste, religion and their future have been told in many popular stories and songs of that time.

Diversity Visa (DV)—the Most Sought-after Immigration Programme: A programme to increase diversity in the US population was initiated in 1995, and since then, the diversity visa, popularly known in Nepal and Nepali language as DV, was provided to 50,000 people through a lottery system. In Nepal, this has been one of the most sought-after programmes with close to a million people applying each year. For the last five years, the number of successful DV applications for Nepalis has ranged from 3247 to 3504. In 2017, 3477 diversity visas were issued, making it nearly 7 per cent of the total DVs issued that year.[10] Nepal's 8,92,961 applications out of 14.4 million total was ranked behind five other countries.[11] When nearly a million out of 20 million able-bodied people, or 5 per cent of the population, apply for visas in the quest to migrate out of Nepal, it reflects the mindset of the Nepali people.

The DV concept created its own industry, from places to fill forms to portals that market success rates. Online portals and others have raked in millions, helping people fill forms and fulfilling other requirements, such as submitting photographs that fulfil all visa specifications, which is not required, as per the US embassy's continuous communications. Further, many other things started being linked to DVs. For instance, when zero tolerance was introduced for drunk driving, the rumour on the street was that if you were caught three times then you would not get a police certificate, which is required for DV applications. Similarly, when students were burning tyres on the streets or protesting, there were again rumours that the US embassy was tracking all pictures being published on social media and papers regarding protests and any involvement would lead to rejection. By 2018, more than 50,000 Nepalis had settled in the US through the DV programme. They then sponsor their families and also enable them to become US citizens in the long run. The US Nepali is sought after for marriage as it provides the husband or wife an opportunity to become a US citizen and have children who will be born as US citizens. There are agencies that are well known for matchmaking and which do roaring business just on the basis of word of mouth. The Nepali population in the US has increased from just 9000 in 2000 to 1,50,000 in 2015 with 83 per cent of them being there for less than ten years.[12]

Gorkha Programme in the UK: In May 2009, through a historic decision in the UK Parliament, Gorkhas who retired before 1997 with at least four years' service were allowed to settle down in the UK. This included their family members too. Many people took up this offer and moved lock, stock and barrel to leave Nepal to take up the passport of a country which they had served and been willing to sacrifice their lives for. Aldershot, near London, is now referred to as Little Kathmandu or Little Nepal.

## A Passport Is Perceived as the Road to Prosperity

There are four categories of migrants. First, a small number are people who have high-level skills, like doctors, accountants and nurses who migrate to the UK, Australia or Europe. Second, there are students who go to the US, the UK and Australia for education and never return to Nepal. The third category comprises semi-skilled workers—plumbers, carpenters, mechanics, etc.—who migrate to countries in the Middle East, South East Asia or Korea. Finally, there are a significant number of unskilled workers who leave, mostly for India.

The source of inspiration for the bipalis is not hard to identify either: the desire to get away from an existence full of impoverishment and unemployment. The financial success and social respect earned by returning bipalis adds to the allure of working in foreign lands. Lack of strong economic growth, hardly any examples of entrepreneurial success, and the continuation of a feudal system of chakari and nepotism, meant that working in Nepal held no promise or hope. It also made many ambitious young Nepalis look beyond the borders. With the establishment of multiparty democracy in 1990, steps were taken to liberalize the market for foreign labour. The most significant of the democratic government's acts was the decentralization of passport control so that issuing passports was now the responsibility of the district offices. Until then, passports were issued only by the Ministry of Foreign Affairs in Kathmandu. But with decentralization, anyone could obtain a passport from their local district office within a week of applying. The availability and ease of access to passports had an immediate and drastic impact on labour migration. Suddenly, every Nepali had the opportunity to become a bipali.

The Government of Nepal started issuing machine-readable passports (MRP) from 26 December 2010 and had issued 5 million passports till 31 May 2017, earning a revenue of NPR 19.26 billion ($190 million).[13] Nepali passports are expensive, being priced at a minimum of NPR 10,000 ($100) and a maximum of NPR 15,000 ($150),[14] one of the highest prices of passports in the world, on a par with costs in the US and the UK.

## Exploring Destinations: Visa Is the Key

In Putali Sadak, downtown Kathmandu, there is signage that advertises the capacity of a company in delivering visas to many countries. Apart from Australia, the UK and the US, you can find practically every country seen on a world map, from Estonia to Hungary to Poland to Costa Rica. These agencies lure students with the promise of enrolling them in study programmes in different countries for a fee while guaranteeing visas to the respective countries. Advertisements for colleges in Kathmandu do not talk about how good the college is but focus on assuring you that you can get a visa to the UK, Australia or an affiliated country. In the 2017–18 fiscal, the Ministry of Education, Science and Technology (MoEST) disclosed that 93,808 students wishing to study abroad received NOCs from the ministry. The highest number of these students were 51,334 to Australia. It is mandatory for Nepalis who are going for studies abroad in a legal manner to obtain these NOCs.[15] More than 1500 agencies involved in the business of issuing visas are registered with the MoEST.

There are many stories we hear from friends and family on the different sorts of scams that have emerged over the years. One of the interesting ones is the promise of providing a dependant visa through marriage with a student who has a study visa for nursing in Australia. Generally, girls who have the visa get offers from boys whose families are willing to pay the living costs and even a semester's fees to the girl. The agencies then arrange all documents relating to the marriage including photographs of fake functions that are held in the full attendance of families from both sides. The extent to which Nepalis can invest for their children to get a visa baffles many.

Similarly, a much sought-after destination in Europe is Portugal, where there are an estimated 30,000 Nepalis. Portugal provides a gateway to many other countries in the European Union (EU). In recent years, Poland has replaced Portugal as the sought-after destination for Nepalis to get an entry into the EU. More scams appear each day as Nepalis look for greener pastures.

## Money Matters: The World of Remittances

In Nepal, a large part of the rural economy was sustained through remittances from Nepalis in the British and Indian armies, along with other security forces and workers from India. However, interest and accounting of remittances has become even more important as the total remittance crossed the billion-dollar mark in 2005. In 1993, the remittance to GDP was just 1.5 per cent, as recorded in the World Bank report. It swelled to 28.31 per cent in 2018.[16] However, we also need to understand that in Nepal data only starts appearing when institutions like the World Bank get interested, as the Nepal government has never seen the value of data or research. Till 1971, remittances from Gorkhas were higher than receipts from tourism or exports.[17] However, accounts at those times were neither properly done nor disclosed as they are now.

Till 2002, there were no formal channels to remit money to Nepal and it was done through informal channels. There is an extensive informal system, a culture and society of recruitment and money transfer that has developed in Nepal. Migratory patterns suggest that once a person has established himself abroad, he will attempt to draw his relatives and local villagers to the same place. This allows for a semblance of home away from home and provides a social security net in case of sickness or injury. The act of being able to place others in jobs abroad also means an increase in stature for the recruiter back home.

Along with this support network, the collection of relatives and villagers also allows for an easier and cheaper means of money transfer. Usually, when one worker goes home on leave, all other workers within his circle send money home through him. This avoids the cost of transferring money through other informal or formal channels. Workers also tend to use the *hundi* and hawala systems of money transfer, which are informal systems that rely on an informal business transaction mechanism and are often part of money-laundering rackets. The attractiveness of the hundi system is both economic and cultural. Economically, hundi is cheaper, faster, more versatile and more far-reaching geographically than banks or money transfer companies. Culturally, the people who run the system are trustworthy members of the community and there is some tie of kinship, ethnicity or personal relations between the users and the operators. The operators generally tend to make money through a minimal service charge or take advantage of the exchange rate spread. For example, in October, 2016, ten foreigners including Nepali and Chinese hundi agents were caught in Korea by the Gyeonggi Nambu Provincial Police Agency. They were found allegedly operating a 'hundi business' by transferring some $44.4 million over five years from Korea to Nepal.[18]

Effective 29 March 2002, the Nepal Rastra Bank had begun granting licences to private-sector organizations interested in the remittance-transfer business. All commercial banks during that period of time started to get into this business. The usage of formal financial services to receive remittance increased dramatically, and by

2016, 52 per cent of the remittances were received through the formal channel.[19] IME Remit is one of the pioneers in remittance transfers today and boasts of 1,50,000 locations worldwide. Its subsidiary in Malaysia, IME (M) SDN BHD, was bought out by global player Ria in June 2015 and it thereafter expanded to the Middle East.

The United Nations Capital Development Fund (UNCDF) Nepal Making Access Possible Report 2016 that I co-authored examined the utilization of remittances. It is estimated that 57 per cent of Nepali adults who receive remittances spend the money on buying food: only 14 per cent save the remittance money, while only 7 per cent use it to buy land or a house and only 7 per cent use it to invest in business.

The common misconception is that remittance of the value of $7 billion in 2018 is sent by low-skilled workers in the Middle East, Malaysia and South Korea. However, the source of remittance tells a different story. The US emerges as a major source of remittance after Malaysia and this can be attributed to the significant increase of Nepalis in the US after the DV programme.[20] With over 4 million people working in India, the estimates of remittances from India to Nepal can just be guessed.

However, with the increase of Indian workers in Nepal, it is estimated that in 2017 $3 billion was remitted from Nepal to India from 6,00,000 Indian workers in Nepal. This makes Nepal the number eight destination for remittances to India ahead of even Canada and Australia.[21]

## Conflict Pushes, Remittance Surges

The escalation of the Maoist insurgency during the 1990s added yet another incentive for young men and women to seek employment in foreign lands. The sudden rise in foreign workers was a boon in disguise for the Nepali economy. With hardly any economic growth in the country, the growing volume of remittance money flowing in was able to prop up the national economy, enabling it to avoid a complete collapse. The surge in remittance flow also helped bring into public debate the previously little-talked-about economy of foreign labour migration. The growing realization of the volume of money involved in the business of labour migration quickly got the private sector interested. However, the government took almost another decade to establish a body to address the needs of these Nepali workers. The lack of government regulation and worker rights has possibly ruined the lives of countless poor Nepali workers who were cheated by swindlers and shady manpower agencies that allowed for massive amounts of profiteering and large-scale fraudulent activities. Nonetheless, deteriorating economic conditions at home meant that the number of Nepali workers going abroad in search of work kept increasing.

With such a booming labour supply industry, the private sector quickly got into the act both in terms of supplying labour and ensuring proper training and in setting up channels for the flow of remittance money. The objective of manpower or human recruitment agencies is to serve as a link between Nepali workers seeking work and foreign companies looking for workers abroad. These agencies are responsible for matching the worker with a job and arranging visas, air travel and documentation. They are also responsible for conducting medical check-ups, job orientation and training to make sure the worker has some understanding of his job. However, most of these agencies have acquired a poor reputation and are approached with suspicion. This is largely due to a weak government that cannot oversee these companies to ensure they follow standard regulations that protect the workers.

Although manpower agencies have established themselves as the primary channels through which to gain access to foreign employment, the lack of trust in them has emphasized the importance of informal channels. Particularly in India and more recently in some regions of the Gulf, entire Nepali villages have captured the niche market of migrant workers. This has led to local migrant labour monopolies; for instance, it is estimated that almost all Nepali migrant workers in and around the city of Bengaluru are from Bajhang district in Nepal. Such trends have been established in the Gulf as well.

## The World of the NRN

The origin of the phrase 'non-resident Nepalis' is copied from India, where non-resident Indian (NRI) is used. In both countries, the word 'non-resident' actually relates to income tax laws, where a person is not liable to pay income tax if they are non-resident, which meant they spent 180 days outside the country. However, the term in both countries started being used as a substitute for diaspora.

The movement to recognize NRNs began when people of Nepali origin returned to invest in Nepal or returned after a stint in an international organization. The NRNA was established in 2003. At that time, there were less than half a million Nepalis in about forty-two countries and the association had less than 1000 members. These people lobbied hard for new laws to govern NRNs, and finally in 2007 the Non-resident Nepali Act was promulgated and in 2009 the NRN Rules were enforced. The promulgation of these pieces of law technically meant that NRNs, who are not citizens of Nepal, could purchase land, acquire assets and invest in Nepal, and also have dual citizenship in the case of certain countries.

The NRNA through its different regional bodies and chapters has tried to pull the diaspora together but there are many challenges. First, around 2003, the concept of the overseas worker, coarsely referred to as migrant labour, had not gripped Nepal so much. NRNs were still a niche group of people. Second, the NRNA was not envisioned as a political organization, but with 3 million votes up for grabs, they have become one of the significant influencers in terms of the vote bank as well as sources for the funding of political parties. Third, the organization has now become very much like any other organization in Nepal where elections to key positions are fought on party lines and millions are spent to be able to take up voluntary positions. With a fraction of NRNs as its members, the NRNA has not been able to drive the transformation of the role of the NRN. Therefore, the definition of NRN can mean anything from New Rich Nepali to Non-required Nepali.

## Benchmarking the NRNA with Global Organizations

Now that the NRNA has national councils in seventy-five countries and Nepalis in over 100 countries, the organization needs to find global benchmarks and not function like a Nepali NGO that lives from one election to another. The current membership base of 50,000 of the NRNA is only a fraction of the 4.5 million people who continuously need help, support and networking opportunities of different kinds. It needs to see whether it can adopt a global model like the Rotary, where a small city-level, zonal-level, national-level and continent-level organizational structure can be developed.

Further, the organization needs to split between the part that looks after the interests of its members and the part that does charitable work. For the second part, a global foundation needs to be perhaps created that is domiciled in Singapore or the US or a country that has strict governance codes, accountability and transparency. There are many institutions that are willing to partner, but winning trust is going to be important.

It is also important to ensure that the governance structure is fixed, with a voluntary elected council but a strong secretariat that hires the best of the global talent. Money is the least of the issues to bring about this structural change; mindset is the major one!

## Keeping Politics Out

The diaspora has inherited all the problems of Nepali politics, and political parties continue to exist in the diaspora community. Elections are stalled, and various stages of litigation have become common. For Nepali political parties, the large vote bank continues to make their mouth water and they never want to let go of the opportunity of trying to further their penetration. This has brought about a swelling majority of silent folks who just avoid diaspora organizations like a plague. Yes, political parties may recruit a few sycophants who may provide some funds in exchange for favours, but they have left a bad taste as far as the diaspora goes.

If the diaspora community is to stay engaged in politics, why don't they engage in the politics of their adopted country rather than filling up social media with hate comments about Nepal? The elections of Harry Bhandari and Pradeep Dhakal in US local elections in 2018 is a sign of Nepalis getting engaged in the politics of the country they have chosen to be a citizen of.

## Challenges and Opportunities

In this context it is important to understand what some of the key developments within the diaspora community have been.

## Politics of Associations

Once, when attending a diaspora conference, I was informed that there are hundreds of Nepali-related associations in the US, out of which close to sixty are in the Washington DC area, and over seventy in the New York area. The associations are apparently across different professions, ethnic groups and objectives. Many stories are heard about the politics in the associations being similar to what is seen in Nepal. It is still difficult to figure out why a particular designation of a voluntary organization is so sought after. It is very difficult to understand why Nepalis continue to lust after positions in not-for-profits, where they are in principle supposed to actually contribute rather than benefit. Is it because of the fact that due to our feudal past we like to cling on to the concept of the ruler and the ruled, therefore desiring leadership positions to have followers? Is it that designations of such organizations get easy access when you want to connect with institutions in Nepal or the US? Is it true that to really do impactful social work, it is important to have a powerful designation in more than one institution? Is it purely the ego of the human being inside us that leads to continuously wanting to have an identity? The politics of many such organizations have also kept out many younger global Nepalis who want to contribute and make a positive difference.

## Behavioural Issues

There is yet to be a credible study done by a Nepali to understand the behaviour of the Nepali diaspora. During my personal travels and work in different countries, I got to encounter many Nepalis working in menial jobs for leading multinational companies. Some of the observations continuously made me wonder if there was a pattern or a trend around the Nepali way of living. Here are some observations.

There are two distinct groups of diaspora Nepalis at two ends of the spectrum: one that simply wants to be associated with being Nepali or with Nepal, and the other which consists of people who are more Nepali than Nepalis in Nepal. This latter group, irrespective of social or economic strata, finds comfort and solace with family members and members of their clan, mingling little with outsiders. This has resulted in Little Nepal areas in multiple countries. In the US, one can find areas that have people from the same ethnic group and the same district. This has led to children born in the US facing difficulties in integrating with members of other groups. Their food preferences have not changed much as Nepalis are not very fond of going out of their comfort zone of meat, rice, dal and vegetables. Some Indian and Chinese food once in a while is tolerable but you find only a small proportion of people sampling international food. With an increase in the Nepali diaspora, many Nepali restaurants have opened in other countries that follow the hygiene and service standards of Nepal. As I chatted with a restaurateur in Jackson Heights, New York, in one of the twenty-odd Nepali restaurants I chose to visit, I shared my disappointment about how we had waited for them to bring US business and service standards to Nepal, while they have happily transported Nepal's mediocre standards to the US.

Similarly, Nepalis across various income and social segments find weekend time to do barbeques, drink, play cards and talk about Nepali politics. Like their disinterest in figuring out the history, culture and natural beauty of Nepal, they are least interested in the museums, places of natural beauty and cultural places where they actually live. With the growth in their earnings, they are spending on social and religious rituals and competing in the same things that they did when they were back home. Further, with the rise of social media, they keep themselves busy discussing the issues and politics of Nepal, flooding websites with comments about a country they have left.

## Alienating the Young Generation

The audience of events in various diaspora programmes are not different from the ones back home—there are very few young people and women. While it is easy to comment on the old leaders in Nepal not giving in to the new generation over drinks and on social media, it is important to also think how young people will be engaged in diaspora events and leadership. The photograph of thirteen men on stage at a regional event of the NRNA held in Rome went viral. People questioned the absence of women and young people.

Why would second-generation Nepalis in the US come to conferences and listen to politicians making long speeches in Nepali? Why would they engage with an organization with whose website they cannot interact? Usage of Nepali is a cultural tool, but such nationalism is also used as a good veil to cover incompetency, unwillingness to change and lack of desire to compete on global levels.

The difference between Ethiopia and Somalia in Africa is that in the former, the second-generation diaspora kept returning and keeping in touch with their country unlike in the latter, where people just did not care. Nepal's hope lies with the second-generation Nepalis around the world who have better education, financial resources and networks than their earlier generation. Diaspora organizations need to think how to get the second generation excited, either by building exchange programmes, education programmes or work programmes. The clash of generations is everywhere, but it is also very clear from the learnings of many countries that the ones who have done well have understood how to unleash the potential of the second generation.

## The Growth of the Diaspora Market

The increasing diaspora has created two major impacts: one, a large market for visitors to Nepal who come for social functions or visiting friends and family, and the second, the demand for Nepali products outside Nepal. As discussed above, since Nepalis like to be in their comfort zone as far as food is concerned, there has been an increase in the export of Nepali essentials. For instance, the price of timmur or Himalayan peppercorn has increase multifold. Buffalo meat, which used to be half the price of chicken, has suddenly become more expensive than chicken as exports of dry buffalo meat—popularly called sukuti—increased. From dried radish to seeds of green leafy vegetables, the list is endless. An entrepreneur who is producing home-made pickles for the diaspora market shared that her estimate of the export of pickle just to the US was close to $1 million per month. The prices of bottled local pickles in Kathmandu have increased three times in the past five years. Similarly, the demand for traditional clothes has increased and companies have Facebook pages on which you can order them to your doorstep in other countries. During the festival of Dasain, people may gift animals for slaughter at family festivals and conduct pujas at shrines through e-commerce portals; the items required for rituals can be bought online.

Priests who conduct rituals have started being flown into other countries from Nepal as people are also figuring out that with large guest lists and increasing costs in Nepal, it is actually cheaper to organize social rituals and events like coming-of-age ceremonies and marriages in their home country rather than travel to Nepal.

## Diaspora Successes

In a nice bar around Dupont Circle in Washington DC, many young Nepali professionals huddle together to meet and chat. Hosted by Tshering Sherpa, who works with a financial advisory firm, many young folks turn up for the event. I went there to catch up with some young professionals who had spent time at Beed and the Nepal Economic Forum. Some of them work at the World Bank, others work for different global companies while some are pursuing their doctoral studies. It was different from the time I had met young people in the early 2000s during the few months I spent in Washington at a fellowship with the World Bank, when some senior Nepali professionals used to think it was beneath their dignity to meet other Nepalis. Many avoided referring to the fact that they were Nepali. But at this later meeting, the discourse was not about politics in Nepal; it was about different global issues, and the key challenges to global development, be it in the UK or the US. It was music to one's ears.

In every country, there are many Nepalis who have taken up iconic positions. In the US, Prabal Gurung has become a big name in the fashion industry and many others have followed in his footsteps. In Australia, Shesh and Jamuna Ghale feature in the list of richest Australians. Kumud Dhital in Australia was part of the team of surgeons that completed the world's first 'dead heart' transplant. In Germany, Jiba Lamichhane opened a chain of hotels. There are many who have made it to senior positions in global organizations, and it is only a matter of time before we see a Nepali leading a Fortune 500 company. In academics, many Nepalis are now featured in journals and papers. In culture, Nepali writers and artists are making their mark. It is just the beginning; there will be many more to come.

# Nepal's Future in between China and India

India and China are growing rapidly and will continue to do so at a rate that will definitely be higher than the growth rate of many developed nations. By 2050, it is estimated that China and India will be the top two economies in the world in terms of GDP, followed by the US. The economic growth activity that shifted to Asia at the beginning of the twenty-first century will be dominant throughout. The Shanghai–Mumbai axis will continue to dominate the agenda of future markets, economic development and global economic thought leadership. Nepal falls right in the middle of all this. Furthermore, the Association of Southeast Asian Nations (ASEAN) countries have shown consistent growth, and other nations in South Asia, sans Pakistan, are also showing signs of being on the right track. The emergence of Myanmar as an open society and economy will shift curiosity to the region.

China and India controlled 80 per cent of the global trade and economy in the beginning of the second millennium, and by the beginning of the nineteenth century, it was still at around 70 per cent.[1] Thereafter, they were dislodged by the US, and as the industrial revolution began, other nations too began to follow suit as the trade of basic goods was substituted by innovation, technology and manufacturing. Nepal is land-linked with both China and India. It shares an open border with India, and China provides preferential treatment to Nepal's border towns and people. This chapter will therefore examine a fresh perspective on Nepal's economic future vis-à-vis the neighbourhood. In this chapter, an attempt is made to provide a historical idea of what defines Nepal's relations with China and India, how the two countries are transforming, as well as issues of perception and how an integrated approach is required to look at new subregional paradigms and border economic zones (BEZs).

## Historical Perspective

The major economic factor that drove the unification process under King Prithvi Narayan Shah was gaining access and control of the primary trading and financial hub along the trade route between China and India. Throughout the 104-year Rana rule, the oligarchs sought to develop close relations with the British as it served their political interests. The country and its people were kept in isolation while the Ranas opted for a policy of appeasement towards the British. The relationship with China was on the wane after the new route to Tibet through India dislodged the one through Nepal.

India's capital was moved from present-day Kolkata, which was in proximity to the Himalayan neighbours of Bhutan, Nepal, Sikkim and Tibet, to New Delhi in 1912. Kolkata then also had easy access to Burma, then part of British India, through what is now Bangladesh, as well as India's north-eastern states, an economically vibrant region. The shift of the capital from Kolkata changed the relationship of India with the Himalayan kingdoms forever. New Delhi has never been able to understand its relationship with countries that are distant from its thoughts, culture and economic sphere of influence. The Ranas could not cultivate a relationship with Delhi as they had with Kolkata, a city where they had tremendous influence, owning prime real estate at the heart of the city and maintaining close friendships with the rulers and families of those times.

The Sino-Indian war of 1962 brought Nepal's importance into the equation as the buffer that both countries did not mind. If India and China had to extend their armies on the border with Nepal, it would have been a big cost for both sides. So keeping Nepal happy and secure continued to be in the best interests of both parties. With the cooling down of tensions between China and India, and the opening of China's markets in 1978, China was more than happy to have India handle the domestic and political issues in Nepal. China's only interest in Nepal was to ensure that Nepal accepted the One China policy, and it did not want any activities against it on account of Tibet. This was communicated to the Nepali governments, from successive kings to the political leaders. It was only after the earthquake of April 2015 that China started taking an interest in Nepal. And as India imposed a major blockade the same year, China was made to think beyond economic interests and understand the issues that plagued Nepal.

In a face-saving deal to mend relations after the blockade, in 2016, a six-member Eminent Persons Group (EPG) was formed with high-level representation from India and Nepal to revisit the 1950 treaty and suggest amendments and a different framework. The EPG tenure ended on 4 July 2019 and the report they submitted to both prime ministers only had ceremonial value. In an interview, one of the members from the Nepal side, Surya Nath Upadhyaya, indicated that the report would not be acceptable to India as Nepal had pushed the agenda of monitoring the movement of people on the border through identity cards.[2]

With the US receding into its own cocoon, globalization on the world stage was captured by China. Since 2017, it became the enabler of connectivity, world trade and dependency as it pushed the BRI. After the blockade, Nepal reached out to China, and a Protocol of Transit Transport Agreement was signed with China on 7 September 2018. For the first time in over a century, Nepal now had the option of diversifying its transit, trade, investment and economic risks.

## Modernizing the Special Relations with India

For most Nepalis, India remains a destination for education, medical treatment, religious rites and tourism. Of course, it functions as a punching bag for anything that is not satisfactory within their own country. In Nepal, nationalism has for many decades been equated with being 'anti-India', and this sentiment is whipped up regularly by all politicians, whether right wing or left, in order to secure maximum electoral weight. However, the same politicians also believe that their longevity—in or out of power—is decided by New Delhi.

India has remained a key trading partner of Nepal since time immemorial. It enjoyed considerable influence in Nepal because of social, cultural and linguistic proximity. Trade flourished due to Nepal's dependence on India as a landlocked country and also because of the open border between the two. Since India's independence, India has accorded 'special relation' status to Nepal, which guides its Nepal policy till date.

Nepal signed a Friendship Treaty in 1913 with British India to get access to the nearest transit point of Kolkata. Nepal and India signed the first bilateral comprehensive treaty including trade and transit in the year 1950. This was renewed in 1960 and 1971 subsequently. Thereafter, in 1978, the trade and transit treaty was bifurcated and a separate transit treaty was signed. The new treaty recognized the transit right of a landlocked country, which is separate and permanent in nature and different to bilateral trade arrangements.

In 1989, the transit treaty of 1978 was unilaterally abrogated by India. India also refused to sign a separate transit treaty and thus a trade embargo began. After the restoration of democracy in 1990 in Nepal, India and Nepal signed separate transit treaties with major provisions of renewal. In 1999 the transit treaty was signed with the provision of automatic renewal every seven years. These treaties, however, were limited to tariff and duty concessions. Such benefits are thought to be transitory in nature and have not contributed significantly to sustainable trade between the two nations.

The Indo-Nepal Treaty of 1996 allowed duty-free access to Nepali exports, and Nepal gained from the new arrangement as it benefited from the low duties it imposed on raw material imports compared to prevailing tariffs on many products in India. Nepal was able to import raw materials at lower costs, process the products and export them to India. Tariff reduction by India, ahead of its scheduled liberalization programme and under her own trade policy reform agenda, has neutralized the benefits conferred by the various trade treaties.

Political instability in Nepal has been a major hindrance to Indian investments and a key concern in New Delhi. Although many key business companies entered the Nepali market from the 1990s onwards, the fragile polity in Nepal created hurdles for Indian businesses. Some big names did contribute immensely in various sectors in Nepal, but investors remained threatened and insecure in a country engulfed in civil strife. Even the post-2006 situation was not very encouraging as political players strived to fulfil their own interests rather than the interest of the foreign investor.

Most Nepalis, including those who were educated in India, view India as a troublemaker and a bully. Agreed, Nepal is geographically small, but Nepalis tend to forget that they are also the forty-eighth-most populated country in the world with a population that is nearly one and a half times that of Australia, and only a few millions less than that of Canada. They continue to think of their country as being at par with Sikkim or Bhutan, both of which have less than 3 per cent of Nepal's population. Their own belief in being a 'small country' complicates their relations with India. Further, the firm belief held by Nepalis—that India wants to meddle in the internal affairs of the country—has not been quelled by India. The blockade enforced from September 2015 to January 2016 in fact further strengthened it.

Over the years, the Indian presence in Nepal has been huge. With over $1 billion in investment, it is the biggest source of total foreign direct investment. It has made huge contributions in terms of employment generation, revenue generation and industrial development and also been able to establish and operate various ancillary industries in Nepal, including packaging, agriculture and transportation. On the other hand, Nepal has no major investments abroad. All Nepali investments in India are through the informal hawala[3] route. There is a law that prohibits Nepalis from investing outside Nepal.

While it is important to understand that formal Indian investments in Nepal have dwindled, the informal sector comprising a vast majority of Nepalis of Indian origin continues to grow, as people living in small Indian border towns move towards larger cities and the capital of Kathmandu to make investments.

The anti-India sentiment invoked mainly by political players for domestic political support has resulted in labour problems and the closure of Indian companies in Nepal. Over the years, this has discouraged the flow of formal Indian investments to Nepal. But the majority of Nepalis, especially those living in the bordering region, have and will continue to look at India as a safety net for jobs, education, healthcare and other business opportunities. Further, Indian culture, especially Bollywood and television serials have influenced the culture in Nepal. Instead of traditional manda (mandala)[4] in the Kathmandu valley, Nepalis have switched to drawing rangoli[5] during Tihar. Marriage rituals have also been influenced as functions carry on for multiple days, complete with Bollywood song and dance sequences. Men drinking Indian whisky brands and women wearing Indian-style wedding clothes dancing to Bollywood numbers do not mind engaging in India-bashing. There is a strong dependence on India in terms of the economy and culture which has led to a more complex relationship between the two countries.

## India's Image Issue

When one visits the Indian embassy in Kathmandu, the staff at the gate speaks to you in Hindi rather than Nepali or English (which are spoken at the Chinese embassy). The image of the Indian embassy being as important as the Narayanhiti Palace perhaps did not go down well with many people. However, there are people who have propagated this image through chakari at the embassy. Nepali is also a language recognized by the Indian Constitution, so why doesn't the government deploy Nepali-speaking staff from India, as it does with Bengali-speaking staff in the Bangladesh embassy? The condescending manner in which some embassy officials speak to Nepalis across different sectors has always hurt the pride of Nepalis. Such themes feature regularly in print and social media. While some ambassadors have been able to bring about reform, others have compounded the problem even further. They travel with multiple security personnel, demand restaurants to be emptied when the ambassador is visiting for a meal, etc. The body language of such security folks in a city with ambassadors from multiple other countries that do not behave in this manner has not helped in resolving the issue.

The small team size of the Indian embassy has been an impediment to its functioning. There are very few senior-level staff members who are burdened with handling many areas of work. Unlike in the past when a posting to Nepal was seen as prestigious, a must-have posting before becoming a foreign secretary in India. By 2018 it was not seen as a preferred destination from a career-building perspective. Therefore, it did not attract the best talent. Further, India uses its intelligence unit, the Research and Analysis Wing (R&AW), extensively to engage in political interferences and manoeuvres within Nepal. Books like *Prayogshala*[6] by Sudheer Sharma, editor at *Kantipur Daily*, provide much insight on how R&AW gets entangled in Nepali issues. In the years of transition from 2006 to 2018, there were many events apart from the blockade that expressed India's dissatisfaction over the Nepali Constitution. Among those, the involvement of India in appointing a tainted government official to head the anti-corruption body, and continuous efforts to keep K.P. Oli out of power will be remembered as the two most significant events that changed the fate of the Nepal–India relationship.

India had many opportunities to undertake small actions to gain the confidence of the Nepali people, but it has not been able to do so. For instance, after the hijack of the Indian Airlines aircraft in December 1999, India suspended operations of its airlines in Nepal for six months, and later instituted a security check at the boarding gate of the aircraft. After twenty years, this extra security check protocol has indicated India's possible lack of trust of Nepali security agencies and people. When India can entrust a larger number of Nepalis to be part of the Indian army and fight under the Indian flag, it is strange that such moves continue.

India's aid to Nepal has been strictly bilateral, implemented at its own wishes without consulting the Nepal government. It has also refrained from routing it through Nepali government agencies like other bilateral and multilateral support. It was only after China moved part of its aid through the United Nations Development Programme (UNDP), that India followed suit, for tokenism purposes. Nepal's Ministry of Finance lists India in the third spot in terms of providing aid to Nepal; in 2018, it provided $78 million.[7] While the proportion of aid from an Indian GDP or budget perspective has diminished significantly over the years, it also formed only a small portion of Nepal's $30 billion GDP in 2018. From being completely dependent on Indian aid in the early 1950s, Nepal has moved on to being an aid recipient of multiple development partners. This has also impacted the relationship.

## India's Act East and Neighbourhood Policies Fail to Impress

In India, like in Nepal, a lot of lip service is paid to issues, with some initial momentum and then no follow-up. India, post-liberalization in 1991, embarked upon a Look East Policy which was aimed at integrating it north-east with ASEAN. After 2014, Prime Minister Narendra Modi rechristened the slogan as 'Act East'. In India's 26 January 2018 Republic Day celebrations, all ten ASEAN heads of state were invited as chief guests. PM Modi also embarked on the Neighbourhood First policy by inviting all SAARC heads of state for his installation as prime minister in May 2014, and as a symbolic gesture, he made his first overseas visit as prime minister to Bhutan.

While think tanks have implemented innumerable programmes around the future of these policies, and even with the government impetus to promote both the Act East as well as Neighbourhood First policies, there have been very few visible changes on the ground. With the political upheaval in the Maldives and Sri Lanka, and Bangladesh reeling under political challenges, and unsuccessful attempts at leveraging the change of leadership in Pakistan in 2018, the vast gap between India's intent and action could be seen.

## Relationship Mishap: Downhill from 'Modi-fication'

Modi-fication: In August 2014, Prime Minister Narendra Modi visited Nepal as part of his Neighbourhood First policy, seventeen years after an Indian prime minister had last been there for an official visit. He received great hospitality from the people of Nepal and reciprocated by speaking of the sense of confidence with which India viewed Nepali sovereignty, making the popular references to the Buddha being born in Nepal and Mount Everest being in Nepal. He was also clear that Nepal's water belonged to Nepal and India was willing to work together with it. Transport treaties were signed that saw a surge of Indian tourists travelling to Nepal by road, and project agreements were signed for two hydroelectric power plants. The Indian prime minister also pledged a $1 billion credit line. When PM Modi returned in November to attend the SAARC summit, Nepalis again saw him as a global leader who was willing to help his neighbours. The quick Indian response to the Nepal earthquake for relief and an additional commitment of $1 billion for reconstruction further solidified this view. June 2015 was perhaps the high point of Nepal's relationship with India.

Blockade Begins: Nepal promulgated its Constitution on 20 September 2015, therefore ending one of the most expensive processes both in terms of time and resources. While the Constitution was promulgated with the overwhelming majority of the Constituent Assembly, issues like rights of women and representation and demarcation of federal provinces were controversial. India disapproved of this Constitution, and on 22 September 2015 imposed restrictions on the movement of petroleum products and other essential goods from India. As per international norms and protocol on landlocked countries, India is supposed to provide uninterrupted movement of goods destined for Nepal, Nepal being a landlocked country. It is not clear what prompted India to make such a move, but two months after the imposition of the blockade (which was officially not accepted as one by India), Nepal was reeling under an economic crisis. The economic impact of the blockade has far outweighed that of the earthquake. After the earthquake, economic growth for 2015–16 was revised downwards by 1.5 percentage points from 4.5 per cent to 3 per cent. However, due to the blockade, economic growth was negative 0.8 per cent, pushing down growth by 3.8 per cent: more than two and a half times higher than the impact of the earthquake. The 2015 blockade was the third one imposed by India, the previous ones being in 1969 and 1989.

## Growing Importance of China

Today, China has not only emerged as the second largest economy in the world but it also assumes the status of a world power. Its rapid economic growth together with its political management is perceived by other countries with inspiration, anxiety and fear. The West-perceived Chinese 'string of pearls'[8] strategy in South Asia is looked at with great trepidation by many countries. But China has always been an interactive power for Nepal, either directly or through Tibet.

Nepal's 'special relations' with India did not deter Nepal and China from establishing diplomatic ties in 1955, which in essence created a new understanding of the new geopolitical dynamics. In the 1960s, Nepal seemed to have reaped some benefits from the then developing animosity and conflict between India and China, but China at no point exerted pressure on Nepal to keep its relationship with Nepal at par with India. It is a widely accepted view in Nepal that the Chinese leaders were basically guided by pragmatism, which was manifested throughout in its foreign policy. The only security concern that China has in Nepal is regarding Tibet, for which it has persuaded every government in Nepal to keep a check. Nepal, on its part, has upheld the One China policy and has repeatedly reassured China that Nepali soil will not be used for any anti-Chinese activities.

Soon after Parliament was dissolved and King Mahendra's authoritarian rule began, China and Nepal signed another Peace and Friendship Treaty in 1960. In 1961, Nepal signed a border treaty and also agreed to the building of a highway route that would connect with China. All this signalled a drift away from India, but post the 1962 war between India and China, Nepal signed a 'secret' agreement with India in 1965 that allowed Nepal to only import arms from India.[9] Since the formalization of diplomatic ties, China has assisted Nepal in development endeavours and activities ranging from building infrastructure such as roads, bridges, power projects and communications to industries, health, water resources, education, sports, etc. China has also agreed to provide assistance to Nepal for the construction of a dry port along the Kodari highway to facilitate trade with China via Tatopani. Nepal in 2018 also acquired Internet through China which reduced the dependency it had on India. This improved bandwidth and services tremendously.

## China's Soft Diplomacy

China's soft diplomacy has increased in Nepal over the years. The Confucius Institute, a Chinese government initiative that started in 2007, provides Mandarin language classes at very low rates. Volunteers from this institute travel to different parts of Nepal to teach Mandarin to primary-school students for free. They also have a programme in Nepali on FM radio that translates and broadcasts news as seen through Chinese lenses. There is an English-language weekly published out of Kathmandu each week and *China Daily* has been introduced in partnership with other publications. Global Times and CGTN, China's international television channels, have also become popular.

Arrangements were made for thousands of Nepalis, mostly youths, to visit China as part of multiple work or exchange programmes. There are study abroad programmes financed by Chinese government agencies at Tribhuvan University. Similarly, scholarships have increased because many journalists have been visiting China. Due to lower costs, many Nepali students prefer China for medical studies, with around 300 students going there for this purpose each year.[10]

The biggest change in Nepal has been that the Chinese have started to boldly engage with the Nepali people, trying to understand their language and culture and also working with other international agencies in Nepal. For instance, the consular section of the embassy has many staff and officials speaking in Nepali. In 2017, the Chinese embassy for the first time started working with UNDP Nepal to disburse a portion of their aid for post-earthquake reconstruction. On 8 March 2019 at the International Women's Day celebrations, the recently arrived Chinese ambassador, Hou Yanqi, put up a performance of Nepali dance—this was her first public appearance after being appointed.

Tourism is another area that has seen a lot of Chinese proliferation, with tourists coming to Nepal especially to visit Lumbini and other places of natural beauty. With more tourists visiting China and China promoting itself as a transit destination for Nepal to travel to the Americas and Australia, more flights have been introduced between Kathmandu and Chinese cities than between Kathmandu and Indian cities. While India continued to bring about policies that discouraged people from transiting at Indian airports, China furthered its Nepali-friendly image, even having Nepali-speaking crews in flights. By mid-2019, there were more flights per week between Nepal and China than Nepal and India.

China and Nepal accorded Most Favoured Nation (MFN) status to each other in 1990 and have also extended preferences in trade. In 2001, Nepal was Tibet's top trade partner as exports of food and construction material to Tibet rose. But trade with mainland China remained one-sided. The huge trade deficit of NPR 114 billion is of great concern for Nepal as the trade deficit with China has been growing at a much faster rate than with India.

## China's Renminbi

China's rise also needs to be understood from how its currency has performed in global markets. Since it allowed its currency to float in 2006, the renminbi or RMB has appreciated by 41 per cent by 2017 in trade-weighted terms since 2005. In real (inflation-adjusted) terms, it has appreciated by 48 per cent. That's a lot of appreciation, and this is likely to continue despite capital outflows and reserve losses. The appreciation of the RMB is mainly due to faster GDP and income growth than the West—China continues to grow three times faster than the developed world. The RMB will continue to trend north accordingly.[11] Many analysts compare the RMB situation to that of the US dollar in the late 1960s and 1970s; it went on and managed to unseat the UK pound as the global currency of doing business in the mid-1970s. On 1 October 2016, the RMB became the first emerging market currency to be included in the IMF's special drawing rights basket—the basket of currencies used by the IMF in East Asia. For instance, in Cambodia and Laos, it is not surprising to find shops displaying prices in RMB apart from the local currency and the US dollar.

For Nepal, which has its currency pegged with the Indian rupee through a fixed exchange rate, it is important to monitor the situation. If Chinese investment, trade and business continues to rise then Nepal might also need to think of shifting to a currency basket.

## The Change in Tibet and Beyond

The sparsely populated but resource-laden Tibet Autonomous Region with a landmass the size of Western Europe holds a special place in China's southern drive. For example, Tibet holds close to 30 per cent of China's fresh water reservoirs (more than 100 billion cubic metres underground and as much on the surface), 30 per cent of the forest and biodiversity land (which is 10 per cent of the total Chinese landmass), massive river systems (twenty major ones and 100 others), vast amounts of minerals (100 mineral resources and 3000 deposit sites), and hundreds of miles of grasslands. The US, for example, converted vast expansive grasslands in the midwest (about 250 million acres) into productive farmland and urban cities by taming the river. China also plans to build 100 dams in the Tibetan plateau, which is going to change the Tibetan landscape in a significant way.

Some notable infrastructural developments in Tibet are 25,000 km of major and minor highway networks, a spectacular railway line linking Beijing to Lhasa (4000 mi), a 1000 km oil pipeline, and many more to come. This infrastructural development in Tibet also holds strategic value for India. China has been investing billions in Tibet, thus opening a potential market for India as a supplier of 'materials' for Chinese projects in Tibet. In some respects, getting supplies from India through Nepal would be cheaper and easier for China than hauling it from the east coast. An annual tourist volume of more than 30 million Chinese travelling to the Tibet Autonomous Region every year can also be a potential lucrative market for Nepal.[12] Tibet, with a population of just over 3 million—one-tenth of Nepal's population—has a GDP of $20 billion, two-thirds of Nepal's GDP.

## China's Belt and Road Initiative

China's BRI is a strategic security and investment tool for China to ensure that new routes of transit for petroleum products and food security are opened. At the same time, it has avenues to push further investments, transfer technology to countries and boost manufacturing at home for exports. Seen sceptically and perceived by many as a tool for China to enhance its political prowess, time will be the judge on how effectively it will be able to navigate the challenges that come with being an overseas donor and investor on a large scale.

The BRI was launched in 2013 by President Xi Jinping in Kazakhstan. It designates eighty-four countries in the programme and has made $434 billion of investments in five years in existing projects and an additional $138 billion in greenfield projects. It operates with a three-pronged approach. The first, most visible, deals with 'hard' infrastructure, which includes roads, railways, ports and telecommunications projects. The second is 'soft' infrastructure, which includes investment and trade agreements as well as efforts to smooth customs clearance, and also efforts to promote the use of RMB. The third area of activity is the promotion of cultural ties.

## China and India Coming Closer Like Never Before

The strengthening of relations between China and India is one of the least discussed elements in Asian geopolitics. Between 2014 and 2019 Prime Minister Modi and Chinese President Xi Jinping have met sixteen times. There is now more trade and investment activity between China and India than ever before as they try to achieve a $100 billion target by 2020. Indian investments in China have increased. Tata Sons, which began with a mere $200 million in turnover in China, now has revenues of $12 billion, employing more than 10,000 people.[13] Similarly, there are other Indian groups spreading their wings in China but no studies on this are available.

Chinese investments in India have increased substantially. Industry-watchers share that after demonetization, to stem the falling prices of real estate, $16 billion in investment came from China to India—this was routed through different countries, and therefore official sources in India put this number at $8 billion.[14] Especially in the area of technology, e-commerce and communications, Chinese companies have invested in all major ventures in India. Indian mobile phone manufacturing and sales is dominated by Chinese companies, and forays have been made in construction also. The fact that a Chinese company has been contracted by the Indian government entity Indraprastha Gas Limited to construct gas pipelines in sensitive north-east India demonstrates the easing of business and investment relations between the two countries. Similarly, air connectivity between China and India is increasing and in 2018 there were forty-two weekly flights which would have increased further.[15] The exchange of visitors and scholars has increased, and Indian students form a significant proportion of foreign students in China, with the country starting to establish global learning centres to attract international students. Statistics from Project Atlas show that by 2015, the number of Indian students studying in China was 16,694, compared to 765 only ten years ago.[16] For instance, in 2016, more Indian students went to China for medical studies than to the UK.[17]

A section of people in both China and India believe that these countries that dominated global business and trade till the eighteenth century should be working more closely to form a formidable alliance to counter the influence of the US and European powers. However, there are also narratives on India's active role in the Indo-Pacific alliance to counter China. The latter narrative is the one that is more reported and discussed.

## The World of Perception

Nepalis view their own country at par with Sikkim or Bhutan, both of which are physically small compared to Nepal, and have less than 3 per cent of Nepal's population. Similarly, people in Delhi view Nepal like they view Bhutan. Apart from India occupying the largest pieces of real estate in both capitals for their embassies, they need to realize there are no commonalities.

India's rise as an economic superpower is generally endorsed with the images of high-rise development in Gurgaon, or the new campuses of IT firms in Bengaluru. For Nepalis, the border posts are an accurate representation of India. When they cross the border into various towns across India through Indian customs or immigration offices, they wonder how this country can be an economic superpower. They are yet to see Gurgaon and Bengaluru, where transformational economic activities are taking place!

For instance, a Nepali in Kakarvitta in the east who has witnessed the transformation of their village from a few huts into a flourishing municipality wonders why India has not changed when looking at a border town. People in Delhi and even Kolkata have no idea how the border town in Naxalbari in West Bengal looks and the fact that government establishments there still function out of temporary structures built decades ago.

However, someone who has also seen the border at Tatopani north of Kathmandu into China then starts to believe China's growth story as s/he starts visualizing how Shanghai or Beijing will look when even a small border town like Khasa looks so imposing.

## Understanding Thy Neighbour

For every ten seminars conducted in Delhi on Nepal, there is hardly a single one conducted in Beijing, which Nepalis see as an alternative force in our geopolitics. We forget that we are far away from the hustle and bustle of Shanghai and Guangzhou. An average Nepali can name at least ten Indian cities, five Indian movie stars and speak at least fifty words in Hindi. Now take that across the border: how many Chinese cities, actors and words in Mandarin can Nepalis utter? The cultural proximity with India has perhaps created a relationship that is so dependent that it can simultaneously be perceived as being difficult. However, in a globalizing India, it is important to understand what Nepal means to a young Indian. People are found struggling when asked fundamental questions on Nepal in quiz shows, such as the name of its capital or prime minister. At times, when I talk to young Indians about Nepal, they talk about it as being only a honeymoon or pilgrimage destination for their parents' generation. For a truck driver driving an Indian licence plate vehicle into Nepal, it is the guys harassing him at check points that form his impression of a Nepali. Hence, it is not the folks in Delhi and Kathmandu who are seen as the real Indian or real Nepali! The challenge in fostering better Nepal–India ties means work needs to be done on not only a government-to-government or business-to-business basis but more at a people-to-people level. Only a bond between the people of both countries can cement a sustainable relationship. We need to understand who represents a Nepali for an Indian and who is an Indian for a Nepali. For a migrant Nepali worker in India crossing the border, it is the harassing police officers who represent India.

For a country at the global economic forefront, security is paramount, and as bureaucrats in South Block or the Indian Foreign Office compete for positions to specialize in, looking at the US, Europe or China as rewarding careers, the only Indian government interest remains with security and intelligence agencies. For security agencies in India, Nepal is another country that can be used as a conduit for terrorists or anti-India activities. The knee-jerk reaction of closing the border seems to be a more viable one for India so it does not have to make it an open border, which is more beneficial for both parties. We need to consider the large number of Nepalis in the Indian army who continue to die and the mental state of the nearly 10 million Nepalis who consider India their home. What does it cost to have this open border compared to the spending on fences that sovereign nations like to build? The challenge is not to shut it but to ensure that the economic benefits of the open border benefit both sides.

In Delhi, you hear of Sinophobia more than even in Kathmandu. In key intellectual circles, questions on China's influence in Nepal are asked by everyone, whether it is the supposed intelligentsia (which comments on the Nepali Constitution without having read it), the hotel manager or the saree dealer in Karol Bagh, Delhi. The journalist, editor and analyst circles in New Delhi have been paranoid regarding the Chinese influence in Nepal. The paranoia is similar to the depiction of villains in Bollywood movies who have links with Pakistan's ISI, or the Hollywood movies of a few decades ago where everything wrong that happened was connected with the Soviet Union.

## Communism in Nepal Came from India, Not China

The biggest feature of the Nepali communist, ignored by parachute analysts, is that communism came to Nepal through Kolkata and not straight from China. Therefore, what we see in Nepal is the West Bengal version of communism rather than a Chinese one. The communist movement in West Bengal has been about multiple factions that keep splitting and coming together, rather than being one single and unified party. At one point in time, people had lost count of how many communist parties in Nepal were overground and underground.

The communist movement in both India and Nepal has been about rent-seeking on positions and selling rhetoric and hypocrisy. It has been about talking about the Red Book during the day and on other diametric subjects later. This is in stark contrast to the Chinese societal model of hard work and encouraging entrepreneurial pursuits.

Moreover, Nepali communists, especially the former insurgents, still talk about Mao and the Maoist ideology. In China, Mao is a word best avoided and is jarring for the current key leadership. Over the years, when a majority group within the ruling party in China decides on an issue, people with opposing views accept the decision and do not challenge it. You can debate on an issue but after a decision is made, you have to abide by it. Nepali communism has been about continuous infighting and creating fiefdoms rather than accepting an individual's leadership.

The recent rise of the Nepali communist has been due to empathy and support from the communist parties of India that were part of the United Progressive Alliance between 2008 and 2013, a critical juncture in Nepal's transition. The Maoists, while underground, received tacit support. With the communist parties in India in disarray now, Nepali communist leaders are looking for options. With the co-chair of the NCP, Pushpa Kamal Dahal, in line to succeed Prime Minister K.P. Oli, other leaders such as Madhav Nepal and Jhala Nath Khanal, who became prime ministers earlier with Indian support, are trying to look for options in China.

Unlike the other nations on the border, China has been that neighbour for India with whom it does not have any commonality— political system, colonial history, language, food or culture. The size of one's eyes continues to be a factor in judging the difference between an Indian or a Chinese! Folks in Delhi were surprised to learn that the Indian Institute of Management in Shillong, Meghalaya (which is in India), now offers a joint MBA programme with Ocean University in China. This is really the need of the hour as north-east India needs to prepare for the connectivity that emerges as subregional market paradigms develop, making political boundaries irrelevant.

## Towards East South Asia: BBIN

When the SAARC nations met in Kathmandu in November 2014 for its fourteenth edition and could not get the Transport Agreement finalized, another alterative was mooted where four countries would go ahead to implement a Motor Vehicle Agreement (MVA). An association of Bangladesh, Bhutan, India and Nepal (BBIN), took shape and the agreement was signed in June 2015. I have perceived this event as a mark of integration in 'East South Asia', a phrase I started using to denote the region comprising Nepal, Bhutan, Bangladesh and north-east India. The region has enormous potential that can be harnessed best through cooperative and competitive engagement amongst the constituent member states. It is imperative that the momentum created by the BBIN–MVA is carried forward and built upon. Given the geographical proximity of the nations, their similarities in culture, and parallels even in spending patterns, it makes good economic sense to strengthen connectivity in East South Asia.

To provide a perspective to this region, it is important to note that the distance from Kathmandu to Guwahati, the economic epicentre of north-east India, is only 1000 km, which is the same distance as from Kathmandu to Delhi. Guwahati is also closer to Yangon than to Delhi. However, our perceptions of distance make it seem it's not the case. As road and rail infrastructures improve, there is tremendous potential for easier movement of people and commodities across the region. When there is increased economic activity across borders, political borders will likely become less relevant.

The potential of sectors in East South Asia is similar irrespective of the country, be it in hydropower, agriculture, tourism or service. This provides a lot of room for intra-regional learning and interactions. There are opportunities for businesses that have developed competencies in certain sectors to expand further beyond national borders as these areas are similar to the ones they operate in.

## Hurdles to Integration

Across the globe, geographical borders have the potential to serve as literal gateways that open up states to trade and commerce with one another. The possibility of utilizing such potential, however, remains far-fetched in the region. In South Asia, for example, even as Nepal shares a 1580-km-long open border with India, the border points act more as a barrier than a bridge. The border is seen as a regulated outlet that has been bestowed as a facility to Nepal. The lack of any formal framework restricts the movement of goods. For instance, handicrafts, which is one of Nepal's main exports and has a large market in north-eastern India and Bhutan, cannot be exported through the Kakarvitta/Naxalbari border in eastern Nepal, which is geographically the closest point through which those markets can be reached. The Indian side lacks the required framework to let these items move across the border. Similarly, apples from Bhutan are yet to find their market in eastern Nepal because of the lack of a framework for formal trade between Bhutan and Nepal. Therefore, this perishable product is instead exported to markets farther off in India. Such obstructions not only raise the cost and make exporting cumbersome for traders willing to operate within the bounds of the law, but also encourage the proliferation of informal trade, which does not benefit artisans and farmers but makes middlemen rich at the cost of government revenues. We can learn from East Africa, where with integrated customs points that are open round the clock, trading partners have increased bilateral trade volumes. Similar developments are also seen in the ASEAN countries.

Valuable goods which are usually subject to significant import duties are smuggled across the India–Nepal border during the time that the border remains closed. Estimates suggest that illegal trade along Nepal's southern border with India amounts to almost 40 per cent of Nepal's foreign trade.[18] At the same time, the closure of border points for long hours restricts the volume of trade that could take place between the two countries. If the border points are kept open, this malaise of rampant rent-seeking will be checked and make the governments gain in the form of increased revenues from import duties. This will, of course, require stringent and effective border patrolling through the coordinated efforts of both sides.

## Open Borders, Interdependent Livelihoods

The open border between Nepal and India has allowed for the unrestricted movement of people, helping shape their way of life along the area. It provides a variety of opportunities to people on both sides as they can travel across to work, attend school or access medical facilities. In a single day, an estimated 20,000 people cross the border through the Kakarvitta crossing alone. This movement of Indians and Nepalis across the border, whether for day-to-day activities or for longer-term employment, goes far back in the history of the two countries' bilateral relations.

However, a lesser known fact is that in Nepal, there are also a significant number of workers from Bangladesh, employed mainly as manual labour in Kathmandu's construction sector. Brick factories in eastern Nepal also employ Bangladeshi workers, sometimes more than 1000 in factories in Jhapa, Morang and Sunsari. These examples show that although labour mobility through formal channels remains low, the demand exists and is significant enough to warrant the creation of more formal mechanisms. The free movement of labour across borders is a key component of any integration process. The establishment of formal channels ensures that these workers will be protected from exploitation by abusive agents. At the same time, the governments can keep a database of movements and use it to keep a tab on criminal activities that might take place through this channel. After all, encouraging mobility does not mean being lackadaisical about security; proper documentation and regulation should ensure that the security of any of the sovereign states is not compromised. Easier mobility through formal channels will incentivize more citizens to move across borders and seek employment most suited to their skill sets. The result is, at least potentially, higher productivity for the region and increased socioeconomic benefits for citizens.

There is also the matter of access to services such as health, from which people both sides of the border benefit mutually. For example, patients from India travel to Lahan in south-east Nepal for eye treatment. The well-known Sagarmatha Choudhary Eye Hospital (SCEH) in Lahan is quite easily accessible from Bihar; almost 90 per cent of the patients who come to the hospital are Indian. Medical tourism to SCEH has become so popular among the people of Bihar that travel agents and other organizations offer 'treatment package tours' for Indian patients to travel to Lahan. Thousands of patients are brought to the hospital from different parts of north India by organizations operating package tours for procedures like cataract surgery.

## Connecting People through Old and New Media

One of the things that connects the people of East South Asia easily and perhaps even all of South Asia is Indian television: Indian soap operas, in particular, enjoy huge popularity across the region. Access to Indian satellite TV has provided an opportunity for companies to advertise their products and services and reach out to their target markets. Further, the rapid expansion of information and communication technologies (ICT) has meant greater people-to-people interconnections in the region, which remains one of the most crucial prerequisites to connectivity and regional integration. The percentage of the population connected to the Internet in different parts of the region has increased tremendously, with the proliferation of mobile devices with Internet connections.

## Summarizing Policy Suggestions[19]

In a paper I wrote for the Observer Research Foundation (ORF) for strengthening connectivity and integration in BBIN, I spoke of three areas of reforms.

1. Transforming Borders: Rather than becoming points of control and harassment, borders should be points of facilitation. Border points between countries in the region should be more welcoming to trade and commerce and serve as a bridge rather than a barrier to meaningful engagement. For this to happen, policies for having integrated customs points and keeping border points open round the clock with all the required frameworks should be in place.
2. Better and Well-connected Infrastructure: Infrastructure development should be based on a regional view of things rather than a constrained border-enclosed vision. The BBIN countries should work towards building and improving physical infrastructure so that connectivity increases not just on paper but in terms of the volume of goods and services traded, reduction in travel time, and lowering of transport fares. A BBIN air network with fifth freedom rights[20] should be instituted to foster better air connectivity in the region.
3. Free Movement of People, Goods and Services: Easier movement of labour between borders with proper documentation can

prevent undue exploitation of workers by agents, help in curbing cross-border criminal activities, and bring workers within the tax net. Proper documentation and regulation should ensure that there is no compromise on security due to movements of labour. Easier market access for labour, goods and services will increase competition for local labour and businesses, thereby incentivizing productivity; consumers also stand to gain from greater competition among service providers. Policies that formally allow people, goods and services to move across the borders freely form the foundation for better connectivity and integration and should, therefore, mark the starting point for strengthening connectivity among the BBIN countries.

## Towards Border Economic Zones

Borders have become geometric lines that create opportunities for governments—and more specifically, unscrupulous officials—to benefit. Customs and security staff are said to be willing to pay for jobs at border posts, where they can extract payments from travellers, turning crossing points intended to facilitate movement into impediments to communication and movement.

Ordinary people are frequently harassed as they fetch basic commodities to and fro. Sometimes, people are even killed in the name of maintaining security. The deadlier the security threat, the more opportunity there is for security personnel and others to extract payments from people for whom border crossings are a necessity of everyday life.

For instance, Nepali farmers trying to cross into India to sell ginger are told to have their products tested by a laboratory in a city they have not heard of. Fruit sellers from Bangladesh are told by Indian officials to send their produce 1000 km to Varanasi for testing. Indians going to an eye clinic in eastern Nepal are harassed by Nepali security officials.

Across South Asia there are multiple disputes related to borders and security, and customs personnel have surely played a role in making frontiers a money-minting machine. When a security system seeks rent in this way, cartels emerge offering to fix anything—from the price of unloading a bag of potatoes off a truck to the exorbitant fares for short-distance transport by rickshaw or taxi. People are often left at the mercy of middlemen, touts and opportunists.

## Connectivity 'Clusters'

In the later part of the twentieth century, free trade zones (FTZs) and special economic zones (SEZs) emerged as a way of overcoming the pernicious effects of excessive taxation and regulation on trade and economic activity. SEZs and FTZs create zones where labour laws, tariff structures and legal requirements are different from other areas. There is now an opportunity for a similar approach to overcome excessive regulation of borders.

The creation of BEZs could facilitate the growth of connectivity clusters on both sides of the regional borders. For instance, on Nepal's eastern border with India, the tea-growing industry spans both sides, taking in the Nepali region of Kakarvitta and the Indian region of Naxalbari. Both could be included in a BEZ in which tea and other agricultural produce could be grown and harvested on both sides of the border and processed at a factory located within the zone. Radical changes to regulations would be required in both Nepal and India, but path-breaking regulatory frameworks have already been created for FTZs and SEZs, and it should be possible to do the same for a BEZ.

Security issues could be resolved through the use of digital technology to develop cheap and reliable ways of identity-checking. In Nepal, citizens must pay $100 for passports—a sum with which they can buy smartphones that could be used for communication and money storage as well as proving identity.

BEZs can be used as a tool to develop better relationships between India and Nepal, which has been challenging not only at the

national level but even at the open borders which have been prone
to negative perceptions. BEZs could be particularly useful for India,
whose large population and economic weight obliges it to find new
ways of managing its relations with its smaller neighbours—not least
to improve its image with bigger countries.

## Towards Making InChiNep Work

There are times in history when new economic growth models
emerge. This could well be such a time.[21] For Nepal, rather than a
yam between two boulders, it should look at being a bridge between
two countries that will be controlling 35 per cent of global GDP in
2050. It must shed its 1950s discourses and look at what is essential
to make the relationship a win-win for all. A former Indian minister
had coined the word 'Chindia', and I would like to create another
one, 'InChiNep', to look at Nepal taking India and China together
in its journey towards economic prosperity. Nepal is having one of
the best moments in its history with its geographical position being
better than ever. When we draw a flight path from Mumbai to
Beijing on a map, Kathmandu is literally at the centre. Nepal needs
to leverage its position as it did a thousand years ago!

# 12

# Capitalist Welfare State: In between Capitalism and Socialism

The discourse and debate around capitalism and socialism has been going on for a very long time. While the world has emerged from a Cold War that was based on countries believing in these two ideologies, it is still a matter of heated debate which of them will better deliver development, economic growth and improved livelihoods.

I look at capitalism and socialism from the perspective of someone scanning the social, economic, business and cultural environment. In my understanding, capitalism means an open-source software which people can plug into and take advantage of in a free market, with varying moments of demand and supply and free movement of goods, services and people, where the state plays only the role of a regulator. While in socialism, the state takes on the burden of everything from selling bread at the same price throughout the country to ensuring that everyone goes to the same schools and hospitals, and earns the same wages and spends the same amount in the same environment.

There are proponents of both these ideologies, but over the centuries, we have realized we cannot take a binary look at the issue. In the land of the Buddha, perhaps we need to take a middle path.

I first propagated the concept of a capitalist welfare state—a state that believes in private enterprise as well as in the welfare of its citizens—in my essay 'State of Nepal'[1] in 2001 and thereafter elaborated on the same in my earlier book, *Unleashing Nepal*.[2] In this chapter, we will examine the different ways in which Nepal has adopted the definition of socialism and capitalism along with the challenges that come with it and the way out. Further, we will examine the components required for Nepal to pursue its journey of becoming a capitalist welfare state. After understanding Nepali perceptions on these ideologies, we will look at the role of the government, private sector, development partners and community-based organizations along with the reforms required to work towards better integrating Nepalis into the global economy. These reforms range from regulating NGOs to fostering competition between various local governments to allowing Nepalis to invest outside Nepal.

## Nepali Perceptions of Socialism and Capitalism

When the Constitution of Nepal was promulgated in 2015, if there was one issue that the majority of the big parties agreed on, it was that of Nepal being a socialist country. Like many countries in Asia, it decided to pursue a 'socialism-oriented' economy. This concept is yet to be understood through government interpretations, but it is generally linked to being sort of a mixed economy where the private sector and the public sector can coexist. Further, Nepal has also given importance to cooperatives in the building of the economy.

As two of the main flanks of Nepali communism—the Maoists and the Communist Party of Nepal (Unified Marxist–Leninist or UML)—formed an alliance to run the country from 2017 to 2022 under the unified Nepal Communist Party, the economic environment will be more socialism-oriented rather than communism-oriented. According to traditional Marxism, socialism is just a transition between capitalism and communism. Currently, the functioning of the party marks it as a left social democratic party rather than a communist party.

Post-1950, Nepal, under the influence of India's first prime minister, Jawaharlal Nehru, decided to adopt a mixed economy but was skewed towards an increased government role rather than the private sector. The revolution in China, influenced by the then USSR, was pursuing socialism to the hilt. In Kolkata, the Indian hotbed of communist revolution was being built, and that influenced the communist movement in Nepal. The Nepali Congress pursued one variety of socialism and the communists another. Both, for over seventy years, have been fighting to prove who is more socialistic and can conserve the status quo rather than making progress. They also compete on who can engage better in distributive economics, curtail free enterprise and open investment policies. By 2018, the Rastriya Prajatantra Party (RPP) was the only party that openly propagated liberal economic policies.

Socialism is seen as the utopian concept we read about in mythology and religion which promised equality and happiness. However, in those stories we also get to see the disparity between the ruler and the ruled. Kings in Hindu mythology are seen as having all powers under them—the executive, the legislature and the judiciary along with being the commander in chief of the army. This was the case in Nepal with the Shah kings, and while they discussed the prosperity of the people, there was no intent in changing the way they looked at the privileges which were theirs by birth. The same concept was repeated in Republican Nepal, where some people continue to think they are higher than others and they must maintain this position to ensure a functioning society. Therefore, more people competed to be more than equal, and more distortions were created in society as people tried to usurp power in the name of socialism through all means including taking up arms and fighting a protracted battle against the state.

Socialism in Nepal is also about being myopic and inward-looking. With a strong conservative culture of caste-based hierarchy, alienation of women and age as a basis of judging seniority and competency, the Nepali model of socialism has evolved over the decades. I see it as a strategy of using nationalism to fend off everything relating to integrating with the world. Leaders can integrate, but not the people! Rules are written separately for the ruler and the ruled, and the best excuse for not getting things done has always been due to *punjiwaadis* or capitalists in Nepali. For instance, each stockbroker in the Nepal Stock Exchange (NSE) was till 2018 allowed to use only two computer terminals provided by the NSE. This was the Nepali model of socialism. Allowing a broker to have unlimited terminals based on capacity of investment was seen as a capitalistic move.

Capitalism has been associated with order and discipline, cleanliness, tidiness and a sense of purpose. In May 2010, former Prime Minister Pushpa Dahal, in an outrage against the failure of Maoist cadres to capture Kathmandu city, talked about how the people of Kathmandu were *sukila-mukila*, prim and proper, which meant they were leaning towards capitalism. Initially, the influence of Nehru in India, which was later picked up by Bollywood films, projected capitalism as a villain. Socialist revolutions were discussed around the world as there were revolts against capitalism and its destructive power. This continuous drilling of thought processes has led to the acceptance of business leaders, who can be very exploitative towards labour and do not follow the law but function as parliamentarians for a socialist political party in Nepal. Further, many who come to Nepal to work in the development sector ensure that they can romanticize the concept of socialism by making it anti-capitalism. This fits very well into the strategies of political and business leaders who plan to be considered more equal than others in the name of socialism.

## Communism Is Not Indigenous

Nepali socialism is also rooted more in communism like in South East Asia, rather than the socialism one learns about in Scandinavia.

The former forces equality on people, while the latter uses market and state regulatory mechanisms along with better civic sense and citizen responsibility to achieve a narrow inequality gap. Nepali socialism has been more like crony capitalism, where the lines between business and politics blur.

The way Nepalis have embraced communism as an antithesis to globalization or Westernization is very peculiar. Karl Marx, Lenin and Stalin were never Asian thinkers. Even Mao borrowed the communist ideology from Marx. In Nepal, communism is propagated as an indigenous ideology and projected as if it has nothing to do with the Western world. Paradoxically, Westernization and capitalism are used as synonyms. Whenever a discourse on communism takes place, especially in Nepali, communism is always pitted against Western influences. For instance, in August 2012, the CPN (Maoist) cadres started a campaign to change the name of educational institutions that had English names. However, the same party cadres are fine with their party offices filled with images of Marx, Lenin and Stalin, and they continue to use English initials in their names. For instance, the current prime minister goes by his English initials, K.P., and there are many other communist leaders who are referred to in the same way. This has also been the case for the Congress, whose iconic leader Bishweshwar Prasad Koirala was referred to as B.P. These behaviours promoting dichotomy make understanding Nepal's political economy even more difficult.

## Towards a Capitalist Welfare State

We cannot look at everything from the binary perspective of either capitalism or socialism, but we can work towards finding the best of both worlds and tailoring it to suit Nepal, such as finding a middle path to become a capitalist welfare state—one where the state believes in private enterprise as well as the welfare of its citizens. In such a state, doing business is easy with the state taking responsibility for the alleviation of poverty and introducing various programmes which are funded by increased taxes resulting from increased income activities.

## Wealth Creation to Combat Poverty

One of the primary benefits of entrepreneurship and a vibrant economy is that the creation of wealth it stimulates inevitably leads to poverty alleviation. Government initiatives alone have consistently proven to be of limited success in tackling poverty. Even in countries like China, where the government is set upon the task of poverty reduction, it did so by promoting business and liberalizing its economy. The simplest way of ensuring wealth creation is to create free, fair and competitive markets, which are accessible to all levels of society, class and caste. Although this is an idealistic vision, it retains a level of structural realism that utopian societies such as those envisioned by the Maoists in their early conflict days cannot match. The structural resilience and flexibility of democratic and market-oriented governments in comparison to ideological communist regimes attests to the more successful strategy of the former. Many studies of economic growth of countries in the past decades have shown that countries pursuing the opening of markets have more economic growth, job creation and prosperity than those who closed their markets and promoted local businesses in the name of nationalism.

The primary reason that an open society is more likely to create wealth is that people in it are secure in the knowledge that their rights—to do business, create wealth and earn—are all protected by the law. I assert that wealth cannot be created without the existence of a private sector that has the right to do business. In this, wealth mimics democratic governance as it is created by the people, for the people and belongs to the people who earn it. Poverty can be understood as the state of not being able to achieve subsistence, therefore, it is a complete lack of wealth. Wealth is a luxury beyond subsistence.

It is created by first creating investment and job opportunities, entrepreneurial assistance, a secure business environment and stable political governance.

People who live in poverty do not and cannot create wealth. A subsistence level of existence restricts people in terms of opportunities and capabilities and forces them to focus only on survival. It is also important to distinguish between being wealthy and being rich—wealth is not just richness, but the ability to become richer through the investment and utilization of one's riches. Wealth is created by people working above the poverty line, individually or through the creation of small enterprises and cooperatives. The first prerequisite for wealth creation is to ensure that people at the bottom of the pyramid are assured of basic necessities. Only then do they have the luxury of exploring opportunities, taking small risks, and engaging in wealth-creating activities in the economy.

Alternatively, wealth can be created through the creation of employment opportunities in large enterprises in addition to creating opportunities via medium, small and micro enterprises (MSME). Enterprises require capital investments, making wealth a prerequisite for the creation of additional wealth. Poverty can only be reduced when it is possible for those without wealth to take part in the project of wealth creation, either through employment or individual entrepreneurship. Therefore, the twin-pronged approach of creating wealth through creating job opportunities in large enterprises and creating entrepreneurs in MSME must be pursued.

Neither a government dependent on foreign aid nor a plethora of development agencies can generate wealth as they are not in the business of wealth creation and can only disburse money. Poverty can only be addressed when the poor can participate in the private sector through ownership as shareholders or as employees in large enterprises or as self-employed people in MSME. The poor can only participate in wealth creation if barriers to their entry into the private sector are reduced. There needs to be a level playing field where the government, donor agencies and civil society can best serve the interests of the Nepali people.

## Role of Government

The government in a capitalist welfare state has two significant roles. One is ensuring that it provides an environment for private enterprise to flourish; the other is ensuring equitable delivery of welfare to all its citizens. The government needs a clear understanding of its role as a regulator and as a service provider.

The government must realize, understand and believe in ensuring and protecting economic freedom as non-negotiable as it is directly correlated to economic growth.

## Let the Government Do Less

In Nepal, the journey of cities and how they have grown can be taken as a good example to show that the lesser the government intervention, the better the growth. 'Government doles, political protection doesn't create better cities or towns; people do.'[3] Prabhakar Rana, Chairman Emeritus of the Soaltee Hotel, used to cite the example of Narayanghat, 200 km west of Kathmandu, and the rest of the Chitwan area's development compared to Bara and Parsa that received much more government funding. Gurcharan Das in his book *India Grows at Night* gives the example of how Gurgaon, the satellite city next to Delhi, grew at a phenomenal pace compared to the ones planned by the government such as Faridabad and Ghaziabad. Therefore, people who think that cities which get more federal budget funds or government attention do well may be misguided. It is instead the cities that have the least government interference which do well as they have lesser barriers and hassles for entrepreneurs and businessmen to operate effectively.

Hetauda in the central region of Nepal is one such example of a city which was given a lot of government attention. Regrettably, it is now nothing more than a transit point. Another example is Mahendranagar, which had an airport built for hunting by the royals, and has now been relegated to a transit point—compare this to Dhangadhi, which is built by MSME entrepreneurs. Therefore, the government needs to change its role from being a controller of businesses to that of a facilitator. It can work with businesses to create a regulatory environment and ensure that global benchmarks and deliveries are met. For instance, it should let the private sector run banks, but there need to be penalties if their ATM machines do not clock 99.5 per cent efficiency, like in South Africa; similarly, companies must be fined heavily for not delivering on their promises. So let the bottled water plants be run by the private sector, but the government must enforce strict international norms on product quality and take on cartels if they gang up to defy government regulations.

## Government to Ensure Safety of Citizens

Perception of safety is very important for a business. Despite being a hotbed of politics, for instance, Chitwan has seen very few disruptions, and businesses there feel secure. Multinational companies have set up factories and tourism has grown. Even during the worst days of the insurgency, this area did not face shutdowns or similar problems like other cities.

Post the ten-year conflict, many new cities emerged across the country, from Udlabari in the east—where people from the eastern hills descended to avoid the troubles—to places like Gorusinghe in the west, which became a safe haven for people fleeing volatile zones of insurgency in the area. After the protracted Terai movement, many moved out of Janakpur and into Bardibas, about 20 km away, which developed as a transit point for the new highway to the east that started operations in 2015, showing how businesses are not interested in the discourse of ethnicity or politics. The relocating of businesses from Birgunj, which borders Bihar, to Butwal, which borders Uttar

Pradesh, also speaks volumes of how perceptions of border safety across different states in India affect ease of doing business in Nepal.

Business houses and entrepreneurs want to do business and will shift to areas that they perceive as safe and secure. The government and politicians need to understand that bad news breeds negative perceptions, which is ultimately detrimental for business.

## Leave Entrepreneurs to Build Business Ecosystems

Many times we feel that the government should be setting in place an ecosystem for businesses, but in reality it is the entrepreneurs who build it. Governments tend to build ecosystems that do not create a level playing field, which foster rent-seekers who never transform into entrepreneurs. In the far west, Nepal itself is facing challenges because of the abundance of developmental organizations and NGOs. On the other hand, in Chitwan in the west and Birtamod in the east, we see far less of the organizations that try to throttle entrepreneurship.

When Nepal is engaging in making federalism work, perhaps a case study on the development of cities like Narayanghat and Butwal will be good to learn exactly what makes them centres of business. If there are good businesses run by entrepreneurs, then more jobs are created. Local job creation means there are more young people wanting to get an education and training that fosters the business of education. This ensures the development of a more sustainable ecosystem and the government needs to ensure that it does not disrupt this.

## Leveraging Technology for Regulation

In Rwanda, from 1 January 2019, all land papers are signed with QR codes to replace electronic seals, stamps and signatures. In Estonia, 30 per cent of people voted using i-voting or electronic voting services and their governance website claims that 99 per cent of public services are available online 24x7, saving 800 years of working time.[4] Cambodia has an efficient electronic visa process and one of the most efficient systems for domestic mobile payments in Asia. Electronic filing of papers and digital signatures are used in many countries. At airports, efforts are made to have less human interface and allow the smooth movement of people by using face recognition software. Airports in Beijing and Istanbul are already at the forefront in implementing these new technologies. Payment of taxes through various electronic modules has increased net tax and revenue collection. Borders are now regulated through X-ray machines and cameras, with movement across borders becoming easier. In education and healthcare, governments have leveraged technology to improve service delivery as well as supervision. The challenges of regulating e-commerce transactions over the Internet and digital space will become even bigger as the world will start accepting the realities of bitcoins and other platforms. From 'I know it all' regulators, the government needs to become a facilitator that moves with the times.

Additionally, the government has to understand the value of outsourcing and explore the possibility of outsourcing select regulatory functions to credible international companies. It has to accept that outsourcing the customs function at the international airport to an international firm or outsourcing the auditor general's function does not compromise the nation's sovereignty.

## Getting Out of the Cartel Economy

The government plays a key role in breaking cartels. For instance, the signing of the agreement on 29 October 2018 between Nepal and Malaysia for sending labour to Malaysia at zero cost broke the jinx of manpower cartels controlling labour supplies from Nepal. Similarly, if the government allows ride-hailing services like Uber, it would break the transport cartels. The operations of Tootle and Pathao, two bike-hailing services, have provided a new cost-effective and efficient way of transportation in the Kathmandu valley and beyond.

The government has to ensure that conflict of interest is understood as people doing business cannot be leading parliamentary committees or representing regulatory authorities. For instance, as seen in the past, owners of banks should not be chairing committees drafting laws on banks, and business people should not be sitting on investment boards as that allows them to gain access to feasibility studies and other documents that they can replicate quickly. Further, penalties, fines and other restrictions must be strictly enforced for cartel-like behaviour. In the long run, probably all business associations should be slowly disbanded to convert and create knowledge-sharing platforms to be run by think tanks and research organizations.

## Towards a More Ambitious Private Sector

The future of the private sector in leading the nation in the goal of wealth creation depends on its ability to realize its own inadequacies. The main quality the private sector needs is ambition—it has to be ambitious enough to take on the global economy. For this, it needs to step outside the box of protectionism, believe in itself and develop the necessary capabilities and competencies to compete on the global stage.

A vibrant private sector is the engine of growth which generates decent jobs and increased opportunities for more inclusive and green growth. While the government can empower poor people through regulations, funding and providing public goods, the private sector can also provide services and generate much-needed employment in the country. A large and formal private sector can also be a strong advocate for policy reform and a force for good governance, establishing a virtuous circle in which an improving business environment brings in private sector growth, which in turn strengthens governance reforms.

A growing private sector creates new stakeholders like new investors, employees and customers in the economy, bringing about a more pluralistic society that can lead to a more accountable political system. The combination of greater competition, market forces and the profit motive can lead to better use of Nepal's human capital and material resources.

The private sector needs to forge alliances with multinationals, seek foreign capital and technology, venture beyond the country and bury protectionist attitudes. Simultaneously, it has to work on developing professionalism, embracing technology and building contemporary administrative structures that follow ethical codes and believe in making adequate disclosures. Although regulating the private sector is the responsibility of the government, it is the private sector that must step up to the plate and dictate the most appropriate regulatory frameworks to ensure that best-practice models are being followed. Global economic entities prefer to do business with firms from nations with regulatory models that match international standards.

It will be important to build strong private sector institutions which will assist the government in policy formulation and act as advocacy bodies for industries, in contrast to its current dependence on political nexuses, kowtowing and lobbying for individual gains. These institutions should be led by business people but managed by professionals. They should target policies that support fair competition and expansion opportunities. They need to invest more in think tanks and research institutes for policy formulation, along with ensuring improved data and information to enhance decision-making. This will require a paradigm shift within the private sector.

The private sector can have a significant impact on the political system and be effective in curbing political corruption. The root cause of corruption lies in the inability of political parties to raise funds legitimately. This forces them to resort to taking political donations in return for favours. The private sector needs to work with the government to formulate policies that enable the funding of political parties legitimately and, most importantly, accountably and transparently. Each business should be given the right to contribute a certain percentage of their profits or turnover to a political party, thereby ensuring proper tax disclosures. Politicians should be legitimately allowed to collect such contributions, which should be tax deductible. Political parties should be mandated to issue financial audits and public disclosures of their collections and expenses. Therefore, when laws emerge favouring a certain business, one can look at the connection between the business, its contribution to a political party and government action. Thereafter, legal and other measures can be initiated to locate such incidents. Currently, it is impossible to trace money given to a party to a business and the favours businesses get.

## Privatize the Private Sector

Unfortunately, in Nepal, the private sector has lagged behind even the government in reforming itself. The private sector needs to move away from the rent-seeking, power-and-opportunity-grabbing mindset and develop long-term sustainable practices to ensure profitability and growth and make an impact on society. Three key areas of reform for the private sector are: First, the segregation of ownership and management is a must, and there is no other option but to corporatize and inculcate professionalism. The second requirement is succession planning for family businesses. Global benchmarks in strategy, accounting and tax practices need to be embraced to gain a comparative and competitive advantage. Third, it needs to place emphasis on the importance of contributing to society, be it in terms of moving towards a circular economy or making environmental causes a part of its strategy, and not resort to mere tokenism.

In the last decade, the image of the private sector has taken a hit as it has been associated with being the root cause of corruption and is frequently accused of getting away with delivering substandard goods and services at high costs. The private sector and business people must lead by example. They have to repackage themselves for the public eye as responsible citizens of the nation and shed their image of profiteering and racketeering. Businesses have to present themselves as professional entities with long-term goals that prosper along with the nation and not as rent-seeking arbitrage units.

## Donors: Make Your Exit Plans

The concept of donors and aid should be done away with rather than enabling it to find newer modes of engagement. Like the transformation we are seeking in the mindsets of the government and the private sector, a serious makeover is called for in the thinking of the donor world. Like Rwanda has planned for the phasing out of donor assistance by 2025, Nepal should set a timeline for development partners to be in business in Nepal. While multilateral investment agencies of the World Bank, ADB and other institutions would surely have a larger investment role, the cottage industry development partners need to make plans to shut shop.

Multilateral, bilateral and international donors have a big role to play in facilitating Nepal's transformation into a capitalist welfare state and in the alleviation of poverty through wealth creation. They have to play a supporting role to the government and private sector but should avoid taking the lead like in many instances in the past where it has led to political complications.

Aid targets should be assessed by the number of sustainable interventions completed rather than by the number of interventions planned. It is essential that donors make an effort to coordinate activity amongst themselves. Along with this, governance, management and financial structures within the development community need improvement. This means public disclosure of receipts and expenditure that is as good as if not better than that provided by publicly traded companies. An amount of $10 million per annum needs to be fixed as the minimum amount of financial aid that can be offered by donors. Transparency in procurement processes, in the hiring of staff and in contracting service providers, is also a must. Finally, a code of ethics must be defined and strictly adhered to, be it rules relating to travel, hotel stay utilization, conferences, seminars, allowances or other rules that are generally governed by employment contracts and organization rules. It is also important that all the money provided by donors is regulated through the government treasury, thereby giving no leeway to individual donor countries or institutions to bypass the government.

Further, privately managed philanthropic funds should become a reality in Nepal, where donors, especially NGOs, as well as multilateral and bilateral aid agencies, would have the choice of giving money to such funds, as this will ensure that overheads of managing the money are minimized. For instance, after the 2015 earthquake, there were agencies that spent 35 per cent of their money on overheads while there were also those who were operating at less than 5 per cent overhead costs. Nepal needs to encourage the latter variety.

Donors also need to review the successes and failures of past programmes. Over the years, development partners have engaged in several public–private partnership ventures in conjunction with business associations and government agencies. In 2005, DFID funded the FNCCI Anti-corruption project to assist Nepali businesses to operate more ethically and set up self-regulating systems that discourage corruption. It will be important to take stock of the successes and failures of such programmes of development partners so that successful ones can be replicated.

## Limiting the Role of Cooperatives

There have been many successful cooperative movements around the world. Closer home, the milk cooperative movement which transformed the state of Gujarat in India is a prime example. In many countries, cooperatives of agriculture producers have been able to transform the lives of farmers. However, cooperatives cannot be used as a tool to replace the private sector.

In the Nepali context, cooperatives are basically private organizations that are not regulated like the private sector and enjoy the perception of being a public sector organization with overtures of nationalism. For instance, banks are regulated by the central bank, while cooperatives are not. But even so, some of these unregulated cooperatives can be larger than banks.

Nepal needs to limit cooperatives to areas where community mobilization is required; in rural areas or in the small and medium agriculture sector. Cooperatives that operate in an unregulated manner in Nepal are impediments to economic growth and should be phased out. It should also be mandatory for them to be registered so that the government can regulate their actions.

## Towards Robust Home-grown Community Service Organizations

One of the biggest achievements of Nepal over the past two decades has been the emergence of a plethora of grassroots organizations that have helped in the transformation of livelihoods. For instance, the community forest user groups that have a combined strength of 1.2 million households[5] manage NPR 1 billion without much supervision.[6] While urban centres were reeling under sixty hours of power cuts every week in the past decade, many of Nepal's villages were enjoying twenty-four-hour electricity from the microhydro-projects they built. In areas where the state utility is absent, communities are paying market prices to ensure there is an uninterrupted supply of electricity.

The key strength we need to pick up from community-based organizations would be their understanding of local skills and networks, local innovation and thought processes and their desire to be a part of the process of unleashing Nepal's potential. The government, aid agencies, NGOs and private enterprises need to harness these strengths collectively and not compete with each other.

## Regulating NGOs

It is also essential to use multi-pronged strategies to tackle the regulation of NGOs. First, the Trust Act, drafted more than twenty years ago, needs to be promulgated with timely changes to ensure that families and others who want the trust structure do not have to use the NGO route. There are many family members who want trustees to undertake a business or activities on behalf of the beneficiaries. Similarly, there must be provisions for family and religious foundations. The current Guthi[7] Act must be expanded to accommodate provisions beyond ownership of land, whether owned by family or religious institutions.

Second, the Social Welfare Council (SWC), the successor of the autocratic regime's entity, the Social Service National Service Committee (SSNSC), which was a control agency, needs to become a facilitation agency for INGOs and NGOs. The SWC's greed for making money formally and informally needs to end.

Third, if NGOs are doing business, they should be registered under the provisions of Chapter 19 of the Companies Act to operate. Fourth, there have to be provisions for the registration of small civil society organizations (CSOs) that spend annually below a certain prescribed limit by just registering themselves with local bodies. Fifth, a national discourse is necessary on why we need so many associations. If they are just a front for cartels, then surely they must be disbanded. Sixth, we need to question whether the patronage bestowed on youth clubs and other entities that were a source of keeping the Opposition out during the Panchayat days is still necessary or whether they should now be merged with local governments. The youth clubs in Nepal are associated with taking premium public plans through land grants or leasing them for building properties and managing them. These have become rent-seeking entities that operate under political patronage.

Finally, transparency will be key when it comes to the question of declaring funds or the affiliation of people. INGOs can show the way by putting up their financials and conflict-of-interest declarations in public domains. These processes should be similar to those of public companies.

## Doing Business in Federated Nepal

One of the key challenges for Nepal up to 2030 will be to make federalism work. There are some key areas that need to be looked at in achieving this. First, there are many global lessons to learn, but it remains to be seen how we can adapt to those lessons. For instance, in New York, mayors have spent a lot of time leading transformations in many areas of public life: from school systems to security concerns to providing information on public services in different languages (170, to be precise). The façade of buildings in Manhattan are being given a heritage makeover, and many of the train stations are being integrated with new commercial buildings. We see that in relatively new East Asian cities like Bangkok and Singapore, shopping and office complexes are integrated with train and bus stations. Nepal needs to explore what would be the best benchmarks for deliveries made by local governments. For instance, it would be worthwhile to learn from Singapore how to have an efficient public transport system, or from within Nepal, learn from the city of Dharan how to keep a city clean.

Second, governance is key. With Nepal converting villages into municipalities at a rapid pace, it also needs to ensure governance structures in these municipalities and see that their vision extends for decades. Rwanda's capital city has the Master Plan 2040 in place, and the same is being replicated in smaller cities and towns. There is a tremendous amount to be learnt from how a third-world city can have first-world cleanliness, greenery and open spaces. Kathmandu, along with other cities and towns in Nepal, needs a serious plan that can be executed. Cities in many parts of the world have undergone tremendous makeovers and transformation, with rivers being cleaned, open spaces created, and tree plantation carried out on a large scale to ensure greenery.

Third, the cost of federalization has to be reduced after the larger outlay of costs in initial years, as it is important that this does not become an additional cost of doing business. Rather than increased costs, there has to be an emphasis on fostering competition between different provinces and local governments to attract investments and grow their economies.

## Refining and Embracing Globalization

Globalization can be understood as the seamless process of integration between global markets and citizens worldwide. It is important to understand globalization not just from the perspective of the market economy but also from a sociocultural perspective as the simultaneous globalization of attitudes, ideologies and practices. From human rights campaigns to animal rights activism, from religion to the horrors of terrorism, and from the spread of culinary delights to the sound of music. For Nepal, the challenge is not just one of market integration but of identifying and capitalizing on its unique brand and identity so that it can contribute to and benefit from the socio-economic process of globalization.

For Nepal to truly capitalize on the advantages that globalization has to offer, it needs to fundamentally reorient and rebrand itself on the world stage. It can no longer stick to its old aristocratic views of isolationism and protectionism and must embrace the dynamic, flat and horizontal structure of the twenty-first century. Nepal has to lock the symbols of its archaic past into world-class museums within the country and start marketing and leveraging the sacred symbols of culture that are housed in such museums. It has to preserve history and meaning—not as an impediment to progress but as a tool for marketing. It is critical that Nepal and the Nepali people participate in this new age of consumerism and remain in tune with changing fads and fashions. In participating in the global community, Nepal must also understand the nature of consumerism and learn how it can best utilize its unique location and history. Its rich history and culture make it ideal for tourism while its location has massive potential for production and industry in both the agricultural and energy sectors.

Nepal even needs to make some changes so it can get in line with the preferred practices the world over. First, it has to change from the archaic Bikram calendar and start using the Gregorian calendar which is used worldwide. It then has to get in sync with global financial markets and let the sun shine on a weekly Sunday holiday in addition to Saturday instead of the ridiculous half-day on Friday. It needs to institute a five-day work week, but operate 24x7 otherwise and also ration out public holidays. It needs a stricter work ethic and a working schedule that does not end at 4 p.m. during winter just because it gets dark early. Second, Nepal's financial year cannot continue to be as unique as its national flag. It needs to either follow the January–December or July–June calendar rather than requiring a host of points to explain which date of the Bikram calendar it begins with in July and which date it ends at. The Bikram Sambat is not constant in the number of days in a month in each year. Third, Nepal's time zone needs to be set to something that has a thirty-minute interval and not a fifteen-minute interval. Currently, Nepal is +5.45 ahead of GMT—this should be either 5.30 or 6 hours. In these times, when conference calls are the way to do business, the fifteen-minute intervals create a tremendous nuisance. Fourth, the introduction of daylight saving time during the summer months by pushing the clock back by an hour means that offices, schools and other establishments can begin an hour earlier. This would not only utilize the productive hours of the morning but also provide more hours in the evening for people to use leisure time productively. Energy savings of an hour in the evening in power-starved Nepal would be a big contribution to the economy. Meanwhile, in the winter, there will be no need to close offices at 4 p.m., especially in cities where transportation is available. Finally, Nepal needs to fully support the installation of English as the primary national language for all Nepali people so that Nepalis are fluent in the language of globalization. Importantly, this does not mean forgetting other languages and dialects, but understanding that a common language without historical baggage in Nepal can only be an asset to a country that is trying to make its way into the global mainstream.

The reasons for the above recommendations are apparent—globalization cannot occur within the confines of a national system and context. The Nepali economy needs to be integrated into the global economy and Nepal must realize it cannot dictate the rules of engagement because it plays a relatively minor role. As a country, Nepal is competing with all the other developing countries for limited global economic resources, whether it is foreign aid, foreign investment, tourists or trade. If the Nepali economy is unsuccessful in reorienting itself, it will be relegated to the far fringes of the global economy. Nepal as a nation and the Nepali people as members of a global community must realize that integration into the global economy will be difficult if we use a calendar that occasionally has only eleven months.

Nepal must also learn from the experiences of other developing countries that have integrated into the global economy. For instance, the closure of airports in Thailand for a week in December 2008 highlighted the need for seamless global flight operations and the fallout of failing to achieve that goal. The closure of the airports pushed the supply chain of computer suppliers in the US out of gear and cost the Thai economy as well as computer companies in the US a considerable amount of money.

## Nepalis Should Be Allowed to Invest Abroad

Nepali citizens should be allowed to invest outside Nepal in an organized way to ensure the country takes advantage of the globalizing world. For example, a businessperson in eastern Nepal has a great understanding of the market in nearby Siliguri or Sikkim in India, while one in far western Nepal understands the opportunities across the border in Uttarakhand. Neither of them particularly understands opportunities in Kathmandu, yet that is where they can invest legitimately—not in their neighbouring countries' markets.

Currently, investments abroad are all illegitimate as they contravene the Foreign Investment Prohibition Act of 1964 which stipulates that no Nepali can invest outside Nepal. This needs to be replaced by a Regulation of Investment in Foreign Countries Act, which will benefit the state in the same manner as allowing the establishment of money transfer firms. Economic and financial prudence suggests that Nepalis should be allowed to invest in the economic growth of China, India and other neighbouring countries. The Nepali national investing in a Nepali fund that invests overseas would have the benefit of getting returns that will not be limited to the Nepali economy. We should not prevent Nepalis from availing this world of opportunity outside Nepal. We need to recall that India's growth in the past couple of years has been fuelled by Indian investments abroad, wherein Indian investors have been able to increase the value of their portfolios through the growth of assets in the developed world.

The fewer restrictions the government places on the flow of money, the greater the benefit to general investors. In the same way that Nepal became the first South Asian country with a digital telephone exchange in 1985, it could become the first South Asian country to be a hub for digital financial exchange. Reforms are not rocket science—a copy of the *Doing Business Report*[8] published by the World Bank that ranks countries based on the ease of doing business provides a list of best practices in this regard, emulating some of which will take Nepal a long way on the road to economic success. A good score in the Doing Business Report, coupled with a better ranking in the Human Development Index and the achievement of sustainable development goals, will truly reflect Nepal's journey towards becoming a capitalist welfare state.

# III

# Action Time

We have spoken about Nepal's journey of nearly 1200 years, and have been able to contextualize it in various aspects. It is now time to understand what needs to be done in specific terms. This is the focus of the next three chapters.

What does it mean for Nepal to be located between India and China? This needs articulation through a vision that will give a sense of the direction in which Nepal should head, the resources it needs and the changes it needs to embrace. What does Nepal need to do to become a middle-income country by 2030? In terms of sectors, hydropower, agriculture and tourism (or HAT) is always talked about, but now the discussion needs to expand to include services and infrastructure.

The realization in Nepal has been that money and education do not necessarily deliver a better society, and it becomes important to articulate what type of society Nepal should aim for, while pointing out the simple things we never tend to ponder upon.

In the final chapter, the emphasis is on societal transformation via individual transformation, and both of these as a means to economic transformation. There are many countries Nepal can learn from in terms of what to do and what not to do to unleash its potential.

# Vision 2030 and Beyond

In Nepal, the English term 'vision' is used loosely to mean just 'a thought', thereby relegating a word with deep meaning and implication to rhetoric. It is very difficult to discuss 'vision' in the real sense. Nepalis generally don't hire architects to plan a house or consultants to figure out business plans. They never begin with the end goal in mind, contrary to the preaching of leadership guru Stephen Covey, the author of the bestseller *The Seven Habits of Highly Effective People*. The concept of using maps has never been completely internalized, and even in the days of Google Maps, people need to be given directions, which they will most probably not understand correctly. Events in Nepal are not planned, and neither is life. While religion and culture teach one to plan beyond this current life through rituals and ceremonies, there is little emphasis on straightening out the big picture. It is too much about living in the present. In terms of spirituality this may be wonderful, but in day-to-day matters it can pose a challenge.

However, successful countries do function on the basis of vision. The success of Singapore and Malaysia has been attributed to them defining a long-term vision and achieving it. Scandinavian and European countries have done it well too, be it planning their own lives or that of the communities they live in. In Africa, countries like Rwanda follow their long-term visions to the hilt. Therefore, in this chapter, we try to force discussions that will take people out of their usual comfort zones and think of where Nepal will be in 2030, 2040 or even 2050, and what that will mean for its residents. Every country needs a vision statement so that there is motivation to make greater efforts. Having a national development strategy and clearly defined roles and responsibilities of the central, state and local governments, private corporate sector and other organizations will be an essential step in building the country. Being thorough about potential risks and bottlenecks is always safer. Vision 2030 will provide long-term alternative policy scenarios on the future course of development in Nepal at different points in time up until the target year.

## The World and Nepal in 2050

In 2050, Nepal's next-door neighbours China and India are going to be the two largest economies in the world with an estimated doubling of their real GDP in the next twenty years. So, China and India, at $59 trillion and $44 trillion respectively, would be global leaders ahead of the United States at $34 billion—based on purchasing power parity (PPP) computations.[1] Another of our close neighbours, Bangladesh, would be ranked twenty-third as per the projected accelerated growth.

It is estimated that Nepal's population would have tapered off at around 36 million people by 2050, while the world population would have inched closer to 10 billion. There would be a significant demographic shift compared to today. For instance, 31 per cent of the population of Nepal was under fifteen years of age in 2018, and this will reduce to 17 per cent in 2050. However, the proportion of people above age sixty-five will increase from 5 per cent to 13 per cent.[2] This means that over the years, the number of people who earn will reduce while the number of dependants will increase. This will have a major impact on social service delivery, especially healthcare.

Nepal needs to look positively at the scenario emerging in the world in 2050, as nearly 35 per cent of the global GDP will be housed between China and India. These two economic powerhouses will create enough opportunities for Nepal, especially as it is linked by land to both. Therefore, it is imperative that there is a long-haul planning process to look at how Nepal wants to leverage the situation over the coming decades.

Like many other countries, Rwanda, for example, that have embarked on a Vision 2050 idea, Nepal needs to perhaps look at how it will deliver the same vision of prosperity to its people by 2050 with equal emphasis on capital, asset utilization, parameters of human development, and of course, happiness.

## Why 2030?

When a vision is decided upon, there is a certain perspective of alignment to global goals that are being followed closely. In this case, for Nepal, using the Sustainable Development Goals (SDGs) of the United Nations as a reference point would not only ensure that it has the necessary tools of measurement but also allow it to compare itself with other countries. The year 2030 also looks like something that can be planned for and does not make the planning process nebulous, especially in the context of the ever-changing pace of communication, technology and global geopolitics.

## The World in 2030

The world in 2030 is expected to have a population of around 8.5 billion, which means more than a billion more people on the planet compared to 2018. China would have become the largest economy in the world, overtaking the United States, and India would be third. Emerging markets will comprise 50 per cent of the global GDP and account for 70 per cent of growth. While poorer countries with younger populations will generally rise up the rankings quickest, better education, healthcare, the rule of law and technology can still maintain the higher positions of countries with shrinking working populations, as should be seen in the likes of Thailand and some of the central Eastern European countries.[3]

The world would have changed in many ways. On the one hand, innovation, technology and artificial intelligence would have changed our lives forever. On the other, the perceptions around human needs and wants, greed, the shift from a linear to a circular economy, climate change and other things that impact human evolution would have bought about new dimensions to life, its purpose, and what it means to have a fulfilling life.

With the use of artificial intelligence to sharpen analysis, human capabilities would have transformed. The world of self-driving cars would be the norm and flight times would have reduced with breakthroughs in technology. Human healthcare would be challenged by the need to take care of more older people as life expectancy increases, but it will be aided by advancement in medical sciences that will allow us to 3D-print and transplant organs. There will be more breakthroughs that will lead to many current must-haves being banished to the museums, like typewriters, pagers and fax machines were a while ago. The desire of the human mind and body to experience and explore will open new vistas. When we look back, we realize that the top jobs of today did not even exist ten years ago. Acquisition of knowledge and skills will transform along with how human beings interact. There are many analyses, discussions and debates being undertaken to look at the world in 2030. Nepal cannot be isolated from this and therefore has to plug into the discourse.

## Nepal: A Middle-Income Country by 2030

There are multiple factors to consider regarding the progress of a nation. The global benchmarks are set around GDP and per capita income growth, and there are many other criteria to be met that will be discussed later. In this section, the discussion will focus on GDP and per capita growth. For Nepal to graduate to a middle-income country by 2030, when the country's population will be around 36 million, it needs to be a $100 billion economy with a per capita income of $2500. To reach this mark, it needs over 8 per cent growth each year. Economic growth can only occur if there are investments in infrastructure, entrepreneurship development, income and employment generation. This would require an investment of about $7–8 billion each year. Domestic investment capacities do not exceed $2 billion a year at present, which means Nepal needs foreign investment. I worked with a member of the National Planning Commission, Swarnim Wagle,[4] in 2016 and wrote a piece on how this growth must be led by the private sector. Many parts of the discussions in this chapter are based on this report[5] I prepared for the ADB.

## Nepal Economic Vision 2030 (NEV 2030)

The three pillars to this vision document prepared by the National Planning Commission have been regarded as Generating Prosperity, Sharing Prosperity and Sustaining Prosperity. Generating Prosperity: Identification of long-term sources of economic growth in Nepal is an important factor to start with. Sharing Prosperity: The next step would be to determine institutions to ensure that economic development gains are shared across the country as well as across socio-economic parameters such as gender, regions, social groups and age groups. Sustaining Prosperity: Protection of the achievements till date is necessary in order to move forward in the future, and to do this, there needs to be speculation about the emerging threats that will make the economy unstable.

The core vision is to see Nepal graduate into a middle-income country by 2030, alleviate poverty and raise the living standards of people along with sustainable development and social justice. In order to do this, there needs to be mobilization between domestic and foreign investments. There must also be reforms under each major sector to ensure the required changes are made.

## The Enablers: What Will Ensure the Vision Is Achieved

Acknowledging the need to improve income, productivity and working conditions in different sectors is an important component of growth and poverty reduction agenda in Nepal. Nepal's economy needs transformation and coordinated reforms in order to achieve the 2030 goals. There is a linkage between reforms, investment and growth which needs strong assistance from the private sector in order to pursue Vision 2030. In this regard, it is also important to understand how resources are going to be allocated towards it. These would include managing the large investment requirement, fostering entrepreneurial culture, corporatization, following global and regional dreams, undertaking key reforms and managing access to resources.

Large Investment Requirement: The World Bank and the IMF have projected Nepal's economy to grow at just under 5 per cent until FY 2019–20, which will hold it back from achieving the target of graduating to a developing country by 2022. Despite this we cannot ignore the fact that Nepal has already met the LDC (least developed country) graduation criteria this year on two of the three points.[6] The two requirements that Nepal has fulfilled are the human asset index and the economic vulnerability index. However, we are far behind in the third and most important criteria: income.

To achieve such growth, investments should not be driven by the government or donors but by the private sector, especially through foreign direct investment. Taking the above hypothesis, it is envisaged that $7–8 billion would have to be invested each year to provide the necessary stimulus to the economy to grow at the desired levels.

Fostering Entrepreneurial Culture: In Nepal, there are many projects that can be government-driven but are executed by the private sector. For instance, in the case of issuance of smartcard-based driver's licences—the government can easily afford this, but instead chooses to wait years for an aid agency to assist and finance such a project. Promoting private-sector enterprises to execute such projects will help foster entrepreneurial culture. Such a culture has a relationship with not only economic growth but also with building social capital, primary sources of innovation and job creation. It will give an opportunity to create institutions that will train people, especially after the earthquake, since people will need money to restart their lives, be it for building livestock inventory or a seed bank and agricultural inputs. Heritage site restoration will require thousands of skilled and semi-skilled workers who can be paid salaries at par with what they earn in the Middle East.

Nepal needs devolution of government, a statutory granting of power for policy implementation or creation at the local level in line with the federal structure. Fostering entrepreneurial culture will lead the way for this. Besides, it will also have a direct influence on internationalization of technology, human resource and capital and information flow.

Nepal needs to examine the provisions in the Constitution related to economic issues. The country needs to understand that poverty alleviation and economic growth can only take place through wealth creation, which cannot be achieved by cooperatives, donor money and grants. Wealth can only be created through a proliferation of MSMEs, employment in private-sector companies and projects that involve large investments. This will lead to an entrepreneur-friendly environment which will promote and foster the growth of those who are willing to compete with global and regional companies. The government needs to step in to ensure that inequality is regulated, consumer rights are protected and a level playing field is provided for all.

Corporatization and Global and Regional Dreams: Over the years, there has been a lot of talk about corporate governance scandals, including those at WorldCom and Daewoo. This has affected capital markets worldwide and raised the issue of accountability, transparency, policies and ethics. These issues have therefore been linked with the business environment, and the private sector has been advised to be part of the solution. For instance, Nepal will be open to many more foreign direct investments in the coming years when the Power Trade Agreement between Nepal and India leverages the private sector. This will not only help the hydropower sector grow but also assist in the big transition from it being one of the worst countries to do business in to a country with massive potential.

Doing business in Nepal is expensive. It has unskilled labourers and low productivity, and frequent strikes or slowdowns make it even more difficult for any business to function smoothly. This has a bigger effect on foreign investments as investors see this as a barrier. It is also very important to have a well-educated labour force and a flexible labour market that puts productivity and merit above unwarranted rights and protection.

## Towards Structural Reforms

We discuss here five key areas of reforms towards ensuring that NEV 2030 is achieved. These are distinct from what typically multilateral agencies would prescribe and are contextualized in terms of Nepal's requirements.

Tax Reform: Currently, a business in Nepal pays 25 per cent income tax apart from 13 per cent value-added tax and 5 per cent taxation on dividends earned. Besides that, businesses have to set aside 8.33 per cent of salaries as a bonus for Dasain. There is a further 10 per cent service charge levied on customers. Further, there are new social security benefits that have been introduced by the new Social Security Act of 2018. While there has been significant improvement in the tax payment system and service, there remains room for improvement in terms of service delivery. Incentives on taxes to encourage businesses to invest more and employ more people should be explored. Further, increasing the tax net is critical to increase the tax base. Nepal needs to learn from many other countries and leverage technology relating to the payment of taxes: by making payment through electronic methods popular and electronic billing machines mandatory, depositing collected tax directly into government revenue accounts, and giving bill-payers in a restaurant or store an electronic receipt from the tax authorities. Currently, mobile phone penetration in Nepal is close to 100 per cent and therefore payment systems using mobile platforms should be explored.

It is imperative that the issue of inheritance tax is looked into. In Nepal, inheritance, especially of land and its disposal, continues to be a major income source for people. Therefore, beyond a certain threshold, this should be taxed so that investments in non-productive assets like land and gold can be reduced and the money can flow into productive sectors.

Land Reform: Landownership taxes should be based on the market value of land where the owners are taxed on the basis of value rather than size of plots. Land revenue management requires a shift from a land area paradigm to a land value paradigm, allowing the government to determine a system based on land value that maximizes its revenue. This revenue can in turn finance or subsidize housing schemes or provide agricultural land for the poor. Additionally, as stated above, an inheritance tax can be levied on the transfer of ownership of land beyond a certain value, thereby not only increasing revenue streams but also helping transform the mentality of the urban Nepali who lives off rents from ancestral properties.

To initiate such land reforms, it is necessary to improve the process of recording and tracking land ownership. Therefore, the first set of reforms would be to make all land records and transactions electronic. Further, it is important that all land records are consolidated to ensure all land held by an individual or company throughout the country is monitored through a single account.

It is also imperative that land is divided into different zones for agricultural, commercial or residential purposes with proper guidelines. For commercial agriculture to thrive, large-scale holdings by companies should be allowed and proper monitoring done to ensure that the provisions are not violated. Similarly, guidelines should be provided to ensure that there are adequate open spaces and landowners adhere to disaster management requirements.

Capital Market Reform: Nepal has never been able to leverage capital market reforms. As a country that needs cash and funds, it needs to look for ways to encourage the raising of money since it will reduce the burdens on the state.

While there have been significant developments like making paperless trading a reality in the stock market and a system of functional mutual funds, this has not been able to excite international players. It is imperative that capital market reform explores the participation of foreign institutional investors (FIIs) in secondary markets through the stock exchange to begin with and then extending it to primary markets. Further, Nepali companies should be allowed to list on stock exchanges outside Nepal. This will ensure that regulations for companies in Nepal are brought up to world-class standards, requiring companies to follow international regulations in terms of governance and disclosure. This will help firms in Nepal to not only be at the same level as international players but will also allow them to compare and contrast their positives and drawbacks. Keeping that in mind, insider trading and other violations of laws should also be strictly dealt with to ensure that these practices are discouraged.

Labour Reform: Labour reform needs to look at changes in the Labour Act and Trade Union Act in order to deal with fundamental issues such as wages being linked to productivity, output and performances. The world is moving from the concept of job creation to income generation with a working population that does not want to stick to a single job till retirement, and instead prefers to combine jobs and entrepreneurial pursuits. The Social Security Programme of the government announced in December 2018 has added a burden for firms as they are required to make further investments for social security of employees. Over time, political affiliations of workers' unions should be done away with, along with the system of collective bargaining. Strong labour courts should be able to settle disputes between employer and employee, handing out verdicts that can be strictly adhered to. For Nepal's next level of economic growth, it is important that it learns from countries like Malaysia that have been able to push labour reforms and implement systems that are fair as well as ones that can be strictly enforced. Currently, companies in Nepal spend very little on human resource development, therefore, spending on learning and development needs to be accelerated through legal provisions.

Financial Sector Reform: The political–business nexus always hinders reforms. The global financial crisis of 2008 illustrated that the financial sector is a difficult one to regulate; however, this doesn't mean that reforms should be frozen just because the government wants to play a zero-risk game. The number of financial institutions in Nepal has increased but there is still a challenge in terms of access to finance. Laws are required to make financial institutions more transparent and use financial instruments like leasing, guarantees, venture capital funds, social enterprise funds, impact funds and private equity in the best possible way.

The financial world in Nepal must move beyond banks and start looking at a variety of players that invest in equity and mobilize money through different instruments. Further, it is important that the focus shifts to service delivery and utilization of technology, be it online banking, branchless banking or mobile banking. The capacity of the regulator has to be enhanced to be able to monitor service delivery. For instance, data on ATM downtimes and server downtimes, cybersecurity and checking on software upgradation will be important to ensure that the regulator and the financial institution can keep pace with changes in systems, processes and technology. Financial services require integration, and the role of insurance as a tool for risk reduction and hedging should not be overlooked.

## Vision Requires Access to Resources

In order to implement a vision, access to resources is paramount. This section on access to resources has been divided into three parts: access to financial resources, access to technical resources, and access to human resources.

## Access to Financial Resources

Nepal's financial sector has extended and the number and types of financial intermediaries have grown rapidly in the last twenty years. The Government of Nepal has recognized the importance of a properly functioning financial sector as a key driver for reducing inequality and poverty. New reforms have made access to finance more stable, but it is still limited in many parts of Nepal. Informal sources are more prominent and famous in Nepal than formal ones—for example, the usage of insurance and electronic payment services is rare. This might also be a result of poor infrastructure and literacy rate.

One of the long-term objectives in Nepal is to achieve a larger extent of financial inclusion, to deliver financial services at an affordable cost, especially for those who are disadvantaged and in low-income groups.

Supply of Financial Services: The Government of Nepal has tried pushing formal financial services for small businesses and low-income households, and also introduced directed lending programmes for the promotion of formal services. Despite these efforts, access to formal financial services is declining. Similarly, access to bank infrastructure has also decreased significantly. Even when remittance was being sent back to Nepal by migrant workers, there was no increase in access to formal financial services because informal services such as hundi were being used.

Demand for Financial Services: The usage of banks is dominated by the urban wealthy. Only 26 per cent of Nepali households have a bank account, and for 18 per cent, cooperatives and financial NGOs are providers of deposits. Family and friends make up the highest percentage as an informal source provider of loans to households. The reason for this is that the formal sector—banks—cannot provide households with the required amount on time. In the case of the rich, who also have a high rate of informal service usage, their transactions require quick access, which is again a problem in formal institutions. In terms of small businesses, because they need working capital, informal institutions are quicker in providing loans than formal ones. Regarding remittance, less than 8 per cent is saved in financial institutions, with the rest used in daily consumption and to repay loans.

Overall, the scenario of demand and supply shows that even with the effort of the government, in Nepal formal financial institutions are not favoured by Nepalis. Small firms and low-income households especially do not have a compatible relationship with them as informal institutions work better.

## Access to Technical Resources

There is rapid growth in the private and non-government sector working in various aspects of technology. There are over eighty science-and-technology-related professional organizations operating in the country, with the largest membership in medical and engineering associations. These organizations have provided services to development efforts. Institutions for policy formulation, education and training, consultancy services, testing and standardization, research and development, extensive services and promotion are established. Nepal has strengthened its basic infrastructure, which has helped the country better utilize modern technology. Some good examples of this can be seen in the communications, health, engineering and agriculture sectors.

There have also been significant achievements in Nepal in the technology sector, comparable to the development of hydropower by Nepali entrepreneurs. Similarly, we have also seen several professional educational institutions focused on technology. By 2030, the strengthening and development of technology will result in strong partnerships and effective implementation of policies.

## Access to Human Capital

Human resource is one of the most important assets of an organization. For generations, the importance of human resource was overlooked. In Nepal, there was and still is a lack of a systematic approach towards human resource development in business organizations. There are hardly any personnel dedicated to human resource management, which is reflected in the allocation of budgets for human resources in annual programmes. Even though the importance of human resource has started making an impact on various organizations now, it has still not received the amount of attention it needs.

Focus on human resource is key to staying ahead of the competition, as the concept of Total Quality People (a measure of people with character, integrity, good values and a positive attitude) holds the key to a successful enterprise. However, in Nepal, we notice that training people is not regarded as an investment and is the first to be targeted when there is a budget cut. This has made a huge impact on the increase in migration for employment outside Nepal. Workers want to travel across borders just to have better training which gives them better opportunities. This makes access to human resource a constraint for Nepali business organizations. Studies have shown that in the past decade, lack of appropriate pay, perks and differential pay structures compared to international organizations in Nepal are amongst the reasons a number of people do not return after completing their studies abroad.

## Achieving Vision 2030

To achieve the overarching goal of a prosperous Nepal by 2030 keeping in mind the above enablers, I have drawn up a list of eleven key recommendations. Many of these are based on my recommendations in the report prepared on leveraging the private sector and investments.

## Getting a Credit Rating for Nepal

If Nepal is to realize its ambitions of graduating to the status of a middle-income country by 2030, it will need very large investments every year.[7] The mobilization of national savings and foreign aid will in no way be enough for investments of that magnitude, therefore Nepal has to look at global financial and capital markets. This makes the requirement of a credit rating for Nepal mandatory.

In a country where politics is not viewed as stable and even a bare minimum enabling environment of strong rule of law is absent, it is difficult to imagine why people would be willing to invest in such large proportions. Furthermore, in the absence of a credit rating from global giants like Moody's or Standard & Poor's for Nepal, international investors have an added uncertainty to deal with. Further, the absence of a credit rating impacts insurance adversely as there are no Nepal-specific products available in the global insurance market.

Nepal should work towards getting a credit rating assigned to itself as accessing large amounts of global capital without it is unrealistic. While Nepal could initially seek assistance from development partners, in the long term such dependence will not be sustainable. Aligning with global benchmarks of getting credit ratings from agencies will be the first step towards making access to global capital easier.

## Dismantling Cartels and Keeping Private-Sector Bodies Away from Regulatory Ones

Lack of competition and stifling entry barriers have prevented the Nepali private sector from having a level playing field. Consequently, big international players and firms are virtually absent from the market. Cartels and syndicates which have unofficial affiliations to various political parties have been the biggest stumbling block to reforms and attracting international investors.

One of the most cited examples in Nepal is that of the public transport syndicate which has for long tried to prevent the entry of businesses which seek to offer better than existing services at competitive prices. Similarly, the presence of business association members in the regulatory agency's board has been a major barrier for meaningful reforms to take place due to the inherent conflict of interest. For instance, an airline association member should not be sitting on the board of the regulating agency. This is sheer conflict of interest and prevents regulators from making the industry more competitive.

Reforms first need to come from legislation. There must be rules and regulations which prevent conflict of interest and bar members of professional and business associations from taking charge of or being part of regulatory authorities. Legislation should aim at making entry and exit from businesses easy and foster competitiveness in the private sector. Anti-competitive practices such as cartelling should be outlawed and have punitive consequences.

## Integrating with Global Markets

In order to reap the benefits of globalization, Nepal needs to recalibrate its position vis-à-vis the rest of the world. Increased opportunities for trade and business will expose it to previously unchartered avenues for growth and take maximum advantage of its comparative and competitive advantage. Increasing engagement with the global economy will not only open up new vistas, attracting investments into the country, but will also heighten the relevance of the country in international affairs.

Integrating with global markets would mean that companies in Nepal will have to gear up for global competition. This will require firms to adopt global standards in human resource management, governance, audits, social media outreach and all aspects of organizational and institutional practices.

The private sector needs to bear in mind that opening the floodgates of international competition does not harm them but presents unique opportunities that had for so long been veiled under isolationism. Opening up to the world economy means that businesses from Nepal which can match global standards and compete globally can go on to become leaders in their respective industries. This should get the private sector excited rather than making it lament over increased competition.

Legislative changes which allow international management, audit and human resource management companies to operate in Nepal will be an important step towards helping the Nepali private sector become globally competitive. Easier modalities need to be set for the repatriation of profits for these companies.

## Leveraging Regional Markets and Consortiums

South Asia remains one of the least integrated regions in the world where intra-regional trade accounts for less than 5 per cent of the total trade.[8] With the creation of alternative subregional cooperation platforms like BBIN and a more eastward-looking grouping of countries in BIMSTEC (Bay of Bengal Initiative for Multi-Sectoral Technical and Economic Cooperation), it is an opportune time for South Asia to integrate meaningfully and enjoy gains from regional trade. Nepal is uniquely positioned in this regard to leverage various regional markets and consortiums not only because it is a part of a sprawling market in South Asia but also because it is often envisioned as a potential link between China and South Asia.

Nepal should seek to make the most of every regional cooperation framework that it is a part of and aim to proactively expand its trade relations with other countries. While negotiating trade agreements in regional or international settings, better homework and preparation on the part of negotiators will go a long way in helping Nepal get the maximum out of each deal. As discussed in Chapter 10, Nepal needs to pioneer the concept of BEZs to be able to look at markets beyond its own international boundaries.

## A Financial Services Authority as Regulator

Banks form only a section of the financial sector lending platform for access to formal finance. Within the formal sector itself, there are other non-banking financial institutions, products and services like venture funds, equity funds, hedge funds, collective investment schemes, electronic transfer platforms, guarantee and leasing products, etc. There is an absence of regulatory bodies for regulating such non-banking and capital-market-related financial products and services. As financial deepening occurs and the use of such products grows, it should be met with reasonable regulations so as to protect customers, prevent undue market power accumulation by certain players and ensure an overall enabling environment for financial services to develop further.

There is a need for a legislative framework for the creation of a body entrusted with the responsibility of regulating non-banking financial institutions. Along with creating a strong institutional set-up, there will be a need for well-trained and highly professional human resources to drive such a body. Therefore, investments in human resources for non-banking financial sector regulation must also be made a priority.

## Promote Policy Institutes, Research and Training Centres

For long in Nepal, economic development has been shaped by politics rather than the other way round. Policies are often crafted by politicians who have the next election in mind rather than the macroeconomic and fiscal stability of the country and its long-term economic interests. Similarly, borrowed development models which might not necessarily take into account local realities as well as social and cultural milieus are likely to deliver below-par results. This is not to discount the need for global standards and operating procedures, but there is a need to blend local insights with global expertise and come up with prudent solutions to Nepal's developmental woes.

Policy institutes, research think tanks and training centres for economic policy development which can blend local and global knowledge to come up with innovative policy prescriptions to Nepal's socio-economic challenges should be acknowledged as key stakeholders in policy formulation.

Global examples have shown how important such think tanks are in policy development. International ones like the Brookings Institution, Chatham House, Carnegie Endowment for International Peace, Council on Foreign Relations and Brookings Institute are the leading institutions whose policy prescriptions and research outcomes have impacted the global political economy immensely. Their studies serve as a valuable asset for governments in forming policies.

Closer home, think tanks in India like the Observer Research Foundation and Centre for Policy Research have been influential. Nepal needs to provide an enabling environment for such policy think tanks to operate in the country so that objective and expert analysis of policy and far-reaching policy prescriptions can be drawn from them.

There are already a number of such institutions within the country, but lack of adequate resources often limits their scope of work and restricts their capability. Similarly, lack of access to proper data from government sources restricts the scope and quality of research that such institutions are able to perform. Furthermore, governance structures, human resource management and audit systems of such institutions are generally not at par with global standards. Given the culture of political patronage in Nepal, a key challenge for such institutions will be to steer clear of undue political influences and produce objective and unbiased policy prescriptions and research outcomes.

To help such institutions overcome resource constraints, the government should explore options of granting tax concessions to businesses and firms which contribute financial resources to them. Similarly, the government can support them by providing a facilitating environment for operations—one way of doing so could be easing data sharing with research institutions so that their research yields better results. International community support will also help overcome resource constraints and put these institutions on the world map. Equally important is for such institutions to adopt global standards in governance, audit, human resource management and research quality.

## Improve Ease of Doing Business

The Ease of Doing Business Index produced by the World Bank, and many other indexes like the Global Competitiveness Index, provide international investors a perspective on the business environment of the country. In 2018, Nepal dropped many places on the Ease of Doing Business Index to rank at 110, compared to its best performance of 94 in 2015. Similarly, Nepal ranks 88th in the Global Competitiveness Index published by the World Economic Forum. This suggests to international investors that Nepal is increasingly becoming an unfavourable destination for capital. Nepal should develop a clear strategy and strictly implement policies which would help improve its rankings and place it on the investors' radar.

Rwanda in east Africa has been able to push its rankings to 29 in the Doing Business Report.[9] The Rwandan example can be a major learning resource for Nepal. The first prerequisite for such an improvement is a strong political will and commitment for undertaking and following through with reforms so that the business environment becomes more conducive to capital. Ratings such as the Ease of Doing Business Index should be seen by the government as a yardstick to measure the efficacy of its reform agenda, and a dip in ratings should evoke prompt policy reforms.

Nepal needs bolder reforms in policy which seek to aggressively crack down on provisions that make doing business difficult. The country needs to have a clear roadmap and should set targets to be achieved in the short, medium and long term.

## Reform Insolvency Laws and Facilitate Easy Exit from Businesses

In Nepal, once a person starts a business, it is very difficult to shut it down. It is imperative that like the ease involved in starting a business, closing one down should also be made simple. While laws relating to insolvency exist, the practical implementation has been poor. Furthermore, contradictions between different Acts like the Insolvency Act and the Banking and Financial Institutions Act have compounded the challenges of insolvency proceedings. Similarly, insolvency in Nepal is perceived as a criminal act on the part of individuals or companies, while in reality, it might not necessarily be the case. Such perception prevents companies from filing for insolvency. Ineffective monitoring by the Company Registrar's Office (CRO) of various companies also leads to companies which should be filing for insolvency going unnoticed.

There are a number of issues relating to insolvency in Nepal. Inconsistencies between different legislations hinder easy insolvency practices. Similarly, given that insolvency in not a very easily accepted practice here and even companies which should be filing for insolvency tend not to do so, further challenges exist in terms of limited know-how of the legal documentations and procedures involved. There is a shortage of both liquidators as well as judges who are skilled at handling insolvency cases. Special training should be imparted to lawyers and judges so that insolvency procedures are not mired with practical problems. Inconsistencies between different legislations need to be addressed promptly.

## Ensure Policy Consistency

The biggest complaint from international investors has been the inconsistency in Nepal's legal and institutional framework. There are international companies that have not been able to repatriate dividends. There are also knee-jerk reactions from regulators that impact the investment climate. For instance, the central bank issued a guideline in 2018 for prior approval for hiring foreign consultants and stipulated that these consultants be paid only after their job was complete. No international consulting firm of repute would work without an advance payment. This shakes investor confidence. Efforts should be made to ensure that there are policy consistencies, and any changes should aim for better facilitation rather than restrictions.

Frequent changes in laws can have a grave impact on companies which have made significant investments in the country. For instance, increasing the level of foreign direct investment from $50,000 to $5,00,000 in April 2019 has put many investors in a difficult situation. There should therefore be legislative arrangements for indemnifying parties which have made investments above certain thresholds in case of legal provisions changing. Policies and legislations must be crafted with long-term impacts on business and the investment climate in mind because frequent changes only deter investor confidence. Punitive frameworks to combat corruption should be made stricter and enforced more effectively. Policy consistency should be regarded as a key element in attracting more investments.

## Leveraging the Himalayan Opportunity

In the role of the secretary general of the Himalayan Consensus Summit, I was involved in hosting four annual conferences in 2016, 2017, 2018 and 2019. The Himalayan Consensus Summit brought together people around the world to ideate on a variety of issues that impacts one-third of humanity living in the region. The political boundaries across the fragile Himalayas have impacted the lives of many. Birds do not see the boundary when they fly, neither do the animals that cross over to different regions, nor do dust pollutants when it comes to impacting the health of millions. Countries have been secretive about data on river flows or movement of people, but the time has come for discussions with a regional focus rather than a focus on an individual country.

Towards a Himalayan Charter: Former foreign secretary of India and former ambassador to China and the US, Nirupama Rao, proposed a Himalayan grouping with a charter that will delve into areas of mutual cooperation and action. She reflected on the principles of Panchsheel (five principles) that China and India signed sixty years ago. Recognition of shared boundaries, shared ecologies, cross-border connectivity and sustainable development challenges is important. The fragile Himalayan space needs to be protected, and the heritage, both tangible and intangible, needs to be conserved. David Molden, director general of the International Centre for Integrated Mountain Development, proposed a Himalayan council to work on issues relating to the future of the Himalayas.

What is required is a platform for Track II dialogue involving both China and India to work together on economic issues and figure out ways to further strengthen cooperation. The global landscape has changed since 2016 with the US getting preoccupied with domestic issues and Brexit bringing about a new set of discourses, and the free movement of people across geographies being questioned. As Prof. Mahendra P. Lama, an eminent Himalayan scholar, says, we need a platform for discussing how to make China's BRI and India's Act East policy work—and the Himalayas are at the centre of the two initiatives.

The vortex of economic growth in the Himalayan region is its topography, landscape and abundant natural resources endowed by nature. However, the future of growth is also dependent on humans being mindful of the fragile ecology and environment. The challenge also is to ensure growth does not invite more conflict and being able to read early warning signs for conflicts as well as crises, whether induced by nature or humans. History tells us that sharp changes in livelihood patterns and economic transformations can bring about challenges of a different nature.

## Thinking Global: From Fragile to Frontier Destination

In May 2013 at the Global Private Equity Conference in Washington DC, I had presented my thoughts on how erstwhile fragile countries are becoming a frontier destination for investments. In the last three years, Rwanda has emerged as one of the top investment destinations in Africa. Ethiopia and Ivory Coast are now in the race. Liberia and Sierra Leone, which were hit by the Ebola crisis, are trying to rebuild. In South East Asia, Laos and Cambodia are slowly but surely spending money on infrastructure projects to boost growth. Erstwhile war-torn countries in Eastern Europe are now proudly talking about putting problems behind them and pushing for prosperity. Like many countries, more and more of us in the F2F (fragile to frontier) discourse feel that income is probably not the only measurement required to look at nations.

In Nepal, income from assets does not matter as it is the appreciation of their value that does. People are more than happy to stash gold and let prices go up. In the stock market, people do not think of cash dividends but are interested in capital gains earned through bonus shares which increase the value of the investment. Rental on properties is a small fraction compared to their value. In the US, properties earn 6–10 per cent yearly on the value of the property as rent, but in Nepal, this number is less than 2 per cent. Rent is inconsequential as the focus is on the appreciation of property value. The disposal of assets is important when expenses are to be incurred, be it for a wedding, international school fees or medical emergencies. Further, any disposable income is channelled into buying more assets; it does not matter whether it is unproductive land or gold that stays inside the vault!

The importance of the asset value and its spiralling increase is important to understand how fragile countries cope.

Nepal has the right ingredients to move from being fragile to a frontier market. First, it has a big population, the forty-eighth largest in the world in 2018—more than that of Australia—with a bustling national capital region of about 5 million people. With half the people under the age of twenty-five, it will continue to up its consumption—Nepali consumption patterns are somewhat similar to South East Asia rather than South Asia. Second, communication connectivity, linking farms to markets, and positive trends in education and health will create more urban centres in rural areas. Third, we are seeing more young people return to Nepal after education and exposure abroad—they are becoming entrepreneurs and will drive the change.

Nepal can become an investment destination for four distinct types of investors. First, high net worth individuals who have a soft corner for Nepal will move from supporting NGOs to encouraging social entrepreneurship. Second, foundations in Europe which have small funds that are just making a couple of percentage points a year are in search of new destinations to increase returns on endowments—many investors I have personally met in the last decade belong to this category. Third, there is a new breed of investor advisers who are looking at to-be-frontier markets; they are the ones who are structuring funds in Afghanistan, Nigeria and Iraq. Nepal, they tell us, has a better geographical location than most other fragile nations. Finally, the new rich that are emerging in the hinterlands of India that cannot go to Delhi, Mumbai or Kolkata with just Rs 5–10 crore in Indian currency ($1–2 million) will find Nepal an attractive destination. These investments are already happening informally; it is to be seen how they can come in through official routes.

Globally, it has been observed that countries that are fragile emerge to become the new frontiers of investments, be it after World War II or regional conflicts. There is a popular saying amongst the investment community, you should invest before the blood in the street dries up. Once the blood dries up, there will be many players that come in. Like traders from centuries ago to investors in the last century, those who have been able to identify countries, evaluate the risk and invest are the ones who have benefited the most.

## Reimagining Brand Nepal

Nepal needs to reimagine Brand Nepal to achieve its envisioned economic growth and prosperity. It needs to dream and continue to pursue its dream. The concept of Brand Nepal has to do with the larger image of Nepalis living across the world, irrespective of their passport or country of residence. The transformation has to be led by changing the perception of Nepal in millions of Nepalis living around the world. The closed definition of being 'Nepali' through citizenship or the practice of questioning someone's Nepaliness or *Nepalipan* has to go. The narrative has to be one that speaks of Nepal's importance in the world, such as its link by land to China and India, the two global economies that will comprise 35 per cent of the global GDP by 2050. In the last section of this chapter, we will reimagine this journey to achieving Vision 2030 through a four-pronged approach.

First, Nepali icons must be leveraged, regardless of where they live and work. The biggest brand for Nepal would be the identity of the Nepali youth that will take on the service sector of the world, be it in hospitality, retail or IT outsourcing. These omnipresent and talented youth with smiles that can win the world at hotels, restaurants, banks, shopping malls, cruises and hospitals in Nepal and around the world will be the country's brand. There are already Nepali fashion designers who have made it to the front cover of *Vogue*, a Nepali works for NASA, and Nepali bands and artists have captured international recognition. This is but the beginning; the youth of Nepal are just awakening and they should be able to chase their dreams. Once that happens, Nepal will be known for its efficient, effective and smiling workers and professionals, in sectors ranging from hospitality to art, from financial services to scientific research. This will be the country's brand and what Nepali people are identified with. The day this starts to happen, Nepal's potential will have been unleashed.

Second, the outlook of Nepalis on Nepal must change from being landlocked to being land-linked. Nepal needs to understand its geographic location and familiarize itself with its own terrain. Kathmandu is closer to a seaport than Delhi is—it lies a mere 800 km from Kolkata compared to Delhi, which is 1490 km from Kolkata. Similarly, if we look at the industrial belt of Birgunj in the border area of Nepal, the distance to the markets of Delhi is a mere 780 km. If Nepal were to establish a BEZ in Mahendranagar, a border city in far western Nepal, it would be as close to Delhi as Delhi is to the Indian city of Jaipur. It would be closer to Delhi than the other Indian cities of Kanpur, Lucknow and Allahabad. The markets of north-east India can be more easily serviced by the Nepali border towns of Birgunj, Jogbani or Kakarvitta in the east than they would be by the geographically more distant northern Indian states. What can be ascertained from this geographic analysis is that Nepal is ideally situated to serve as a trading and manufacturing nexus for most of north India.

Similarly, in the north, Lhasa, capital of the Tibetan Autonomous Region of China, is soon to be a mere 770 km rail journey from the border town of Kerung in Tibet, just across the Nepali border. With the completion of China's rail link, it would mean that only 900 km separate Kathmandu from Lhasa and a mere 1100 km separate Lhasa from the Indian border town of Raxaul.

Third, there should be a push for 'hi-gration'. Migration is a reality we all live with and it is important to move it up the value chain. People who are leaving the country for a better future must do so with better skills and training along with the right value systems. Even if we assume 2 million people are sending remittances back home, just a $10 a month increment due to better skills will result in $240 million additional remittances a year. Contrary to the reports of the parachute consultants, remittances will not reduce, nor will migration. Nepalis will find newer places to work and migrate. With the population ageing in the industrial nations that led growth in the latter half of the twentieth century, they will be forced to hire people from other parts of the world. Japan in December 2018 announced they will start taking workers, and Nepal was a country it was willing to take people from. Further, with Africa opening up and requiring time to get their skill-sets right, we will see the current trends of Nepalis moving to Africa for supervisory and junior management jobs. The work of different development partners in Africa will continue in a big way, and Nepalis have done well in this field, which means we will see them lead the hi-gration transformation. With job markets not knowing what are going to be the top jobs in 2030, the global workspace is wide open.

Fourth, there should be a focus on Brand Smile. One of the things Nepal has to offer that is completely indigenous, human and heart-warming is its 'brand smile'. This natural instinct has led to Nepalis finding good opportunities in the service sector, be it in healthcare as airline flight attendants or restaurant stewards. The smile is not something that is taught to them; it comes on its own, and the success of the tourism industry is often attributed to this phenomenon. Combining 'brand smile' with skill development can create one of the foremost service sector workforces, especially bearing in mind that by 2030, out of the 35 million people in Nepal, 17 million will be under the age of twenty-five. Vision 2030 has to meet the aspirations of these smiling Nepalis.

14

# Making 'HATS and I' Happen

## Infrastructure in addition to Hydropower, Agriculture, Tourism and Services

If Nepal wants to pursue Vision 2030 for becoming a middle-income country and start building a strong capitalist welfare state, it needs to explore key areas and sectors. With Nepal being land-linked to China and India, the two economic powerhouses, it can explore areas where it has competitive and comparative advantages.

The discourse around key sectors brings us back to what we have been discussing for more than half a century. The big three tangible sectors remain hydropower, agriculture and tourism, but two other sectors, services and infrastructure, are also part of the mix now. With the growth potential of migration and thus remittances increasing, infrastructure will be key to economic growth.

While I have discussed many of the sectors in my previous book, *Unleashing Nepal*, in this chapter I try to provide a few additional lenses.

## Hydropower to Power Energy

Nepal has lived in a dark paradox for decades. Nepal built its first 5 KW hydropower plant in 1911, at the same time when the technology was being explored in other parts of the world on a commercial basis. The estimated potential of hydropower in Nepal is 84,000 MW—as per a dissertation paper by water resources expert Hari Man Shrestha in 1966—with half of it being commercially exploitable. This has been the reference point for hydroelectricity potential over the years.

Despite all this potential, Nepal did not build hydropower plants on its own and waited for aid to do so. In the 1990s, laws were finally made to allow private investments in hydropower. Nepal also received diesel generation plants as aid and used imported diesel to run these plants. After the conflict began and people started migrating to Kathmandu and urban centres along with increased demand due to growing economic activity in urban centres, there were better income levels that meant they could afford electricity. Further, with the building of roads, transmission lines were also built, increasing distribution to parts of Nepal that had never seen electricity. Nepal then started undergoing serious forced power cuts, termed as load-shedding, with their durations peaking at up to eighteen hours a day. Politicians, planners and business people discussed the potential of hydropower in rooms with electric lights powered by either diesel generators or battery-powered inverters. For decades, power remained only on slides in PowerPoint presentations. It was only in 2016 when Kulman Ghising took over as the managing director of the NEA, the state utility, that the load-shedding woes ended due to skilled management of demand, coupled with better negotiation with India on imports, paving the way for supply keeping pace with demand. On the eve of Tihar, the festival of lights, in November 2018, he announced that Nepal would be lit up to its fullest—this is exactly what happened as he watched from a control room in Kathmandu.

The hydropower potential therefore needs to be viewed from multiple perspectives. In the following section, we will examine the four key issues to bear in mind in this regard.

## Need for an Energy Discourse and National Energy Policy

In Nepal, the discourse around energy is mixed up with the discussion on hydropower. For its growth, a country needs to first identify sources of energy and its demand and supply, distribution, costs and benefits. Hydropower development is only a part of the overall energy discourse but in Nepal the cart has been put in front of the wheel. Therefore, the primary objective should be to embark upon preparing a National Energy Policy with hydropower development being a key component. This should also include components related to solar energy and energy that can be produced through biomass, waste, wind and other sources.

## Understanding Energy Demand and Its Management

Nepal's energy consumption is dependent on the import of petroleum products using precious foreign exchange. The energy policy needs to examine sectoral demand and thereby look at energy substations. If energy is required for cooking and this is currently serviced predominantly by firewood, liquefied petroleum gas (LPG) and kerosene, the policy must address how electricity can be used to substitute these. Similarly, if diesel is the source of energy for transport vehicles, the development of railways and ropeways based on electricity needs to be examined. Another point to explore is if large-scale construction can only be facilitated by diesel generators, how can distribution be recalibrated to meet such requirements? These are the key questions to consider as we go forward.

In Nepal, energy consumption, especially of electricity, is low, and the country ranks in the bottom ten countries in the world in terms of electricity consumption, which is determined on the basis of linear growth assuming a certain increment each year. The state utility does not look at demand from the perspective of growth of the economy, changes in life patterns, urbanization, development of infrastructure and changes in the way people live, move and work. Today, even in a small eatery, it is not surprising to find eight to ten pieces of equipment running on electricity. The process of lighting at workplaces has changed and there is a proliferation of large-format stores that need a lot of lighting. People have more rooms in their houses and are buying electrical equipment as prices have declined. There is more consumption of electricity in public spaces and events. More importantly, there is affordability. With the low cost of air-conditioning equipment, its use is becoming more and more popular. With domestic help getting expensive and people moving towards nuclear families and living in apartments, there will be more families using dishwashers and cleaning robots in future. Each office and residence building that has security guards to open and close doors will shift to electronic systems that do not require manpower.

The concerned government agency has its task cut out. Undertaking a major study on the future of electricity demand based on latent demand has never been looked at. If people realize that they have no electricity supply constraints, people will plan and think differently. Currently, Nepal consumes, per capita, 15 KW per person per day or 134 KW per person per year. This is one-twentieth of the global average of 309 KW and 2674 KW. This means that if Nepal is to consume electricity at par with the global average, it will need twenty times more supply, which means it must start building hydropower plants to produce electricity for domestic consumption. This would also change the way electricity plants are built. Rather than waiting to sign power purchase agreements (PPAs), merchant plants with direct contracts with local distribution companies can be an option.

Finally, the energy policy will be required to look at renewable energy as a priority and preferred source which means there will have to be a drastic reduction in the energy produced by petroleum products. The use of renewable energy will have to be incentivized, either by allowing the sale of solar energy tapped by individual households to grids or giving benefits to urban centres that prohibit the usage of vehicles running on fossil fuels. With breakthroughs in technology relating to electric vehicles, and countries announcing deadlines on a shift to electric vehicles, there will be a need for charging station networks.

## Towards Regional Leadership

Nepal has to be a regional leader in the generation of hydropower to meet its own energy demand as well as benefit from creating a regional electricity market. Hydropower continues to be an energy source that can be stored, and with the concept of reverse pumping, it can be used as the most stable source of energy. While hydropower can fetch higher prices due to its storage value, regional energy markets will provide even better opportunities. The demand in Bangladesh and India for electricity peaks in summers and for Nepal it peaks in winters. With differentiated tariffs, Nepal can fetch better prices for electricity in summers and import electricity in winters from grids at lower costs. For this, the development of an electricity trading platform is essential. It is in Nepal's interest to push for an electricity market, and with China's interest in pushing infrastructure, connectivity in the north can also be another extension for the Nepali electricity market.

In Nepal, when there are discussions about hydropower, the oft-used Nepali phrase is *'Jhola ma khola'*. The literal translation of this is 'the river in one's bag', referring to licence-holders carrying licences of run-of-river projects and going around to get investors. This has led to hydropower licences being linked with political patronage and creating an environment where people are more than happy to rent-seek in this respect rather than develop hydropower plants. It is also done by some international players who have acquired licences through teaming up with politically connected local partners, thus getting a backdoor entry into projects.

Money has been raised by developers from local markets through the issuance of shares despite poor credit rating scores, roping in many international investors, especially from China and India. The absence of a trading mechanism and market has made all producers sell to one buyer: the state utility, which has a most complicated financial situation.

Worldwide, we have seen many innovations in hydropower, with improvements in the technology used in construction as well as maintenance. Turbines are becoming more efficient, and the same source of water can now provide more energy than earlier. From managing operations through cloud technology and monitoring safety deep inside dams using high-tech equipment, there have been many technological breakthroughs. Nepal needs to continue adopting such transformational developments. It can aim to develop competencies around development, operations and maintenance of hydropower plants and use its expertise to not only operate plants in Nepal but also in other parts of the world, like some Nepali knowledge workers are already doing in parts of Asia and Africa.

Therefore, many reforms are required for hydropower investments to be more feasible and successful in the long term. First, there has to be an electricity market and trading platform that plants can sell to so that they are not dependent on a single monolithic utility. Second, having a credit rating is important to ensure there is a global insurance market that will specialize in Nepali risks—after ports, hydropower plants carry the highest risk of construction and operation. Third, there has to be a separate legislative and institutional framework for international investors so that they do not have to follow the same risk patterns as other investments. Further, the Nepali government has to outsource firms to negotiate with investors on its behalf. Finally, the role of the community is important as water in the river is a community resource. It has to be compensated not in the form of free shares, but through improving livelihoods through the usage of electricity and the creation of tourism and jobs at project sites.

## Recalibrating Transmission, Distribution and Tariffs

It is important to improve transmission and distribution to multiply the potential of Nepal's hydropower. It is common to see a house being built first, followed by connecting roads, then water and sewerage pipes and then electricity connection. This order has been followed in hydropower plant development too. First, the location of a plant is determined and then transmission lines are built. Distribution to consumers takes place only in the end. Therefore, when a Special Economic Zone was built in Bhairahawa, no industries could start production as there was no electricity. With an empowered local government, the process will have to start with demand-mapping at local levels and identification of demand centres, which will have to be connected by transmission lines and networked for hydropower plants to plug into. A complete overhaul is necessary.

The end consumer has to be at the centre of policy, whether the consumer is a household, a hotel, an industry or a large township. The process of acquiring a connection should not require officials' palms to be greased. Payment systems also need to be rejigged. In Rwanda, people can buy prepaid cards and recharge meters as one recharges cellphone balances. If this is made possible, a villager would not have to pay a huge sum of money to get an LPG connection along with the cost of cylinder transportation when they can just recharge electricity meters based on consumption. It is also vital to ensure there are different plans to suit consumers. People don't think of cellphone usage in minutes any more; they are buying packages at designated prices to suit their plans. So, if people are willing to take advantage of peak and off-peak tariffs, let them do so. Differentiated pricing should also be introduced. Why should a person in rural Nepal pay the same price for electricity as a consumer in Kathmandu? Differentiated pricing can include subsidies from local governments to attract industries and businesses that create and offer jobs.

The unbundling of the state utility, NEA, along with restructuring the institutional framework has already taken place. The realignment of responsibilities and powers between federal, provincial and local governments will be key moving forward.

## Unleashing Agriculture

The most effective way to improve the lives of the millions mired in poverty is to support agriculture in developing countries. Most of the world's poor are farmers and people who spend much of their income on food. Transforming a country's agriculture sector can create jobs, raise incomes, reduce malnutrition, and kick-start the economy on its path to being a middle-income one. In fact, almost every industrialized nation began its economic ascent with an agricultural transformation. Recent examples include Brazil, China and Vietnam, each of which at least doubled the value of its agriculture sector within twenty years of starting its transformation process. Many other countries in Africa, Asia and Latin America are also on this path.[1] Nepal should also use agriculture as a tool.

When we are talking about unleashing the potential of agriculture, we need to broaden the definition to include not only basic agriculture produce like fruits and vegetables but also cash crops, forest products, livestock, animal products, dairy, fisheries and other activities that have to do with the cultivation of land and breeding of animals. In Nepal, the definition of agriculture has long been limited to rice and sustenance farming of other crops, and the broader definition is slowly being more widely understood only of late. Agriculture products in some parts of Nepal are still traded under the barter system, and only after increased connectivity through roads and communication has the market for agricultural products widened, with Nepal exporting as well as importing produce in large quantities. In this section, we examine five key focus areas.

## Understanding Consumption

The discussion around the potential of agriculture should also be viewed from the perspective of the changing lifestyle of people across the country. While there are parts of Nepal that continue to see rice as a luxury item to be eaten at Dasain or other celebrations, there has been an unprecedented transformation in consumption patterns of agricultural products in the majority of Nepal, thereby pushing people towards the lucrative sector of agriculture from other businesses as well as increasing imports to unprecedented levels.

What poverty-brokers don't understand is that Nepal is a country of nearly 30 million people. So even if 5 million have left the country, and 5 million are not financially secure, there are 20 million people eating two meals each day, which means 40 million meals are served in Nepali households each day. The composition of such meals is changing at a rapid pace. For instance, even two decades ago, in rural Nepal a meal could be rice and dal, or meat curry and rice. Today, a meal in an ordinary household is like that of the feudal lords of yesteryears. Rice with dal, a vegetable or two, achar (pickle) and other condiments. Fruits and raw vegetables in salads have become a must. Egg is consumed each day and so are milk and milk products. Meat consumption has gone through the roof, and due to the increased demand for exotic products, the consumption of rabbit meat, ostrich and trout fish is also growing. As a country obsessed with malnutrition data due to the business of selling poverty, there are no institutions to track the transformation in terms of consumption. Data on better livelihoods will put the business of poverty out of business.

The concept of eating out has exploded. It used to be a taboo to eat out due to casteism—not always being able to know the caste of a cook—which made people desist from even travelling. But this has now changed. Even if just 5 per cent of meals are consumed outside the household each day, we are talking about 2 million meals a day! This would mean around a billion dollars a year, at an average cost of NPR 150 per meal. Eateries have mushroomed, there is better road connectivity and more people travelling for work and pleasure, which has led to highway eateries popping up across the country. More women have joined the workforce and become entrepreneurs, and are not consigned to the kitchen in households. Online food delivery services have pushed open the market further.

Two decades ago, Nepali coffee was just a concept—today it has become a cultural epitome of transformation, with coffee shops opening across the country, even in rural areas, adding a crop that was never in any consultant's plan three decades ago. Even a decade ago, the honey and mushrooms produced in villages used to be only for Kathmandu, Pokhara and a few urban markets, but today they are consumed in the production centres as well. In a visit to western Nepal in 2018 on an assignment on agriculture, I was amused to hear how households were consuming half a kilo of honey each week due to kids using it as a substitute for jam and sugar. The commercial market for agriculture has increased multifold.

The discourse around agriculture has to be understood not only from the perspective of the producer, the intermediary and the market, but also from the perspective of a market that is driving all the other markets. In the absence of planned growth, Nepali agriculture has not been able to cope with increasing demand and therefore there is a reliance on imports. Further, some Nepali habits are peculiar—the kiwi fruit is preferred just because it is imported and expensive rather than a fruit that grows in Nepal. When avocados became expensive, the demand soared, and the price of lauka (gourd) increased multifold when India's FMCG guru Baba Ramdev started to prescribe it for better health. Further, when the export of traditional Nepali products like herbs, forest produce and pickles to the large Nepali diaspora began, the markets got distorted. So, the next agriculture plan has to put the market and consumption at the centre and work backwards towards the producer.

## Understanding the Production Side

In a South Asian democracy, the farmer is the best example for proving how far political parties can go with their distributive economics. Election promises would earlier comprise free seeds, irrigation projects, loan waivers and doles of all kinds. However, among those who get all the government freebies, very few want to get into agriculture despite it being commercially lucrative. During one field visit in 2017, a farmer in the successful agricultural area of Kapurkot, Salyan, made a very powerful statement. He said that by investing less than NPR 20,000 a ropani[2] in a year, he could make a minimum of NPR 60,000 by growing and selling vegetables. Good crop planning, resulting in better prices and more intense time requirements, along with investments, could fetch as much as NPR 1,25,000–1,50,000. This, he said, could be additional income along with what is earned through routine farming activities and livestock. He wondered how one could complain about one's labour when it was rewarded so well. Farmers definitely earn more than what people send back from Qatar or Malaysia, but hard work is not something that is looked upon favourably. A farmer who makes half a million rupees from his farmland a year has less social status than the guy who draws half that money working in an NGO! The image of the farmer being associated with illiteracy, poverty and backwardness has made people take up other professions and businesses as soon as they have some savings from their agriculture business. It is vital to introduce vocational training programmes so that people can consider agriculture a viable career. The appreciation of agriculture also needs to be taught at schools.

Therefore, the commercialization of agriculture, allowing large-scale investments, pooling of land and partnerships with communities, can only improve the productivity and efficiency of the sector. This can be extended to supply chain management, processing and value addition. For instance, tomato farmers can be organized under a large company, with constituent members as shareholders as well as seasonal workers pooling their produce. This can create a sizeable volume that can provide inputs to a processing plant for tomato ketchup or a factory producing tomato soup powder. The scale must increase in a big way.

## Looking at China and India as Markets

Nepal can leverage its position between China and India through exporting agricultural products to these large markets. Since rice is not a high-value crop, Nepal can import all the rice it consumes from them and in turn export high-value agricultural products like vegetables and fruits. Indian vegetables enter the Nepali market freely through the porous borders each day, but Nepali vegetables face quarantine procedures and other hassles on their way to India. World-class laboratories have to be set up that can provide certification to products so that they meet quarantine requirements in India and elsewhere in the world. Nepali mid-hill vegetables command high prices and are sought after in Indian border towns due to their taste and texture. There are other high-value products that have big markets in both China and India. For instance, cheese made in Nepal is sought after, but its export has been a challenge due to certification issues. Similarly, high-altitude exotic organic products are seeing unprecedented demand across the world, and Nepal can grow many of them at a commercial scale. Hence, the agriculture plan must be driven from the market perspective of demand.

## Relooking at Productivity

Though Nepal's eastern parts bordering the Indian hills of Darjeeling produce the finest tea in the world, there needs to be a rethink on the production process. It is clear that a fourteen-year-old girl these days would not want to sacrifice her career and education to pluck tea leaves like her mother or grandmother did. We need to understand that labour-intensive agriculture practices will move from being mass-market to niche-market, with high value being recovered for labour. Therefore, for mass markets, in the absence of mass labour, there have to be investments in technology. For instance, robots could pick tea leaves, like the automation that is being seen in picking olives and grapes.

The core of agriculture production is about managing supply chains and the ability to meet demand at consumption centres. For that, the management of the production cycle and inventory is key. More industrial-scale planning is required to ensure that farmers have control over where and how final products are sold. With online platforms and digital payments, it should be possible to remove the intermediaries who have made fortunes fleecing both farmer and consumer. This will also boost productivity and efficiency.

## Benchmarking to International Practices

A mushroom farmer in far western Nepal was showing me a YouTube video downloaded by her son on mushroom production in Europe. She asked me how she could get such a machine. It will be important for Nepali products to follow international benchmarks, especially as the costs of getting the required certifications and understanding the processes have all reduced considerably due to technology and low communication costs. The farmers can learn online, get certifications from visiting affiliates from nearby countries, and join an international community of people who are pursuing similar products.

In agriculture too, it is the cartels that are the regulators rather than the government, fixing prices of eggs, meat and vegetables without any consideration of quality. Producers who believe in quality cannot fetch a better price, and non-adherence to international standards will not allow them to extract a premium. Bringing about a complete overhaul in this regard will be possible through domestic players tying up with international and regional players who produce world-class products. These would then go on to disrupt the market and dismantle the cartels.

## Unleashing Tourism

Nepal's major foreign currency earner since it opened up its economy has been tourism. This has not only created income for the government through climbing fees, trekking fees, fees to national parks and other fees, but it has also created jobs directly and indirectly. Tourism has ensured that Nepal has an identity in the world, a positive one where people talk about the natural beauty, landscapes and friendly people. Now, we will look at the five major areas where recalibration is required to ensure that Nepal benefits from tourism with the least cost to its fragile ecology and environment.

## Shifting from Product to Experience

Nepal's history of tourism goes back many millennia, with people from India and the now Tibet Autonomous Region in China coming here for pilgrimages, visiting holy shrines in the Kathmandu valley and other prominent sites. So, Nepal has been handling religious tourism for around two thousand years, since the family and disciples of the Buddha started travelling to the Kathmandu valley. But the strong caste system that treated people with white skin—Europeans, and later, Americans—as outcastes made Nepal unfriendly for travellers from these regions. These foreigners were seen as people who ate cow meat, and therefore, it was considered scandalous to come into contact with them or anything they touched. This made it technically impossible to host a foreigner in one's house. It was only after Jang Bahadur's visit to England that these rules were relaxed; hence, in the early part of the twentieth century, more foreigners started visiting Nepal. It is also important to understand that in Nepal, from a cultural standpoint, Indians are not considered foreigners or *bideshi*. Tourism numbers started being formally recorded after the end of Rana rule in 1950, with another item being added to its existing list of attractions: the mountains. Nepali tourism has therefore been product-driven.

Nepal's entry into the global tourism market was as a high-end destination. So the friendly, smiling Nepali automatically became a major comparative advantage as rich tourists from the US and Europe started visiting. Later, as the backpackers descended in the 'hippie age', the differentiator remained good service. You could smoke pot freely in many parts of the world, but in Kathmandu you could do it differently: hanging out with folks who owned small places in the by-lanes of what was then called Freak Street, and also having nice conversations with those serving you. When Thamel began to blossom, people came back to their favourite watering holes and restaurants because of their bond with the locals. Tourists came despite the dilapidated infrastructure, health hazards and limited options. Even now, in some iconic Thamel institutions, there are remnants of the old service culture.

In religious tourism, there is the belief that people don't repeat destinations. This is like the attitude of the highway eateries, which do not see people as repeat customers. Therefore, fleecing the customer or tourist becomes part of the business strategy. I remember vividly how tourists in the city of Benares in India were referred to as ATM cards to be swiped at every opportunity. It is not very different in Nepal, where vendors, cabbies, guides and agents do not want to drop an opportunity to make that extra rupee from the tourist. Tourism that is defined from the perspective of being a product market looks at the short-term perspective only.

Nepali tourism needs to graduate from being a product to an experience, making people visit multiple times to sample a host of products and services. It is not about a particular temple, but about its history and heritage that makes it more than a place to take pictures at. The world is moving from a focus on product to experience and many such platforms are emerging that focus on experiences. With Swiss national Monika Schaffner, we coined a term, 'mindwalk', which is an experience she delivers by taking tourists to various parts of Nepal on a journey of the mind. Trekking is a physical exploration, but mindwalk means going beyond the physical. With interest in nature, culture and spirituality increasing like never before, Nepal is at the cusp of unleashing another set of tourism experiences similar to what it did with trekking.

Further, even large global tourism companies are not selling products, but experiences. Airbnb is selling accommodation and other experiences, Uber and other transport companies are selling commuting experiences, TripAdvisor is selling experiences relating to destinations, cuisines and others. They all have one thing in common: they don't own any assets, but are all dependent on the experiences of the people who interact with their portal. Nepal has the opportunity of taking the lead in selling experiences through a convergence of different services and products. For instance, the culinary experience can be a combination of hotels, restaurants, community spaces and other components that deliver unforgettable moments.

## Understanding the Market: China, then India

The United Nations World Tourism Organization (UNWTO) projects that the outbound market in 2030 will be around 1.8 billion,[3] with China leading with 400 million people. It is very interesting to note that at the beginning of the new millennium, China's outbound was just 10.5 million, which grew at an astronomical pace to 156 million in eighteen years![4] China's spending on tourism in 2017 was $257.7 billion, the highest in the world as per the UNWTO report, nearly double of what the US spent that year. India, interestingly, does not feature in the top ten.[5] In Nepal in 2001, just 8738 tourists came from China of the total arrival of 3,61,237 tourists—less than 2.4 per cent.[6] This increased to 1,34,362 in 2018, an excess of 10 per cent of the total. If we are to assume that the China volume till 2030 will grow to 400 million, even a proportion of 1 per cent visiting Nepal means it can expect 4 million tourists just from China.

For the Chinese, Nepal is a new destination as it is associated with Buddhism and nature. They see Nepal as a novelty, a Shangri-La that is yet to be explored, and one which opens up many connections with the inner self. This is in contrary to Indians, who see it as an extension of their own country where they can travel without a visa, where their language is understood, and the food habits are similar. With the massive development of infrastructure in air transport facilities, connectivity is not an issue—as mentioned earlier, Nepal already has more weekly flights with China than with India.

The Indian market for Nepal is taken for granted and not much effort is made to sell itself as a tourist destination. With the relaxation of the foreign exchange regime in the 1990s in India, the world has opened up for Indians who can get better deals in South East Asian countries and the Middle East, where there are more options for entertainment and shopping. Nepal remains, for the Indian market, a pilgrimage destination for the old and a holiday destination for friends and families. The other segment of Indian tourists is the people who have inhibitions about travelling to other countries due to issues of language, culture and food. They favour Nepal and have started to discover the depth of its culture, heritage, natural bounties and adventure challenges. This is the segment Nepal needs to focus on.

India's outbound tourism will also increase but at a much slower pace than China's. Nepal can look at the latent demand of tourists from India who are connected with it by improved roads and have to travel a shorter distance when travelling to Nepal than some parts of India. Even though after the alcohol ban in Bihar, it has become difficult to distinguish between genuine tourists and people who drive across the border for a drink. The opening of airports in Bhairahawa and Pokhara should drive volumes as more regional flights will operate from there to Indian cities. Further, India agreeing to more connectivity with Nepali airports from its smaller cities would bring more tourists to Nepal who otherwise spent more on flights than on hotels. For instance, a Dimapur–Guwahati–Biratnagar flight can connect eastern Nepal and an Ahmedabad–Delhi–Nepalgunj flight can bring tourists to western Nepal.

The big advantage for the Indian market remains the ease of entry as no visa is required, the Nepali currency is pegged to the Indian rupee and there are no stark cultural contrasts. Nepal must leverage this to the fullest.

## Choosing Quality over Quantity

Nepal's tourism has always been fixated on numbers. The million tourists target has floated around since the early 1990s but was only achieved two decades later in 2018. However, the average number of days and the amount of money a tourist spends has fallen considerably. From $180 per day in 1980, it has fallen to around $44 in 2018.[7] The debate of quality versus quantity has not been looked at from a policy perspective as the private sector which is involved in the tourism industry pushes the government to keep a regulatory environment where the industry stays insulated from international standards, norms and practices. Therefore, the rhetoric on quantity has become easier as increasing numbers just requires lowering prices. At low prices, a service provider does not have to deliver quality and can get away with anything. This mindset has allowed premium Nepali products and experiences like Everest climbs, treks, conservation park visits and religious and cultural tourism experiences to be sold for a song.

The advent of multiparty democracy brought about the exploitation of worker unions by political parties to create disruption in enterprises in the name of worker rights. Some international agencies loved to fund this transformation of labour in the hospitality sector at the cost of industry. People who did not know the difference between a refrigerator and an oven started to become key union leaders without ever having worked in a hotel. On the ownership side, traders found business cards stating an association with a hotel or restaurant prestigious. So, many people who never had a love for travel or hospitality suddenly became hotel and restaurant owners. Then the service charge row began in the early 2000s, later getting sorted out as owners saw how they could manipulate it for some extra bucks.

Thus, the downslide of the hospitality industry began. People who provided great service and pathetic service got the same share of service charge. Frustrated, many good workers left Nepal, and you can meet them in restaurants and hotels in the Middle East, the UK or the east coast of the US. The disruption in the tourism business caused by 9/11, the insurgency and the frequent closures (bandas) by political parties did not help the cause of better service. Client profiles also changed. A country that differentiated itself from other destinations with its service quality and attracted high-end tourists is now keeping them away with deterioration in service.

Therefore, the policy debate needs to happen on why Nepal should move towards quality tourism to protect its fragile environment and to ensure revenues from a lesser number of tourists. With a formidable market developing in China that has a serious interest in Nepali tourism experiences, it is essential to recalibrate it as a destination that is not cheap and where quality is preferred over quantity. Nepal need not replicate Bhutan's policies, but it can surely learn from how Bhutan has been able to preserve its fragile environment through various policies emphasizing protection of natural and cultural resources.

## Domestic Market: The Biggest Market

The domestic tourism market has grown in a big way since the insurgency ended, especially after the Maoists were defeated in the second Constituent Assembly in 2012. Road connectivity, increase in ownership of vehicles and the peer pressure to post travel pictures on social media has pushed people to travel more. Further, many Nepalis who have travelled the world are now discovering Nepal's natural bounty and cultural richness.

The Nepali domestic tourist does not demand much when travelling. The staple dal–bhat is a must, and beyond that if the menu offers momos, chilli chicken and chowmein (noodles), it is enough. Alcohol is more important than food, and now high-end single malt whiskies are available in highway eateries where getting a bottle of drinking water from a credible company may not be possible. Meat is very important, and barbeques of all kinds will suffice. There are not many demands on hygiene, good sanitation and service. Nepalis are adaptable!

The only challenge with Nepali tourists is like their Indian or Chinese counterparts—they can be very noisy, blaring music till late at night, and not very interested in ensuring civic public behaviour in their kids. The behavioural issue has of late become a bigger challenge, and prompted me to use the 4 Ds to identify a Nepali tourist: drinks, dinner, dance and dangdung (meaning fight). This has posed challenges for establishments that receive foreign tourists.

The Nepali market will grow as affordability and lifestyle changes take place, but it will be equally important to educate people on acceptable public behaviour. Perhaps it is time to integrate this as part of the curriculum in schools and implement it at school-trip levels so that it has a sustained impact. Else, while the size of markets is not comparable, we may go the India way, where the component of international tourists is very small and establishments are happy with like-minded domestic ones. In 2018, for 1.6 billion domestic tourists in a country of 1.3 billion, India handled just 10 million foreign tourists.[8]

## Recalibrating Service

Relooking at the quality of service is key for the next leap of growth. Whenever I attend a function at a Kathmandu hotel or spend a night at one of the getaway destinations close to the valley, I observe the way service is delivered at each step—be it the guy who gets the tea in the morning or the housekeeping staff member who speaks loudly on the phone when a conference is going on. I also like to reflect on the beginning of my career at the Soaltee Hotel—which was then an Oberoi-managed property—and the way benchmarks for service were defined. I have developed this obsession with service observations in the many hotels I check into and the many restaurants I visit. Today, portals like TripAdvisor have become a platform where people co-create content with the focus generally remaining on service. As the design of hotel rooms become homogenous and there is more similarity in the menu cards of restaurants, the only differentiator is service.

The hotel and restaurant business only delivers the best when there are discerning clients who want the best and are willing to pay for it. From a personal interface with a single client, it has changed to an interface with the key person who makes the decision on where a conference will be held or at which hotel a dinner will be hosted. The mushrooming of development agencies post-1990s saw hotels and restaurants receiving more customers for junkets, training, seminars and conferences. Then financial institutions—be it banks or cooperatives—became the next big spending segment. The decision-making shifted to the guy who decides on procurement. Incentive structures started to become critical.

Like the night bus passengers who eat wherever the driver deems fit, the decision never rested on the customer, but an intermediary who made the final decision. Customer feedback was ignored for establishments learnt how to keep the decision-maker happy. Service expectations plummeted and low quality service became the norm. For example, a development worker who attends scores of events a year at different establishments has no service expectations from these places—but when it comes to paying from his/her own pocket to take his/her family out, they would never visit the same places. Service only improves and benchmarks are recalibrated when the customer demands the best service for the best price. Establishments compete on price and not on service. The change in profile of international tourists does not help in this matter either, as it is only the more price-sensitive segments of Indian and Chinese tourists that are increasing.

Recalibration is essential for the long term. Many people in the hospitality industry tell me there is no point in investing in services because customers do not value them. But in the past couple of decades, if there are some establishments that have done well and expanded, it has been due to innovation and service quality. For example, look at Chandan Kayastha and his chain, Roadhouse Café, along with the Temple Tree property in Pokhara. If more people raise the bar, others will follow, similar to how the basic layout and design of eateries changed post the Jhamel era. Recalibration will only ensure that in the long run, entrepreneurs and workers can make more money for devoting the same amount of time in a business. Else, customers not caring for service and providers not wanting to provide better service in an ecosystem where the powerful decision-maker is indifferent will diminish any chances of Nepal increasing the quantity and quality of tourists, both domestic and international. This is not only a necessity but an opportunity too as the global tourism industry is being recalibrated by travellers who love to share experiences online.

## Why Services?

With little competitive and comparative advantages in manufacturing, Nepal will have to continue to focus on the service industry, both domestically and internationally, especially in terms of producing a workforce that goes abroad to learn. This is important due to human capital formation; labourers learn from the best in other countries and apply the techniques back home. However, there is always the problem of fewer workers coming back to Nepal due to its lack of labour management and poor living standards. With a population of 30 million, Nepal is the forty-eighth most populous country in the world and also one of the youngest twenty-five. Given the ageing populations of developed countries, Nepal has the potential to produce trained human resources for the world that will not only perform mundane manual labour but also move up the value chain very quickly.

Within Nepal, increased consumption and urbanization is creating many domestic jobs in the service sector; however, low productivity and labour issues remain problems. With formal businesses increasing—large-format retail stores, restaurants, schools, hospitals and service companies—productivity along with service orientation remains a challenge. However, with increased competition and cartels not being allowed to hold sway, it is expected that improvements will be made on this front.

Nepalis working in other countries have earned respect for their hard work and loyalty outside Nepal. The biggest assets of the Nepali people remain their ubiquitous smiles and charm, which have made them successful in the hospitality as well as nursing/caregiving sectors around the world.

## Technology as a Job Creator

The general attitude is that technology and automation will take away jobs, but on the contrary, sectors have expanded with automation. The banking sector was seen as a human-resource-intensive job and it was feared that the introduction of technology in this sector will make people redundant, but more jobs have been created with automation and digital financial platforms. The proliferation of e-commerce has pushed for more job creation in the service sector, be it in packaging, logistics, supply-chain management, warehousing or back-end services. Young Nepalis are already involved in many business process outsourcing jobs, from transcription to back-office management to process management. These are only going to increase as the difference between service and products morphs further in the future.

Jobs that involve interacting with humans will become the premium jobs. With technology infusions, humans will interact more with machines, but many will still like to deal with real people. Beyond a certain point, technology can become a challenge. People will not mind paying a premium to speak to a banker in person or to check in at an airport with the help of an actual person. When you are investing a fair bit in furniture or branded apparel, you will prefer to have contact with a human for quality assurance. Full-service hotels and restaurants already command a premium. There will be new areas in health, wellness, and mind and body rejuvenation, where the service will be delivered by a human. Nepali youth are already one of the most preferred service providers and this will only grow.

## Building Infrastructure for Economic Growth

There are many studies that correlate infrastructure development and economic growth. It is estimated that every $100 of investment in infrastructure increases private sector output by $17.[9] In China, the policy of building infrastructure to create jobs has been pursued. Even in the US, it is believed that a $100 billion investment will result in a million jobs.[10] A World Bank estimate of Nepal's 'infrastructure gap' pegs investment needs this decade at between 8 and 12 per cent of the national income to achieve Nepal's medium-term ambition of graduating to a middle-income nation by 2030.[11] However, the current levels are at a dismal 2–3 per cent.[12] Experts put this requirement at $30–40 billion in the coming decade. However, we are yet to have the mindset that is required for a global view on infrastructure projects that goes beyond financing and includes safety, security, sustainability and service.

## Understanding Linkages between Land and Money

Large infrastructure projects, whether in transport, energy, housing or social infrastructure, require land to be acquired. And generally, these are fragmented agricultural holdings that are providing livelihood opportunities to many. In any land acquisition deal, people with political backing get into the fray and make the biggest chunk of money. As in agriculture or other small-scale production, the middlemen benefit the most, and they have little to lose if deals do not go through. We have seen end-recipients suffering, as a bunch of brokers appears to make money on an opportunity. In Kolkata, during the 1980s, it took two decades to build a few kilometres of a metro track, while for the Delhi metro, more kilometres of the track have been built each year than in the previous year. Similarly, in Rwanda, the government has embarked on a fifty-year plan for land acquisition for roads and other infrastructure.

There is no way we can get soft money and aid to build infrastructure. All infrastructure projects have to be financially viable, and if there are shortfalls, the government should step in to make it worthwhile for investors. Financial closure, involving international financial institutions, is not easy. In Nepal, we tend to think that there are scores of financial institutions queuing up to invest. But Nepal needs to reach out to them, which it has never done. The risk of doing business in Nepal is high due to unpredictability. Meanwhile, countries in Asia and Africa are making big pitches for projects and ensuring that investor risk is reduced. Nepal needs to follow suit. The primitive controls of foreign exchange through stricter laws and regulations by the Central Bank does not exude confidence for international debt and equity investors.

The financing of these projects has to be done by international lenders, whether they are multilateral development financial institutions or others. Such organizations would like to see the investment environment improve beyond what is committed to or promised at investment summits. Infrastructure is built on the basis of extensive planning, and it is again important to get the best planners who can see the requirements over the next couple of decades. Further, we need to understand that infrastructure is a permanent investment with little recourse to financial institutions in case a project fails. So there must be an environment of safety, adequate insurance and risk-mitigation guarantees against local political goons to ensure projects are not delayed.

## Understanding Areas for Development

With the aim of reaching $100 billion in GDP by 2030, the required investment of $7–8 billion a year would be mostly in infrastructure. This could be in different sectors like road and air transport, trade facilitation, sustainable urban development, economic corridors, energy generation, transmission and distribution systems, along with water development and management.

There have been many studies in the past, and now it is time to update them for better implementation. Further, Nepal needs to get the world's best companies to build and operate infrastructure. The way Nepal has converted its airport to a bus terminal when the world is building bus terminals that look like airports is a continuous reminder of how crony capitalism is promoted in the name of nationalism. International firms must be vetted properly. Further, when multilateral agencies are involved, they should be able to voice their dissent when the going gets tough. For instance, in the Melamchi water project, the ADB has not been able to exert pressure on the government to implement it in a timely manner, apart from failing to abide by social and environmental guidelines.

## Harnessing Skills and the Private Sector

In Nepal, while there are many agencies putting money into infrastructure development, little skilled labour is available in the construction sector, with many migrant workers from India seen across sites. In a billion-dollar project, thousands of workers who can perform different activities are required. With increased mechanization of the construction process, more people are needed who can handle equipment and are tech-savvy. Most of the skilled construction labour force has been lost to different parts of the world. A programme needs to be developed to bring them back.

One of the major problems in Nepal relating to infrastructure projects is the lack of clarity over the role of the local private sector partner. The tendency of a local sponsor—who should be putting his own money as equity—resorting to commissions on equipment supply, car hire or hotel accommodation brings about tremendous issues of trust with international investors and financial institutions. The Nepali private sector needs to decide whether it is in the role of sponsor for a project, or of a commission agent taking a cut out of everything possible. Many Nepali hydro projects have not moved forward as local companies have not been able to figure out a clear role.

A delayed infrastructure project is a dead project. A year's delay can eat away all profits as additional financing costs make projected surpluses vanish. In Nepal, government-sponsored projects get delayed as more money is made at different levels if this happens. We need to ensure that projects start and finish on time.

# 15

# Unleashing Transformation

In my previous book, *Unleashing Nepal*, most of the recommendations revolved around what the government, private sector, development partners and civil society could do, with prescriptions given for various organizations. In this chapter, I try to put the Nepali, whether they are outside or inside Nepal, at the centre and see what can be done and what needs to be done. The focus has to be on major behavioural change that will supplement changes in the social, economic and financial status of the country.

Often, countries with bountiful resources and financial strength may not provide the same level of lifestyle to their citizens. For instance, countries in the Middle East and Scandinavia have similar income levels but contrasting levels of freedom, human rights, women's rights, apart from cultural and natural bounties. There are many countries we can learn from. Therefore, it becomes important to put into perspective the required transformation at the human level to achieve a positive transformative impact on the people. Beed Management, the company I founded in 2008, has as its tagline the phrase 'In the business of positive transformation'. In this chapter, we will examine how we can unleash such a transformation.

I look at a few pivotal areas and reflect on what is happening and what can be done to ensure a societal transformation that will support improved living standards, increased disposable income and never-ending increases in the price of assets, especially land. In this chapter, we will look at Nepal's future potential in three parts. First, we will explore the lessons we can learn from other countries. Second, we will see how societal transformation is the key to economic transformation, and finally, we will see how Nepal's high-potential human capital can be leveraged, which will be beyond skills and knowledge, through a transformation in societal behaviour.

## Learning Lessons

The challenge for Nepal has been that leaders spoke about benchmarks without really understanding the need for them; therefore, they were never achieved. Just after the 1990 Jana Andolan, Nepali Congress leader Krishna Prasad Bhattarai became the prime minister. I heard him from close quarters a few times, rattling on about how Nepal would turn into another Singapore, and be known for its extreme cleanliness. As a young professional who worked at the Soaltee Hotel back then, I used to wonder how a person who chewed paan so incessantly that his teeth were stained and who had perhaps never learnt the importance of oral hygiene could possibly make the whole city or country clean. Perhaps there was no internalization of the process of benchmarking and then delivering.

In the quest of learning lessons from different countries, I try to collect my impressions that have formed parts of opinion pieces in newspapers. Among them are lessons from Rwanda and Singapore.

## Lessons from Rwanda

Rwanda has never ceased to baffle me, and Nepal has lots of lessons to learn from it. This East African country that is smaller than Bhutan with half of Nepal's population has become one of the top five investment destinations in Africa. I travelled to Rwanda for the first time in January 2012 and then fell in love with it; so much so that our firm expanded its operations there and started consulting on various projects. I have had the chance to meet and chat with many people and see with my own eyes how a country can transform in just six to seven years. So, here are six lessons Nepal can learn from Rwanda.

Think Big: In Rwanda, when you start discussing a project, it's never small. I remember being told in 2013 about the new international airport that they were building for $6 billion, equal to the GDP of that time. I kept wondering how they could plan and achieve this. It's about execution. In 2018, I learnt that the first phase would be ready by the end of 2019, and the airport would be positioned as a regional airline hub. Rwanda's national carrier, Rwanda Air, which had a fleet size smaller than Nepal's official carrier in 2012, had by 2019 added multiple destinations and secured approvals for direct flights to the US.

Rwanda's tourism is anchored around the viewing of mountain gorillas. Eighty passes are available each day at $1500 for each pass, and is overbooked on many days. This means it attracts high-end tourists. To further the meetings, incentives, conferences and exhibitions (MICE) business, a convention centre has been built in the middle of Kigali at $400 million, funded by a Eurobond issue. The centre has hosted major global and regional events, providing a major boost to tourism. This is in contrast to the 'party palace' mindset in Nepal where small minds think of small projects and deliver even smaller results.

The proud moment in Rwanda in 2018 was the deal Rwanda Tourism signed with English football club Arsenal. As part of this three-year sponsorship deal, the words 'Visit Rwanda' featured on the jersey sleeves of the club's players. This is expected to give a tremendous boost to the image of the country, similar to what Thailand received when it started sponsoring and (later) buying football clubs in Europe. With a viewership of 3 billion people, reaching out to a large number of audiences is a step Rwanda believes is important for tourism. While in Nepal, we feel that sticking a Visit Nepal logo in taxis and restaurants in Nepal will get us more tourists.

Take a Leadership Position: President Paul Kagame of Rwanda is seen at a number of major global events, be it the World Economic Forum or G7 meetings. In Moscow, he was at the opening of the FIFA World Cup in 2018. Rwanda hosted the FIFA Council meeting in October 2018. It leverages its position as head of the African Union and knows how to use global networks. Rwanda is hosting the Commonwealth Heads of Government Meeting in 2020 despite the fact that it was never a British colony and took membership of the Commonwealth just eight years ago. The former French colony took over the leadership of the Organization of French-speaking countries (OIF) in 2018. Despite a chequered past between France and Rwanda since 1994, President Kagame met President Emmanuel Macron in 2018 to renew ties. Rarely is a country at the hub of both Commonwealth and Francophone activities.

Rwanda wants to take a leadership position in whatever it does, be it leading Africa in the discourse on climate change or taking up cleanliness campaigns. In 2016, it started distributing medicines in remote areas through drones. From January 2019 began the issuing of QR codes on land registration documents instead of stamps and signatures, again pushing the cause of digitization. Its digital payment systems are at par with Scandinavian countries.

Backed by security and safety records, the mindset is like that of Singapore. It strives to be on the global centre stage as a hub for business, trade, commerce and connectivity.

Create Trust: Contrary to Nepal, which does not have any plans to end foreign aid and assistance, Rwanda has planned to eliminate it by 2025, therefore pushing for more foreign investments to create jobs.

In 2013, Rwanda made its maiden $400 million Eurobond issue, raising $3.2 billion, an oversubscription of eight times. It requires a lot of guts to go out in the international market to raise money, but it has not looked back. It has been able to consistently improve its image—jumping places in the World Bank Doing Business Report, and ensuring that it continues to remain in the top five investment destinations in Africa. This is in complete contrast to Nepal, where belief in the country's potential, capacity and people is quite underestimated.

Ensure Rule of Law: When a motorcyclist violates a traffic rule, pedestrians get together and hand the violator over to the police. Rwandans take pride in abiding by the law and if you are seen throwing trash out of your car while driving, someone can just text your licence plate number to the cops. The cleanliness in the city, the ban on plastic shopping bags, and strict traffic rules can only be possible through implementation of the rule of law. The capital, Kigali, one of the safest cities in Africa, enables women to take cabs or walk around at any time of the night without fear. For Nepalis, a red light is just a suggestion to stop, and not a law. The key learning is that if citizens follow the rule of law and co-work to enforce it on other citizens, the changes it can bring are more than any series of constitutions.

Have a Positive Attitude: It is difficult to hear a 'no' from Rwandans. They even try to articulate negative reactions in a positive way. So, in meetings, they will not say things like 'This will not work' or 'This will not happen'. When you are used to hearing 'no' in the corridors of bureaucracy and politics in Nepal, it becomes difficult to comprehend the 'can do' attitude. In Rwanda, one person will refer to another, and tell you what you need to be careful about, but they want to see projects built and improvements delivered. They are in a 'learner' mode, where they want to learn what is happening in different parts of the world and how they can make the same thing happen in Rwanda, rather than in a 'judger' mode to tell you why it would not happen. Ask a bureaucrat or businessperson in Nepal, and they will tell you why Nepal is not a great destination to invest even though their lives have improved several times over because of their businesses.

Maintain Cleanliness and Order: One of the first things that strikes anyone who visits Rwanda is how clean it is. At the airport, you are scrutinized for plastic bags, and if you are carrying any, they are confiscated. The streets are clean. Building good drainage and service ducts for wires is as important as building roads. The key is that they have been able to maintain what they have built. Painting road markers is not an indication of completion of roads like in Nepal; it is a perennial exercise. Construction sites are asked to clean even barricades built with GI sheets. Toilets in offices, whether government or private, are as clean as the ones in restaurants. Roadside eateries may not have swanky toilet installations like in Nepal, but unlike Nepal, these are kept clean. Cleanliness is a day-to-day habit integrated into life, not once a year like on World Environment Day.

The biggest difference between Rwanda and South Asia is that it has learnt to perceive cleanliness as a part of the social order and a tool of equity. We have grown up learning that to be neat and clean and orderly is a capitalist behaviour; therefore, if you are to be a socialist, there has to be a sense of disorder. Filth, dirt and squalor has long been seen as a sign of socialist equity in our part of the world. But socialism can be clean and orderly too.

## Lessons from Singapore

If Rwanda learnt from Singapore, why can't Nepal? What are the three things we can learn from Singapore?

Consistency Matters: Singapore got its underground metro railway at the same time as Kolkata flagged off the first metro train in India.

Over the next quarter-decade, while Singapore built nearly 200 km of a system that makes Europe and Japan envious, Kolkata has not even doubled its capacity. Singapore believed in the public transportation system being a means to bring about efficiency and let people travel seamlessly for $5 or less per day—something that has been impossible in a country like Nepal. Singapore has built a network of buses that drop you less than ten minutes walking distance from the place you live, thereby not making it necessary for people to buy cars. Because neither automobile companies nor auto dealers lobbied for solutions based on personal automobiles, Singapore has been able to burn less fossil fuel, which has contributed to minimal pollution. With a large area of forest cover, it continues to be an environmentally friendly city state. Therefore, it is not about making one-time speeches and inaugurations, it is about being able to manage the city with consistency.

Maintenance and Planned Growth Is Key: In Singapore, maintenance and planned growth is taken seriously. Spending on maintenance is as important as building new structures. Everyone takes pride in cleanliness and regular maintenance of structures and spaces. However, in Nepal, unfortunately, even the painting of zebra crossings is a one-time activity. Perhaps it is a reflection of our personal and social behaviour of doing everything on a project basis. Restaurants and cafes are mushrooming around the country, and in their opening month, some of them look like the restaurants in Singapore. Three years later, they start resembling eateries in Tier III Indian cities. People who are in the project mode of running their own household then start running the nation, and national priorities become limited to their priorities. Women who operate and maintain households are never in a decision-making position, while men who have never managed a household can't seem to manage a nation.

Every Citizen Is a Tourism Brand Ambassador: The Nepal Tourism Board was established in 1998, a year after the establishment of the

Singapore Tourism Board. I still recall the days when Renton de Alwis, who worked with the Singapore Tourism Board establishment through a UNDP project on partnership for quality tourism, came to Nepal hoping to replicate what worked in Singapore. With much fanfare the tourism board was established, only to be converted into another government department. After twenty years, Singapore doubled its annual arrivals from 7 million people to 15 million. Its tourism receipts went up from $7 billion to over $25 billion. What Singapore earns annually from tourism is more than Nepal's GDP. It embarked upon the Tourism 21 vision statement in 1997, and stuck to it. Nepal, in the same period of time, is discussing how to handle 1 million tourists, with multiple tourism cartels finding ways of keeping cartels and the people running them alive rather than bringing about transformations that were thought of in 1997.

When we were working on an assignment on tourism assessment for Rwanda, a country that likes to be inspired by tourism, we learnt how Singapore converted each of its citizens into a tourism ambassador. Anyone you meet can tell you about tourist destinations in detail and guide you to the user-friendly apps and websites. Contrast that to Nepal, where we keep wondering how many Nepali leaders across different walks of life have actually paid an entry fee and visited the Patan museum. The big lesson is that for tourism to succeed, it is not only good infrastructure that is important, but it is also vital to make every citizen a tourism brand ambassador. This is a zero investment project that does not require donors; it just requires citizens to believe that they need to know about tourist spots in their own country.

## Societal Transformation Key to Economic Transformation

Politics will not change if the society does not. A person who does not use a clean toilet or keep their toilet at home clean cannot be expected to keep the toilet in his office clean once s/he becomes a minister. A parent who shouts slogans on the streets protesting students not being allowed to cheat will not be against cheating once s/he becomes an elected official. A person who wields all his power to get ahead in a temple queue will surely not be against putting certain files on top of the heap for a sum of money once s/he starts to wield political power. These changes in mindset and behaviour are fundamental to changes in society and achieving economic transformation.

In this section, we examine this from the perspective of how we need to see the glass half full, how we need to inculcate a value system, how a prospering society cannot be judged by money only and good aesthetics also reflects cleanliness of the mind.

## From Glass Half Empty to Glass Half Full

The infectious negativity in Nepali society has created a situation where everyone is more occupied in seeing the glass half empty rather than half full. Businesspersons who have just closed their financial year with 30 per cent growth in revenues and profits complain about how the year has been bad. They complain endlessly about Nepal even though they have made millions, even billions, in this country. Multinational companies and foreign investors who have made fortunes out of doing business in Nepal, either by selling things to Nepalis or using Nepali labour to produce items for export, also complain a lot. Companies that put in a million dollars are sitting on valuations of hundreds of millions in a couple of decades. But every time a potential investor meets them, they have only negative things to say.

There has been an unprecedented growth in the number of Nepali people who have gone through formal education, from engineering and medical degrees to PhDs. At the same time, wealth has been created for millions of Nepalis, and the valuation of their wealth has gone through the roof, particularly with the rise in real estate prices all over the country. With 86 per cent of Nepali families owning land, it has impacted practically everyone. The ownership of shares that keep growing in value has been another way of wealth creation.

It is difficult to even find three people within friends or families that are worse off than they were ten, fifteen, twenty or twenty-five years ago. However, the people who are better off in terms of education or wealth have also complained the most.

It makes me wonder if businesspersons will stop complaining only after they can double their wealth each month! I asked one complaining professional I met whether he could have ever imagined twenty years ago when he started his career that he would be earning so much money, driving a fancy vehicle and giving his children the best possible education, all on a legitimate income! I go to restaurants where waiters earn a minimum of NPR 30,000 and an equivalent amount in service charges but still complain of low pay. I talk to cabbies in Pokhara and they complain that they can only make around NPR 40,000 a month for working just one shift of eight to ten hours. Is it that our expectations are too high and therefore we cannot meet them? Or is it that our gambling genes from time immemorial, as depicted in our religious scripts, like the Mahabharata, make us want to see income and wealth multiply at an unprecedented speed. What is the change that is required?

## Inculcating a Value System

The democratization of corruption that began with multiparty democracy in the 1990s has made people aim for political positions and rent-seek on that basis, rather than carrying out entrepreneurial pursuits. Why not, if one's lifelong benefits flow from the state even for convicts and jailbirds? Societal values have eroded and people do not even feel a loss of face when their names and photographs appear in newspapers as loan defaulters; there is no rejection of people who are charged for corruption and no help is available for innocent people who are framed.

I met a Nepali professional living in the US for the past fifteen years who had come to Kathmandu for a family event. He was disgusted that two former ministers who had served jail terms were invited for the event. The big question he had was that if he were to return to Nepal permanently, how would he explain these value systems to his kids who had been born and raised in the US?

The same goes for the discourse on citizenship. The 2015 Constitution does not provide equal rights to women. A woman who is married to a Nepali man can get citizenship but a man married to a Nepali woman cannot get citizenship. This attitude is more to do with how upper-caste Nepali male chauvinists see this as a matter of politics than value judgement. For people who have daughters and no sons, what will happen to their property if the daughters marry non-Nepali nationals? Scores of people are facing this tough situation. The only argument people have is that women are taking their property rights both as daughters and daughters-in-law.

I grew up in an age where you listened to your parents and there was little room for disagreement. In school, when my principal entered for the Monday morning assembly at 8.15 a.m., there was pin-drop silence. You could almost never get away with indiscipline. Religion, culture and practices were followed without questioning. Later, I worked in an organization where strict discipline flowed from the top, and any compromise with rules could cost you your job.

The new generation today has evolved with less of these internal points of reference. Therefore, they ape those who are successful. The pinnacle of success in Nepali society is to be a political leader, perhaps become a minister, drive a vehicle with red lights flashing and security folks in tow, with everything yours for free—you do not have to pay for anything, the gifts flow, donors take you on junkets, you stay in hotels you would never otherwise be able to pay for, and then get away with practically all the intentional mistakes you make. You do not have to feel accountable to anyone! It is really important to inculcate the right value systems in present and future generations.

## A Prospering Society Is Never Judged by Money Only

I take this example to illustrate the issue of societal transformation. In August 2017, when the embassy of the Republic of Korea in

Kathmandu organized a beautiful evening of music, it had some of the best contemporary talent from Korea perform at a hotel banquet hall. This was in contrast to what I saw in Bhutan at the ninth edition of the Mountain Echoes festival in August 2016. The main venue was the hall at the Royal University of Bhutan, a simple structure that could house a large number of people.

When the BIMSTEC meeting took place in Kathmandu in August 2018, it was a moment of shame for Nepal—a $30 billion economy hosted one of the most shabbily organized international events ever. In 1988, when Nepal was just a $4 billion economy, the first SAARC summit was held in a spruced-up convention hall that was perhaps one of the best in South Asia, while the visiting heads of state were put up at newly built suites at the Soaltee Hotel. Three decades later, the fact that Nepal did not have a decent set of rooms or a hall to host the BIMSTEC summit speaks volumes about how it has squandered time and opportunities in the myopia of power struggle and mediocre ambitions. During the visit of Chinese President Xi Jinping in October 2019, only the part of the city he would travel through was beautified overnight. When all the décor was taken down the next day, comments observing the same filled social media pages.

The Royal Nepal Academy hall in Kamaladi was built decades ago and remains one of the few options for hosting events in the city, apart from City Hall and the Birendra International Convention Centre. The centre will hopefully be vacated after the elections to Parliament are completed. The fact that hundreds of organizations conduct programmes at these venues and accept the state of the toilets and other facilities reflects how Nepali society looks at hygiene, sanitation and aesthetics in their day-to-day lives. The development business has always been seen as a short-term one, and building long-term options is never a priority. Therefore, programmes were initially conducted at star hotels till the increased pricing became prohibitive, forcing a shift to other venues. The business of banquet halls, popularly known in Nepal as 'party palaces', is modelled on the aesthetics of the Tier II and III cities of Bihar and Uttar Pradesh in India. This has become an acceptable benchmark of aesthetics and class in a country where a few centuries ago the Malla kings had commissioned some of the finest structures. The stench in the toilets is a hallmark of these banquet halls, where the standards of hygiene, sanitation and quality reflect what the government, private companies and NGOs in Nepal have been used to. Torn tablecloths, shabby service and staff emanating body odour that makes you want to puke have been the norm. Following rules about parking space, safety and security, sanitation and noise levels and acoustics have never been a priority.

## Providing a Good Experience Is the Key

I wonder what Nepalis aspire for. I look at the way people conduct their social functions, at makeshift structures created in their homes. I have seen them in rich and poor households alike, across religions, castes and ethnicities. The common thread is that there is a project mindset—'let's get it done'. It is about quantity and not quality. It is about having 5000 guests but not ensuring that the guests have parking or food. It is about showing off to family members or friends or colleagues. The priorities are all messed up.

We miss out on small things. We do not care for what makes an experience special. Millions are spent on flower arrangements and decoration, but no attention is paid to toilets. The state of toilets at all major hotels and party palaces is pathetic. But people do not complain because they are not used to clean toilets anyway. Further, the concept of keeping a toilet clean for the next user is absent. So this vicious circle of mediocre facilities is accepted as mediocrity reigns.

The world has changed dramatically in the past decade, with technology being used to provide comfort and comfortable experiences, and increasing awareness of issues like energy and water consumption. Nepalis in leadership positions are travelling around the world like never before, but what are they bringing back? It is a big question to ponder on as it seems that most of us leave good habits behind when we depart from airports of foreign lands.

# Good Aesthetics Is a Reflection of Cleanliness of the Mind

People often wonder why meditation centres have nothing written or hung on their walls. It perhaps reflects that the human mind likes simple, clean aesthetics. The image of South Asia is one full of clutter and chaos, which has been sold as a positive brand as vibrant and colourful. But people need to ask themselves why one should get excited about seeing miles of tangled wire or a collage of ugly hoardings. In Nepal, hoardings have been allowed to mushroom, creating one of the ugliest cityscapes in the world. The fact that well-to-do people rent out their window fronts to have ugly hoardings blocking their view speaks volumes about how much money means to people—more than quality of life. No one has been told that glass structures should be cleaned regularly, hence we have fancy glass buildings that are pathetically dirty. When people admire buildings in other countries for their beauty, I keep reminding them that they are cleaned every day. That's what makes the difference. Similarly, we are taught to throw trash in streets, resulting in clogged drains, flooded streets and erosion of roads. In Nepal, we use the word *naali* for drains like we would refer to a trash receptacle. When one lives around dirty drains and dirty windows and looks at ugly hoardings, how can one's mind be clean?

# Aggregation of Border Towns

My colleague Samriddhi Pant, who came to Nepal after her studies in Singapore, had some interesting insights as we crossed from Nepalgunj to Rupaidiah in India. She thought that Kathmandu resembled a border town in terms of how shopfronts and houses were built here. We discussed this topic quite a bit. Yes, all of Nepal perhaps now looks like an aggregation of border towns. Historically, in all trading cities, shopfronts used to line the main street or thoroughfare through which travellers and traders passed. With limited roads, shops and houses on the high street commanded a premium. Temples and resting places were built along these routes.

In the twentieth century, with automobiles proliferating worldwide, roads became the key trading routes, where vehicles would be parked and travellers would spend a night at roadside inns and eat at restaurants.

The replication of the trading route and border town mindset in Kathmandu is visible with encroachment on all open spaces, a lack of parking lots, and no distinction between zones for commercial and residential purposes. While traditional Newa structures before the horse carriage and automobile days focused on community living and community spaces, these were destroyed as everyone wanted to claim every inch of land in a market where land prices skyrocketed every year. Border towns do not believe in open spaces. They are meant for people who are in transit. Everyone is absorbed in the myopia of the moment and long-term planning does not come into the picture. This mindset becomes contagious. Even in industrial estates all over Nepal that are basically capturing high-value land at low lease rentals, the concept is about just having a row of establishments. Travelling across Nepal, one sees that every municipality or village council finds it very easy to build temporary structures on riverbeds and disputed land. The business of replicating border towns and trading streets has been the easiest. In the past forty years, every town and city in Nepal has started to look ugly, far away from the beautiful picture-postcard scenery of the 1970s.

## Change Is Internal

If we are looking for change, it will only happen if each component of society can work towards it. If businesses bring about change by adhering to quality, if educational and health institutions bring about change and start respecting ethics, if professionals change with respect to meritocracy, if individuals change to discourage nepotism and favouritism—if we can start seeing the glass as half full—change will happen! We are the change—change is never external, it is always internal. For Nepal, the challenge now is not about money or degrees or education. The challenge is about the right mindset to think with an entrepreneurial perspective.

It is also about getting the ethical practices right. In 2017, at a Nepal Responsible Summit, there were lots of discussions around ethics and integrity. We need to understand that ethics and integrity are binary, you either believe in them or you don't. It cannot be measured on a scale of one to ten. Therefore, the question emerged as to how one should look at the corporate responsibility of disposing of waste generated by products like noodles packets or packaged food or bottled water. Similarly, how can alcohol companies claim that they support health centres as part of their CSR plans? People who talk about ethics are engaged in the food chain of extraction of resources.

A common sight in Nepal is tipper trucks that extract natural resources and ferry them. The other is bulldozers that are deployed to extract resources in the name of building roads. Tipper and bulldozer terrorism is rampant. River beds are contracted for low amounts of money to people who are either politicians-turned-businesspersons or businesspersons-turned-politicians. They engage in the extensive extraction of natural resources and ferry these across in the tippers. Stretches of roads are destroyed by these heavily loaded vehicles. However, they enjoy impunity from prosecution by the police and other agencies as cartels have tremendous political clout.

In a country where citizens do not have a culture of knowing the source of construction materials like the source of agricultural products, these issues never become a point of public discourse. Extensive extraction facilities on riverbeds are creating irreparable damage but of course putting up 'Open Defecation Free Zone' signage is easier. The world has been built on natural resources, there is no debate on that. But this needs to be regulated by a policy framework.

Nepal's disdain for public spaces, disregard for ecology and the environment, deepening of entitlement culture, the lacking culture of philanthropy, the proliferation of gambling, the drop in productivity along with rise in arrogance and fall in humility represent major issues. There must be some way to educate people so that they believe in values, compassion and respect for other humans. It is also important that Nepalis build an outlook and value system that is global and will allow talented citizens to return to Nepal, not for the sake of nationalism, but because of better opportunities.

No law or rule will really eradicate corruption, neither will creating super-government agencies. The change will have to come from small steps—such as not submitting food bills when alcohol was consumed, not extending a work trip by a day just to get that one day's travel allowance, being transparent about giving a contract to a friend or family member. Small steps are the only way to start!

A person who changes for the better and who can take up the challenge of politics can perhaps change Nepal for the better. For instance, we can link the discourse of productivity with holidays. Holidays in Nepal are declared at the drop of a hat, either when a prominent personality dies, or a dignitary is visiting, and work culture is rarely based on productivity. The government is one of the largest job providers, yet workers have seldom learnt to be productive. There are teachers who do not go to classrooms and doctors who do not practise in hospitals where they are assigned. Some of these teachers, doctors and workers become leaders and start drawing up plans in conjunction with people in the bureaucracy. It seems like the whole nation has grown up in a culture that has a tremendous disregard for meritocracy, productivity, professionalism and ethical practices. Along with the home-grown catalysts creating holiday junkies, there were two additional sectors that furthered this trend: private businesses like schools and financial services, and the development sector. Thus, there is an immediate need to introspect on how to push productivity and change the work culture.

Throughout its recent history—from the establishment of democracy in 1990 to the abolition of the monarchy in 2006—change is now being seen in Nepal as people seize responsibility for their own fate. For instance, the 2015 earthquake in Nepal generated an unprecedented sense of collective responsibility for the future. Nepal's youth in particular showed themselves to be incredibly creative, collaborative and altruistic. We also saw walls of social status crumble and new relationships emerge across economic and caste lines.

There are three ways in which we can change this culture and rehabilitate mindsets. First, the government needs to think of ways to create an atmosphere where productivity and efficiency is its end goal. Second, change agents in the private sector need to form an alliance to come up with workable solutions that they can implement with voluntary agreement from workers. Finally, a mass uproar is important, as shown in May 2010, when people, tired of strikes and shutdowns, defied them till strikes that paralyse at least Kathmandu and other big cities have become memories of a distant past.

This change can also be undertaken once we understand that human capital is the key differentiator, and learn how to manage talent and build credibility.

## Human Capital, the Differentiator

One of the key challenges in the coming decades will be to see how Nepal can unleash its human capital and transform the way people are viewed, making them enablers rather than pall-bearers of transformation. Take the banking industry as an example.

In the early 1990s, with private banks being allowed to operate in Nepal, there was a big disruption in terms of how service was delivered. From paying a small under-the-table bribe to withdraw your own money from a government bank, now you could make the banks come to you. There were more options for people as credit cards and consumer loans started being issued. People who would never have been able to afford a car or a house could hedge future earnings to fund these luxuries, or even spend on higher education for children. It was one of the key catalysts in reducing inequality in a country where there was only a small middle class. Now we have come to a similar juncture where the market needs another disruption keeping the consumer in mind. Many people in my office talk about how they, their family members or their friends find that going to a bank is like going to a government office. Social media pages are full of complaints about financial institutions and their service delivery. Someone in my office questioned me about why front-office people in banks look so sad and wondered if there could be programmes on making people working there smile. It has become important to introspect on how human capital can be made the differentiator in a market that is seemingly becoming a big oligopoly rather than a free market. We can examine this through six different perspectives.

Disruption Is Key: When private healthcare services began in Asia, hospitals started recruiting staff from hotel management institutions along with trained nurses. In India, some banks have already started recruiting staff from the hospitality industry—gone are the days when only business schools were a source. In the US, most of the investment banking staff now come from liberal arts colleges. These are students who have understood many aspects of human life, anthropology, sociology and behaviour, and can transition to finance easily. We also have business school students who perceive that they deserve to get better jobs for higher pay even though they do not have a basic understanding of society or human behaviour. In financial institutions, it takes longer for business school graduates to learn soft skills than liberal art graduates to learn finance. Technology is only as good as the person using it. We tend to believe that having the best technology platforms will deliver the best, but this is not true. Leaders across many fields use the best smartphones and laptops, but that does not make them the best communicators. It is important to understand that the future will be led by people who disrupt.

In Nepal, we cook up our own concoction of an enterprise. For instance, the functioning of banks in Nepal is different from how banks around the world work. Banks in Nepal thrive to provide better returns to their owners who in turn would have pledged their shares for other businesses. Trading of shares gets more attention than banking itself. This is the case across all sectors. Till we are able to adopt global benchmarks and do away with Nepali benchmarks based on mediocrity and nationalism, it will be difficult to bring about change. Industries are being disrupted by firms they never thought belonged to their league. A telecom company can give money transfer firms a run for their money, peer-to-peer lending platforms can give a bank's lending arms a tough time, and firms that provide both debt and equity to projects give its project finance business competition. These alternatives are being thought up by people who are thinking beyond their jobs, promotions and bonuses. They are pushing new global standards and changing the way banking is done.

Why a Ministry of Human Capital Is Needed: A paradigm shift is required in how we look at people—not just as labour that will help the investor earn, but as a co-traveller in one's journey. Different skill-sets are needed to handle businesses that have to compete with firms from different parts of the world. Companies need to invest a lot in getting people's attitudes right. Learning and development cannot be limited to ticking boxes, opening subsidiaries and siphoning money. Management of financial capital will only be possible if we manage our human capital well. We have seen that money does not resolve everything, otherwise Nepal would not be reeling under financial problems. There are more and more stories of corruption in broadsheet dailies each day, and the society is getting quieter as they realize that the government, which is sharing the spoils, will never respond to it. We need to ponder over the changes required and how we can get people involved with the discourse on ethics as we move ahead.

Nepalis Can Perform: On a Qatar Airways flight from Washington Dulles airport to Doha, the senior cabin director spoke to me in Nepali and welcomed me aboard. After a brief conversation, I came to know that she had been working with the airline for ten years. It is not the first time this has happened, and it made me wonder again how Nepalis could perform so well in other countries but not their own. I tried to analyse this further.

Nepalis who have world-class talent don't get trained to deliver world-class services. The same Nepalis who work for global airlines, financial institutions, hospitality chains, medical service providers and infrastructure companies around the world are able to do so. Nepalis are general managers of hotels in China, Europe and the US, and they are also at the helm of infrastructure companies and service providers like railroads in the US and irrigation systems in Africa. There are Nepalis who are seen as the best performers in global airlines, and are sought after medical service professionals. They are as good as they are trained to be.

Professionalism Begins At the Top: There are generally two types of organizations, one kind that is owner-driven and the other kind that is run by professional management on behalf of the owner. In Nepal, it is rare to find the latter—even when the owners have left the operations to a professional team, performance is limited to the imagination of the person who is driving the organization.

In Nepal, the quality of services has plummeted mostly due to the limited understanding of professional managers or business owners. Hotel owners are observed being part of the festivities at events rather than overseeing the proceedings. At banks, bank directors, owners and senior management do not bother to use online banking systems, so they have no way of seeing how their online platform is performing. In government services, it is worse. For instance, ministers and government officials go through VIP channels, and hence they do not know the plight of passengers at baggage claim. When they are out of power, they will surely never pay to travel, so they will never have the real airport experience and figure out the difficulties that ordinary people face.

Therefore, it is important to have good management at the top—whether a business is driven by the owner or professional management—to change the way people are trained and service is delivered. In the early 1990s, the entry of global firms in advertising, market research, banking, insurance, manufacturing and hospitality changed the way Nepalis worked. They trained the work force to become global resources, and some of the people who were trained during those times are now leading global firms.

Self-development Is an Investment: In Nepal, when we talk about training, people ask what they will get to go for a training session. This is as absurd as restaurants asking customers to come to restaurants and them asking if they will actually get paid to eat. The multiple NGOs and their funding agencies have converted the training process into something that people should be paid to undertake. Training sessions are conducted to tick boxes in log frames and planning documents.

We need to change our thoughts on what self-development is and why it is important to take investments seriously. We have relegated training programmes into events to get certificates. People are interested in going for training only if it is outside the country and they get a free trip out of it.

The Future Is All about Individual Potential: With artificial intelligence ready to compete with human minds, the humans who continue to evolve are the only ones who can take on the future. They understand the need to get better and are willing to invest time and financial resources for the same. Despite the development of machines, machines continue to be controlled by the humans.

Nepal has the advantage of having half its population under the age of twenty-five, and they can be moulded to take on the world with the right intervention and guidance. If Nepalis can be trained to be successful workers elsewhere, Nepali firms can take on the challenge of developing Nepalis for Nepali companies to take over the world.

## Managing Talent

We have to get people ready for jobs that don't exist yet: In the US, discussions across companies are being driven not by which market to focus on or how to raise funding, but how to undertake talent management. This is true across all segments of for-profit and not-for-profit organizations. Even mom-and-pop stores and small operations are a part of this discourse, with disruptive innovation, artificial intelligence and developments in communication. Talent has gone beyond its traditional definition to encompass a broader sense of human capital ability. The biggest challenge remains how to hire people and train them for jobs of the future. If we look at the top ten jobs in the US nowadays, many of them did not even exist ten years ago. Similarly, what students learn in the freshman year of an undergraduate programme in some fields is obsolete by the time they graduate. Further, the discourse has moved from job creation to income generation.

The New CEO: When I began my career three decades ago, it was generally folks like me in accounting and finance who made it to the CEO's post. It was not hotel management graduates who were heading hotels or engineers who were heading energy companies. Because the focus was so much on the financial health of a company and the objective was dominated by financial goals, it was quite natural for the chief financial officer (CFO) to be seen as the de facto CEO before actually becoming one. Thereafter, the marketing folks dominated the scene, and it was the chief marketing officers who were most likely to get CEO jobs. (I got a diploma in marketing because I thought it was essential to move ahead in my career and life.) In the early 2000s when disruptive tech companies emerged, the chief technical officers became the de facto CEOs, even taking over marketing and finance. If we look at lists of the top business people in the world, we will see they are dominated by people with a techie bent of mind. Companies like Tesla took building and selling cars into the software space, in contrast to traditional automobile companies. Uber went on to run a large network of vehicles without owning even one, while Airbnb began operating hospitality businesses without owning a hotel.

Now there seems to be a tectonic shift happening, with human resource and talent managers seen as next in line to become CEOs.

You may get your finance, marketing and technology right, but if you do not get your people right, then you are going to face challenges. Many people in the top tier of business are shifting to take on roles within the human resource function as they feel that this will be the future trend. Never before has so much been written and discussed on these issues.

Artificial Intelligence (AI) and Talent: The role of AI is set to be the next big disruption, with Google and other tech firms talking about it being far 'more profound than electricity or fire'. When Sophia the robot came to Nepal in March 2018 and interacted at the Himalayan Consensus Summit, it was amazing to see how a human-made machine surpassed human capacities. It is believed that AI will make many jobs redundant. For instance, one of the big questions people ask is what will happen to the millions of truck drivers once driverless trucks become the norm.

However, I personally believe that AI is changing how people work, but it will not replace humans. In fact, taking repetitive and boring jobs away from humans will make them more productive. A person's every movement can be tracked, along with the interactions happening in his or her computer, thus providing amazing levels of feedback. Customer service, which is so hard to monitor, can now be analysed through the data feed received through cameras. AI will assist talent acquisition, management and productivity, and perhaps monitor emotions and intangibles like mindfulness and awareness, thus changing the world of talent management forever.

What It Means for Nepal: In Nepal, any new innovation often means that either a government agency will crop up or a cartel in the veil of an association will emerge—so perhaps a Talent Management Board or Talent Management Association of Nepal will be established! However, Nepal has a lot to gain if it gets talent management right and doesn't use the traditional ways of approaching issues. Firms and organizations in Nepal have always been driven by finances or media attention. This has to change. Investment in talent and human resources, along with its management, is dismally poor. Currently, the human resource function is seen as a clerical one. Talent is getting sourced globally, and Nepalis will have to compete with people from other parts of the world. Nepali workers will have to compete with Bangladeshis and Indians on construction sites, for instance. More websites are being developed outside Nepal for Nepali firms, more Nepali books are printed outside Nepal, and with virtual currency becoming a reality, one may shun local bankers with attitude problems in favour of virtual platforms that are being managed elsewhere.

The pace of change is now moving at an alarming rate, similar to the disruption that emails, the Internet and mobile phones brought into our lives in the late 1990s and the turn of the millennium. India's image and opportunity got recalibrated during these times. Perhaps in this next big churn, Nepal can arrive on the global stage with its great youth talent and aspirations.

## Building Credibility

If we are to take advantage of the fact that we have a Constitution and an elected set of representatives, we need to work hard towards building a credible society. This can help make leaders accountable when they go up for re-election in 2022.

First, like-minded folks must be found in each field to build a pressure group to discuss important issues. For instance, we need to question whether it is important for a minister to inaugurate an event. Is it important for him or her to speak? Is it important for one to attend a programme just because a minister is in attendance? Does the attendance of a minister mean that it is important? This culture began when the country only had one television channel, and if you wanted that government media organization to cover your event, you had to invite a minister, but it doesn't need to go on. Similarly, think of whether you want sofas in the front row for the supposed VVIPs, or if there should be more people on the stage than in the audience. A lot of people don't like these practices, but it is time to put one's foot down!

Second, we need to build credible institutions that will not be impacted by changes in government or people. We need to have think tanks that do research and analysis and produce useful information and trends. We need stronger educational institutions that will not rely on political patronage and union power, but have the rigour to inculcate values in students.

Third, we need to ensure that the youth learn what is right and what is wrong from their parents first and school later. Which means even parents need to be educated on what is wrong and what is right. I watch the parents looking out for the schoolbus from their second-floor window. They only accompany the child to the bus once it gets to their doorstep, resulting in huge traffic jams. The child must be taught to walk to the bus stop, ending the culture of insisting on privilege even if it inconveniences others. If you think it is okay to serve alcohol at birthday parties to the friends of your fifteen-year-old child or you think it is okay to give thousands of rupees to your sixteen-year-old to book a table at a club, then you cannot complain when trouble begins. In Nepal, a lot of money comes in from assets that one has inherited rather than hard work.

Hence, it is not the big things that need to change in Nepal, it is the smaller things around us. Perhaps then everyone will stop finding excuses.

Finally, we have to get our sense and sensibilities right. Within two generations, Nepal, like many other countries, has moved quickly in integrating itself to the ever-globalizing world, but the key question to ask is whether our sense and sensibilities are also moving towards twenty-first-century norms. The luxury of travelling by air, bikes, cars or in buses, communicating with gadgets, eating out at restaurants, shopping in large-format stores, watching movies in halls that have the best technologies and attending programmes have reached the common Nepali in the past three decades. However, we are yet to learn basic ways to deal with situations. Tourism comments have singled out Chinese and Indian tourists as the most difficult ones to handle and now Nepalis are getting added to the list. Money can buy space in hotels and restaurants, tickets to the cinema, mobile phones and recharge cards, but one must invest in good behaviour too, or the identity of a country can get associated with all kinds of negative things.

All the sectors that have been discussed are related to each other and cannot be viewed in isolation. Tourism and agriculture, for instance, rely on energy and infrastructure, while services cuts through all the other sectors. To implement Vision 2030, the development of these sectors has to be pursued in an integrated manner.

# Acknowledgements

A book is a compilation of observations, stories and thoughts. Many people have inspired the observations, stories and thoughts that have gone into this book. There were hundreds who ignited new perspective, new learnings and new ways of viewing issues. They were people seated next to me in airplanes or in immigration or security queues. They were people with whom I spent time chatting at bars, trains and coffee shops. They were people I interviewed in the course of assignments and those who attended consultative meetings and discussions I was moderating. They were students and participants who asked interesting questions at talk programmes. They were the faithful folks who continued sending me comments after an opinion piece got published. They were the ones I follow on different social media platforms who share interesting articles and readings with me. I am grateful to all of these people who helped shape my thoughts.

In the course of work and conversation, I have been fortunate to meet many stellar diplomats, organization leaders and change agents who questioned the status quo. Learning about other countries, cultures and solutions helped me create a multidimensional approach to understanding issues. Literary festivals, conferences and events provided the perfect platforms to expand my curiosity. With the expansion of Beed's operations in other countries, there were more lessons to learn and challenges to be compared to Nepal. And there were many friends with whom I talked endlessly about everything under the sun. A big thank you to them.

Many people in my career have inspired me, but foremost amongst them is Prabhakar Rana, former chairman emeritus of the Soaltee Hotel. He is an epitome of selfless leadership from whom I learnt how to take a long-term view on issues and the importance of integrity to be able to survive the long haul. I miss him greatly. Gurcharan Das, Bibek Debroy and Namita Gokhale continue to inspire me. Kul Chandra Gautam is another person I look up to and confer with when I seek answers.

In the course of working on my book, the team members of Beed and the Nepal Economic Forum supported me extensively and gave me latitude to take time off to get the writing process going. Many of them functioned as my sounding board when I had to cross-check data and information; I often got them to read portions. Aman Pant has provided immense support in the writing process by reading drafts and providing comments.

A big thank you to Ranjana Sengupta, associate publisher at Penguin Random House India. I began the journey with her with *Unleashing Nepal*, and we ideated a lot on the structure of this book. Thank you to Shreya Chakravertty for ensuring the book took this final form, and to Anushree Kaushal for the coordination.

Finally, my wife, Alpa, and my daughter, Suyasha, were extremely supportive and patient with me during my long hours working on this book. They forgave my preoccupation and obsession with research and writing, and later with reviews and edits. Their candid feedback has shaped the way I go about life, and the change has always been for the better. A big thank you to you both.

# Notes

## Introduction

1. Satya Mohan Joshi, *Buddha Khojdai Chin Pukda Phela Pare Arniko* (Setopati, July 2018), https://setopati.com/social/163879
2. *Arthat Arthatantra* (Kathmandu: Nepalaya Publications, 2018).
3. https://kathmandupost.com/money/2017/03/31/tourism-pumped-rs177b-into-nepals-economy

## Part 1
## Chapter 1: Nepal Chronicles Its Existence: Nepal Era, 879 CE

1. The Bikram calendar is a solar calendar which is sixty-two years ahead of the Gregorian calendar. It begins and ends in mid-April. It is also occasionally inconsistent—the number of days in a month may vary, as determined by astrologers.
2. Newas were the inhabitants of the Kathmandu valley and were also spread across different parts of Nepal. In this book, the word Newa has been used to denote the group that the author belongs to. Their language is also called Newa.
3. The goddess Tara, one of the Bodhisattavas, is regarded as the goddess of compassion.

4. Satya Mohan Joshi, *Buddha Khojdai Chin Pukda Phela Pare Arniko* (Setopati, July 2018), https://setopati.com/social/163879

5. Bahas are communities that are built around a Buddhist monastery and have a consecrated Buddha. A commune or sangha lives around it.

6. https://www.penguinrandomhouse.com/books/132261/the-travels-of-marco-polo-by-marco-polo/9780307269133/

7. 'Marco Polo and His Travels', http://www.silk-road.com/artl/marcopolo.shtml (accessed May 2019).

8. Baburam Acharya, *Prachinkalko Nepal* (Krishna Acharya, reprinted 2006).

9. Nepa Mandala is referred to as the Kathmandu valley ruled by the Mallas.

10. Gopal Singh Nepali, *The Newars* (Mandala Book Point, reprinted 2015), p. 14.

11. Prista Ratanapruck, *Market and Monastery: Manangi Trade Diasporas in South and Southeast Asia* (Harvard University, 2008).

12. *Sikh Heritage of Nepal* (Kathmandu: BP Koirala Foundation, Embassy of India, 2019).

13. The varna system was like the caste system but also included Buddhist priests among the upper castes of Brahmin, Kshatriya and Vaishya.

14. Gopal Singh Nepali, *The Newars*, p. 147.

15. Conversations with Jigmed Namgyal, the heir to the last ruler of Ladakh.

16. Michael Aris, *Bhutan: The Early History of a Himalayan Kingdom* (Aris & Phillips, 1979), p. 344.

17. Karma Phunsto, *The History of Bhutan* (Random House India, 2013).

18. Bahas are communities that are built around a Buddhist monastery.

19. Prof. Todd Lewis, 'Buddhism, Himalayan Trade and Newar Merchants', http://buddhim.20m.com/8-4.htm

## Chapter 2: Shah Rule: From Regional Hub to Isolation, 1776–1846

1. Sanjay Upadhya, *Nepal and the Geo-Strategic Rivalry between China and India* (Routledge Studies in South Asian Politics, 2012).

2. Adam Smith, *The Wealth of Nations* (London: W. Strahan and T. Cadell, 1776).

3. Prithvi Narayan Shah, *Divya Upadesh* (Nepal: Government of Nepal, Ministry of Information and Communication, Information Department, 2003).

4. Birtas were given only to Brahmins during Prithvi Narayan Shah's time, but other castes had also started getting them by the time his descendants were ruling.

5. Birta land grant recipients.

6. Ijara was a farm revenue system to derive revenue from agriculture.

7. Ludwig F. Stiller, *The Rise of the House of Gorkha: A Study in the Unification of Nepal* (Human Resource Development Centre, 1995), pp. 242–43.

8. M.C. Regmi, *Kings and Political Leaders of the Gorkhali Empire* (Orient Longman Limited, 1995), pp. 12–14.

## Chapter 3: Shah Puppets: Rana Autocracy, 1846–1950

1. In the official records of the British army, the soldiers were referred to as Gurkhas, while in India they are called Gorkhas. The word refers to inhabitants of the Gorkhali kingdom.

2. Sagar S.J.B. Rana, *Singha Durbar: Rise and Fall of the Rana Regime of Nepal* (Rupa Publications India, 2018), p. 48.

3. Subodh Rana, http://historylessonsnepal.blogspot.com/2013/03/the-b-c-conundrum.html (accessed May 2018).

4. Conversations with Prabhakar S.J.B. Rana.

5. 'Laypersons' is referred to in Buddhism to denote householders who have a close relationship with the ordained sangha and provide material and economic support to temples and monasteries.

6. Deepak Gyawali, 'Yam between Bhot and Mughal', in *State of Nepal*, Kanak Mani Dixit and Shastri Ramachandaran, eds (Himal Books, 2005), p. 212.

7. Ram Sharan Mahat, *In Defense of Democracy* (Adroit Publishers, 2005).

8. Ibid.

## Chapter 4: Shahs' Rise and the Fall of the Partyless Panchayat: 1950–90

1. https://en.wikipedia.org/wiki/Chief_of_the_Nepalese_Army

2. Sujeev Shakya, *Unleashing Nepal* (New Delhi: Penguin India, 2013), p. 31.

3. Devanagari is a left-to-right script whose alphabets are based on the ancient Brahmi script.

4. A plan initiated by US Secretary of State George C. Marshall to reconstruct Western Europe and thwart communist expansion, https://history.state.gov/milestones/1945-1952/marshall-plan

5. Compiled from the Ministry of Finance Economic Survey.

6. https://thewire.in/diplomacy/nepal-india-relations-china (accessed May 2018).

7. Library of Congress, 'A Country Study: Nepal', http://lcweb2.loc.gov/frd/cs/nptoc.html (accessed January 2009).

8. In India, the privy purse was a payment made to the ruling (royal or lower) families of erstwhile princely states as part of their agreements to first integrate with India in 1947, and later to merge their states in 1949 whereby they lost all ruling rights.

9. Sujeev Shakya, *Unleashing Nepal*, p. 51.

## Chapter 5: Fall of Shahs: Restoration of Multiparty Democracy, Conflict and End of Shah Dynasty, 1990–2008

1. Anjali Puri and Manoj Dahal, 'Import Duty', *Outlook*, 18 January 2009.

2. The Fabian socialist model follows the model of democratic socialism adopted by the Fabian Society that pushes for gradual transformation rather than a revolution.

3. Compiled from the Ministry of Finance Economic Survey, 1994.

4. The Lewis Model is a development model of a dualistic economy, consisting of rural agricultural and urban manufacturing sectors.

5. Kanak Mani Dixit, 'Bahuns and Nepali State', *Nepali Times*, 19 October 2001.

6. Sujeev Shakya, *Making Private Sector an Engine for Growth* (DFID, 2008).

7. *Village Development Committees
†Municipalities
‡District Development Committees

8. Chakka jam literally means the jamming of wheels, prohibiting vehicles from plying the roads. Banda/bandhs are temporary shutdowns in all commerce enforced by the organizers of street-level agitation.

9. Min Bahadur Shrestha and Shashi Kant Chaudhary, 'The Economic Cost of General Strikes in Nepal', *NRB Economic Review*, 2016.

10. Institute of International Education, http://www.iie.org/Who-We-Are/News-and-Events/Press-Center/Press-Releases/2011/2011-11-14-Open-Doors-International-Students (accessed January 2013).

11. Deepak Thapa and Bandita Sijapati, *A Kingdom under Siege* (The Printhouse, 2003).

12. Crisis Group Asia Report No. 104, 'Nepal's Maoists: Their Aims, Structure and Strategy', 2005.

13. Government of West Bengal, India, 'West Bengal Industrial Policy' (1978).

14. Kedar Subedi, '*Suraksha bina ko suraksha karcha*', *Himal Khabarpatrika*, 13–27 February 2005.

15. Ibid.

16. Ibid.

17. Ibid.

18. Bhaskar Gautam, Purna Basnet and Chiran Manandhar, *Mauwadi Virodh: Sashatra Sangharsh ko Avadhi* (Martin Chautari, 2007).

19. Ibid.

20. Ibid.

21. UNHCR, UNHCR Nepal Factsheet, November 2008, http://www.un.org.np/unhcr/docfile/2008-12-16-unhcr-nepal-fact-sheet.pdf (accessed January 2009).

22. Dasain, the annual festival celebrated around October, where the sacrifice of the goat is common.

23. Interview with Chairman Prachanda, *Maoist Information Bulletin* 4, 15 September 2003, Communist Party of Nepal (Maoist) via http://www.cpnm.org/new/English/documents/information_bulletin-4.htm (accessed January 2009).

## Chapter 6: Years of Transition: 2006–18

1. This book was a compilation of the quotations and speeches of Mao Tse Tung, chairman of the Communist Party of China. It was referred to as the 'Little Red Book' and distributed extensively in 1965.

2. Bhojraj Pokhrel and Shristhi Rana, *Nepal Votes for Peace* (Cambridge University Press India, 2013).

3. Constitution text, http://www.lawcommission.gov.np/en/archives/987
4. *Kathmandu Post*, 'Norwegian Company Pulls Out of Tamakoshi III Project', 3 January 2016, http://kathmandupost.ekantipur.com/news/2016-01-03/norwegian-company-pulls-out-of-tamakoshi-iii-project.html

## Chapter 7: The Leap: The 'Unleashing Nepal' Journey, 2006–18

1. Alex Gray, 'These Are the World's Fastest Growing Economies in 2017', WEF, 9 June 2017.
2. Sujeev Shakya, *Unleashing Nepal* (Penguin India, Revised 2013).
3. United Nations Office of the High Commissioner for Human Rights, Nepal Conflict Report, 2012.
4. Compiled from data by the Ministry of Finance.
5. *Spotlight*, 'SEE Results 2076: Private Schools Maintain Lead', 28 June 2019.
6. Compiled from Trading Economics, https://tradingeconomics.com/nepal/school-enrollment-primary-male-percent-gross-wb-data.html
7. Compiled from MDG Achievement Fund, http://www.mdgfund.org/node/922
8. National Planning Commission, 'Nepal and the Millennium Development Goals Final Status Report 2000–2015', 2016.
9. 'Heli' is used in Nepali to refer to helicopter rides, which have of late become a sign of high social status.
10. A festival of colours celebrated with sprinkling colour and coloured water.
11. One anna is one-sixteenth of a Ropani. A Ropani is 5174 square feet.

## Part II

## Chapter 8: Cartelpreneurs: The World of the Nepali Private Sector

1. Declaration or proclamation from the Rana rulers.
2. Gorkhaland is a separate state of the Gorkha (Nepali) people that was demanded from India, comprising the hills of Darjeeling district and the Dooars.
3. Sujeev Shakya, 'Fragile to Frontier', *Kathmandu Post*, 14 May 2013.

4. Nepal Economic Forum, 'Understanding the Cartel Economy', March 2018.

5. Ministry of Finance, Government of Nepal, Economic Survey, 2016–17.

6. S. Dhungana, 'NRB to Raise Daily Gold Import Quota to 20 Kg', *Himalayan Times,* January 2017.

7. Organization for Economic Cooperation and Development, 'Hard Core Cartels', 2000.

8. Shrinkage loss refers to gasoline loss due to shrinkage and evaporation when it is transported from locations with a high temperature to cooler places.

9. S. Dhungana, 'Fuel Dealers Withdraw Protest as Govt Hikes Loss Compensation on Fuel Transport', *Himalayan Times,* August 2017.

10. S. Giri, 'Private Water Suppliers Halt Work; Valley Hit', *Kathmandu Post,* June 2013.

11. S. Ghimire, 'NBA, NIC Asia Bank Accuse Each Other of Unfair Practices', *Republica,* March 2018.

12. S. Ghimire, 'Durbar Marg Traders Shut Down Stores to Protest Govt Monitoring', *Republica,* September 2017.

13. Nepal Economic Forum, 'Understanding the Cartel Economy', December 2017.

14. *Kathmandu Post,* 'Sajha Bus Vandalised', January 2017, http://kathmandupost.ekantipur.com/printedition/news/2017-01-20/sajha-bus-vandalised.html

15. *Kathmandu Post,* 'Meterless Taxi Drivers Protest in Pokhara', January 2018.

16. *Kathmandu Post,* 'Petrol Pumps Go on Strike', August 2017.

17. *Kathmandu Post,* 'UML, Maoist Centre MPs Block HPE Bill', October 2017, http://kathmandupost.ekantipur.com/news/2017-10-13/uml-maoist-centre-mps-block-hpe-bill.html

18. A. Dahal, 'MPs Influencing Parliamentary Decisions in Clear Conflict of Interest', *Republica,* July 2016, http://www.myrepublica.com/news/1810

19. Nepal Economic Forum, 'Political Economic Analysis of Business Houses in Nepal', November 2017.

20. Anil Giri, 'Foreign Ministry Officials Miffed at Govt's Envoy Picks', *Kathmandu Post,* February 2017.

21. Rupak D. Sharma, 'How Did Palm Oil Become Nepal's Top Export Item from Zero Export in 2017', *Himalayan Times*, September 2019.
22. Indicated in a confidential valuation report.
23. Nepal Economic Forum, 'Political Economic Analysis of Business Houses in Nepal', November 2017.
24. Ibid.
25. Ibid.
26. Ibid.
27. Ibid.

## Chapter 9: Donorpreneurs and the Business of Development

1. Eugene Bramer Mihalay, *Foreign Aid and Politics in Nepal: A Case Study* (Himal Books, 2002).
2. As per SWC, 46,235 NGOs are registered with them, http://www.swc.org.np/wp-content/uploads/2017/08/ngo_rec.pdf (accessed 2 January 2019).
3. Scott Morris, 'The Biggest Club You've Probably Never Heard of', Center For Global Development, 4 December 2018.
4. Dan Steinbock, 'How the Belt and Road Could Change the 21st Century', *Telegraph*, 24 May 2017.
5. Sujeev Shakya, *Unleashing Nepal* (Delhi: Penguin India, 2013).
6. Ibid.
7. The Dalit Welfare Organization describes Dalits as de facto 'untouchables' of contemporary Nepal.

## Chapter 10: Global Nepalis: The World of Migration, Diaspora and Remittance

1. A mandatory purification ritual taken to re-enter Nepal .
2. David Seddon, 'Lest We Forget', *Nepali Times*, November 2018.
3. Garden Court Chambers, 'The Launch of the Gurkhas: The Forgotten Veterans', https://www.gardencourtchambers.co.uk/news/the-launch-of-the-gurkhas-the-forgotten-veterans (accessed May 2019).

4. C. Mishra, L.P. Uprety, T. Panday, 'Seasonal Agricultural Labour Migration from India', Centre for Nepal and Asian Studies, 2000.

5. Khukris are weapons that are associated with the Gorkhas/Gurkhas of India and Nepal.

6. Bipali is Shakya's neologism which combines the 'bi' from the Nepali word 'bidesh' (foreign country) with the 'pali' from Nepali.

7. Nepal Economic Forum, 'Nefport: Migration Special', January 2017.

8. Compiled from information from the Ministry of Labour, Employment and Social Security.

9. Ramyata Limbu, 'Nepal Migration: Fake Identities in Search of Prosperity', IPS News Agency, August 1996, http://www.ipsnews.net/1996/08/nepal-migration-fake-identities-in-search-of-prosperity (accessed May 2019).

10. Compiled from US Department of State, Bureau of Consular Affairs, https://travel.state.gov/content/dam/visas/Statistics/AnnualReports/FY2017AnnualReport/FY17AnnualReport-TableVII.pdf (accessed May 2019).

11. Ibid.

12. Pew Research Center, http://www.pewsocialtrends.org/fact-sheet/asian-americans-nepalese-in-the-u-s/ (accessed May 2019).

13. *Himalayan Times*, 'Five Million Nepalis Obtain MRPs', June 2017.

14. Compiled from the Ministry of Foreign Affairs, Department of Passports.

15. S. Dhungana, 'Australia Is Most Preferred Study Destination for Nepalis', *Republica*, 6 November, 2018.

16. Compiled from World Bank Data, https://data.worldbank.org/indicator/BX.TRF.PWKR.DT.GD.ZS?locations=NP (accessed May 2019).

17. Rajendra Dahal, 'Nepal's Remittance Bonanza', CESLAM, 2010.

18. Dhananjay Shah, 'Hundi in South Korea Nepalis Remittance Channel', *Himalayan Times*, 27 July 2017.

19. UNCDF, 'Making Access Possible Nepal: Detailed Country Report, 2016.

20. Bibek Subedi, 'Malaysia Top Remittance Sending Country to Nepal', *Kathmandu Post*, 5 August 2016.

21. Ishani Dasgupta, 'How the Mix of Remittances is Changing for Indians', *Economic Times*, 1 July 2018.

## Chapter 11: Nepal's Future in between China and India

1. Notes from Growing Industrial Interconnections and Globalised Companies International Conference on Globalisation of Knowledge Development and Delivery, Third Annual Conference of the Forum for Global Knowledge Sharing, New Delhi, 17–18 October 2008, https://www.pardos-marketing.com/paper_l02.htm (accessed May 2019).

2. Interview with Surya Nath Upadhyaya, *Kantipur Daily*, 2 September 2019.

3. A traditional way of transferring money.

4. Mandalas are traditional Newa drawings.

5. Rangolis are patterns that originated in India, drawn on the floor or ground using different materials.

6. Sudheer Sharma, *Prayogshala* (Fineprint Books, 2013).

7. Compiled from the Ministry of Finance, http://portal.mof.gov.np/portal

8. A perceived geopolitical strategy of China to encircle the Indian Ocean

9. Southasia Program at the Hudson Institute, History of India-Nepal Relations, http://www.southasiaathudson.org/history/

10. Amrit Kharel, 'Doctors Who Graduated from Chinese Medical Schools Doing Well in Nepal', Xinhua, 21 May 2013.

11. DBS Group Research, 'China the rise and rise (and rise) of RMB', February 2017.

12. Xinhua, 'Tibet receives more than 30 mln tourists in 2018', January 2019.

13. Shared by the Tata Sons China CEO on 5 December 2018 at the first round of the Silk Spice Road Dialogues convened in Beijing at the UNDP China office with the UNDP, Center for China and Globalization and the Himalayan Consensus as co-hosts.

14. *Times of India*, 'China Says Its Investment In India Crossed 8 billion', 26 April 2018.

15. *The Hindu*, 'India China Aviation Officials Discuss Increasing Air Connectivity', 2 June, 2018.

16. Cao Siqi, 'More Indian students coming to China as result of new preferential policies', *Global Times*, 1 January 2018.

17. Hemali Chhapia, 'China gets more Indian students than Britain', *Times of India*, 7 January 2018.

18. B.K. Karmacharya, N. Taneja and S. Sarvanathan, 'India's Informal Trade in SAARC Countries: Case of Nepal, India and Sri Lanka', *South Asia Economic Journal* 5.1 (Jan–June 2004): 27–54.

19. Sujeev Shakya, 'Strengthening BBIN Connectivity Market Signal For Policymaking', ORF Issue Brief 129, February 2016.

20. ICAO defines as the right or privilege, in respect of scheduled international air services, granted by one State to another State to put down and to take on, in the territory of the first State, traffic coming from or destined to a third State.

21. Sujeev Shakya, 'In Southasia the Time Has Come for Border Economic Zones', *Nikkei Asian Review*, April 2017.

## Chapter 12: Capitalist Welfare State: In between Capitalism and Socialism

1. Kanak Mani Dixit and Shastri Ramachandaran, eds, *State of Nepal* (Nepal: Himal Books, 2001).

2. Sujeev Shakya, *Unleashing Nepal* (New Delhi: Penguin Books India, 2013).

3. Ibid.

4. E-Estonia, https://e-estonia.com/solutions/e-governance/i-voting (accessed May 2019).

5. Department of Forestry, 'Achievements', http://www.dof.gov.np/achievements

6. K.C. Rajendra and Aasha Khattri, 'Contribution of Community Forestry in Reducing Rural Poverty in Nepal', http://www.tropentag.de/2008/abstracts/full/147.pdf

7. Guthi is an organizational system that is prevalent among the Newa community that functions both as social organization and social security commune.
8. These annual reports are published by the World Bank and are available at http://www.doingbusiness.org

## Chapter 13: Vision 2030 and Beyond

1. PWC, 'The Long View: How will the global economic order change by 2050?', February 2017.
2. Compiled from the World Population Data of the Population Reference Bureau, http://www.worldpopdata.org/map
3. Janet Henry, 'The World in 2030', HSBC, September 2018.
4. He went on to become the vice chair of the National Planning Commission from August 2017 to February 2018.
5. Sujeev Shakya, 'Nepal Economic Vision 2030: Leveraging Private Sector Growth and Investments', ADB, August 2016.
6. Ibid.
7. Sujeev Shakya, 'A wounded economy', *Kathmandu Post*, 24 November 2015.
8. World Bank, 'Regional Integration in South Asia', 3 October 2015.
9. World Bank, Doing Business 2019, http://www.worldbank.org/en/region/sar/brief/south-asia-regional-integratio

## Chapter 14: Making 'HATS and I' Happen

1. Sara Boettiger, Nicolas Denis and Sunil Sangh, 'Successful Agricultural Transformations: Six Core Elements Of Planning and Delivery', McKinsey and Company, December 2017.
2. A Ropani is 5174 square feet.
3. UNWTO, Tourism Highlights 2017, https://www.e-unwto.org/doi/pdf/10.18111/9789284419029 (accessed May 2019).
4. Oliver Smith, 'Rise of the Chinese Tourist', *Telegraph*, April 2018.
5. UNWTO, Tourism Highlights 2018, https://www.e-unwto.org/doi/pdf/10.18111/9789284419876 (accessed May 2019).

6.  Ministry of Culture, Tourism & Civil Aviation, tourism statistics 2012, p. 23.
7.  *Kathmandu Post*, 'More tourists are visiting the country but they are spending less money', May 2019.
8.  http://tourism.gov.in/sites/default/files/Other/ITS_Glance_2018_Eng_Version_for_Mail.pdf
9.  Josh Bivens, 'The Potential Macroeconomic Benefits from Increasing Infrastructure Investments', Economic Policy Institute, July 2017.
10. Jeffrey M. Stupak, 'Economic Impact of Infrastructure Investment', Congressional Research Service, January 2018.
11. World Bank, 'Nepal Systematic Country Diagnostic', February 2018.
12. Asian Development Bank, 'Meeting Asia's Infrastructure Needs', 2017.

# Index

Acharya, Shailaja, 91
acquisition of knowledge, 298
Acute Immune Dependency
    Syndrome (AIDS), 208–9
Adi Shankaracharya, 5
Age of Enlightenment, 23
ageing populations, 344
agrarian economy, 25
agriculture: benchmarking to
    international practices, 335;
    commercialization of, 332–
    33; core of production, 334;
    crop planning, 333; labour-
    intensive practices, 334;
    understanding consumption,
    330–32: understanding the
    production side, 332–33
aid money, leakage and wastage
    of, 202
Airbnb, 337, 372
Aishwarya, Queen, 68

All Party Mechanism (APM),
    118, 125, 130
Anglo-Nepal war, 28–29, 32,
    222
Annapurna Conservation Area
    Project (ACAP), 154
anti-competitive practices, 310
anti-English tirade, 49
anti-India activities, 260
anti-India sentiment, 53, 248
anti-Rana crusade, 43
architectural marvels, ix
armed police force, formation of,
    105
Arniko, 6–9, 221
*Arthat Arthatantra*, xi
artificial intelligence, 298,
    371–73
Arun III project, 154
'*Asare Bikas*', 130
'ashan grahan' ritual, 150

Asian Development Bank (ADB), 134, 205–6, 284, 299, 348

Asian Tigers, 74

Association of Southeast Asian Nations (ASEAN), 243, 250, 264

aviation, 40, 167, 193, 201

Baba Ramdev (FMCG guru), 332

bad practices, institutionalization of, 213

Bahas, 7–8

Bahun Business Barons, rise of, 163–64

Bangladesh, 13, 143, 180, 224, 244, 249, 251, 262, 264, 267, 296, 327

Bangladesh, Bhutan, India and Nepal (BBIN), 262–63, 266–67, 311

bankers, 79–80, 374; banking monopoly, 79; competition, 79; premium customer service, 79

Bankers' Association, 177

Banking and Financial Institutions Act, 315

bankruptcy, 28–29, 82

Bankruptcy Act, 82

Banks and Financial Institutions Act, 182

Bar Association, 152

barber associations, 180

Basnyat, Singha Bahadur, 209

Beed Management, xvi, 350

behavioural issues, 239–40

Belt and Road Initiative (BRI), xii, 9, 207, 245–56, 257, 317

Berlin wall, fall of, 72

'Bhagbanda', 118, 172

Bhandari, Bidya Devi, 151

Bhandari, Harry, 238

Bhatbhateni Supermarket, 192

*bhatta pratha*, 213

Bhattarai, Baburam, 96, 114

Bhattarai, Krishna Prasad, 74, 104, 351

Bhrikuti, Princess, 4, 7, 221

Big Bash League, 146

Bikram calendar, 290

Bikram era, 3

bilateral transit agreement, 128

Bill and Melinda Gates Foundation, 207

BIMSTEC (Bay of Bengal Initiative for Multi-Sectoral Technical and Economic Cooperation), 311, 361

Biratnagar Jute Mills, 60

Birendra, King, 53, 66–71, 73, 107; constitutional monarch, 71; economic reforms, 67; equidistance card New Delhi, 73; massacre of, 71; non-aligned policy follower, 66; royal patronage and business, 68

birta land system, 26, 52

*birtawals*, 25–27

Bishwakarma, Karna Bahadur, 178

black waters, 33–34

blockade, 19, 29, 55, 117, 119, 126, 128–29, 133, 245, 247, 249, 252

'body shops', 217

border economic zones (BEZs), 244, 267–69, 312

border towns, aggregation of, 363–64

Borobudur temple, 14

Brahminism, 5

brand Nepal, 320–21

'brand smile', 322

bribery and commissions, 59

British East India Company, 10, 27–28; administrative system, 27

British Overseas National Passport (BONP), 228

Brookings Institute, 313

Buddhism, 4–7, 10, 37, 199, 338

Buddhist missionaries, 5

budgetary spending on security, 101

bulldozer terrorism, 152, 155, 365

bureaucracy, 43, 59, 82–85, 114, 118, 163, 182, 203, 216, 218, 354, 366

Burmese Citizenship Act (1964), 224

Bush, George, 106

business associations, lackadaisical attitude, 171

business–bureaucracy–politician nexus, 85

capitalism, 21, 23, 37, 58–59, 72, 103, 120, 158, 163, 197, 270–71, 273–74; alternatives to, 120, 163; balance with communism, 59; binary perspective, 274; crony capitalism, 172, 274, 348; European, 22; expansion of, 197; free-market capitalism, 21, 23; liberal market capitalism, 72; loss of faith in, 58; perceptions of, 271–73; rise of, 37. *See also* Westernization

capitalist welfare state, 82, 158, 270–71, 274–75, 277, 284, 292, 323; role of donors, 284; role of government, 277

CARE, 205

Carnegie Endowment for International Peace, 313

cartels, 95, 149, 159, 169, 172–84, 190, 194, 205, 268, 278, 280, 287, 310, 335, 344, 357, 365; all-pervasive, 178; cartelpreneurs, 159, 177–78, 183; conflict of interest, 181; cost, 178–82; dismantling, 310; economy, 159, 173, 179, 280–81; election funding, and, 183; exploited social media, 179; key characteristics, 178; omnipresent, omnipotent and omniscient, 180; politics of, 182; proliferation of, 172; transport cartels, 131, 176, 280

caste purification ritual. *See pani patia*

caste system, hierarchy of, 36, 272

Centre for Policy Research, 313

Chabahil, 4

*chakari*, xiii, 42, 57, 68, 82, 150, 249; feudal system of, 230; institution of, 42–44

*chakka jam*, 87–89, 99–100

chambers of commerce, 169, 174

Charumati, 4

Chatham House, 313

Chaubisi Rajya, 17

Chaudhary, Binod, 181

*China Daily*, 254

China Development Bank (CDB), 207

China: Belt and Road initiative, 256–57; building infrastructure policy, 346; GDP growth, 243, 296–97; growing importance of, 252–53; influence in Nepal, 260; interest in Nepal, 245; investment in India, 257; land-linked with Nepal, 244; multiple work or exchange programmes, 254; Nepali-friendly image, 254; Peace and Friendship Treaty (1960), 253; preferential treatment, 244; relationship with, 244; Renminbi appreciation, 255; soft diplomacy, 253–55; tourism spending, 338; tourist volume to Nepal, 256

Chola dynasty, 14

Christian missionaries, 20

citizenship rights, 128

civil code based on caste and class, 37

Civil Service Act, 84

civil war, 48, 165

climate change, 216, 298, 353

coalition governments, 81

coalition politics, 113

cocktail circuits of Kathmandu, 136

code of ethics, 284

cold war, 55, 165, 270

Columbus, Christopher, 14

Commission for the Abuse of Authority, 173

Commission for the Investigation of Abuse of Authority (CIAA), 130, 152

communism, 49, 59, 112, 197, 261–62, 271, 273–74; as an antithesis to globalization, 274; ideology of, 112; as in indigenous ideology, 274; rise of, 49; in USSR, 59; West Bengal version of, 261; in Western Europe, 197

Communist Party of Nepal (Maoist), 71, 110, 113, 115–16, 139, 274

Communist Party of Nepal (UML [Unified Marxist–Leninist]), 81, 110–11, 113, 116–17, 181, 271

community forest, 217–18, 286

Companies Act, 60, 82, 165–66, 287

Competition Promotion and
    Market Protection Act, 176
Confederation of Indian
    Industries (CII), 186
Confederation of Nepalese
    Industries (CNI), 171, 174
conflict of interest, non-
    declaration of, 212
conflict resolution, 120–21, 129,
    149, 206, 216; business of,
    120–21
conflict-of-interest declarations,
    287
connectivity 'clusters', 268–69
conservative Hinduism, 220
Constitution: constitutional
    monarchy, 150;
    Constitution-writing, 114,
    122, 126; drafting, 106;
    flaws, 119–20; gender
    inequality, 128, 360; Indian
    dissatisfaction, 249, 252;
    interim, 44–46, 51–52, 165;
    mania, 118–19; political
    document, 119; protest
    against, 128; provisions
    related to economic issues,
    301
constitutional monarchy, 70,
    150
construction-friendly laws, 153
consumerism, 49, 78–79, 289;
    nature of, 289
contractual hiring of
    administrators. See ijara
    system
convertible currency, 48

cooperative movement, 163, 190,
    285
cooperatives, 98, 120, 163,
    190–91, 216, 271, 276,
    285–86, 301, 307, 343
corporate culture, 185
corporate governance scandals,
    302
corporate industrialization, 98
corporatization, 161, 300, 302
corruption, 59, 73, 80, 84, 99,
    104–5, 125, 131, 168, 172,
    210–11, 249, 282, 285, 359,
    366, 369; built-in incentive
    for, 210; democratization of,
    359; punitive frameworks to
    combat, 316; root cause of,
    282–83
'cottage industry of development',
    211
Council on Foreign Relations,
    313
Covey, Stephen, 295
credibility building, 374–76
credit rating, 79, 309, 328
currency curry, 46–48
customer-oriented work,
    treatment of, 188

Dahal, Kamal, 113
Dahal, Pushpa Kamal, 98, 113,
    115, 262, 273
Dalai Lama, 15
Das, Gurcharan, 277
Dasain festival, 241
'Dash Maoist', 113
datrisansthan, 199

David-and-Goliath battle, 29
demand–supply gap, 168
democracy: 'democracy industry',
    123; flirting with, 50–55;
    restoration of, 71, 91, 154,
    246
demonetization, 257
destination weddings, 149
Deuba, Sher Bahadur, 115–17
development, arrival of aid,
    196–97
development: concept of, 196;
    development assistance,
    key challenges, 209–11;
    development partners.
    *See* donors; first aid
    package, 197; imported
    bikas and original bikas,
    198–99; Marshall plan
    implementation, 196–97;
    understanding development,
    198
DFID, 205, 285
Dhakal, Pradeep, 238
Dhital, Kumud, 242
diaspora market, growth of,
    241–42
differentiated pricing, 329
differentiated tariffs, 327
diversity visa (DV), 229–30, 234
*Divya Upadesh*, 23, 26
Dixit, Kamal Mani, xv, 51, 61
*Doing Business Report*, 292, 314
domestic investment capacities,
    299
donation campaigns, 200
donors, 195

donors, 81, 91, 102–3, 120, 125,
    131, 170, 195–96, 199,
    201–3, 205–6, 209–10,
    213, 284–85, 300, 357, 360;
    donor making, 199–200;
    donorpreneurs class, creation
    of, 216; evolution of
    assistance, 200–2; make your
    exit plans, 284–85; Maoist
    attack on, 105; successes and
    failures of past programmes,
    285
Durbarmarg Development Board,
    178
duty concessions, 169

Earth Summit, 154
earthquake, 118–19, 124–27,
    129, 206, 245, 252, 254,
    285, 301, 366; charity money
    and goods, 125; collective
    responsibility for future,
    366; credibility of the prime
    minister's relief fund, 125;
    disaster preparedness testing,
    126; free text and phone calls,
    125; lost their lives, 124;
    observations and lessons,
    125–26; relief work, 125;
    relief workers, 126; silver
    lining of, 127; temporary
    protection status (TPS),
    126
Ease of Doing Business Index,
    314–15
East India Company. *See* British
    East India Company

easy exit from businesses, 315
Ebola crisis, 318
e-commerce transactions, 280
economic liberalization, 74–77
economic opportunities, 41, 221
economic protectionism, 23
Economic Vision 2030 (NEV
    2030), 299–300
economic vulnerability index, 300
economics of mercenaries, 41–42
education: community-owned
    schools, 63; educational
    consultancy industry, 93–
    94; educational monopoly
    of Tribhuvan University,
    94; foreign education,
    92–94; higher learning,
    private institutions of,
    94–95; improvements
    to, 92; low quality of
    government education, 92;
    new national education
    plan, 63; private schools,
    93–95, 103, 179
elections 2017, 116–17
Eminent Persons Group (EPG),
    xii, 245
employment-intensive economy,
    193
end of the conflict, 139
energy demand, 325–27
energy savings, 290
English boarding schools,
    expansion of, 94
entrepreneurial culture, 300–1
entrepreneurship development,
    209, 299

environment, business of, 154–55
environment-related issues, 155
Essential Goods Protection Act
    (1955), 177
ethnic exoduses, 224
exchange rate, 47–48, 191, 233,
    255
extraction facilities on riverbeds,
    365

Fabian socialism, 58–59, 74
fast track road, 130
'father of democracy'. See
    Tribhuvan, King
favouritism, 364
federalism, 118, 122, 279, 288;
    ethnicity-based, 132–33; key
    areas, 288
federalization, cost of, 288–89
Federation of Nepal Gold and
    Silver Dealers Association
    (NEGOSIDA), 175
Federation of Nepalese National
    Transport Entrepreneurs
    (FNNTE), 174
Federation of the Nepalese
    Chambers of Commerce and
    Industry (FNCCI), 170–71,
    173–74, 182, 186, 285
feudal lords, 24, 31, 96, 331
feudalism, 22
Fewa Boat Association, 175
financial resources, access, 306–7;
    demand for financial services,
    307; supply of financial
    services, 306–7
Financial Services Authority, 312

'First World', 197
fixed exchange rate policy, 48
flow of remittance money,
    channels for, 235
FNCCI Anti-corruption project,
    285
foreign aid, 49–50, 68, 197, 202–
    3, 208, 210–11, 217, 276,
    291, 309, 353; economic
    implications, 50; impact
    on real estate, 213; limited
    impact, 217; tremendous
    impact of, 50
Foreign Countries Act, 292
foreign debt, 210
foreign direct investment, 91,
    101, 132, 148–49, 167, 247,
    300, 302, 316
Foreign Investment and One-
    Window Enterprise Act
    (1992), 75
Foreign Investment and
    Technology Transfer Act
    (1992), 75, 169
Foreign Investment Prohibition
    Act (1964), 292
Forestry Master Plan, 217–18
Forestry Sector Policy, 217–18
fragile polity, 247
fragile to frontier (F2F), 172, 318
Franklin, Benjamin, 23
free trade zones (FTZs), 268

Gacchedar, Bijay, 115
Gama, Vasco da, 14
gambling, proliferation of, 365
Gampo, Songtsen, 4

Gandaki scheme, 202
Gandhi, Indira, 226
Gandhi, Mahatma, 43
Gandhi, Rajiv, 67, 72
Gandhi, Sonia, 73
*gau bikas samitis*, 84
Gautam, Kul Chandra, 211
Gautama Buddha, 6–7, 10
gender demographics, 216
gender mainstreaming, 144, 216
George Cross medals, 223
Ghale, Jamuna, 242
Ghani, Ashraf, 211
Global Competitiveness Index,
    314
global dreams, 300, 302
global markets, integrating with,
    310–11
Global Private Equity
    Conference, 318
global standards, 40, 132, 191,
    311, 313–14, 369
globalization, 49, 148, 167,
    184–86, 245, 274,
    289–91, 310; benefits of,
    310; liberalization, 167;
    professional competencies
    and, 184–86; refining and
    embracing, 289–91; socio-
    economic process, 289
Golden Temple (Hiranyavarna
    Mahavihara), 6
gora supremacy, 212
Gorkha Programme in UK, 230
Gorkha rulers, 20
Gorkhaland movement, 67, 162,
    224

Gorkhapatra Sansthan, 192
Gorkhas, 17, 34, 97, 223, 226, 230; active recruitment into British army, 34; remittances from, 232; success in foreign armies, 226
great depression, 58–59
greener pastures, 36–37, 149, 232
guise of associations, 174–76
Guru Nanak,11–12
Gurung, Harka, 65
Gurung, Min Bahadur, 192
Gurung, Prabal, 242
Guthi Act, 287
*guthi land grants*, 26
Gyeonggi Nambu Provincial Police Agency, 233

harnessing skills, 348–49
hawala route, 233, 248. *See also* hundi business
Health Profession Education (HPE) Bill, 181
Hetauda Cotton Textile Mills, 62
high-caste wives, 35
'hi-gration', 321–22
hill community, 128
Hillary, Sir Edmund, 64
Himalayan Consensus Summit, xvi, 316, 373
Himalayan Java–a coffee shop, 192
Himalayan Kingdoms, 15–16
Himalayan opportunity, leveraging the, 316–18
Hinduism, 37, 48, 57, 199, 220
'hippie age', 336

historical modernity, 8
home-grown community service organizations, 286
Hong Kong ID, 228
hospitality industry, 340, 343, 368; downslide of, 340
hotel industry, 184
human asset index, 300
human capital, 101, 282, 344, 351, 367–72; access to, 308–9; banking industry, 367; disruption is key, 368–69; individual potential, 371; ministry of human capital, 369; Nepalis performance, 369–70; professionalism at top, 370–71; self-development, 371
human development index, 135, 292
hundi business, 233
hydroelectricity, 39, 76, 324
hydropower, 70, 73, 77, 91–92, 129, 131, 165, 200, 210, 263, 293, 302, 308, 323–29

*ijara* system, 27
illegal trade, 99, 264
imperial history, 9–10
imperialism, 96, 103, 106, 215
import tariffs, 75
import-licensing, abolished, 75
*In Defense of Democracy*, 42
InChiNep Work, 269
India Connection, 10–11
*India Grows at Night*, 277

India: Act East and neighbourhood policies, 250–51; aid from, 250; blockade, 252; Chinese investment, 257; cultural proximity with, 259; dissatisfaction over the Nepali Constitution, 249; education, 246; foreign exchange regime, 338; friendship treaty (1913) with British India, 246; GDP, 243, 296–97; image issue, 248–50; Indo-Nepal treaty (1996), 247; investment by, 247; key trading partner, 246; land-linked with and Nepal, 244; medical treatment, 246; neighbourhood first policy, 251; open border with, 244, 263; outbound tourism, 339; –Pakistan war, 224; protectionist policies, 166; religious rites, 246; response to earthquake for relief, 251; 'special relation' status, 246; tariff reduction by, 247; tourism, 246; trade and transit treaty (1950), 246; transit treaty (1999) with automatic renewal, 246; twelve-point agreement, 109

Indian Airlines aircraft, hijack of, 90, 250

*Indian Idol*, 145

Indian Pale Ale (IPA), 15

Indian Premier League, 146

Indo-Nepal Trade and Transit Treaty, 186

Industrial Enterprise Act (1974), 67, 75

Industrial Enterprises Act (1962), 166

industrial revolution, 33, 37, 243

industrialization, 39, 74, 197

inflation, 47, 255

informal trade, proliferation of, 264

information and communication technologies (ICT), 266

infrastructure, building, 253, 346

Insolvency Act, 315

instability, 103, 201

insurgency, 67, 95, 97, 99, 101–6, 120, 135, 155, 206, 278, 340–41

Interim Government of Nepal Act (1951), 45

intermarriages, 16

international airports, xiv

International Finance Corporation (IFC), 171

International Labour Organization (ILO), 86

International Monetary Fund (IMF), 76, 134, 203, 255, 300

International Women's Day celebrations, 254

intra- and inter-party fights between the Madhesi parties, 133

investment risk for doing business, 102
isolation, 14, 18, 40–41, 52, 189, 244, 376
isolationism, 289, 311
isolationist policies, 23
Italian Renaissance, 14

*jagir* system, 25–26, 83, 85
Jain, Rajeeb, 145
Jana Andolan (1990), 70, 72–74, 82, 84, 87, 351; chakka jams, 87; markets liberalization, 148, 167
Jana Andolan II, 110
Jefferson, Thomas, 23
Jinping, Xi, xii, 117, 257, 361
job creation, 275, 279, 301, 304, 345, 372; local, 279
job creator, 345; banking sector, 345; e-commerce, 345; hotels and restaurants, 345; new areas, 345
Joshi, Satya Mohan, x, 7
judiciary, failure of, 157
Jung Bahadur, 30–35, 37, 39, 41, 162; audacity and daring, 39; British alliance, 33; intelligence on the China, 32; offensive against Tibet, 32; voyage to Europe, 33

Kagame, Paul, 353
*Kantipur Daily*, 249
Kantipur Publications, 192
Kapilvastu, 4, 6, 10, 220
Karki, Sushila, 130

Kashmiri Muslims, 12
Kashmiri Takiyah, 12
Katawal, Rookmangud, 113
Kathmandu and Tibet, treaty between, 5
Kathmandu-centric governance model, 83
Kathmandu-centric Nepal, 40
Kathmandu University Act (1991), 94
Kayastha, Chandan, 343
Kerung, Treaty of, 21
Keynesian economic model, 76
Khan, Kublai, 6–8, 14
Khanal, Jhala Nath, 113, 262
Khas language, 37
*khey bhaye (Khas* language*)*, 17
*khukris* (utility knife), 226. *See also* Gorkhas
King Mahendra Trust for Nature Conservation, 68, 108, 154
*kipat land*, 26
Koirala government, liberal bent of, 54
Koirala, B.P., 43, 50–51, 54–55, 74, 274; belief in socialism, 54
Koirala, Girija Prasad, 71, 75, 80, 104, 110
Koirala, M.P., 50–51
Koirala, Sushil, 115
Kot massacre (1846), 31
Kunwar, Balbhadra, 34

Labour Act (1992), 86, 304
Labour Court Laws, 86

labour management, 344
Lai, Chou En, 55
Lall, K.B., 58
Lama, Mahendra P., 317
Lamichhane, Jiba, 242
Lamichhane, Sandeep, 146
land and money linkages,
    346–47
land disputes, 28
landownership system, 22, 38
LDC (least developed country)
    graduation criteria, 300
Left Alliance, 117
left-leaning distributive economy,
    119–20
legacies of conflict, 97–98
Lenin, 274
Lewis Model, 77
'Lhasa Newas', 16
liberal capitalistic model, 85
liberal market economy, 74,
    77–79; agricultural boom,
    77; alcohol and cigarette
    industries, 78; road networks,
    78; trade routes, 78
life expectancy, 142, 298
Lissanevitch, Boris, 64
Litigious Society, 151–52
living standards, 299, 344, 351
Livre des Merveilles du Monde
    (Book of the Worlds
    Marvels), 8
look east policy, 250
Lucknow Loot, 34–35
Lucky Man, The, 34
Lumbini Development Trust,
    68

machine-readable passports
    (MRP), 231
Macron, Emmanuel, 353
made in Nepal products, 187
Madhav Kumar Nepal, 113, 262
Mahat, Ram Sharan, 42, 69
Mahendra, King, 51, 54–61,
    63–66, 68, 108, 154, 253;
    autocratic quasi-democracy,
    59; 'one country, one
    language' policy, 63;
    panchayat system by, 174;
    public sector, 58
Malla caste, 13–14
Manmohan Memorial Academy
    of Health Sciences, 181
manpower agencies, 182, 235
Maoists: conflict, 91; demands
    for a Constituent Assembly,
    106; extortion and tax
    racket, 98; guerrillas,
    97; inability to defeat
    army, 109; infrastructural
    damage, 100; insurgency,
    234; Nepali Maoist trade
    unions, 99; peace talks with
    government, 106; People's
    Army formation, 96; political
    and administrative capacities,
    97; revenue, 98; state's war
    against the, 100; struggle,
    96; success of, 97; terrifying
    image, 139; violence, 98,
    104; war efforts, 97
Marco Polo, 8–9
market capitalization, 136, 189
marriage rituals, 248

Marwaris, advent of, 161–63
Marx, Karl, 274
maternal health goals, 141
Matwalis, 17
medical tourism. *See* tourism
mediocre services, 213
mediocre standards, 240
Melamchi water project, 348
Middle Marsyangdi hydropower
    project, 211
migration, 7, 23, 36–38, 143,
    157, 220–25, 227–28,
    231, 235, 308, 321, 323;
    diversity visa (DV), 229–30;
    Gorkha programme in
    the UK, 230; hardships,
    challenges and separation,
    220; Hong Kong ID,
    228; illegal channels, 227;
    internal migration, 222–23,
    225; mass migration,
    101; perception of, 222;
    permanent migration, 228;
    preferred destination, 226;
    primary reasons, 227; protect
    identity and cultural stifling,
    37; remittances and, 157;
    timeline, 221–23; types of,
    227; way of life, 225–27
millennium development goals
    (MDGs), 141
mixed economy, 57–59, 271–72
modernization projects, 40
Modi, Narendra, xi, 117, 129,
    250–51, 257
Mohamad of Ghazni, 10
Molden, David, 317

monarchy, abolition of, 366
money-laundering rackets, 233
Moody, 309. *See also* Standard &
    Poor
most favoured nation (MFN)
    status, 255
motor vehicle agreement (MVA),
    262
Mount Everest, 64, 251
Mountain Echoes festival, 361
multi-language dictionaries, 41
multilateral development banks
    (MDBs), 207
multiparty democracy, 71, 80,
    84–85, 137, 172, 174, 230,
    340, 359
Muluki Ain (1854), 37

*nagar palikas*, 84
Namgyal, Phuntsog, 15
Namgyal, Shabdrung Ngawang,
    15
National Defence Council, 105
National Energy Policy, 325
National Private and Boarding
    Schools Organisation
    (NPABSON), 182
Naxalite war, 97
Nehru, Jawaharlal, 43, 54,
    58, 272; staunch belief in
    liberalism, 59
Nepa Mandala, 9, 11–14, 17
Nepal Aid Group, 203
Nepal Association of Foreign
    Employment Agencies, 182
Nepal Bank, 78, 204
Nepal Business Forum, 171

Nepal Communist Party (NCP), 117, 181, 262
Nepal Companies Act, 60, 162
Nepal Economic Forum, xvi, 171, 178, 242
Nepal Electricity Authority (NEA), 91, 324, 329
Nepal Forum of Environmental Journalists (NEFEJ), 154
*Nepal Idol*, 145. *See also Indian Idol*
Nepal Oil Corporation, 177
Nepal Petroleum Dealers Association, 177
Nepal Rastra Bank, 148, 233
Nepal Rastra Bank Act (1955), 47
Nepal Reconstruction Authority (NRA), 127
Nepal Responsible Summit, 365
Nepal Sambat, x, 1, 3–4, 37
Nepal Stock Exchange (NSE), 76, 273
Nepal Tourism Board, 356
Nepal Trust for Nature Conservation, 108
Nepal's Napoleon. *See* Jung Bahadur
Nepali films, 144
Nepali-language author, 146
Nepal–India relationship, xi, 167
Nepal–Thai Chamber of Commerce and Industry, 175
nepotism, 60, 82, 103, 230, 364
new caste system, 19–21
Newas, 13, 16–17, 19–20, 38, 83, 160–61, 163, 222;

Newa families, 35–36; Newa language, ix–x; Newa rulers, 20; Newa script, 9; rise and fall of, 160–61
Nick Simons Institute (NSI), 218
non-aligned movement (NAM), 55
non-aligned philosophy, 69
non-resident Nepali (NRN ), 160, 221, 236–37
Non-resident Nepali Act (NRNA), 236–37, 240
Non-resident Nepali Association (NRNA), 228
non-resident Nepalis, arrival of the, 165
non-violent movement, 43

Observer Research Foundation (ORF), 266, 313
Ohashi, Ken, 204
oil boom (1970), 226
Oli, K.P., 55, 111, 115, 117, 129, 249, 262
One China policy, xi, 245, 253
One Day International status, 146
'one language, one religion', 37
online banking or mobile banking, 190
open borders, 244, 264–65, 269
open defecation free zone, 365
open extortion, 139
open moment, 110–11
opium war, 32
oral traditions, 37
Orban, Viktor, 117

Ostrom, Elinor, 218
overseas migration, 225
own land vs. lord's land, 38–39

Padmasambhava, 4
*pajani* system, 24–25, 27, 31–32
Pala dynasty, 3
*Palpasa Café*, 146
panchayat, 55–56, 174;
    constitution, 57;
    government, fall of, 72, 74;
    'party-full panchayat' system,
    111; 'party-less panchayat'
    unitary system, 111; policy,
    69; rule, 54, 56–57, 70;
    royalist vision of, 57
*Panchsheel* (five principles), 317
Pandey families, 21
*pani patia*, 222
Pant, Samriddhi, 363
paragliding associations, 180
Parliament of the Privatization
    Act (1994), 76
'party palaces' (banquet halls
    business), 136, 138, 361–62
Pashupati Development Trust, 68
Pashupatinath temple, 11–12,
    49, 73
passport: advent of, 220;
    decentralization of, 230–31;
    democratization of, 137;
    restrictions on issuance, 226
patronage of labour, 131
peace accord (2006), 120
peace dividends, 129–32
peace talks, 106
People's Army, formation of, 96

People's Liberation Army (PLA),
    97–98
People's War (1996–2006),
    95–97, 103
petroleum dealer associations, 180
petroleum products, taxes on, 140
pilgrimages, 12–13, 336
Plassey, Battle of, 10
police structure, 104
policy consistency, 316
political instability, 80–81, 157,
    247
political patronage, 287, 327,
    375; culture of, 313
political turmoil, 88, 105, 166, 201
political–business nexus, 305
politics of associations, 238–39
politics of business associations,
    169–72
polygamy, 35
Ponzi schemes, 216
post disaster nothing achievable
    (PDNA), 127–28
Potala Palace, 15
power purchase agreements
    (PPAs), 326
power-sharing agreement, 117
power trade agreement, 92, 302
power vacuum, 51
'Prachandapath', 98
Praja Parisad, 43, 51
'Prajapatra', 162
*Prayogshala*, 249
preferential policy, 62
Private and Boarding Schools
    Organisation (PABSON),
    182

private banks, 367
private sector: ambitious, 281–83;
certificate of origin, 187;
challenges of, 159, 183–84;
competitiveness in, 310–11;
contribution to GDP,
159; economic growth, 75;
expansion, 79; focus, 189;
future of, 281; government's
emphasis, 67, 148;
government's receptiveness,
186; growth period of, 166;
harnessing skills and, 248;
history of, 159–60; impact
of development sector, 215;
impact on political system,
282; importance of, 157;
investment in infrastructure,
346; investment in tourism,
65; involvement in
hydroelectricity generation,
76; journey of, 165–69; key
areas of reform, 283; labour
migration business, 235;
multinationals alliances,
282; myopic lobbying, 168;
outside Nepal, 167; paradigm
shift, 282; participation of,
76; policy reform advocacy,
281; poor's participation,
276; privatization of ,
283–84; promotion of
enterprises, 301; quality
required, 281; regulating
the, 282; remittance-
transfer business, 233; roads
development by, 66; role

of, 120; stagnation of, 193;
stakeholders creations, 281;
tool to consolidate power,
60–63; value of, 193
privatization policy (1991),
76
Privy Purse, abolition of, 66
procreation and categorization,
35–36
procurement policies, 214
procurement processes,
transparency in, 284
productivity discourse with
holidays, 366
professional competencies,
184–86
prohibitive cost of war, 100–1
'project mentality', 216
protectionism, 172, 176, 281,
289
protectionist monetary economy,
23
protectionist policies, 24, 56, 62,
169
Protestant revolution, 37
psychological impact of war, 101
public–private venture, 61, 285
publishing, 95, 146, 213
Putin, Vladimir, 117

quality of life, 141–43;
achievement of millennium
development goals (MDGs),
141; healthcare access,
142–43; infant mortality,
141; life expectancy, 142;
poverty reduction, 141;

primary education access, 142

quality vs. quantity, debate, 340

*Rakam land grants*, 26

Ramachandaran, Shastri, xv

Rana regime: isolationist policy, 52; resentment against, 40

Rana rulers, 4, 7, 33, 37–38, 43, 57, 61, 223

Rana, Gaurav SJB, 46

Rana, Madhukar, 204, 210

Rana, Mahavir Shumsher, 43, 51

Rana, Mohan Shumsher, 40, 55

Rana, Prabhakar, 55, 64–65, 67, 70, 107–8, 277

Rana, Shumsher Jung Bahadur (SJB), 46

Ranabhat, Taranath, 107

Ranas, decline and fall of, 39–40

Rao, Nirupama, 317

Rastra Bank, 47–48

Rastriya Banijya Bank, 204

Rastriya Prajatantra Party (RPP), 115, 272

real estate developers, 152

real estate prices, 112, 140, 358

*Red Book*, 112, 210, 261

referendum (1979), 69

reforms: agrarian reforms, 97, 200; better and well-connected infrastructure, 266; bubble of, 80; capital market reform, 76, 304; economic reform, 221, 203; financial sector, 79, 305–6; free movement of people, goods and services, 266–67; insolvency laws, 315; key areas of, 283; labour reform, 304–5; land reform, 198, 303–4; market-oriented reforms, 148, 167; political reforms, 97; tax reform, 75, 302–3; transforming borders, 266

regional dreams, 300, 302

regional leadership, 327–28

regional markets, leveraging, 311

Regmi, Khil Raj, 111, 114

regulating NGOs, 286–87

remittances, 134, 221, 232–34, 321, 323; from Gorkhas, 232; IME Remit, 234; interest and accounting of, 232; surges, 234–35; utilization of remittances, 234

rent seeking: behaviour, 175, 177–78; culture, 149; job, 26; mentality, 24–28; society, 155

resources sharing, disagreements, 202

restaurant and coffee shop business, 146–47

Rinpoche, Guru, 5

risk management, 189

risk of doing business, 347

role of cooperatives, limiting the, 285–86

*roti–beti* ('bread–daughter'), 16

'Royal Lady'. *See* Bhrikuti, Princess

royal massacre, 71, 90, 106–7
Royal Nepal Airlines, 65–66, 201
Royal Nepal Army, 106
Ruit, Sanduk, 142
rule of uncertainty, 111–12
run-of-river projects, 327
Rwanda, 297, 351–55;
    cleanliness and order, 355;
    FIFA Council meeting,
    353; leadership position,
    353; meetings, incentives,
    conferences and exhibitions
    (MICE) business, 352;
    positive attitude, 354–55;
    rule of law, 354; think big,
    352; tourism, 352; trust,
    353–54; Vision 2050,
    297

SAARC summit, xi, 251, 361
safety of citizens, 278–79
Sagarmatha Choudhary Eye
    Hospital (SCEH), 265
Sakhwa, Sankhadhar, 3
Sakya Lama, 7
Salt Trading Corporation, 61
Sambat calendar, 4
Save the Children, 205
Schaffner, Monika, 337
'Second World', 197
secularism, fundamentals of, 118
securities board, 76, 182
security issues, 268
selling uncertainty, business of,
    134–36
sepoy rebellion (1857), 33–35, 41
service sector, domestic jobs in,
    344

Seven Habits of Highly Effective
    People, The, 295
shadow ministers, 117
Shah dynasty, ix–x, 9, 24, 43, 71,
    108–9; fall of, x
Shah kings, 4–5, 9, 17, 36, 45,
    60, 83, 154, 272
Shah, Hrishikesh, 56
Shah, Prince Dravya, 17
Shah, Prithvi Narayan, 17–21,
    23, 25–27, 70, 244; astute
    tactician, 20; economic
    rationale, 20
Shakyas, 6, 14, 220
Sharma, Chudamani, 152
Sharma, Sudheer, 249
Sherpa, Tenzing Norgay, 64
Sherpa, Tshering, 242
Shrestha, Raj Krishna, 34
Shrestha, Ram, 143
Shumsher, Chandra, 41, 223
Shumsher, Juddha, 40
Shumsher, Padma, 40
Shumsher, Suvarna, 43
Sikkim, annexation of, 53, 162
Silk Road, 9
Singapore, 11, 74, 237, 288,
    295, 351, 353, 355–57, 363;
    consistency matters, 355–56;
    every citizen is a tourism
    brand ambassador, 356–57;
    maintenance and planned
    growth, 356; minimal
    pollution, 356; public
    transportation, 356
Singapore Tourism Board,
    357

Singh, Deepak, 61
Singh, Ranjit, 28, 34
Singh, Tripurawar, 51
Sino-Indian war (1962), xi, 58, 167, 245
Sino-Nepal war (1792), 28, 33
Sinophobia, 260
Sita, 10
small business elite, 148, 167–68
Smith, Adam, 19, 21
smuggling, 62, 99
social inclusion, 115, 118, 216
social indicators, 141
Social Security Act (2018), 302
Social Service National Service Committee (SSNSC), 287
Social Services National Coordination Council (SSNCC), 68
Social Welfare Council (SWC), 217, 287
socialism, 54, 103, 119, 158, 165, 270–74, 355; binary perspective, 274; model of, 273; myopic and inwardlooking, 272; perceptions of, 271–73
societal transformation, 111, 293, 351, 357–58, 360
socio-economic challenges, 313
special economic zones (SEZs), 268, 329
special relations with India, 246–48
Spice Silk Road, 5
sports, 145–46, 205, 253
Stalin, 274

Standard & Poor, 309
Standard Chartered Bank, 185
state apathy, 104–5
State of Nepal, xv
state of toilets at hotels, 362
stock exchange, establishment of, 76
Stok Palace, 15
structural problems, 35
structural realism, 275
structural reforms, 302–6; capital market reform, 304; financial sector reform, 305–6; labour reform, 304–5; land reform, 303–4; tax reforms, 302–3; See also reforms
structural resilience, 275
Suez crisis, 56
Sugauli Treaty (1816), 223
sukuti (buffalo meat), 241
sustainable development goals (SDGs), 292, 297
'sycophancy' traits, 150
syndicate, 111, 118, 125, 130, 149, 172–73, 177, 310

talent management, 371–74; artificial intelligence (AI) and, 373; new CEO, 372
Talent Management Association, 373
Talent Management Board, 373
Tara Management Private Limited, 108
Tara, Goddess, 4
tax concessions, 314
tax holiday, 166

tax revenues, 140

tax scam, 152. *See also* Sharma, Chudamani

taxi associations, 180

Tayyip, Recep, 117

technical resources, access to, 307–8

technocrat government, 111, 114

technology for regulation, leveraging, 279–80

Thamel institutions, 337

Thant, U., 56

Thapa families, 21

Thapa, Bhekh Bahadur, 58, 218

Thapa, Bhimsen, 30

Thapa, Kamal, 115

'Third World', 197

Thompson, J. Walter, 168

Thulung, Narada Muni, 51

Tibet Autonomous Region, xii, 256, 336

Tibetan Buddhism, 4, 7, 221; popularity of, 9

Tibetan refugees, 224

Tibetan writings, 4

Tobgay, Tshering, 124

Tokha Chhahare Minibus Enterprise Association, 175

Tokha route, 175

total quality people, concept of, 308

totalitarian rule of upper-caste, 36

Tourism Act, 64

Tourism: associated destination with Buddhism and nature, 338; behavioural issue, 342; Chinese interest, 341; client profiles, 340; customer feedback, 343; disruption in, 340; domestic market, 139, 341–42; entry into global tourism, 336; heavily dependent on, 187; history of, 336; hotel and restaurant business, 342; medical tourism, 265; recalibration, 343–44; religious tourism, 12–13, 336–37; Tourism Master Plan, 64–65

tourist tax, 112

Trade and Transit treaty with India, 52

Trade route between China and India, 244

Trade Union Act, 86, 304

trade-specific associations, 172

trading and manufacturing nexus, 321

trading route, replication of, 364

transit agreement, 72, 166

transit transport agreement, 245

transport agreement, 262

transportation, 66

travel advisories, negative, 90

travel industry, 184

travel processes, 220

*Travels of Marco Polo, The*, 8

'treatment package tours', 265

Treaty of Sugauli (1812), 13

Treaty of Sugauli (1816), 21

trekking, 335, 337

Tribhuvan, King, 43–45, 50–51, 71, 107

Tribhuvan University, 63, 94–95, 182, 254
TripAdvisor, 337, 342
Trump, Donald, 117
Trust Act, 286
'two-laddoo' syndrome, 84

Uber, 180, 280, 337, 372
understanding areas for development, 347–48
under-the-table bribe, 367
United Nations Capital Development Fund (UNCDF), 234
United Nations Development Programme (UNDP), 250, 254, 357
United Nations membership, 52
United Nations Millennium Summit, 141
United Nations Mission for Nepal (UNMIN), 120
United Nations, quest for membership, 55
United Nations World Tourism Organization (UNWTO), 338
United Progressive Alliance, 261
United States, 40, 49, 55, 59, 67, 93, 117, 121, 196, 296–97; aid by, 49; competition with Soviet Union, 55; concept of committees, 121; Great Depression, 59; King Birendra's 67; Nepali students in, 93

*Unleashing Nepal*, xii–xiii, xvi, 134, 138, 271, 323, 350
Upadhyaya, Surya Nath, 245
US Peace Corps, 212
USAID, 205–6
USSR, collapse of, 72

Vajrayana Buddhist faith, 5, 7
value system, 321, 358–60, 366
Varanasi connection, 48–49
Victoria Cross awards, 223
village development committees (VDCs), 100
VIP culture, prevalence of, 150
visa, 31–32, 175, 227–29, 231–32, 280, 338–39
Vision 2030, 295–96, 300, 320, 322–23, 376. *See also* Economic Vision 2030
*Vogue*, 320
*Voice of Nepal*, 145
voluntary employment programmes, 98

wage war, 5, 24
Wagle, Swarnim, 299
war economics, 98–100
wealth creation, 155, 275–77, 281, 284, 301, 358
*Wealth of Nations, The*, 21–22. *See also* Smith, Adam
Westernization, 274. *See also* capitalism
'white skin', 211, 336
*Who Wants to Be a Millionaire*, 145
women, role of, 37, 143–44

World Bank Doing Business
    Report, 354
World Economic Forum, 134,
    314, 353
World Environment Day, 355
World Trade Center attack
    (9/11), 90, 106
World War I, 35, 41, 223;
    Gorkhas' remittance to
    economy, 223; Nepali
    soldiers in British army, 223
World War II, 35, 41, 162,
    196–97, 223, 319; demise of
    colonialism, 196; economic
    growth, 197; role of Nepalis,
    223

Yadav, Ram Baran, 113
Yadav, Suryanath Das, 51
Yatayat, Sajha, 179
young generation, 240–41
Younghusband, Francis, 5
youth clubs, 287
youth, waste of, 89–90
Yuan dynasty, 6

'Zhikha', 16
zilla bikas samitis, 84
zone of peace, 66, 69–70